THE FEAR
OF THE
LORD IS
WISDOM

THE FEAR
OF THE
LORD IS
WISDOM

A Theological Introduction
to Wisdom in Israel

Tremper
Longman III

Baker Academic
a division of Baker Publishing Group
Grand Rapids, Michigan

© 2017 by Tremper Longman III

Published by Baker Academic
a division of Baker Publishing Group
P.O. Box 6287, Grand Rapids, MI 49516-6287
www.bakeracademic.com

Paperback edition published 2024
ISBN 978-1-5409-6882-1

Printed in the United States of America

The Library of Congress has cataloged the hardcover edition as follows:
Names: Longman, Tremper, author.
Title: The fear of the Lord is wisdom : a theological introduction to wisdom in Israel / Tremper Longman III.
Description: Grand Rapids : Baker Academic, 2017. | Includes bibliographical references and index.
Identifiers: LCCN 2017003345 | ISBN 9780801027116 (cloth)
Subjects: LCSH: Wisdom literature—Criticism, interpretation, etc.
Classification: LCC BS1455 .L66 2017 | DDC 223/.06—dc23
LC record available at https://lccn.loc.gov/2017003345

Baker Publishing Group publications use paper produced from sustainable forestry practices and postconsumer waste whenever possible.

To our new granddaughters:

Ava Rae Longman (born July 8, 2016)
Emerson Foster Longman (born July 10, 2016)

CONTENTS

Acknowledgments

My interest in wisdom in the Old Testament began during my studies at Yale University in the late 1970s. As I was defining and exploring the genre of Akkadian fictional autobiographies for my dissertation under Professor W. W. Hallo, I found some autobiographies that ended with wisdom admonitions. As I will explain in chapter 9, these Akkadian compositions were similar in form to Ecclesiastes. I soon had an offer to write a commentary on Ecclesiastes, and then over the next couple decades, I also wrote commentaries on Proverbs, Job, Song of Songs, and Psalms, all of which in one way or another helped me to gain a better understanding of the concept of wisdom in the Old Testament.

Being an advocate for and practitioner of christological or christotelic interpretation, my interest in wisdom in its discrete setting within the Old Testament led me to study wisdom in the New Testament as well. Furthermore, since I try to write in a way that will be helpful for clergy, I have also pondered the relationship between ancient biblical wisdom as it informs wisdom today (thus appendix 1).

I want to thank Baker Academic and in particular Jim Kinney for the opportunity and encouragement to write this book, which is a synthesis of years of studying biblical wisdom. I have worked with Jim for a number of years now and consider him not just my editor but a close friend. He not only encouraged me to write this volume but has also guided me through the entire process. I also want to thank Wells Turner and his team for an excellent job of editing the volume.

I appreciate and give credit to the countless students to whom I have taught wisdom literature at the undergraduate as well as the graduate level. The very first course that I taught in 1981 was on Psalms and wisdom and indeed in the coming spring 2017 semester I will again teach that course. Naturally, the version of the course I will teach next semester is significantly different, and hopefully much better informed, than the one I taught in 1981.

I always want to thank my wife, Alice, for her great support over the years. She epitomizes wisdom in her life. We are also so thankful for our three sons, their wives, and also our four granddaughters. I have already dedicated previous books to our older granddaughters Gabrielle (now 11) and Mia (now 7), daughters of our son Tremper IV, so it is my pleasure to dedicate this book to our two newest granddaughters: Emerson Foster Longman (daughter of Timothy and Kari) and Ava Rae Longman (daughter of Andrew and Tiffany). Love to all you girls. May you grow up in the fear and wisdom of the Lord.

ABBREVIATIONS

General and Bibliographic

AB	Anchor Bible
ANET	*Ancient Near Eastern Texts Relating to the Old Testament*, ed. James B. Pritchard, 3rd ed. (Princeton: Princeton University Press, 1969)
BBR	*Bulletin for Biblical Research*
BCOTWP	Baker Commentary on the Old Testament Wisdom and Psalms
BIBD	*Baker Illustrated Bible Dictionary*, ed. Tremper Longman III (Grand Rapids: Baker Books, 2013)
BN	*Biblische Notizen*
BZAW	Beihefte zur Zeitschrift für die alttestamentliche Wissenschaft
ca.	*circa*, about
CBQ	*Catholic Biblical Quarterly*
CEB	Common English Bible
chap(s).	chapter(s)
ConBOT	Coniectanea Biblica: Old Testament Series
COS	*The Context of Scripture*, ed. William W. Hallo, 3 vols. (Leiden: Brill, 1997–2002)
DJD	Discoveries in the Judaean Desert
e.g.	*exempli gratia*, for example
esp.	especially
ESV	English Standard Version
ET	English translation
EuroJTh	*European Journal of Theology*
EvQ	*Evangelical Quarterly*
FOTL	Forms of the Old Testament Literature
Heb.	Hebrew
HTR	*Harvard Theological Review*
HUCA	*Hebrew Union College Annual*
i.e.	*id est*, that is

JAOS	*Journal of the American Oriental Society*
JBL	*Journal of Biblical Literature*
JETS	*Journal of the Evangelical Theological Society*
JHNES	Johns Hopkins Near Eastern Studies
JSOT	*Journal for the Study of the Old Testament*
JSOTSup	Journal for the Study of the Old Testament Supplement Series
JTISup	Journal for Theological Interpretation, Supplements
MT	Masoretic Text
NCB	New Century Bible
NIB	*The New Interpreter's Bible*, ed. Leander E. Keck, 12 vols. (Nashville: Abingdon, 1994–2004)
NICOT	New International Commentary on the Old Testament
NIDOTTE	*New International Dictionary of Old Testament Theology and Exegesis*, ed. Willem A. VanGemeren, 5 vols. (Grand Rapids: Zondervan, 1997)
NIV	New International Version
NIVAC	NIV Application Commentary
NJB	New Jerusalem Bible
NLT	New Living Translation
NRSV	New Revised Standard Version
NT	New Testament
OBO	Orbis Biblicus et Orientalis
OT	Old Testament
OTE	*Old Testament Essays*
OTL	Old Testament Library
RevQ	*Revue de Qumran*
SBLDS	Society of Biblical Literature Dissertation Series
SBLSymS	Society of Biblical Literature Symposium Series
SJT	*Scottish Journal of Theology*
STDJ	Studies on the Texts of the Desert of Judah
THOTC	Two Horizons Old Testament Commentary
TLB	The Living Bible
TOTC	Tyndale Old Testament Commentaries
v(v).	verse(s)
VT	*Vetus Testamentum*
VTSup	Supplements to Vetus Testamentum
WBC	Word Biblical Commentary
WTJ	*Westminster Theological Journal*
ZAW	*Zeitschrift für die alttestamentliche Wissenschaft*

Old Testament/Hebrew Bible

Gen.	Genesis	Josh.	Joshua	1 Kings	1 Kings
Exod.	Exodus	Judg.	Judges	2 Kings	2 Kings
Lev.	Leviticus	Ruth	Ruth	1 Chron.	1 Chronicles
Num.	Numbers	1 Sam.	1 Samuel	2 Chron.	2 Chronicles
Deut.	Deuteronomy	2 Sam.	2 Samuel	Ezra	Ezra

Neh.	Nehemiah	Jer.	Jeremiah	Jon.	Jonah
Esther	Esther	Lam.	Lamentations	Mic.	Micah
Job	Job	Ezek.	Ezekiel	Nah.	Nahum
Ps(s).	Psalm(s)	Dan.	Daniel	Hab.	Habakkuk
Prov.	Proverbs	Hosea	Hosea	Zeph.	Zephaniah
Eccles.	Ecclesiastes	Joel	Joel	Hag.	Haggai
Song	Song of Songs	Amos	Amos	Zech.	Zechariah
Isa.	Isaiah	Obad.	Obadiah	Mal.	Malachi

New/Greek Testament

Matt.	Matthew	Eph.	Ephesians	Heb.	Hebrews
Mark	Mark	Phil.	Philippians	James	James
Luke	Luke	Col.	Colossians	1 Pet.	1 Peter
John	John	1 Thess.	1 Thessalonians	2 Pet.	2 Peter
Acts	Acts	2 Thess.	2 Thessalonians	1 John	1 John
Rom.	Romans	1 Tim.	1 Timothy	2 John	2 John
1 Cor.	1 Corinthians	2 Tim.	2 Timothy	3 John	3 John
2 Cor.	2 Corinthians	Titus	Titus	Jude	Jude
Gal.	Galatians	Philem.	Philemon	Rev.	Revelation

Old Testament Apocrypha/Deuterocanonical Books

Add. Dan.	Additions to Daniel (= Pr. Azar., Sg. Three, Sus., and Bel)
Add. Esth.	Additions to Esther
Bar.	Baruch
Bel	Bel and the Dragon
1–2 Esd.	1–2 Esdras
Jdt.	Judith
Let. Jer.	Letter of Jeremiah (= Baruch chap. 6)
1–4 Macc.	1–4 Maccabees
Pr. Azar.	Prayer of Azariah (often cited as part of the Song of the Three Jews)
Pr. Man.	Prayer of Manasseh
Ps. 151	Psalm 151
Sg. Three	Song of the Three Jews
Sir.	Sirach
Sus.	Susanna
Tob.	Tobit
Wis.	Wisdom (of Solomon)

Other Ancient Sources

T. Job	Testament of Job

PROLOGUE

What is wisdom in the OT? The redemptive history claims that God works in a special way through Israel to reach the world (Gen. 12:1–3).[1] That special relationship comes to focus in Israel's covenant relationship as well as the law expressed within the framework of the covenant. The prophets insist on exclusive worship of Yahweh, the God of Israel, and they condemn any who might worship another God. The priests protect God's holiness by "guarding" that covenant (Deut. 33:9).

Upon initial reading, books that speak about wisdom—particularly Proverbs, Job, and Ecclesiastes—feel significantly different than books based on redemptive-historical, covenantal, legal, prophetic, and priestly traditions. Or that is certainly the impression one gets from the writings of those who have studied wisdom over the past number of decades. Scholars have talked about a distinctive wisdom tradition that is markedly different than the rest of the OT.[2] Wisdom, so the argument goes, is practical not theological, universal (consonant with ancient Near Eastern wisdom) not particular to Israel, tied to creation theology not redemptive history or covenant.

This book intends to explore wisdom in the Bible. We will focus on the OT, Israel's wisdom. Ultimately, however, our study is a work of Christian biblical theology; thus, we will continue by examining how the NT appropriates the wisdom of the OT.

1. For how the promises to Abraham reverberate throughout the redemptive history of the OT and into the NT, see Clines, *Theme of the Pentateuch*.
2. Examples include the classic study of wisdom by von Rad, *Wisdom in Israel*, and the recent book by Brown, *Wisdom's Wonder*.

At the heart of our study is the question of the nature of wisdom in the OT. Is the contemporary assessment of wisdom accurate, which views it as universal rather than particular, practical rather than theological, and based in creation theology rather than redemptive history? Very recently scholarly voices have been heard questioning what we might call the overarching consensus of the past decades. In particular, the work of Will Kynes and Mark Sneed, though differing in significant respects, have challenged the idea of a distinctive wisdom tradition, school, or genre as commonly perceived by scholars working in the field.[3] This book owes much to their stimulating insights, though I do not find myself persuaded completely by their perspectives and will interact with them, as well as the ideas that they challenge, throughout this book. However, at this beginning stage I will simply state that even if they are correct that there is no specific wisdom tradition, school, or genre, there is a concept of wisdom in the Bible that is worth exploring and that will be the subject of this book.

Without making the claim that Proverbs, Ecclesiastes, and Job constitute a distinct genre (though see appendix 2 for my discussion of genre theory as it relates to the question of wisdom literature), there are still obvious reasons to begin such a study by a close look at wisdom in these books. The preface to Proverbs (1:1–7) states that the purpose of the book is "to know wisdom and discipline" (1:2a) and "to give to the simple prudence, to the young knowledge and discretion" (1:4) as well as to make the wise even wiser (1:5). In our chapter on Job, we will demonstrate that the book is best understood as a wisdom debate between Job and his friends, as well as Elihu, with all of them the losers and God the winner. Wisdom also plays a central role in the book of Ecclesiastes. As we will see, an unnamed speaker addressing his son (12:12) points out that the main speaker in the book, Qohelet, "was a wise man" (12:9). The book will evaluate the nature of his "under the sun" wisdom. While all three of these books differ from each other and each will nuance our understanding of wisdom in different ways, they strikingly all agree, as we will point out in the chapters that follow, that the heart of wisdom is the "fear of the Lord." Thus, our first three chapters (part 1, "The Heart of Wisdom: Proverbs, Ecclesiastes, and Job") will be:

1. Proverbs: The Fear of the Lord Is the Beginning of Wisdom
2. Ecclesiastes: Fear God, Obey the Commandments, and Live in Light of the Coming Judgment
3. The Book of Job: "Behold, the Fear of the Lord Is Wisdom" (Job 28:28)

3. See their contributions in Sneed, *Was There a Wisdom Tradition?*

While these three books have the most pervasive and intense presentation of wisdom in the OT, there are a number of other books or parts of books that also speak of or illustrate wisdom. We will have to tread carefully here, though, because, as in particular Kynes has stated, there is a tendency in scholars to treat everything as wisdom. Indeed, as we will later point out, an argument can be made that there is a pervasive wisdom dimension to most if not all of the OT, since the transmission and final form of texts were the product of scribes who themselves, like Qohelet, were considered "wise" (*ḥākām*). Thus, after treating Proverbs, Job, and Ecclesiastes, we will go on to look at wisdom in select psalms, Deuteronomy, Song of Songs, and certain historical narratives, in particular the stories of Joseph and Daniel as well as Adam and Solomon.[4] We will cover these books (part 2, "Wisdom Elsewhere in the Old Testament") in the following chapters:

4. Other Sources of Wisdom: Deuteronomy, Psalms, Song of Songs, and Prophecy

5. Joseph and Daniel: Paragons of Wisdom

6. Adam and Solomon: From the Heights of Wisdom to the Depths of Folly

Once we have gathered the textual materials that are most relevant to the study of wisdom, we will then examine a series of issues that will question the contemporary understanding of how wisdom fits into the rest of the canon. There is no question that wisdom has distinctive emphases that make it different from the other traditions of the OT, but we contend that these differences have been overemphasized to the point of distortion. The sages are not an alien presence within the Bible but rather another voice bearing witness to Yahweh along with the prophets, priests, and those who write of God's mighty acts.

Our initial foray into wisdom (chaps. 1–3) will already have shown that wisdom is not just a practical (and ethical) category but is deeply theological ("the fear of the LORD is the beginning of knowledge," Prov. 1:7). Afterward, we will continue questioning the depiction of wisdom as universal, rather than particular, by exploring the following issues (part 3, "Israel's Wisdom: Cosmopolitan or Unique?"):

---

4. The subject of wisdom in historical narrative is not limited to the topics we will cover, but we believe that the stories of Joseph, Daniel, Adam, and Solomon are high points. For an interesting recent study, see Firth, "Worrying about the Wise."

7. Sources of Wisdom: Experience, Observation, Tradition, Correction, and Ultimately Revelation
8. Wisdom, Creation, and (Dis)order
9. Israelite Wisdom in Its Ancient Near Eastern Setting
10. Wisdom, Covenant, and Law

The study of these topics will reinforce our understanding that wisdom strikes a distinctive but not discordant note with the rest of the OT. With this background we will turn our attention to a series of issues that will deepen our understanding of wisdom in the Bible. First, we will examine the relationship between wisdom and reward: the question of retribution. On a surface reading of Proverbs, one might (and many do) claim that the way of wisdom leads to prosperity while the way of folly leads to failure and punishment. The books of Job and Ecclesiastes undermine the supposed connection between wisdom and reward, but are Proverbs and Job/Ecclesiastes at odds with each other? We will follow this with a look at two debated topics: (1) the social setting of wisdom and (2) wisdom and gender. Was there a specific social setting for wisdom, and can we identify it? The fact that a book like Proverbs depicts a father instructing his son about life and personifies divine wisdom as a woman raises questions about wisdom and gender (part 4, "Further Refining Our Understanding of Wisdom").

11. The Consequences of Wise and Foolish Behavior: The Issue of Retribution Theology
12. The Social Setting of Wisdom
13. Wisdom and Gender

After this thorough look at wisdom in the OT, we will then look at its afterlife in two parts. We begin with intertestamental wisdom with a focus on Sirach (Ecclesiasticus), Wisdom of Solomon, Baruch, and the Dead Sea Scrolls. We will follow that with a chapter dedicated to the NT's appropriation and development of OT wisdom. That chapter will include both the presentation of Jesus as the ultimate sage and an examination of the nature of Christian wisdom (part 5, "The Afterlife of Israel's Wisdom").

14. Intertestamental Wisdom from the Apocrypha to the Dead Sea Scrolls
15. New Testament Wisdom

We will end with two appendixes, the first of which will draw together our main conclusions and present our understanding of the nature of OT wisdom in its broader (Christian) canonical context as well as its continuing significance for life today. The second appendix will turn to the question of genre. As mentioned above, in the light of new challenges to the idea that there is a genre of wisdom literature, we have decided to explore the concept of wisdom instead. However, in the appendix I will make a case for retaining the category wisdom literature, based on a more fluid understanding of genre.

Before moving on, we need to make clear our approach to Scripture, which will bear on the focus and shape of this present study. Our exploration of wisdom in the Bible will be synchronic and not diachronic, or in other words, canonical rather than historical-critical. We will be talking about these books in their final form and in the terms in which they present themselves. In my mind there is no doubt that all OT books (with the possible exception of Nahum) have a compositional history and that most, if not all, books found their final form very late in the postexilic period. While a diachronic study is possible, it is also extremely speculative. And in any case, as Childs and others have pointed out, the final forms of the books are the Scriptures of the church.[5]

5. Representative of Childs's canonical criticism is his *Biblical Theology*.

PART 1

THE HEART OF WISDOM

Proverbs, Ecclesiastes, and Job

The title of this book, *The Fear of the Lord Is Wisdom: A Theological Introduction to Wisdom in Israel*, announces that it is a study of wisdom. But what exactly is wisdom in the OT? Since at least the mid-nineteenth century and the work of Johann Bruch, scholars have spoken of "wisdom literature"; wisdom as a genre of literature distinct from, say, the Historical Books and the Prophets and Law.[1] Granted, the health of wisdom as a genre has waxed and waned from its nineteenth-century origins until the present moment, but even today most scholars would affirm that Proverbs, Job, and Ecclesiastes form the core of wisdom literature. Some scholars of the genre would add other texts, including a number of wisdom psalms and the Song of Songs. Others would go further and place the Joseph narrative,

---

1. Bruch, *Weisheits-Lehre der Hebräer*.

Esther, Daniel, and certain other historical narratives and even prophets in this literary category.

In recent days, however, the idea of a wisdom genre has come under serious question. Will Kynes presents the most persuasive case that wisdom should not be considered a genre. He rightly indicates that there is no evidence that the so-called wisdom books were considered a genre in antiquity or even really until the mid-nineteenth century and Bruch's work. That said, he also recognizes that this is not a sufficient argument against the idea of a genre of wisdom literature, since as a single argument it commits the so-called genetic fallacy, which argues that "an idea's origin can either confirm or contradict is truth."[2] In other words, emic (native) categories are not the only valid ones. Etic (outsider) categories, those formulated by modern scholars, have their utility, as in the use of modern grammatical categories in the description and teaching of ancient languages.[3]

Kynes furthers his argument by pointing out that even the core books (Proverbs, Job, Ecclesiastes) are not easily distinguished generically from the other books of the OT. For instance, he questions the very existence of ideas commonly associated with wisdom as modern constructs imposed on the literature, or at least their distinctive use within a supposed wisdom literature (he names, for instance, creation theology, universalism, empiricism, retribution, and secularism).

He has also noticed that there has been a gradual but persistent expansion of wisdom literature in scholarship. As noted in the second paragraph of this section above, some scholars would include broad swaths of the OT under the rubric wisdom. He sees here an analogy to how scholarship saw the influence of Deuteronomic theology where Samuel–Kings, if not Joshua through Kings, Jeremiah, and other prophets were labeled Deuteronomistic. He then asserts, in the case of wisdom, that if everything is wisdom (a bit of an overstatement), then nothing is wisdom.

Kynes and others thus present questions that a book like mine purporting to describe wisdom cannot ignore. Is wisdom really dead? Is there no wisdom literature? Is there no distinctive wisdom movement? Are there no wisdom teachers or sages to be distinguished from priests or prophets or kings? These are questions we will take up in the following chapters.

But where to begin? Though wisdom as a distinct literary category, movement, or professional status can be challenged, perhaps successfully (as we

2. Kynes, *Obituary*.
3. A point I made as early as 1987 (Longman, *Literary Approaches*) in a book that was reprinted in 1996 with other books from the series in a combined volume titled *Foundations of Contemporary Interpretation* (see esp. 127–28).

will see), there is no denying that the concept of wisdom makes its presence known in the OT. Wisdom is the English translation of *ḥokmâ*, and a person who is characterized by wisdom is called a *ḥākām*.[4]

Accordingly, perhaps it is best to understand this book not primarily as a description of a literary genre but rather as an exploration of the concept of wisdom. Kynes himself will agree with us on this level since he states that his approach "would treat wisdom (now with a lower case w) as a concept similar to holiness or righteousness instead of a genre."[5]

So we will leave open the question of whether wisdom is a genre and embark on a study of the concept of wisdom (for more on wisdom as a genre, see appendix 2). But how should we organize our exploration? Where do we start and how do we progress?

One approach could be diachronic, starting with the earliest texts that speak of *ḥokmâ* and moving on from there until the latest texts. That would be a legitimate, but also a highly speculative, approach, speculative because the dating of texts is both highly complex and extremely controversial.

I have thus decided to approach the question synchronically. This does not mean that I will avoid all questions of when texts were likely or probably composed, but my description of wisdom will not depend on their dating, at least in major points.

I will start then with those texts that speak of *ḥokmâ* most pervasively. While this does not presume that they compose a genre, this does lead us to start with the three books that are, as we have noted above, considered the core of a supposed wisdom genre.

The first question we are going to ask is, what is the nature of wisdom? We start with Proverbs, which announces in its preamble (1:1–7) that it intends to make its readers wise.

4. The question of whether *ḥākām* is used as a professional category will be addressed in chap. 12.

5. Kynes, *Obituary*.

1

PROVERBS

The Fear of the Lord Is the Beginning of Wisdom

The book of Proverbs is a book of instruction and, like its ancient Egyptian counterparts (see chap. 9 below), begins with a preface, which states the purpose of the following chapters in terms of their intended effect upon readers:

> The proverbs of Solomon, the son of David, king of Israel—
> to know wisdom and discipline;
>   to understand insightful sayings;
> to receive the teaching of insight,
>   righteousness, justice, and virtue;
> to give to the simple prudence,
>   to the young knowledge and discretion.
> Let the wise hear and increase teaching;
>   let those with understanding acquire guidance,
> so they may understand a proverb and a difficult saying,
>   the words of the wise and their enigmas.
> The fear of Yahweh is the beginning of knowledge,
>   but fools despise wisdom and discipline. (1:1–7)[1]

---

1. All translations of the book of Proverbs are from Longman, *Proverbs*.

The lengthy purpose statement of the preface begins "to know wisdom." The Hebrew word commonly translated "wisdom" is *ḥokmâ*. *Ḥokmâ* is the word used most frequently in Proverbs to denote the hoped-for consequence of reading the book of Proverbs, though there are many other closely related words found in the preface as well as throughout the book, words like "discipline" (*mûsār*), "understanding" (*bînâ*), "insight" (*haśkēl*), "prudence" (*'ormâ*), "discretion" (*məzimmâ*), and others. Truth be told, we struggle to find the exact nuance of these words (thus the variation among translations),[2] but they all seem to be aspects of the broader concept of wisdom, and thus our focus will be an overarching understanding of wisdom in the book of Proverbs.

What Is Wisdom according to the Book of Proverbs?

We have to look not only at the preface but also the contents of the teaching of Proverbs in order to discover the meaning of wisdom. As we do so, we will see that wisdom is not a simple concept. Our description of wisdom in Proverbs will unfold on three levels: practical, ethical, and theological. While we will present wisdom separately as practical, then ethical, and finally theological, we should state right at the beginning that in Proverbs the three are deeply intertwined. No one can be truly wise unless one is wise practically, ethically, and theologically.

The Skill of Living: The Practical Level

When people think of the book of Proverbs today, they often think of it as a repository of advice about how to navigate life. Proverbs is a book that gives nitty-gritty instructions about how to avoid pitfalls and maximize success understood as having and maintaining robust relationships with others, maintaining personal health, and working in a way that will ensure a life-sustaining income (if not riches).

While we will see that certain excessive expectations of wisdom along these lines are wrong-minded (see chap. 11), it would be an error to deny that the teaching of Proverbs intends to impart advice that indeed has such purposes. Consider the following examples:

> A slack palm makes poverty;
>   a determined hand makes rich. (10:4)

2. For the best effort so far to refine our understanding of the nuances of the various words used for wisdom (and folly), see Fox, *Proverbs 1–9*, 28–44.

Here the wisdom instructor commends industriousness as the route to material success, while warning against laziness, which will lead to disaster.

> A winking eye brings trouble,
>> but those who reprimand with boldness bring peace.[3] (10:10)

Here we have advice about how to maintain peace in a relationship when someone has done something wrong. In the second colon the wise teacher advises a straightforward reprimand of the person. The first colon is a bit obscure since we cannot be absolutely certain of the significance of a winking eye. It seems to be in contrast, though, to a bold reprimand, so it likely signifies a tacit acceptance of the wrongdoing on the part of another. The teacher insists that it is actually the reprimand rather than the avoidance of the problem that leads to healthy relationship.

> In an abundance of words, wickedness does not cease;
>> those who restrain their lips are insightful. (10:19)

In this final example, we encounter counsel in the area of speech communication. Good speech is necessary for good relationships. This proverb fits in with others (13:3; 17:28) that advise the wise person to avoid excessive talking. The fewer words the better. Those who talk immoderately only make a situation worse.

These are just three of many examples of proverbs whose purpose is to impart a practical kind of wisdom that helps a person live life well.

Indeed, on this level wisdom is similar to what today we often call emotional intelligence.[4] Emotional intelligence is similar to what used to be called social skills or even street smarts. Emotional intelligence is different from what we often mean when we say that a person is intelligent. The latter concerns a knowledge of facts ("knowing that"), while wisdom entails living life skillfully ("knowing how"). Raw intelligence can be measured by devices such as an IQ test, while emotional intelligence can be measured by tests that indicate a person's EQ.

Emotionally intelligent people, like the wise in the book of Proverbs, know how to say the right thing at the right time. They do the right thing at the right time. They also express emotions that are appropriate for a situation at

---

3. The second colon follows the Septuagint translation, since the Masoretic text simply and almost certainly erroneously repeats 10:9b.

4. Goleman, *Emotional Intelligence*. More recently, see the excellent book by Brooks, *Social Animal*. See more in appendix 2.

the right intensity. Timing is everything in wisdom. Consider the following proverbs that emphasize proper timing:

> It is a joy to a person to give an answer!
>> How good a word at the right time! (15:23)

A response is effective only if it is appropriate for the situation. Our next example illustrates this insight.

> Those who bless their neighbors with a loud voice in the early
>> morning—
> it will be considered a curse. (27:14)

On the surface of it, one might think a "blessing" or positive word would be well received, whether in a loud or a soft voice. However, the wise teacher informs his hearer that if it comes at the wrong time—early in the morning when a person is just waking up—that positive word will not be appreciated.

Note also the following proverbs that show how wisdom and folly are expressed through one's emotions:

> Patience brings much competence,
>> but impatience promotes stupidity. (14:29)

> A patient person is better than a warrior,
>> and those who control their emotions than those who can capture a
>> city. (16:32)

These two proverbs support reticence in the expression of emotions. Losing control of one's emotions leads to ineffective thought and action.

> Those who hold back their speech know wisdom,
>> and those who are coolheaded are people of understanding. (17:27)

This proverb urges self-control in both speech and emotions. Those who are able to exercise self-control are called wise.

Intriguingly, research has discovered that there is a high correlation between emotional intelligence and success in life, with a corresponding low connection between a high IQ and human flourishing. In short, people who have good social skills as described above thrive in relationships and have an easier time getting a job and keeping it. The same research has shown that a high

IQ does not correlate well with these desired results.[5] After all, says Goleman, "academic intelligence offers virtually no preparation for the turmoil—or opportunity—life's vicissitudes bring."[6]

Of course, IQ and EQ are not mutually exclusive characteristics. One can be highly intelligent both academically and emotionally, but it appears that, while the latter alone can bring a measure of life success, the former typically does not.

We turned our attention to the subject of emotional intelligence because of its similarity to biblical wisdom. Proverbs is a book that on the practical level offers to make its attentive reader wise (emotionally intelligent). The research that indicates that emotional intelligence/wisdom results in great benefits makes sense of the biblical sages' connection between wisdom and reward, on the one hand, and folly and negative consequences, on the other, as illustrated by the following examples:

> Wise women build their houses,
>> but dupes demolish theirs with their own hands. (14:1)

The sages frequently use this type of "antithetic parallelism," which is constructed with the use of antonyms rather than near synonyms and addresses the same situation but from opposite perspectives. Here the contrast is between wise and foolish women. The actions of the former lead to constructive results and the latter to negative. Of course, wise women do not literally build, nor foolish women literally demolish, their houses, but rather their respective actions lead to the flourishing or diminishing of their households.

> Those who ridicule the poor insult their Maker;
>> those who rejoice in disaster will not go unpunished. (17:5)

This proverb points the finger at those who mock poor people. The disaster in the second colon refers to the situation that led to their unfortunate circumstances. To rejoice in someone's difficulties is not only unseemly but an insult to the God who made all people, including the poor and those who suffer tragedy. The wisdom instructor warns that such behavior will result

5. The data is presented in an accessible way by Goleman, *Emotional Intelligence*, including a study of Harvard students from the 1940s of varied academic levels who "were followed into middle age." The study discovered "the men with the highest test scores in college were not particularly successful compared to their lower-scoring peers in terms of salary, productivity, or status in their field. Nor did they have the greatest life satisfaction, nor the most happiness with friendships, family, and romantic relationships" (35).

6. Ibid., 36.

in negative consequences for those who so treat the poor. The nature of the punishment is intentionally not specified because it might come in a variety of forms.

The wisdom teachers thus make the same point as those today who describe emotional intelligence. Wise, emotionally intelligent attitudes and behaviors lead to success in life.[7]

The Wise Person as a Good Person: The Ethical Level

In the previous section, we explored the practical dimension of proverbial wisdom. Many people recognize the beneficial value of proverbs for guidance in how to live life. Indeed, for many that is the sum total of the nature of wisdom. Such a limited understanding of wisdom, however, perverts the biblical idea of wisdom.

The purpose of Proverbs is not simply to make someone emotionally intelligent and able to live life skillfully. Proverbs wants to make a person good as well as successful.[8]

We get the first hint of the ethical dimension of wisdom from the preface. In 1:3b we read that the purpose of the book includes the impartation of "righteousness, justice, and virtue." What constitutes these qualities is not specified here, which raises the question of the relationship between wisdom and the law found in the Torah. Both wisdom and law demand certain types of behaviors. God calls for obedience to the law, and the father and Woman Wisdom urge the son to follow the dictates of their advice in Proverbs.

The relationship between wisdom and law has been much debated, with some scholars seeing a close connection between the two and others denying any substantial relationship.[9] Certainly there are differences between commandment and advice. As our study progresses, we observe with even more clarity that the proverb is not universally true but true only when applied to the right situation, while the commandment is always true. However, when the proverb is rightly applied, it has the force of commandment. Perhaps this explains why the vocabulary connected to law is used in the book of Proverbs for the teaching of the father and Woman Wisdom.[10]

---

7. See chap. 11 for further discussion of the relationship between wise behavior with reward and foolish behavior with punishment.

8. Lyu, *Righteousness*.

9. See the classic statement of the two sides in Gemser, "Spiritual Structure"; and Zimmerli, "Concerning the Structure."

10. *Tôrâ* ("instruction/law") is used in 1:8; 3:1; 6:20, 23; 7:2; 13:14; 28:4, 7, 9; 29:18; 31:26; and *miṣwâ* ("command") is used in 2:1; 3:1; 4:4; 6:20, 23; 7:1, 2; 13:13; 19:16.

Indeed, the teaching of many proverbs echoes the requirements of the Ten Commandments, particularly those that regulate the behavior among human beings:

Commandment	Proverbs
Honor father and mother (5th):	1:8; 4:1, 10; 10:1; 13:1
Do not murder (6th):	1:10–12; 6:17
Do not commit adultery (7th):	2:16–19; chap. 5; 6:20–35; chap. 7
Do not steal (8th):	1:13–14; 11:1
Do not bear false witness (9th):	3:30; 6:18, 19; 10:18; 12:17, 19
Do not covet (10th):	6:18

Proverbs is not as explicit on the connection between wisdom and law as the later Wisdom of Solomon or Ben Sira (see chap. 14). In those books Woman Wisdom speaks the law of Moses. However, the roots of this connection are to be found in the book of Proverbs itself.

David Bland has made a major contribution recently in describing the ethical nature of wisdom in his book *Proverbs and the Formation of Character*. He argues persuasively that the proverbs don't simply lead to a change of behavior but encourage attitudes and behaviors that over time become habits that contribute to the transformation of character. As Lyu puts it, "Proverbs instructs that the reader should learn and become wise and righteous. To reach that goal, the learner is expected to go through the reshaping of his inner person. His desires, hopes, and disposition must be reconditioned to reflect the ideal."[11] The son who obeys the advice of his father will become a righteous person, and the one who does not becomes wicked. Second, Bland emphasizes that wisdom is not just for individual betterment but for the benefit of the community.[12]

Throughout the book of Proverbs, righteousness and wisdom are interchangeable terms. One cannot be wise without being righteous. In the same way, folly and wickedness are inextricably intertwined. Foolish behavior is evil. If we understand this, we recognize the ethical dimension of wisdom. But even so, we have not yet arrived at an adequate understanding of wisdom according to the book of Proverbs.

11. Lyu, *Righteousness*, 64.
12. See also Brown (*Character in Crisis*, 47), who puts it this way: "Productive and responsible citizenship within the life of the community is of central concern to the editors who produced the book of Proverbs."

Fearing God: The Theological Level

THE FEAR OF THE LORD IS THE BEGINNING OF WISDOM

Our continuing exploration of the nature of biblical wisdom takes us back once again to the preface of Proverbs. In its climactic concluding verse, we read:

> The fear of Yahweh is the beginning of knowledge,
>   but fools despise wisdom and discipline. (1:7)

This statement is well known; but even so, Proverbs and wisdom have been described by some, scholars as well as laypeople, as nontheological or even secular. We will say more about this below, but first we will unpack Prov. 1:7.

The first six verses indicate the practical and ethical nature of wisdom, but this verse reveals its theological character: "The fear of Yahweh is the beginning of knowledge." This principle is repeated a number of times (sometimes with the variant "the beginning of wisdom") in Proverbs (esp. 9:10, which forms an inclusio in the discourses of the book found in chaps. 1–9, but see also 1:29; 2:5; 3:7; 8:13; 10:27; 14:2, 26, 27; 15:16, 33; 16:6; 19:23; 22:4; 23:17; 24:21; 28:14; 29:25; 31:30) and also in other wisdom passages (for instance Job 28:28; Ps. 111:10; Eccles. 12:13).

"Beginning" can either refer to the foundation on which an edifice is built or can mean the first of a succession of moments. In either case (and both might be meant), the phrase insists that where there is no fear of the Lord, there is no wisdom. One cannot even begin in the enterprise of wisdom without having fear of God.

But why fear? Why not "the love of God is the beginning of wisdom"?

To answer this question, we first explore what exactly is meant by "fear" in this context. The Hebrew word (*yir'at*) can be used of everything from anxiety to horror.[13] There does not seem to be an exact English parallel to the sense in which it is meant here, but "fear" here certainly does not point to the type of fear that makes someone run away and hide like Adam in the garden of Eden (Gen. 3:8). Some suggest that the word should be understood as "respect" (TLB), but that word seems inappropriately weak. Perhaps the closest English word is "awe," but even that word does not quite get it. The "fear" of the "fear of the Lord" is the sense of standing before the God who created everything, including humans whose very continued existence depends on him. The emotion is appropriate for wisdom because it demonstrates acknowledgment that God is so much greater than we are. He takes our breath

---

13. For a helpful and full study of the Hebrew word, see *NIDOTTE* 2:527–33.

away and makes our knees knock together. Such fear breeds humility and signals a willingness to receive instruction from God.

This fear is not the fear that makes us run, but it is the fear that makes us pay attention and listen. Fear of the Lord makes us humble, a wisdom trait, rather than proud and "wise in our own eyes" (3:5, 7; 6:17; 11:2; 15:25, 33; 16:5, 18, 19; 18:12; 21:4, 24; 22:4; 25:6–7, 27; 26:12; 30:1–4, 13). This is why fear rather than love is the appropriate emotion for the wise.

The fear of the Lord inevitably leads to obedience. The one who fears God will follow the advice that God imparts through the sages in the chapters of instruction in the form of lectures and proverbs that follow the preface.

The connection between fear of the Lord and obedience is well illustrated in the life of Abraham. For much of the NT, the Abraham story is read to drive home the important point that our relationship with God is based on faith not obedience. On a number of occasions Paul cites Gen. 15:6 ("Abram believed the Lord, and he credited it to him as righteousness"; see Rom. 4:3, 9; Gal. 3:6) to establish what later theologians would call the doctrine of justification by faith alone.

In their zeal to avoid works righteousness, many Protestant theologians don't know what to do with James's appropriation of the conclusion to the Abraham story found in Gen. 22, the binding of Isaac.[14] Abraham passes this ultimate test of his faith and then hears the angel of the Lord proclaim: "Now I know that you *fear God*, because you have not withheld from me your son, your only son. . . . I swear by myself, declares the Lord, that because you have done this and have not withheld your son, your only son, I will surely bless you and make your descendants as numerous as the stars in the sky and as the sand on the seashore. Your descendants will take possession of the cities of their enemies, and through your offspring all nations on earth will be blessed, *because you have obeyed me*" (Gen. 22:12, 16–18, emphasis added). James uses this story to make his readers understand that faith without works is dead (James 2:14–26).

Thus, from Prov. 1:7a we learn that wisdom requires the right attitude toward God. Step one ("the beginning") of wisdom involves a robust relationship with God. The second part of the verse talks about those who reject wisdom as fools. The rejection of wisdom begins with a rejection of God, as Ps. 14:1 points out:

> The fool says in his heart,
>   "There is no God."

14. Longman, *Genesis*, 286–302.

And then the psalmist goes on to comment on the fool's character:

> They are corrupt, their deeds are vile;
>> there is no one who does good.

We learn in Prov. 1:7 that at its foundation wisdom is a theological category through and through.

We are, however, led to the conclusion of the theological nature of wisdom by more than a single phrase, no matter how repeated and strategically placed. The sages who produced Proverbs further indicated that wisdom requires a relationship with Yahweh through the figure of Woman Wisdom. We thus turn our attention to the role she plays in the book.

WOMAN WISDOM

Proverbs 1:7 is not the only way that the book communicates the deeply theological foundation of wisdom. Throughout the discourses of the first part of the book (chaps. 1–9), we encounter the intriguing figure of Woman Wisdom. Indeed, she makes her initial appearance the second lecture:

> Wisdom shouts in the street;
>> in the public square she yells out.
> At the top of the noisy throng she calls out an invitation
>> at the entrances to the gates in the city she says her piece:
> "How long, O simple, will you love simplemindedness,
>> and mockers hold their mocking dear,
>> and fools hate knowledge?
> You should respond to my correction.
>> I will pour forth my spirit to you;
>> I will make known to you my words
> Because I invited you, but you rejected me;
>> I extended my hand, but you paid no attention
> You ignored all my advice,
>> and my correction you did not want.
> I will also laugh at your disaster;
>> I will ridicule you when your fear comes.
> When your fear comes like a tempest,[15]
>> and your disaster arrives like a storm,
>> when distress and oppression come on you,

15. Reading Qere (šoʾâ) rather than the Ketib (šaʾăwâ).

then they will call me, and I will not answer;
    they will seek me, but they will not find me
because they hated knowledge,
    and did not chose the fear of Yahweh.
They did not want my advice,
    and they rejected all my reproof.
They will eat from the fruit of their way,
    and they will be sated from their own counsels,
For the turning away of the simple will kill them,
    and the complacency of fools will destroy them.
Those who obey me will dwell securely;
    they will be untroubled from the horror of evil." (1:20–33)

Here Wisdom speaks from the most public of places. She is out in the open, in the public square, on top of the wall, at the city gate. Her teaching is not hidden, mystical, secret, or elitist, but rather open and accessible to all. However, not everyone cares. The simpleminded (naive or immature) person, the fool, and, worst of all, the mocker ignore or resist her message.

Wisdom anticipates the time in the future when those who do not listen to her now will turn to her. When crisis hits, they will seek her, but because they ignored her in the present, she will ignore them in their future crisis. The message is clear. Turn to Wisdom now before you need her, before trouble comes.

Fear of the Lord leads people to form a relationship with Woman Wisdom, but fools and mockers do not fear God. Those who reject her will suffer, while those who turn to her will be safe (vv. 32–33).

Woman Wisdom herself speaks in this discourse, and she will speak again (see discussion of Prov. 8:1–9:6), but before looking at these pivotal passages, we will first take note of the way the father speaks of this Woman to his son.

Blessed are those who find Wisdom,
    and those who gain competence.
For her profit is better than that of silver,[16]
    and her yield, better than gold.
Her value is more than pearls,
    and all that you want is not the equal of her.
Length of days is in her right hand;
    in her left are wealth and honor.
Her paths are pleasant paths,
    and all her trails are peace.

16. Literally, "For its profit is better than the profit of silver."

> She is a tree of life to those who embrace her,
>> and those who hold her tight are blessed.
> Yahweh laid the foundations of the earth with Wisdom,
>> establishing the heavens with competence.
> With his knowledge the deeps burst open,
>> and the skies drop dew. (Prov. 3:13–20)

In this discourse the father talks to his son about Woman Wisdom. He urges his son to seek a relationship with her by pronouncing those who do so "blessed" and telling him of the great reward that results. She is more precious than even the most expensive jewels and rare metals. She bestows long life and also the ability to navigate life. After all, Yahweh created the world with her (a point that will be expressed again in 8:22–31). Who would better know how the world worked?

> Hear, sons, fatherly discipline,
>> and pay attention to the knowledge of understanding.
> For I will give you good teaching;
>> don't forsake my instruction.
> For I was a son to my father,
>> tender and the only one of my mother.
> He taught me and said to me:
>> "Let your heart hold on to my words;
>> guard my commands and live.
> Acquire Wisdom;
>> acquire Understanding.
> Don't forget,
>> and don't divert from the speeches of my mouth.
> Don't abandon her, and she will guard you.
>> Love her, and she will protect you.
> The beginning of wisdom: Acquire Wisdom!
>> And above all your acquisitions, acquire Wisdom![17]
> Esteem her highly and she will exalt you.
>> She will honor you, if you embrace her.
> She will place on your head a garland of favor,
>> she will bestow on you a crown of glory." (4:1–9)

17. Many commentators (see Clifford, *Proverbs*, 60) argue that v. 7 is a later addition based on the fact that it is missing from the Greek and that it is awkward to the context and made up of phrases found elsewhere. However, it is not so awkward as to be without possible meaning in the text, and its absence from the Greek could have a number of different explanations, including that the Greek translator did not understand it and then dropped it, as Clifford does. Fox (*Proverbs 1–9*, 175) is not convinced v. 7 is original but does point out in its favor that it is part of a chiastic structure in the passage.

The father again exhorts his son to establish a relationship with Woman Wisdom. Here he uses marital language. He is to love her and esteem her. In return, she will honor, guard, and reward him.

We now turn our attention to the most sustained presentation by Woman Wisdom in the book of Proverbs. In the eighth chapter the narrator, understood to be the father, introduces Woman Wisdom by identifying her location and calling our attention to her speech:

> Does not Wisdom cry out;
>> and Understanding give forth her voice?
> At the top of the high places on the path,
>> at the crossroads she takes her stand.
> By the gate before the city,
>> at the entrances she shouts. (vv. 1–3)

Similar to her first speech, her location is public (1:20–21). Here we have for the first time an emphasis on the elevation of her location ("at the top of the high places"), which, as we move into chapter 9, will prove deeply significant.

The rest of the chapter presents her words as she reveals her character and her actions to them:

> I cry out to you, O men;
>> my voice goes out to the sons of humanity.
> Understand prudence, you who are simpleminded;
>> you fools, take this to heart.
> Listen, for I speak noble things,
>> opening virtuous lips.[18]
> For my mouth[19] utters the truth,
>> and my lips despise wickedness.[20]
> All the speeches of my mouth are righteous.[21]
>> Nothing in them is twisted or perverse.
> All of them are straightforward to understanding,
>> and virtuous for those who seek knowledge.
> Take discipline and not silver,
>> and knowledge more than choice gold.
> For wisdom is better than pearls,
>> and nothing is more delightful than it. (vv. 4–11)

18. Literally, "the opening of my lips is virtuous."
19. The Hebrew has the more specific "palette" (*ḥēk*), though that seems a bit too precise a translation for this context.
20. Literally, "the abomination of my lips is wickedness."
21. Literally, "In righteousness: all the speeches of my mouth."

She opens her speech to all the men who hear her by admonishing them to pay attention to what she has to say. In particular, she appeals to the simple-minded (or immature) as well as fools. Presumably the wise are already listening to her. Her appeal is based on the ethical rightness of what she has to say. She speaks of noble, virtuous, righteous matters, and she eschews wickedness and perversity. Her words will lead to understanding and knowledge. She also encourages them to listen to her because what she has to say is more valuable than even the most precious metals.

> I, Wisdom, dwell with prudence.
>> I have found knowledge and discretion.
> Those who fear Yahweh hate evil,
>> pride and arrogance, and the path of evil.
>> I hate a perverse mouth.
> Advice and resourcefulness belong to me,
>> as do understanding and strength.
> By me kings reign,
>> and nobles issue just decrees.
> By me rulers rule,
>> and princes, all righteous judgments.
> I love those who love me,
>> and those who seek me will find me.
> Wealth and honor are with me,
>> enduring riches[22] and righteousness.
> My fruit is better than gold, even fine gold;
>> my yield than choice silver.
> I walk on the way of righteousness,
>> in the midst of the trails of justice,
> to cause those who love me to inherit substance,[23]
>> and I will fill their treasuries. (vv. 12–22)

Woman Wisdom now describes herself by associating herself with prudence, knowledge, discretion (v. 12), and righteousness (v. 20), while distancing herself from pride and perverse speech (v. 13). She has good advice, and therefore people—and in particular, rulers who are in charge of others' lives—are most

22. Or perhaps "negotiable wealth," according to Hurowitz, "Two Terms," 252–54. If so, it refers to wealth that can be transported during a trip, perhaps for business purposes. In either case, Woman Wisdom claims to be able to make a person rich.

23. This word $y\bar{e}š$ is unique as a noun in Hebrew. It typically has the sense of a copula "there is" or "there was." Hurowitz, "Two Terms," rather argues that it is related to the Akkadian *busu*, which also developed from a verb "there is," and means "valuables, goods, moveable property."

effective if they are related to Woman Wisdom (vv. 14–16). She aligns herself with those who fear Yahweh (see above).

This stanza also declares that those who enter into a relationship with Woman Wisdom will benefit not only in skill of living but also in material goods (vv. 18–19, 21). By emphasizing this connection, Woman Wisdom tries to encourage people to enter into a relationship with her.

> Yahweh begot me at the beginning of his paths,
>> before his works of antiquity.
> From of old I was formed,
>> from the beginning, from before the earth.
> When there were no deeps I was brought forth,
>> when there were no springs, heavy with water.
> Before the mountains were settled,
>> before the hills, I was brought forth.
> At that time the earth and the open country were not made,
>> and the beginning of the clods of the world,
> when he established the heavens, I was there,
>> when he decreed the horizon on the face of the deep,
> when he strengthened the clouds above;
>> when he intensified the fountains of the deep,
> when he set for the sea its decree,
>> wherein the water could not pass where he said.[24]
> I was beside him as a craftsman.[25]

24. "Where he said" is literally "his mouth."

25. The translation of this difficult yet important word is much discussed, and relevant bibliography will be cited herein. The consonantal text of the Hebrew is '-m-w-n, and the Masoretes vocalized the word as 'āmôn, which means "craftsman" or "master craftsman." (For Dahood's defense of the translation "Master Architect," see "Proverbs 8,22–31," 518–19.) However, many readers find this difficult for two reasons. In the first place, Wisdom is never said to actually participate in the acts of creation in this chapter. Second, many people, including myself, would find it troubling if the text presented the picture of a second, separate creator who, along with Yahweh, brought the cosmos into existence. It appears that for these reasons, particularly the second, some scholars, going back at least to Aquila and his Greek translation, repoint the word with a u-vowel, thus 'āmûn, and understand the word as "nursling" or "child." I will briefly mention yet another approach—namely, that of Scott ("Wisdom in Creation"), where he revocalizes the text as 'ōmēn ("binding together") and translates the phrase "I was at his side a living link."

Most scholars agree that the meaning of the word could produce either meaning, provided one is open to vocalic emendation. However, it appears the only real reasons for moving away from the MT "craftsman" are theologically motivated. This is usually not satisfactory, but it is true that we should try to understand this text in the context of orthodox Yahwism. Rogers ("Meaning and Significance") tries to solve the problem by appealing to grammar. He says that we should take the word as appositional to the pronominal suffix, thus "I (Wisdom) was beside him (Yahweh), who is a craftsman."

My own view may be explained as follows. I agree with Rogers that the word 'āmôn refers to Yahweh, but contra Rogers, I also believe it refers to Woman Wisdom. How so? The answer

> I was playing daily,
>> laughing before him all the time.
> Laughing with the inhabitants of his earth,
>> and playing with the human race. (vv. 22–31)

Verses 22–31 are the most difficult in terms of both translation and content. The footnotes indicate and try to navigate the former. What is clear is that Woman Wisdom here declares her involvement in the creation of the world. No matter the details, the implicit message is that humans should want to know this woman because she, better than anyone, knows how the world works, and thus she is capable of helping us navigate life.

One reason this stanza is so difficult is that the NT uses this chapter to describe Jesus. Thus, through the ages interpreters have felt uncomfortable with the idea that Woman Wisdom appears here to have been created or born herself. We will deal with this issue later (see chap. 15).

No doubt, though, attends the idea that Woman Wisdom was present during the period of the creation of the cosmos. She was present before there were the watery deeps or the mountains. She was there and observed the creation of the heavens themselves. Interestingly, the poet speaks of creation utilizing ancient Near Eastern mythological ideas. This is seen most clearly when God sets a limit to the sea, restricting its location. Here (v. 29) the sea is personified as a force that needs control, very similar to the depiction of Marduk pushing back the sea and instructing "not to let her [Tiamat's] water escape."[26]

It is clear that Woman Wisdom observed creation, but the poet likely goes further and indicates that she also participated in it. The question hinges on the meaning of the Hebrew word 'āmôn in v. 30. The philology is discussed above in the footnote attached to this verse, and there it can be seen that I think the predominance of evidence lies on the side of a translation like "craftsman" rather than "nursling," "child," or some other alternative.

> And now, sons, listen to me;
>> happy are those who guard my path!
> Listen to discipline, and be wise,
>> and don't avoid it.

---

to that question rests on the exegesis of Prov. 9:1–6, but anticipating that discussion, I believe that Woman Wisdom is a poetic personification of Yahweh's wisdom; indeed, as indicated by her house's location on the high point of the city, Wisdom ultimately represents Yahweh himself.

Fox ("'Amon Again") suggests reading 'āmôn as an infinitive with the meaning "being raised" or "growing up." The colon would thereby refer to Wisdom's growing up in the presence of God.

26. Lambert, *Babylonian Creation Myths*, 95, citing Enuma Elish, tablet 4, line 140.

> Happy are those who listen to me,
>   watching daily at my doors,
>   guarding my doorposts.
> For those who find me find life,
>   and they gain favor from Yahweh.
> Those who offend me do violence to their life;
>   all those who hate me love death. (8:32–36)

This magnificent poem of Woman Wisdom ends with what is by now a familiar exhortation to pay attention and have a relationship with her. Those who do so will be happy and will live, whereas those who reject her will suffer and die. The decision whether to embrace Woman Wisdom is truly one of life or death. This choice comes to a head in the final chapter of the first part of the book:

> Wisdom built her house;
>   she erected her seven pillars.
> She slaughtered her slaughter, mixed her wine.
>   She also arranged her tables.
> She sends her maidens; she issues[27] an invitation
>   from the pinnacle of the heights of the city:
> "Whoever is simpleminded—turn aside here,"
>   she says to those who lack heart.
> "Come, eat my food,
>   and drink the wine I mixed.
> Abandon simplemindedness and live.
>   March on the path of understanding." (9:1–6)

The narrator introduces the speech of Woman Wisdom by describing her house, her feast, and her invitation. Wisdom constructed her house, and it is a magnificent house, which seems to be the meaning of the seven pillars, a number of completeness and totality. Claims that the seven pillars are a reference to the seven known planets of the day[28] or to the seven discourses in the previous chapters[29] are possible but speculative. That she has built her house reminds us of the later proverb that describes the wise woman as one who builds her own house instead of tearing it down as the foolish woman does

---

27. The breakup of the poetic line differs from the MT, since the *athnach* occurs under the verb "issues." Combined with the question of the significance of the *athnach* is the question of who is the subject of the verb "issues." We understand the subject to be Woman Wisdom and not the young maidens who are sent out. See McKinlay, *Gendering Wisdom*, 46.

28. In Poythress, *Shadow of Christ*, 18.

29. Skehan, "Seven Columns."

(14:1). She has also prepared a feast by slaughtering animals, thus providing meat, and mixing her wine. A meal of meat and wine was a special meal, a true banquet. Having prepared herself for guests, she then sends out her female servants to invite all the men who are going by. Indeed, considering the pervasiveness of the metaphor of the path and that all men—the addressees of the book of Proverbs—are on a path, we are to consider this an invitation to all who read the book of Proverbs.

At this point we note the location of her house, though we will discuss the implications later. Her house is described as occupying "the pinnacle of the heights of the city," again emphasizing her location at a high place (see also 8:2).

The invitation is addressed to the simpleminded (immature or naive, Heb. *peti*), who are also referred to as those who "lack heart." Unlike in modern English, in the OT "heart" refers primarily to the mind and not to the emotions or to courage. The term simpleminded could also be understood and even translated "immature." Thus, the invitees are neither clearly wise nor foolish. They could go either way. Woman Wisdom wants them to come to her feast.

Even today when we invite someone over for a meal, we do so in order to create a deeper relationship with that person. If anything, in ancient Israel to eat with someone is to create closer bonds with that person. And here, where a woman invites men to dine, there is even a stronger emphasis on relationship building. As McKinlay points out, eating and drinking are sexual metaphors.[30] Woman Wisdom wants these men to enter into an intimate relationship with her.

However, before the men, who represent the book's readers, can respond, they receive a second invitation, this one from Woman Folly.

> Woman Folly is boisterous;
>> she is simpleminded but does not even know it.
> She sits at the doorway of her house,
>> on a seat at the heights of the city.
> She invites those who pass by on the path,
>> those going straight on their way.
> "Whoever is simpleminded—turn aside here,"
>> she says to those who lack heart.
> "Stolen water is sweet;
>> food eaten in secret is pleasant."
> But they do not know that the departed are there;
>> that those invited by her are in the depths of Sheol. (9:13–18)

30. McKinlay, *Gendering Wisdom*, 57.

The narrator begins by introducing this second woman, whose name is Folly. She herself is simpleminded but so simpleminded that she is unaware of it. Someone who is simpleminded or immature and knows it can take steps to move toward wisdom, but she lacks any self-awareness. While Woman Wisdom worked to prepare the meal she offered to those who pass by, Woman Folly simply sits at her door. While Woman Wisdom is industrious, Woman Folly is lazy. Indeed, this description of her raises the question whether there actually is a meal at all or whether she is lying. We must also note here—to be explained later—that Woman Folly's house is also at an elevated location, "at the heights of the city."

She appeals to the same group as Woman Wisdom: those who pass by on the way. They are here, as earlier, described as "simpleminded" and "those who lack heart"—that is, people who have come to a point of decision. Will they dine with Woman Wisdom, or will they dine with Woman Folly? Woman Folly offers a meal that is stolen and to be eaten in secret, while Woman Wisdom offers her meal in public. The language connected with Woman Folly suggests a kind of secret knowledge gained illegitimately. After Folly's speech, the narrator notes the dire consequences for those who accept her invitation. They will die and become one of the departed (Heb. *rəpā'îm*), a shade or departed ancestor. They will find themselves in the depths of Sheol, the shadowy place where all the dead go.[31]

THE CRUCIAL CHOICE

Now that we have considered the main texts that inform us about Woman Wisdom and Woman Folly, we should feel the burden of choice. With whom will we dine? Whom will we make an integral part of our life? This is the most fundamental decision we can make. But who are these women? What or whom do they represent?

Their names make it obvious that they are personifications of wisdom and folly, respectively. Indeed, Woman Wisdom, who is the more fully developed figure, embodies all the virtues associated with wisdom. She speaks truth and avoids lies. She hates arrogance. She is industrious, not lazy. The brief description of Woman Folly correlates with the vices associated with foolishness. She is secretive, a thief, and a liar.

So certainly Woman Wisdom and Woman Folly represent wisdom and folly. However, the location of their houses allows us to go further. Their houses

31. Johnston, *Shades of Sheol.*

are on the heights, and Woman Wisdom often speaks from the heights. When one asks whose house occupies the highest place in an ancient Israelite, or for that matter ancient Near Eastern, city, the answer is the deity.

Thus, we may go further and say that Woman Wisdom is not simply a personification of God's wisdom but actually represents Yahweh himself. But if that is true, what about Woman Folly? Her house is also on the heights. Woman Folly also represents deity. In her case, she stands for the false gods and goddesses that rival Yahweh for the affection of the Israelites.

The choice is clear. Do we, the readers, choose to dine with Woman Wisdom, who represents Yahweh? Or do we choose to dine with Woman Folly and thus worship a false deity? In this way the book of Proverbs shows that it understands that wisdom and folly are theological categories.

Conclusion: The Nature of Wisdom in the Book of Proverbs

Much recent thinking about this subject has suggested that wisdom, as opposed to other biblical traditions, has a secular, or at least cosmopolitan, perspective. Zoltán Schwáb has recently collected and analyzed the comments of a number of scholars who apply the category "secular" to wisdom.[32] Here are just three examples he provides:

> Wisdom teaching is profoundly secular in that it presents life and history as human enterprise. . . . [Wisdom] consistently places stress on human freedom, accountability, the importance of making decisions. . . . [Wisdom] is concerned with the freedom, power, and responsibility of man to manage his world.[33]

> The proverbs as such have a universal character. Proverbs can surface anywhere among humankind, just like accounts of creation or the flood. . . . [Proverbs mentioning God] have no specifically theological foundation in an explicitly theological context. Rather, they speak of God in such a manner as would any person without stepping outside of everyday, secular discourse.[34]

Unfortunately, some preachers also hold this perspective, as represented by this quotation from Willimon:

32. Z. Schwáb, *Toward an Interpretation*, 164–74. McKane (*Prophets and Wise Men*; *Proverbs*) is often cited as the scholar who first promoted the understanding that early Israelite wisdom was secular. More recently, Fiddes (*Seeing the World*) sees Proverbs as fundamentally and originally secular in approach.
33. Brueggemann, *In Man We Trust*, 81–83.
34. Westermann, *Roots of Wisdom*, 130.

Generally, I dislike the book of Proverbs with its lack of theological content, its long lists of platitudinous advice, its "do this" and "don't do that." Pick up your socks. Be nice to salesclerks. It doesn't hurt to be nice. Proverbs is something like being trapped on a long road trip with your mother, or at least with William Bennett.[35]

Our understanding of the nature of wisdom in the book of Proverbs is that it is more than practical advice for how to live in the world. Wisdom is ethical and foundationally theological. One cannot be called wise unless one has a proper relationship with Yahweh (Prov. 1:7 and the figure of Woman Wisdom).[36]

This theological understanding of wisdom means that even those proverbs that don't mention God in the second part of the book (chaps. 10–31) are theological. We end with two examples:

> A wise son makes a father glad,
>   and a foolish son is the sorrow of his mother. (Prov. 10:1)

> A slack palm makes poverty;
>   a determined hand makes rich. (Prov. 10:4)

On the surface, these two proverbs seem to be observations with no theological substance. However, they must be read in context that includes the first nine chapters and in particular the decision offered in Prov. 9 whether to dine with Woman Wisdom or Woman Folly, both of whom represent deities. Once the reader recognizes this context, then we must consider Prov. 10:1 to make a theological statement along the following lines. Those who bring joy to their parents are wise, meaning that they are acting like a proper worshiper of the true God. However, those who bring grief to their parents are acting like idolaters. In the case of Prov. 10:4, hard workers are wise and thus in relationship with Woman Wisdom, who represents God, while lazy persons are acting like they are in relationship with an idol.

Thus, Proverbs makes it clear that wisdom is neither secular nor universal, but rather theological and particular to Israel. We now turn to Ecclesiastes to see if our understanding of wisdom rings true for this perplexing book.

---

35. Willimon, *Pastor*, 255–56, quoted in Bland, *Proverbs and the Formation of Character*, 8.
36. In this we agree with Weeks (*Early Israelite Wisdom*, 73): "The theory that early Israelite wisdom was a secular tradition has been examined in some depth and found to be wanting in almost every respect."

2

ECCLESIASTES

*Fear God, Obey the Commandments,
and Live in Light of the Coming Judgment*

We began our exploration of the biblical concept of wisdom with Proverbs since that book presents wisdom in a positive and, relatively speaking, untroubled manner. In the words of the theologian David Kelsey, "Proverbs conveys what we may call the conventions of mainstream Wisdom tradition as it thinks within the framework of a theology of creation."[1]

In the next two chapters we turn to the other two books of the Protestant canon that are considered wisdom—namely, Ecclesiastes and Job. While we will argue that there is no contradiction between Proverbs, on the one hand, and Ecclesiastes and Job, on the other, we will see that there is a definite and clear difference in emphasis and tone. In the final analysis, a view of wisdom that rings true to the Bible (and to life) may be gained only by attention to all three, or—to put it another way—we must ultimately read any one of these books in the light of the others. A canonical approach to interpretation insists on such an understanding.

While it was important for us to begin our study of wisdom with Proverbs, no necessary or logical reason requires us to begin with one or the other of the two books. Thus, we will begin with Ecclesiastes and then continue with a study of Job.

---

1. Kelsey, *Eccentric Existence*, 188. For the connection between wisdom and a theology of creation, see chap. 8.

The Limits of Wisdom "Under the Sun": The Nature of Wisdom in the Book of Ecclesiastes

Meaningless, meaningless! Everything is meaningless![2]

When most people think of the book of Ecclesiastes, this statement comes immediately to mind. After all, the word "meaningless" (*hebel*)[3] occurs over forty times in this relatively short book. The impression that the book of Ecclesiastes concludes that life is meaningless seems odd in a book included in sacred Scripture. This conclusion has not only mystified but also discouraged clergy from preaching and laypeople from studying the book of Ecclesiastes. One's initial impression of the book, however, is not borne out by a close reading, as we will see.

Thus, before entering into an examination of Ecclesiastes's contribution to the theology of wisdom, we begin with a relatively brief orientation to the proper reading of the book. The view presented here is not uncontested, but neither is it idiosyncratic. It is not surprising in the least that scholarly experts of the book differ in their approach to a book that, at times, seems to contradict not only other portions of Scripture but also itself. As I lay out my own understanding of the book, I will indicate what is broadly agreed upon and what is not.

Two Voices, Not One

We begin with what is now a widely held view among commentators on the book. There are two speakers in the book as we know it, not just one.[4] No longer is it fashionable to explain these two voices as simply the result

---

2. Translations of Ecclesiastes come from Longman, *Ecclesiastes*.

3. The nonmetaphorical meaning of *hebel* is "breath, breeze, vapor," but it is never used in its nonmetaphorical sense. The main dispute is over whether *hebel* denotes an ephemeral *meaning* or ephemeral *time*. There are variations among scholars holding the first view. Fox (*Qohelet and His Contradictions*) translates *hebel* as "absurd," while Bartholomew (*Ecclesiastes*) and Enns (*Ecclesiastes*) translate it "enigma." For support of the ephemeral *time*, thus "transient," meaning, see esp. Fredericks, *Coping with Transience*. Fredericks's argument, which departs from the long history of interpretation of this word in Ecclesiastes, seems like an attempt to turn Qohelet into an orthodox thinker. It makes a big difference whether Qohelet is asserting the meaninglessness (or enigmatic nature or absurdity) of life or the transitory nature of life. Interestingly, Seow (*Ecclesiastes*) translates *hebel* in a number of different ways throughout the book. While he believes the context calls for such variation, it seems more likely that the book is using it as a motific word that would have only a single translation. For more on the word *hebel*, see Longman, *Ecclesiastes*, 61–65.

4. Recognized not only by Longman, *Ecclesiastes*, but also Bartholomew, *Ecclesiastes*; Enns, *Ecclesiastes*; Fox, *Ecclesiastes*; Seow, *Ecclesiastes*.

of the history of composition.[5] Even if the so-called epilogue (12:8–14) was added on to a previously existing work, what we have in the canon is the final form of the book, and that is what is authoritative to us and should be the focus of our interpretation.

Though subtle, the presence of two voices in the book is clear.

First, we have the voice of Qohelet. Qohelet transliterates the Hebrew word that identifies the one who speaks in the first person in the body of the work (1:12–12:7): "I, Qohelet." The Hebrew is traditionally translated "Preacher" beginning with the Greek version (*ekklesiastes*) and moving on to the Latin, giving the book its title in Christian tradition. More recent English versions (e.g., NIV, NLT; ESV is an exception) prefer the translation "Teacher," presumably on the ground that "Preacher" is anachronistic for the book's setting in the OT. In addition, as we will see, Qohelet's views are rather edgy for one thought to be a clergy member. To some, he is more like a philosophy professor who raises disturbing questions about life.

However, the Hebrew word Qohelet means neither "preacher" nor "teacher." It is a feminine active participle of the common Hebrew verb *qhl*, which means "to assemble" or "to gather together." Feminine active participles can be used for occupations,[6] and thus a translation more in keeping with the Hebrew is "Assembler" or "Gatherer."

The more traditional translations presume that the name refers to the speaker's gathering a group together, either an ecclesiastical gathering or a classroom, in order to speak to it. However, I think the name is intended not to identify the speaker's role but to further an association (not identification) with the historical Solomon, the purpose of which I will explicate shortly below. After all, the verb *qhl* plays an important role in the Solomon narrative in Kings, particularly 1 Kings 8 (particularly vv. 1, 2, 14, 22, 55, 65) that describes the dedication of the newly built temple where Solomon addresses an assembly (*qāhāl*). Whatever the exact significance of the name or of its connection to the historical Solomon, Qohelet is a pseudonym. It is not the speaker's real name.

Having discussed the main speaker's name, we now return to the discussion of the two voices in the book, the first being Qohelet's. We identify his voice easily because he speaks from 1:12 to 12:7 in the first person.

Seeing that Qohelet speaks in the first person, we take note of the second voice in the concluding section of the book (12:8–14), when the speaker refers

---

5. As did Crenshaw, *Ecclesiastes*.

6. See Ezra 2:55, 57; Neh. 7:57, 59 for the use of the feminine participle as an occupational name. Also that it is an occupational name rather than a personal name may be seen by the addition of the definite article (Eccles. 12:8).

to Qohelet in the third person: "Qohelet, he." This is a voice other than Qohelet's since it is obviously talking about Qohelet, and, as we see in 12:12 ("Furthermore, of these, my son, be warned"), this second speaker is talking about Qohelet to his son.

Noting the clear shift of speaker in the epilogue raises the question of the prologue (1:1–11). We see that 1:1 is a superscription to the book, and 1:2 is speaking about Qohelet, so again we have the voice of the second speaker. This much is clear. The status of 1:3–11 is debated among those who see two voices in the book.

It is true that these verses express Qohelet's viewpoint. These verses, to be sure, articulate the type of frustration that Qohelet bemoans in 1:12–12:7. Thus, some scholars attribute them to Qohelet.[7]

I disagree. Qohelet does not start speaking in the first person until 1:12 ("I, Qohelet, have been king over Israel in Jerusalem"). As my early study of the genre of fictional autobiographies in the ancient Near East demonstrated, 1:12 conforms precisely to the opening line of such an autobiographical reflection.[8] Thus, it is best to understand the entirety of 1:2–11 as a prologue spoken/written by the second wise man to introduce Qohelet's viewpoint. The words are his, but the thought is Qohelet's.

Finally, we should note one more appearance of the second wise man, this time in the body of Qohelet's first-person speech. It is easily overlooked because the second wise man's presence is simply marked by "Qohelet said" (7:29). But this simple phrase indicates that Qohelet's speech is one long quotation. The father is reporting Qohelet's words to his son.

In summary, Ecclesiastes contains a wise father's words to his son (12:8–14) after he introduces him to the thought of a person who calls himself Qohelet (1:12–12:7). The father provides an introduction to Qohelet's words (1:1–11), and thus his voice frames that of Qohelet (leading Fox to call him the frame narrator).[9] I will also use that term to identify this speaker as well as the rather clumsy "second wise man."

Ecclesiastes contains a father's interaction with his son as he presents and then critically interacts with Qohelet's ideas. Thus, to understand the book of Ecclesiastes one must ask two questions. First, what is the message of Qohelet? Answering this question is necessary but not sufficient for proper interpretation of the book. We must then press on to the second question, which is, what is the message of the frame narrator? Since the latter's message

---

7. Seow, *Ecclesiastes*, 46–47.
8. Longman, *Fictional Akkadian Autobiography*.
9. Fox first argues this in "Frame-Narrative."

frames the words of Qohelet and then concludes the book, his perspective is
the message of the book.

Our next step is to answer these two questions. As we do so, we will pay
particularly close attention to how Qohelet and the frame narrator understand the nature of wisdom.

The Message of Qohelet

Qohelet is best known for this search for meaning "under the sun," though
that search is really concentrated in the first part of his speech. He examines work (2:18–23; 4:4–6), pleasure (2:1–11), relationships (4:7–12), wealth
(5:10–6:9), and wisdom (2:12–17) and concludes that meaning does not reside
in any of these. Indeed, as the frame narrator will tell his son, the bottom line
for Qohelet is that "everything is meaningless" (12:8).

There are three reasons why meaning is not found "under the sun": death,
injustice, and the inability to discern the proper time.

DEATH

Of these three, death may be the most debilitating. Death renders all things
meaningless because, for Qohelet, death is the end of the story. He does not
believe in any kind of afterlife. Qohelet's speech concludes with a sad reflection on death:

> Remember your creator in the days of your youth before the evil days come and
> the years approach when you will say, "I have no delight in them," before the
> sun and the light and the moon and the stars grow dark, and the clouds return
> after the rain, on the day when the house guards tremble and the landowners
> bend, and the women grinders cease because they are few, and those women
> who look through the window grow dim; the doors to the street are shut, when
> the sound of the mill decreases, and one rises at the sound of a bird, and all the
> daughters of song are brought low. Moreover, they are afraid of heights and
> the terrors in the path. The almond tree blossoms and the grasshopper drags
> itself along and the caperberry is useless. For humans go to their eternal home
> and mourners go about in the street. (Eccles. 12:1–5)

What interests us in these verses is Qohelet's reflection on growing old and
dying. He sets a somber tone by comparing our aging bodies to a house and
its languishing inhabitants. Just as the house guards tremble (like our hands),
the landowners bend (like our backs), the women grinders cease because they
are few (like our teeth), and the women looking through the window grow
dim (like our eyes), so do our bodies grow weaker and weaker. Other details

of the text also imply the effects of aging on the body. The doors represent bodily orifices that start to shut down, and the caperberry (an aphrodisiac) doesn't work anymore. One loses hearing but is still startled by sudden noises. Hair turns grey like the blossoms of the almond tree, and so forth. In the end, humans go to the grave (their "eternal home").

Qohelet continues his reflection on death using a different image in his final statement that follows:

> Before the silver thread is snapped, and the golden bowl is crushed, and the jar is broken by the well, and the wheel is crushed at the cistern, and the dust returns to the earth as it was, and the spirit returns to God, who gave it. (Eccles. 12:6–7)

Life here is compared to something precious (silver thread, golden bowl) or useful (jar, wheel), but death renders these items obsolete. Finally, Qohelet describes death as a reversal of the process that brought life into existence at the very beginning when God created Adam by breathing into the dust. One should not be tempted to read any sense of eternal life into this statement. Qohelet firmly believes that death ends life and renders everything meaningless.

Injustice

Second, injustice renders life meaningless for Qohelet. After all, if there are no rewards in the afterlife for those who do the right thing or punishments for those who do not, then any benefits and liabilities for good and bad behavior must happen in the present life. However, as Qohelet has examined the world, he concludes that there is no justice in the world: "Both I have observed in my meaningless life: There is a righteous person perishing in his righteousness, and there is a wicked person living long in his evil" (7:15). According to Qohelet, it is not right that the righteous die before the wicked. He therefore advises that people should be neither too righteous nor too wicked (see 7:16).

Qohelet's anguish over injustice is also expressed in 8:10–14:

> Thus, I observed the wicked buried and departed. They used to go out of the holy place, and they were praised in the city where they acted in such a way. This too is meaningless.

Qohelet "observes" that the wicked were not only praised in life but also honored in death. He finds this "meaningless," an injustice. He goes on to draw a moral from his observation: "Because the sentence for an evil deed is not quickly carried out, therefore the human heart is filled with evildoing. For sinners do evil a hundred times and their days are lengthened." In other words, the wicked getting away with their evil only encourages others to do wicked acts.

Suddenly, however, Qohelet seems to change his tune. Indeed, he seems to completely reverse what he just stated when he announces "although I know that it will be well for those who fear God because they fear him, and it will not be well for the wicked, and their days will not lengthen like a shadow, because they do not fear God."

Does Qohelet have a change of heart, finally asserting that there is justice in this life? No. We need to pay attention to the change from "I observed" in v. 10 to "I know" in v. 12. This signals a change from his experience to his theology. What he sees in the world is injustice, but his theology teaches him that the righteous are rewarded while the wicked are punished.

As we read on, his experience trumps his theology. We see this when he follows up his statement of theology with an anecdotal experience. "There is another example of meaninglessness that is done on the earth: There are righteous people who are treated as if they did wicked deeds, and there are wicked people who are treated as if they did righteous deeds." He thus concludes that "this too is meaningless."

Timing

Third and finally, Qohelet's sad conclusion that life is meaningless is also fueled by his belief that, though God created everything for the right time, he does not allow humans to know when that right time is.

That God has made everything for a right time is the subject of the well-known poem found in 3:1–8:

> For everything there is a season,
>   and a time for every activity under heaven.
> A time to be born and a time to die;
>   a time to plant and a time to uproot what has been planted.
> A time to kill and a time to heal;
>   a time to tear down and a time to build.
> A time to cry and a time to laugh;
>   a time of mourning and a time of dancing.
> A time to cast stones and a time to gather stones;
>   a time to embrace and a time to refrain from embracing.
> A time to seek and a time to give up as lost;
>   a time to keep and a time to throw away.
> A time to tear and a time to sew;
>   a time to be silent and a time to speak.

> A time to love and a time to hate;
>   a time of war and a time of peace.

Usually readers isolate these verses of the poem from those that follow, where Qohelet responds to the truth that God has made everything for the right time. Separated from Qohelet's commentary on his observation that God made everything for the right time, vv. 1–8 might be read in a positive or hopeful tone. From Qohelet's comments we get the strong feeling that he is not hopeful but rather frustrated. He begins by asking a rhetorical question: "What profit do people have from their toils?" (3:9). Qohelet sees no profit or certainly not any kind of substantial profit from their toil in light of the observation that God sets the proper time. Why? He goes on to say, "I observed the task that God has given to the human race to keep them occupied. He makes everything appropriate in its time. He also places eternity in their hearts. But still, no one can discover what God is doing from the beginning to the end" (3:10–11). Yes, God makes everything appropriate for its time, and he has given humanity awareness of this truth, but even so, God has not allowed humans to know when the right time occurs. This leads Qohelet to great frustration. As we consider the impact of Qohelet's conclusions on this subject, we need to remember from our earlier study of Proverbs just how important it was for the wise person to know the right time to apply the appropriate proverb.

Thus, for Qohelet, life is ultimately meaningless because of death, injustice, and the inability to read the time. These three themes are taught not just individually but all together in chapter 9:

> Indeed, I devoted myself to all this and to examine all this: the righteous and the wise and their works are all in the hand of God. However, no one knows whether love or hate awaits them. Everything is the same for everybody: there is one fate for the righteous and the wicked and for the clean and the unclean and for the one who sacrifices and for the one who does not sacrifice; as it is for the good, so it is for the sinner; as it is for the one who swears, so it is for the one who is afraid to swear.
>
>   This is evil among all that is done under the sun. For there is one fate for all, and furthermore, the human heart is full of evil, and madness is in their hearts during their lives, and afterward—to the dead! (vv. 1–3)

> Then I turned and observed something else under the sun. That is, the race is not to the swift, the battle not to the mighty, nor is food for the wise, nor wealth to the clever, nor favor to the intelligent, but time and chance happen to all of them. Indeed, no one knows his time. Like fish that are entangled in an evil net

and like birds caught in a snare, so people are ensnared in an evil time, when it suddenly falls on them. (vv. 11–12)

Carpe Diem

Life is meaningless because death is the end of the story and injustice and frustration characterize one's earthly existence. But what is a person to do since life is meaningless? According to Qohelet, one should live life with a carpe diem—"seize the day"—attitude. Qohelet's advice to "seize the day" is found throughout his speech:

There is nothing better for people than to eat and drink and enjoy their toil. This too, I see, is from the hand of God. For who will eat and who will worry apart from him? For he gives wisdom, knowledge, and pleasure to the one who pleases him, but he gives to the one who is offensive the task of gathering wealth to be given to the one who pleases God. This too is meaningless and chasing the wind. (2:24–26)

I know that there is nothing better for them than to be happy and enjoy themselves during their lives. Also everyone who eats, drinks, and enjoys their toil— that is a gift of God. (3:12–13)

So I observed that there is nothing better than for people to rejoice in their work, for that is their reward. For who can bring them to see what will happen after them? (3:22)

Indeed, this is what I have observed to be good: that it is appropriate to eat, to drink, and to enjoy all the toil that one does under the sun the few days God has given to that person, for that is his reward. Furthermore, everyone to whom God gives wealth and possessions and allows them to eat of it and to accept their reward and to take pleasure in their toil—this is God's gift. Indeed, they do not remember much about the days of their lives for God keeps them so busy with the pleasure of their heart. (5:18–20 [5:17–19 MT])

Then I commended pleasure, for there is nothing better for people under the sun except to eat and to drink and to have pleasure. It will accompany them in their toil during the days of their life that God gives them under the sun. (8:15)

Go, eat your food with pleasure, and drink your wine with a merry heart, for God has already approved your deeds. Let your clothes be white at all times, and do not spare oil on your head. Enjoy life with the wife whom you love all the days of your meaningless life, that is, all the days he has given you under the sun, for it is your reward in life and for the toil that you do under the sun.

All that your hand finds to do, do with your power, for there is no action or thought or knowledge or wisdom in the grave where you are going. (9:7–10)

While some scholars detect a note of joy in the carpe diem passages,[10] it is hard to disagree with the majority of scholars who detect resignation, sadness, and frustration in these passages. In other words, the gist of Qohelet's thinking is that since life is difficult and then comes death, we should eke out of life whatever joy we can.

In this regard, we should take particular notice of 5:18–20 (5:17–19 MT). Here Qohelet considers fortunate those who have the wherewithal to carpe diem (not everyone does after all). He is also aware that some, or maybe many, who have the wherewithal do not have the disposition to do so. But even for those who have the resources and the mind-set, what is the ultimate advantage? Those who can successfully live life with a carpe diem attitude can, at least momentarily, forget the harsh reality that life is hard and then you die. End of story.

Qohelet and Wisdom

Qohelet was a wise man (12:9). Indeed, he claims that he was wiser than anyone who ruled over Jerusalem before him (1:16). As acknowledged above in our discussion of the pseudonym Qohelet, there is an intentional association of Qohelet with Solomon, which, before we go further, we can now develop. According to the historical tradition (see 1 Kings 3–4), God gifted Solomon with incredible wisdom. He was "wiser than anyone else" (1 Kings 4:31).

There are a number of signals in the book of Ecclesiastes that the connection between Qohelet and Solomon is not as simple as identity. In other words, Qohelet is not Solomon but rather is associated with Solomon in order to drive home the point of the book that meaning cannot be found "under the sun," including in one's wisdom.[11]

We begin with the simple question, if Qohelet was Solomon, why not simply use that name rather than a pseudonym? The pseudonym associates but does not identify Qohelet with Solomon. Further, as we read beyond the first four chapters of the book, the association between Qohelet and Solomon ends, so that when Qohelet speaks about the king, he is speaking not about himself but about a third party (see 4:1–3; 5:8–9; 10:20). In addition, we should point out that we have no good reason to think, as we turn to the historical

10. Whybray, "Qohelet, Preacher of Joy."
11. As developed at length in Longman, "Qohelet as Solomon."

tradition about Solomon, that he turned back to the Lord after turning away from him at the end of his life (see 1 Kings 11). Finally, there are clear signs that Ecclesiastes was written not at the time of Solomon but at a much later time, during the postexilic period.[12]

If Qohelet is not Solomon, then who is he? There are two possibilities. One is that Qohelet is an actual wise man, who, in order to make the point that all things under the sun are meaningless, explores different possibilities under the persona of Solomon. Or, and I consider this possibility more likely, Qohelet is not a real person but rather a literary construct developed by the author in order to get the reader to think about the meaning of life.

Of course, both of these possibilities raise the question of motivation. What is the purpose of an association between Qohelet and Solomon? I believe the text itself answers that question when Qohelet states: "For what can anyone who comes after the king do but that which has already been done?" (2:12). The figure of Qohelet reminds us that not even Solomon, who had more wealth, pleasure, and (in terms of our present subject) wisdom than anyone else, could find meaning in any of them. The rest of us can live with the illusion that if we only had more—whether of wealth, pleasure, wisdom, or whatever—then we would find satisfaction. Solomon had it all and ended life as a bitter old man.

But now, what about wisdom? Right from the start of his reflections, Qohelet identifies himself as a person of exceptional wisdom (1:16) who is now going to explore the world through his wisdom (1:13) in order to discover the meaning of life under the sun. Even before he takes us through his search, he announces his unhappy conclusion that everything is "meaningless, a chasing after the wind" (1:14). Striking a tone quite unlike that found in Proverbs, he tells his readers, "For with much wisdom comes much frustration; he who adds to knowledge adds to pain" (1:18).

He not only tries to discover meaning in such things as pleasure (2:1–11) through his wisdom but also tries to discover meaning in wisdom itself (2:12–16). He grants a sort of relative benefit to wisdom over folly: "I observed that there was more profit to wisdom than folly, like the profit of light over darkness. The wise have eyes in their head, while fools walk around in darkness" (2:13–14a). In other words, wisdom provides a kind of practical value to living life well. He evokes a picture of the fool trying to walk across a room with eyes closed, bumping into furniture, while the wise person is able to cross the room unscathed, avoiding all obstacles.

Even so, in the final analysis wisdom too is meaningless. Why? Death.

---

12. See Longman, "Determining the Historical Context."

But I also understand that the same fate awaits both of them. I said to myself,
"Even I will meet the same fate as the fool, why then have I become so wise?"
So I said to myself, "This too is meaningless." For the memory of neither the
wise nor the fool endures forever. The days arrive only too soon when both will
be forgotten. How will the wise person die? Like the fool! (2:14b–16)

The wise die and leave no lasting legacy. In the final analysis death renders
wisdom impotent.

Qohelet also points out the limited but ultimately valueless nature of wisdom
through an anecdote of a "poor but wise youth" who is better than "an old and
foolish king" (4:13). According to the cultural sensibilities of the ancient world,
the king has two advantages over the youth. He is old (experienced) and he is
the king (rich and powerful). The youth is of course young (inexperienced) and
poor (weak). Even so, the latter's wisdom outweighs everything, which makes
him "better," and thus he rises from weakness (prison) to power (kingship).

However, as we learned from Qohelet in 2:12–16, wisdom brings no lasting value. The anecdote ends not with the wise young king's success but with
his ultimate failure. In the end, the people were not pleased with him, again
illustrating that wisdom is ultimately meaningless.

Qohelet offers a second anecdote along the same lines in 9:13–16 as an
"example of wisdom" (v. 13). This anecdote again pits a powerful king against
a poor but wise man. The former besieges the city of the latter, but because
of the wisdom of the poor man the city is saved. Wisdom is better than folly
to be sure. But again the example does not end on a happy note, because
"nobody remembered that poor wise man" (v. 15). Indeed, "the wisdom of
the poor man was despised! His words were not heeded" (v. 16).

These reflections lead Qohelet to offer two proverbs that flow from the
anecdote:

> The quiet words of the wise are better heeded
>   than the shouts of a leader among fools.
> Wisdom is better than weapons of war,
>   but one person who messes up destroys a whole lot of good.
>   (9:17–18)

Thus, at best wisdom has limited value in light of death. Wisdom will not
secure justice in this life either: "Indeed, I devoted myself to all this and to
examine all this: the righteous and the wise and their works are all in the hand
of God. However, no one knows whether love or hate awaits them" (9:1). In
perhaps the most startling passage in the book, Qohelet says, "Both I have
observed in my meaningless life: There is a righteous person perishing in his

righteousness, and there is a wicked person living long in his evil" (7:15), leading to the following advice:

> Do not be too righteous and do not be overly wise. Why ruin yourself? Do not be too wicked and do not be a fool. Why die when it is not your time? It is good that you hold on to this and also do not release your hand from that. The one who fears God will follow both of them. (7:16–18)

We have not looked at each and every passage where Qohelet has spoken explicitly about wisdom, but the passages examined represent Qohelet's ideas about the subject. In summary, Qohelet believes that wisdom has some limited value over against folly for navigating life. However, Qohelet believes that death renders even that limited value meaningless. Wisdom does not guarantee success in this life or secure an afterlife.

The Message of the Frame Narrator

Having examined the thought of Qohelet, we now turn our attention to the unnamed wise man who is speaking to his son and whose words frame those of Qohelet. Since he has the first and last word, the message of the author/ book is associated with this voice and not the voice of Qohelet. What does the frame narrator say about life in general and about wisdom in particular?

As described above, the second wise man's words (1:2–11;[13] 12:8–14) frame the speech of Qohelet (1:12–12:7). The prologue simply sets the stage for Qohelet's speech. We hear the frame narrator's perspective in the epilogue, and so we now turn to the epilogue.

In the epilogue, the second wise man speaks to his son (12:12). He uses Qohelet's speech to give his son a lesson on life and in particular where to find the meaning of life. His words to his son are brief but still can be divided into two parts. In the first part (12:8–12) he evaluates Qohelet's reflections on life. In the second part (12:13–14) he tells his son how to live life meaningfully.

He begins the first part by asserting what he considers to be Qohelet's "bottom line": "'Completely meaningless,' Qohelet said. 'Everything is meaningless'" (12:8). While Whybray and others want to say that Qohelet is a preacher of joy, the frame narrator begs to differ, saying that Qohelet's ultimate conclusion is that life is difficult and then one dies.[14]

---

13. Ecclesiastes 1:1 is an editorial superscription.

14. Whybray believes that 12:8 and following are written by a disciple who did not understand his teacher. See Whybray, *Ecclesiastes*, 35.

The father then evaluates Qohelet as a wise man. He begins with "Qohelet was a wise man" (12:9a). If someone is called wise (*ḥākām*) in the book of Proverbs, this is high praise. Outside of Proverbs, though, calling someone a *ḥākām* does not put an imprimatur on everything that person says. Perhaps *ḥākām* here functions almost like a professional designation.[15] In the David story, for instance, Jonadab, who advises Amnon how to lure his sister Tamar into his bed (2 Sam. 13:3; see also Ahitophel in 2 Sam. 16:15–17:29), is called a *ḥākām*. My point is not that Qohelet is evil like Jonadab but rather that to call someone a *ḥākām* does not mean that everything that person says is right. The father goes on to compliment Qohelet by saying that "he taught many people knowledge. He heard, investigated, and put in good order many proverbs" (12:9b). He describes Qohelet with respect, but he is not over-the-top in his description of Qohelet as a *ḥākām*. As Fox puts it, he is a good workman.[16]

Nevertheless, the frame narrator continues his assessment by saying, "Qohelet sought to find words of delight, and he wrote honest words of truth" (12:10).[17] Here the frame narrator affirms the truth of what Qohelet said. How are we to take this positive statement?

I believe that the frame narrator realized that what Qohelet said was true given Qohelet's own parameters. We might remember that throughout his speech, indeed on twenty-nine occasions,[18] Qohelet kept acknowledging that he was trying to find meaning "under the sun." It is not easy to pin down exactly what Qohelet means by this phrase, but it does seem fair to say that, though he certainly is no atheist, he does not allow himself to find meaning by appealing to God or his revelation. As we saw in our analysis of Eccles. 8:10–15 above, Qohelet is intent on finding meaning by "observation" rather than by given knowledge, and he comes up short.

In short, the frame narrator is saying to his son, "Qohelet is exactly right. Life is hard and then you die, if you stay 'under the sun' in your thinking."[19]

15. See chap. 12 for discussion of the sage as professional.
16. Fox, "Frame-Narrative."
17. Here I depart from my translation of this verse in my earlier commentary (Longman, *Ecclesiastes*, 275). In my commentary, influenced by Fox ("Frame Narrative," 97), I proposed a slight emendation that produced a translation "Qohelet sought to find words of delight and to write honestly words of truth." I then went on to propose that Qohelet "sought" to find words of delight and words of truth but failed to do so.
18. Eccles. 1:3, 9; 2:11, 17, 18, 19, 20, 22; 3:16; 4:1, 3, 7, 15; 5:14, 19; 6:1, 12; 7:11; 8:9, 15 (2×), 17; 9:3, 6, 9 (2×), 11, 13; 10:5.
19. Though we cannot be absolutely certain about the exact time the book was composed, it is likely, in my opinion, that Qohelet's under-the-sun viewpoint represents a contemporary Jewish perspective (perhaps Jewish ideas melded with Hellenistic ideas) that this book seeks to criticize.

In other words, the frame narrator exposes his son to Qohelet in order to show the failure of such "under the sun" thinking. He will direct his son to a different (what we might call "above the sun") perspective in the concluding two verses of the book (see below).

The frame narrator moves now to a general assessment of the wise (who are like Qohelet), followed by advice about future interactions with such writings: "The words of the wise are like goads, and like firmly implanted nails are the masters of collections. They are given by a shepherd. Furthermore, of these, my son, be warned! There is no end to the making of many books, and much study wearies the body" (12:11–12).

He uses similes (goads and firmly implanted nails) that are positive but also painful. The frame narrator has exposed his son to Qohelet's thought because he thinks that it will benefit his son, but he also realizes that such exposure is painful. Accordingly, he follows this observation with the advice not to dwell on it. It is good to hear Qohelet's "under the sun" viewpoint, but don't dwell on it.

And that brings us to the second part of the frame narrator's admonition to his son. His first words are abrupt and short, particularly in Hebrew: "The end of the matter. All has been heard" (*sôp dābār hakkōl nišmā'*, 12:13a). It is as if the father is saying to his son, "Enough of this [i.e., of Qohelet's thinking]. Let's get on to what is really important":

> Fear God and keep his commandments, for this is the whole duty of humanity. For God will bring every deed into judgment, including every hidden thing, whether good or evil. (12:13–14)

Thus, the father instructs the son to adopt what we might call an "above the sun" perspective on life. The son is the implied reader of the book; he is the one directly addressed by the father, but all subsequent readers are the actual readers. In other words, when the son is addressed, we stand in his place. What lesson does the father communicate to him/us?

First of all, his final instruction is brief and to the point. He packs a lot of instruction into a verse and a half. His admonition to "fear God" teaches us to establish a right relationship with God characterized by fear. The son/we (the readers) are to "keep his [God's] commands" and so are to maintain that relationship through obedience. Finally, the reader is to live in light of the future judgment. If we were to use anachronistic theological categories, we would say that we have justification, sanctification, and eschatology in a verse and a half.

While such a reading is correct, I suggest that the words of the father evoke another important connection. First, it is necessary to recognize, along with the vast majority of contemporary interpreters, that Ecclesiastes is among the latest books of the OT. It certainly dates to the postexilic period, probably, but not certainly, as late as the Greek period.[20] At such a late date the Jewish canon is coming into shape and is often described as having three parts: Torah (Law), Nebi'im (Prophets), and Ketubim (Writings).

With this background, I do not think it is too much of a stretch to think that the father's words bring to mind these three parts of the canon. "Fear God" makes one think of the Ketubim; "keep the commandments" evokes the Torah; and to live in light of the future judgment makes one think of the Nebi'im. If this is correct, then the father is telling the son and subsequent readers to adopt an "above the sun" perspective by turning to the Tanak, God's revelation to his people.

The Frame Narrator and Wisdom

We turn finally to the message of the frame narrator as regards wisdom, remembering that the frame narrator's perspective coincides with the message of the book in a way that Qohelet's perspective does not (similar to the role the human participants play in the book of Job; see next chapter).

First, we can conclude that the frame narrator believes that the type of wisdom represented by Qohelet has some utility but is in the final analysis severely limited. In 12:8–12 he acknowledges that Qohelet exposes the true but painful reality that life "under the sun" is meaningless. He is wise, but since his wisdom restricts itself to observation, it leads ultimately to frustration.[21]

But, second, the frame narrator himself does not stay "under the sun" but gives his son an "above the sun" perspective that begins with the admonition to "fear God." The admonition to "fear God" evokes Proverbs's statement that the fear of the Lord is the beginning of wisdom.

Some might object that the frame narrator is not alone in urging his hearers to fear God. It is true that Qohelet also advocated the fear of God (Eccles. 3:14; 5:7 [5:6 MT]; 7:18; 8:12 [2×], 13; 12:13). However, as I have argued in much more detail elsewhere, the context of Qohelet's admonition makes it clear that he is advocating not the kind of fear that leads to obedience but rather the kind of fear that would lead a person to run away and hide.[22]

20. As I argue in "Determining the Historical Context."
21. Perhaps one of the most enigmatic statements from the frame narrator about Qohelet is that he has written "words of delight" (12:10). Even the most generous interpretation of Qohelet's thought makes one wonder precisely what the frame narrator is getting at here.
22. Longman, "'Fear of God.'"

Thus, in spite of Qohelet's message, the book of Ecclesiastes presents the same type of wisdom that is based on the fear of God that we discovered in the book of Proverbs. Ecclesiastes makes clear that human wisdom has its limitations. Wise and righteous people do not have a guarantee of living long and prospering, but the goal of the frame narrator is nonetheless to bring his son to an "above the sun" perspective in which he will submit to God, obey him, and live in light of the coming judgment.

We have now examined Proverbs and Ecclesiastes, in many ways two quite different books that have the same deeply theological understanding of wisdom grounded in the fear of God. We now turn our attention to the third book that focuses on wisdom, the book of Job.

3

THE BOOK OF JOB

"Behold, the Fear of the Lord Is Wisdom" (Job 28:28)

Having considered the books of Proverbs and Ecclesiastes, we now turn to Job to further our understanding of the nature of wisdom. When most people think about Job, their first thought is that Job is a book about suffering. Job famously suffers, but the book's primary issue is not the nature of suffering, nor is it interested in answering the question of why we suffer. No, Job's suffering presents the occasion for raising the real issue of the book: wisdom. Job is not a theodicy but rather a wisdom debate. All the human participants in the book present rival claims to wisdom and dispute each other's perspective. Thus, like Ecclesiastes, Job presents more than one voice, and proper interpretation depends on properly situating these varied voices.

Job: The Search for Wisdom

The Prose Prologue (Job 1–2)

In the first few verses, the narrator introduces Job as the epitome of the sage. He was "innocent" (*tām*) and "virtuous" (*yāšār*), words found frequently in the book of Proverbs as characteristics of the wise person. He feared God and turned away from evil, reminding us of the concluding verse of the preamble to Proverbs ("The fear of Yahweh is the beginning of knowledge," 1:7).

Not surprisingly, considering the connection between good character and reward in Proverbs, Job enjoys substantial wealth as well as a large and extremely happy family. His sacrifices on behalf of his family after their happy celebrations are over the top (just in case, not because of known sin). This is to be read not as a sign of spiritual anxiety but as an indication of his sincere piety.

After introducing Job, the narrator's attention turns to Yahweh, who is convening a meeting of the assembly of his angelic council, including one angel who is called "the Accuser" (haśśāṭān). Heaven here is described like a royal court in which the Lord is the king and the angels are his ministers. The Accuser's role in the court is that of God's "eyes and ears" (in other words, his spy service). The Lord meets with him to take his report and wants a special account of his servant Job, whom he describes, in agreement with the narrator, as an innocent and virtuous man who fears God and turns away from evil (1:8).

The Accuser does not disagree with the Lord's assessment of Job's integrity, but he does question Job's motivation. He suggests that the only reason Job behaves in such a way is to gain God's favor and the accompanying rewards. He, accordingly, suggests a test of sorts where God will allow him to remove these rewards and then watch what develops.

God gives the Accuser permission, and the latter departs and removes the external blessings of Job's life by removing his wealth and killing off his children (1:13–20). Job responds as God expected him to react by worshiping God and saying:

> Naked I came from my mother's womb,
>   and naked I will return there.
> Yahweh gave and Yahweh took,
>   blessed be the name of Yahweh. (1:21–22)[1]

The narrator assesses Job's actions by saying "in all this, Job did not sin, and he did not ascribe wrongdoing to God" (1:23).

Unfortunately for Job, however, he has only been through the first round of torment. The Accuser returns to God and tells him that the only reason why Job has remained in relationship with him is because God had forbidden the Accuser to harm Job himself. "Skin for skin" (2:4), the Accuser tells God. That is, of course Job will remain in relationship with God as long as God does not harm Job himself. Thus, God allows the Accuser to harm Job,

1. Translations of Job come from Longman, Job.

though not kill him, and the Accuser follows through by afflicting Job with "boils from the soles of his feet up to his head" (2:8).

Even so, Job stays true to God. He does not abandon his relationship with him, even at the urging of his wife (2:10). Job responds to her by saying, "You are speaking like one of the foolish women. Should we receive good from God and not receive evil?" And the narrator evaluates Job by saying, "In all this, Job did not sin with his lips" (2:10–11).

The prologue ends by informing the reader that Job's three friends—Eliphaz, Bildad, and Zophar—came to sit with him. They sat with him for seven days in silence—and then Job broke his silence.

Job's Complaint (Job 3)

After seven days of silence, Job speaks. He seems to be speaking not to his friends but to the air. His suffering had reached a point where he just had to burst forth in complaint. Job does not directly curse God, but he does curse the day of his birth. He is on the edge, but his speech does not cross the line by rejecting God. He maintains his relationship with God, but just barely.

Some compare Job's speech to the laments of the Psalms,[2] but there is a crucial difference. The psalmic laments are addressed to God; Job's speech is not. In other words, he is complaining, not lamenting. His words are dangerously closer to the grumbling in the wilderness (Exod. 15:22–17:7; Num. 11–25) than they are to the words of the psalmist. The difference is critical since God allows for lament but hates grumbling. He punishes the latter, while he listens to the former. No wonder that the three friends are now mobilized into action.

The Debate between the Three Friends and Job (Job 4–27)

Job's three friends respond to Job's complaint, thus initiating the longest and most well-known part of the book. Eliphaz begins gently: "Should someone venture a word with you, would you be discouraged? But who is able to restrain themselves from speaking?" (4:2).

Eliphaz then proceeds to present an argument that is repeated time and again by the three friends. He begins with the assertion that the wicked get punished:

> Please remember: Who being blameless has perished?
> Where were the virtuous destroyed?

2. Westermann, *Structure of the Book of Job*.

> As I have seen, those who plow iniquity
>> and those who plant trouble harvest them.
> They perish by the breath of God;
>> they are finished off by the blast of his anger. (4:7–9)

In other words, the innocent do not suffer but only those who do wrong. The implication, which will be brought out explicitly in later speeches, is that Job's suffering indicates that he is a sinner.

If suffering is the result of sin, then what is the solution to Job's problem? Repentance.

> As for me, I would seek God,
>> and I would commit my thoughts to God,
> the one who does great and unsearchable things,
> marvelous things, without number. (5:8–9)

> See, blessed are those whom God reproves,
>> so do not reject the instruction of Shaddai.
> For he wounds and binds up.
> He strikes, but his hands heal. (5:17–18)

This first speech of Eliphaz opens up the debate with Job, which runs through at least chapter 27.[3] There are three cycles of speeches. In the first two, the three friends each take a turn, and Job responds to each one in turn. In the third cycle, Eliphaz speaks and Job responds, followed by a very short speech by Bildad (Job 25) and a response from Job, but then Zophar does not speak a third time. It appears that the three friends have run out of steam. Their speeches get shorter and shorter and finally end.

After all, though there are three cycles of speeches, the three friends keep repeating the same argument that Eliphaz presented in his first speech: if you sin, then you suffer; therefore, if you suffer, then you are a sinner. This attitude expresses what we will call retribution theology.

The three friends never depart from their retribution theology. There is no development in their argument; there is only intensification in their vitriol. As we have seen, Eliphaz begins gently, but as time goes on the insults fly. In his first speech, Bildad heightens the rhetoric:

> How long will you continue speaking these things?
>> The words of your mouth are a strong wind. (8:2)

3. We will treat Job 28–31 separately as a monologue by Job.

Zophar later believes that a donkey will give birth to a human baby before Job happens to utter a wise word ("But an empty-headed person will get understanding when a wild donkey gives birth to a human!" 11:12).

But Job can give as good as he gets. While it is hard to read tone in Hebrew, it is difficult to miss the sarcasm in his voice when Job says to the friends, "Truly, you are the people, and wisdom will die with you!" (12:2). While Job insults his friends' wisdom, he asserts his own: "I also have a mind like you. I am not inferior to you" (12:3).

What we have here is a debate about wisdom, and Job's suffering is the occasion for the debate. Who has the proper insight to diagnose and then prescribe a remedy for Job's situation? After all, that is what wisdom does: it helps people navigate life by identifying problems and pointing to solutions. The wise are those who can navigate life well, avoiding pitfalls and maximizing success.

But what is Job's perspective on the matter? Though surprising to realize, Job clearly affirms the same retribution theology as the three friends. He, like the three friends, believes that God punishes the wicked and rewards the righteous. But that is why he is so upset; he knows (and we know that he is right from what the prologue said about him) that he has done nothing to deserve the suffering he is presently experiencing. His affirmation of the retribution principle and his awareness of his own innocence lead him to accuse God of injustice. That is his diagnosis of his problem: God is unjust.

> Though I am righteous, my mouth condemns me.
>   I am innocent, but he declares me perverse.
> I am innocent. I don't know for sure.
>   I loathe my life.
> It is all the same; therefore, I say:
>   "He destroys the innocent and the wicked."
> If a disaster brings sudden death,
>   he ridicules the despair of the innocent.
> The earth is given into the power of the wicked;
>   he covers the face of its judges.
> If it is not he, then who? (9:20–24)

According to Job, God is unjust. That is why he suffers. If so, then what is the solution to his problem? Remember that Job, like his three friends, considers himself wise and able to navigate life. Job's solution, therefore, is to confront God. He wants an audience with God in order to confront God, accuse him of injustice, and demand that he set things right.

And it is in this attitude that we see development in Job's thinking as we move through his many speeches. At first he wants to confront God but does not believe it is worth the effort because God is too powerful and won't care:

> If he crosses over to me, I will not see;
> if he passes by, I will not perceive him.
> If he carries off, who will bring back?
> Who will say to him, "What are you doing?"
> God does not relent of his anger.
> Even Rahab's allies cower toward him.
> How can I answer him?
> How can I choose my words with him?
> Though I am righteous, I could not answer him.
> I could only plead for mercy with my judge.
> If I summoned him, and he answered me,
> I do not believe that he would hear my voice. (9:11–16)

Here he expresses his desire to meet with God, even his determination to do so, but he has no hope that he will be successful even though he is right. However, starting with the end of this very same speech, Job broaches the topic of a third party who might mediate his dispute with God:

> For he is not a person like I am that I could answer him,
> that we will go together into judgment.
> There is no umpire between us
> who would set his hand on both of us.
> He would take his rod away from me,
> and not let his dread scare me.
> I would speak and not be afraid of him,
> though this is not the case with me. (9:32–35)

Even though in his own mind he is convinced that he, and not God, is right, he does not believe he can stand before him alone and be successful. Thus, he wishes there were a mediator, or as I translate the Hebrew *môkîaḥ*, an umpire. At this point he does not think there is such an umpire, but in the final speech of the first cycle, he expresses his continuing desire to confront God and his determination to do so no matter what the consequences:

> But I would speak to Shaddai.
> I would love to reprove God. (13:3)

> See, he will kill me; I have no[4] hope.
>> I will reprove him to his face concerning my behavior.
> This will be my salvation,
>> that the godless will not come into his presence.
> Listen closely to my words;
>> let my declaration be in your ear.
> See, I am prepared for the judgment;
>> I know I am righteous.
> Who is this who accuses me
>> so now I would be silent and die? (13:15–19)

Thus, Job does not surrender his belief that he is on high moral ground with God, who has treated him unjustly. He even returns to the idea of a third party who might intercede on his behalf with God.

> O earth, do not cover my blood;
>> do not let there be a place for my cry for justice!
> Even now, see, my witness is in heaven,
>> and the one who testifies for me is on high.
> My friends scorn me,
>> and my eye drips tears to God.
> He would arbitrate with God on behalf of a person,
>> as between a person and his friend.
> For when a number of years have come,
>> I will go the way from which I will not return. (16:18–22)

Here he does not want to go away silently before he can register his protest. At the very end of this speech, he says that he does not expect to live longer, but he places some hope on the possibility that his case will get a hearing when he starts talking about a witness in heaven who would speak on his behalf and "arbitrate" (from the same root used to form the noun *môkîaḥ* in 9:33, *ykḥ*) between God and himself.

As we read on, we come to what may be Job's most hopeful statement concerning his challenge to God when he says:

> Oh, that my words were written down.
>> Oh, that they were inscribed in a scroll.
> Oh, that with an iron pen and with lead
>> they were etched on rock as a witness.

---

4. Though many translations (e.g., NIV) read the Qere with the scribes (an asseverative *lû*), this reading seems to be wishful thinking of the scribes (and modern translators), and we go with what was written in the Hebrew (the Ketib), which is the negative *lo'* (see NRSV).

> I know that my redeemer lives,
>> and he at last will rise up on the dust.
> After my skin is peeled off,
>> then out of my flesh I will see God.
> I will see him for myself;
>> My eyes will look and not a stranger's.
>> My heart fades within me.
> When you say, "How should I pursue him?"
>> and, "The root of the matter is found in him."
> Be careful of the sword,
>> for his wrath brings the punishment of the sword,
>> so you may know that there is judgment. (19:23–29)

The words that Job imagines written on rock would be his challenge to God's injustice. They would serve as a witness against God, but then, more in keeping with Job's previous statements about an "umpire" and a "witness," he speaks confidently about "my redeemer," who at last would "rise up on the dust." And then after Job's skin is peeled off, he would see God.

No one should deny that this passage is extremely difficult textually, philologically, exegetically, and theologically.[5] Indeed, many modern lay readers quickly but wrongly identify Jesus as the redeemer of the passage, based on a famous aria in Handel's *Messiah*, and the reference to "after my skin is peeled off" to the resurrection of the body after death, but such a reading is impossible (see "Jesus as Woman Wisdom," in chap. 15).

Read in the context of Job's speeches, and in particular the passages that we have just examined concerning a third-party advocate, we should see the reference to a redeemer in this passage as similar to the earlier references to a mediator or umpire between Job and God. These are variant names of someone who would serve as a heavenly witness on Job's behalf. The reference to Job's peeling skin should not be taken as any kind of hope of the afterlife, which Job not only does not affirm anywhere else, but which he explicitly denies (for instance, 14:7–12, where he contrasts humans with a felled tree; the latter can grow back).

But what exactly does Job have in mind in these passages that mention a third-party advocate or helper? Something that Elihu will later say is helpful in our identification. We will look at Elihu in more detail in just a moment, but for our present purposes we should note that Elihu acknowledges that it is just possible, but not very likely, that there would be such a mediator. In speaking of people suffering for their sin, he notes:

5. For a detailed analysis, see Longman, *Job*, 254–55, 259–63.

Their flesh wastes away so it cannot be seen.
  Their bones, laid bare, may not be seen.
Their souls draw near the Pit,
  their lives to those who bring death.
If there is any angel for one of them,
  a mediator, one out of a thousand,
  one who declares what is right for him,
And he is gracious to that person and says:
  "Redeem him from going down to the Pit;
  I have discovered a ransom;
Let his flesh become fresh like that of a youth;
  let him return to his youthful vigor." (33:21–25)

Elihu helps us understand that at this time and in this culture the idea of a third-party advocate refers to an angel, one who could mediate between God and Job and make sure that Job would get a fair hearing.[6]

Once we realize that Job has an angelic figure in mind when he is hoping for heavenly help, we can see the immense irony of the situation. After all, as readers we have been given a glimpse into the divine council in the preface, and we know that there indeed is an angel who has taken an interest in Job—the Accuser. However, the Accuser is acting not on Job's behalf but rather against his interests. In other words, Job has no one who could be called an umpire, mediator, witness, or redeemer. However, his (false) hope for such a figure fuels his growing determination for meeting with God and challenging him. As we will soon see, he will get his chance to meet with God, though the meeting will not go the way he imagines. However, that fateful meeting does not take place right away; rather, we first hear Job deliver a monologue, followed by a totally unexpected appearance of a hitherto unannounced character.

Job's Soliloquy (Job 28–31)

In the third cycle of the debate between Job and his three friends, we saw that the latter were rapidly losing steam. Eliphaz gives a substantial final speech, but Bildad can only manage a paltry six verses (chap. 25), and Zophar, who has been the hottest head among them, has apparently totally burned out,

6. We might also take note of Eliphaz's earlier warning to Job: "Call out now! Is there anyone who will answer you? To whom among the holy ones will you turn?" (5:1). In other words, Eliphaz acknowledges that angels can act as mediators in the type of circumstance in which Job finds himself but believes that since it is so obvious that Job suffers because of his sin, no angel ("holy one") will take up his case.

saying nothing.[7] Thus, it is best to think of Job's speech in chapters 28–31 as a type of soliloquy. He may have an audience, but he is not specifically addressing them, just expressing his thoughts to the open air.

His opening speech (chap. 28) is a powerful and beautiful statement that all wisdom comes from God. He marvels at how precious metals and gems can be extracted from the earth through human ingenuity and effort (vv. 1–12), but these very same humans have no clue as to where to find wisdom ("As for wisdom, where can it be found? The place of understanding, where is it?" 28:12, 20). The source of wisdom is not only hidden from human eyes, but even powerful mythological forces like the Deep and the Sea (v. 14) and Abaddon and Death (v. 22) don't know where to find it.

Only God knows where to find it (vv. 23–27). Wisdom's origin is in God alone. The poem ends, though, showing humans to the one way to acquire wisdom: "Behold, the fear of the Lord is wisdom, and turning aside from evil is understanding" (28:28).

We have heard this before, of course, both in the book of Proverbs (see 1:7 and elsewhere) and in Ecclesiastes (12:13). We are not surprised to see the book of Job add its voice to the chorus. What is mystifying is the placement of this statement in the mouth of Job at this point in the book.

After all, as we will see, the affirmation that true wisdom involves fearful submission to the wisdom of God is the conclusion at the end of the book. Job's recognition of it here does not bring the book to an end or, as the soliloquy goes on, end his own confusion and distrust of God's justice.

For this reason, some have claimed that Job 28 is not a speech of Job but rather the statement of the narrator. However, there is no signal of a change of speaker at the beginning of chap. 28. Accordingly, the best explanation is what Alison Lo called the psychological explanation.[8] That is, Job suffers like many people suffer, and in the midst of our pain, we may have a moment of clarity and calm but then find ourselves soon plunged into darkness once again.

And indeed, after his magnificent praise of God's wisdom, Job once again complains by contrasting his present humiliating situation (chap. 31) with the high status he held earlier (chap. 30). His last speech (chap. 31) is a final protest of his innocence that culminates with the determined and defiant statement that he will indeed boldly seek God and challenge God's treatment of him:

---

7. Rejecting attempts to reconstruct a longer Bildad speech and reconstructing one by Zophar. See the attempts by Zerafa, *Wisdom of God*, 195–96.

8. Lo, *Job 28 as Rhetoric*; see the similar approach in Dillard and Longman, *Introduction to the Old Testament*, 204.

> Oh, that someone would listen to me!
>> Here is my signature! Let Shaddai answer me!
>> Let my accuser write out an indictment!
> Surely, I will wear it on my shoulder;
>> I would bind it on me like a crown.
> I would give him [God] an account of all my steps;
>> I would approach him like a prince. (31:35–37)

We might expect the story to move directly to the confrontation between Job and God. However, our expectations are thwarted by the appearance of a character who has not yet been introduced in the narrative—Elihu.

Elihu's Monologue (Job 32–37)

Up to this point, we only know that Job and his three friends are present during the debate. We have not a hint of an audience to their debate. With the introduction of Elihu, we now know that there is at least one onlooker who has remained silent while the four of them debated the cause and the remedy of Job's suffering. But now that the three friends have run out of arguments, Elihu steps forward to take their place.

Before Elihu speaks, the narrator introduces him:

> These three men stopped answering Job, for he was right in his own eyes. And Elihu, son of Barakel the Buzite, from the clan of Ram, was exceedingly angry with Job. He was angry because he considered himself more righteous than God. He was angry with the three friends because they could not find a response and they thus made God appear guilty. Now Elihu had waited to speak with Job because they were older than he was. But Elihu saw that there was no adequate response on the part of the three men, so he was angry. (32:1–5)

The one thing that the narrator makes clear is that Elihu is angry. He is angry at Job, and he is angry with the three friends. He believes that both sides have dishonored God. Job dishonored God by holding him responsible for his suffering, and the three friends dishonored God by failing to convince Job, which made God look like the guilty party.

Why had Elihu been silent for so long, letting his anger swell to the breaking point? The narrator tells us that it was "because he was young," and indeed when Elihu begins to speak, he makes the same point:

> I am young,
>> and you are aged.
> Therefore, I was very afraid
>> to express my opinion to you. (32:6)

After all, in the ancient Near East, wisdom was associated with the elders, not the youth. Later in chapter 7 we will explore the role that experience, observation, and learning from mistakes play in the development of wisdom, and those who are older have had more time to observe, to experience, and to learn from their experience. Elihu goes on, however, to claim a different type of source for his wisdom:

> It is the spirit in a person,
>   the breath of Shaddai, that gives them understanding.
> The many are not wise;
>   the elders do not understand justice.
> So I say, "Listen to me!
>   I will show you my opinion." (32:8–10)

So Elihu represents a different type of human claim to wisdom, based not on age but on a kind of divine inspiration. How does this play out in the following argument? His speech characterizes him as an angry blowhard:

> For my part, I will answer;
>   I will share my opinion.
> For I am full of words;
>   the spirit in me compels me.
> My innards are like wine with no opening,
>   like new wineskins ready to burst.
> I must speak in order to find relief,
>   I will open my lips to answer. (32:17–20)

His emphasis on himself (notice how many times "I," "my," and "me" appear in the passage) is typical throughout his speech. Also illustrative is the comical picture he draws of himself as someone full of air who needs to find relief by expelling it from his body.

And when we analyze what he says, we see him making the same argument as the three friends. He may emphasize more the disciplinary nature of his suffering (33:12–30), but we see this as early as Eliphaz's first speech (5:17–22). He, like the three friends, settles on the argument that God is not unjust and that Job's suffering is the result of his wickedness:

> Who is a man like Job?
>   he drinks ridicule like water;
> He travels with a band of evildoers,
>   going with the wicked.

He has said, "People get nothing
    out of taking pleasure in God." (34:7–9)

Sensible people will say to me,
    wise people who listen to me:
"Job speaks without knowledge.
    His words are not insightful."
Oh, that Job would be examined completely
    because his responses are like those of the guilty.
For he adds transgression to his sin.
    He claps his hands among us.
    He multiplies his words against God. (34:34–37)

His rather arrogant confidence reaches a pitch when he exclaims:

Have some patience with me, and I will inform you,
    for I still have words to speak on God's behalf.
I carry my knowledge from afar;
    I ascribe righteousness to the one who made me.
For truly my words are no lie;
    perfect knowledge is with me.
Look, God is mighty in strength.
    He does not reject the pure of heart.
The wicked will not live;
    he gives justice to the afflicted. (36:2–6)

Although the first five chapters of Elihu's speech are filled with self-serving statements full of hot air that merely repeat the failed arguments of the three friends, Elihu ends his speech in a way that anticipates the divine speeches to come. However, as Cheney points out, we must read this final section (chap. 37) in light of the much longer first part. When we do, we agree with Cheney that we should not therefore conclude that Elihu is a positive figure, a kind of herald of the coming of God. As he puts it, "the argument that Elihu is not a comic figure because he ends on a serious note is really no argument at all since parody is always a careful admixture of seriousness and buffoonery. If a buffoon ends on a serious note, so much the worse for the serious note."[9] Thus, we understand the lack of any response to Elihu. He says nothing new, and the most biting response one can give a narcissist is to ignore them completely.

But then what is the purpose of including the Elihu speech? We will give a more complete statement when we summarize the teaching of Job on the

9. Cheney, *Dust, Wind and Agony*, 165–66.

subject of wisdom, but for now we can say that Elihu represents yet another human claim to wisdom different than that of either Job or the three friends. He claims a "spiritual" inspiration to his wisdom, and in the final analysis, his wisdom is inadequate.

Yahweh's Speeches and Job's Response (Job 38:1–42:6)

In the debate with the three friends, Job expressed his conviction that his suffering was the result not of his sin but rather, since he suffered despite his innocence, of God's injustice. Thus, the way out of his predicament was to confront God. While at first he doubted that this strategy would work since God was powerful and did not care about the innocent (9:14–20, 32–35), he grew in his determination and confidence that he would succeed if he got his opportunity to address God directly (16:18–21; 19:23–27; and esp. 31:35–37).

When Yahweh finally appeared to him at the beginning of Job 38, his wish came true, but the meeting did not go at all the way that he anticipated. Rather than Job challenging God, God challenged Job.

The narrator introduces God and informs the reader that he is speaking out of a whirlwind (38:1), a surefire indication that God is none too happy with the one he addresses. When God does speak to Job, he characterizes him as ignorant and prepares him for a proper upbraiding:

> Who is this who darkens advice
>   with ignorant words?
> Brace yourself like a man.
>   I will question you, and you must inform me! (38:2–3)

God announces that he will subject Job to a series of questions to expose his ignorance. The purpose of this exercise is to show Job (and those of us who read his story) that he is not in a position to judge God's ways in the world.

Accordingly, God peppers Job with question after question, not even waiting for a reply because it is all too obvious that no human being could possibly answer. He begins by asking questions that could only be answered by God himself as the one who created everything:

> Where were you when I founded the earth?
>   Tell me, if you have understanding.
> Who set its measurements? Surely you know.
>   Or who extended the line on it?

> On what are its bases sunk?
>> Or who set its cornerstone,
> when the stars of the morning sang for joy
>> and all the sons of God shouted gleefully? (38:4–7)

He also asks whether Job is the one who maintains the rhythms of the creation in a way that controls the present chaos. For example, consider what God says concerning the alternation of evening to morning:

> In your days, have you commanded the morning?
>> Can you inform the dawn of its place
> so it grabs the edges of the earth,
>> so the wicked can be shaken out of it?
> The earth is transformed like clay by a seal impression,
>> and its features stand out like a garment.
> Light is held back from the wicked,
>> and their upheld arm is broken. (38:12–15)

The next series of questions have to do with the knowledge and sustaining of wild animals. As an example, here is what God says concerning the mountain goat:

> Do you know the time when the mountain goats give birth?
>> Do you observe the birth pangs of the deer?
> Do you count the months that they fulfill
>> to know that time when they will give birth,
> when they crouch down and bear their young
>> and deliver their fetuses?
> Their offspring are healthy and grow in the countryside;
>> they go out and do not return to them. (39:1–4)

As we come to the end of the first round of God's response to Job, we see that God has no interest in hearing Job's challenge. Furthermore, God does not have any interest in telling Job why he is suffering. Rather, God has put Job in his place, reminding him that Job is not God and culminating this first round by saying:

> Will someone who contends with Shaddai instruct him?
> Let the one who reproves God answer back! (40:2)

At this point Job speaks and announces that he can only remain silent in response to God's challenge:

> I am small; how can I answer you?
>   I have placed my hand over mouth.
> I have spoken once already and will not respond;
>   twice, but I won't add to that. (40:4–5)

Job appeared before God ready to launch a serious case against God, but now that he has heard God, he knows he has nothing to say. However, this response does not satisfy God, and so he continues to put Job in his place.

After warning Job again to prepare himself for more questions ("brace yourself like a man. I will question you, and you must answer me," 40:7), God then clearly identifies the reason for his anger toward Job:

> Would you invalidate my justice?
>   Would you condemn me so you might be righteous? (40:8)

We have clearly seen that in his earlier speeches Job was accusing God of injustice, since Job affirmed the retribution theology of the friends but also knew that he did not deserve to suffer.

God asserts his justice, but he never tries to explain himself to Job. Indeed, he acknowledges that the world is filled with evil and with dangerous threats. He does not rid the world of these elements but rather controls them. On the contrary, God says, Job does not even have power to restrain evil, not to speak of eradicating it.

We see this in God's taunt of Job telling him to take a shot at crushing the wicked, and most memorably we see this in God's descriptions of Behemoth (40:15–24) and Leviathan (41:1–34 [40:25–41:26 MT]). God describes these two creatures, emphasizing their immense strength. He also informs Job that only he can control them. Concerning Behemoth, God says that only he ("its Maker") "can approach it with a sword" (40:19b). He concludes his reflection on Behemoth by asking rhetorically, "Can it be taken with hooks, or can you pierce its nose with a snare?" (40:24). In regard to Leviathan, God begins by exposing Job's (and human) impotence against this magnificent creature ("Can you catch Leviathan with a fishhook? Can you press down its tongue with a cord?" 41:1 [40:25 MT]). God is taunting Job for Job's inability to control Leviathan, something God can easily do. Job cannot play with Leviathan "like a bird" or put it on a leash "for your young girls" (41:5 [40:29 MT]), but God certainly can.

The identity of these creatures has mystified interpreters through the centuries and has led to a number of speculations, some quite outlandish.[10] Upon

---

10. Like young-earth creationists who identify them with dinosaurs.

reflection, it is not feasible to suggest that Behemoth and Leviathan are known animals such as a hippopotamus or crocodile. In the first place, the description of Leviathan as a creature that breathes fire would make no sense (41:19–20 [41:12–13 MT]) for a crocodile or any other known animal. In the second place, we know Leviathan from other biblical texts (e.g., Pss. 74:12–17; 104:26b; Isa. 27:1) as well as extrabiblical texts (the Ugaritic *lotan*) as a multiheaded (or specifically seven-headed) sea monster. In other words, Leviathan is not an actual creature, but the most fearsome sea creature imaginable.

If that is the case, then what about Behemoth? Our understanding of Leviathan as the most fearsome sea creature imaginable draws our attention to the word *bəhēmôt*, which is the plural of the word "animal" (*bəhēmâ*) and almost certainly to be taken as a plural of majesty. Thus, Behemoth is a word that invites the reader to envision the most fearsome land animal imaginable. Thinking of such creatures leads Job (and us the readers) to realize that he is powerless before the forces of the world, but God can control them. Thus, God describes these creatures again to put Job in his place.

And God is successful in his attempt, as Job now responds a second time to God's speech:

> And Job answered the LORD, and said:
> "I know that you can do all things,
>   and no plan of yours is impossible.
> 'Who is this who hides advice without knowledge?'
>   Thus I spoke, but I did not understand,
>   things too wonderful for me that I did not know.
> 'Hear and I will speak.
>   I will question you, and you will inform me.'
> My ear had received a report of you,
>   but now my eyes have seen you.
> Therefore I hold myself in contempt,
>   and I repent in dust and ashes." (42:1–6)

Job begins by acknowledging God's sovereignty, and then he also confesses that he spoke out of ignorance. The latter refers to his charge that God was unjust in how he treated Job. Job is not claiming that he now understands why he suffered, but he is saying that the explanation is above him, and thus he now repents[11] of his actions and stands silent before God.

11. It is true that this traditional understanding of the verb *mā'as* can be challenged based on a number of translational ambiguities. See the excellent description of the issues in Balentine, *Have You Considered My Servant Job?*, 182–83. Like Balentine, I believe that the broader

The Prose Epilogue (Job 42:7–17)

The book of Job began with a prose prologue and now concludes with a prose epilogue. A number of modern interpreters find the conclusion to Job confusing and disappointing.[12] After all, Job had resisted his friends' call to repent and did not believe their promise that if he did, then God would restore him. Here at the end, though, Job repents and God restores him (and more). Were the friends right?

At first blush, the prologue does seem to undermine the message of the book of Job up to that point. But note that God affirms Job and criticizes the three friends:

> And it came about after the LORD spoke these words to Job that the LORD spoke to Eliphaz the Temanite. "My anger burns against you and your two friends because you did not speak correctly about me as did my servant Job." (42:7)

It is only a superficial reading of the book that sees a conflict between Job's repentance and God's criticism of the three friends. The matter becomes clear when we understand that Job was not repenting of anything that led to his suffering in the first place. The book is consistent in understanding that Job's suffering was not the result of sin. Thus, the friends indeed did speak wrongly and harmfully by suggesting otherwise. Job rather repented of his later charge that God was unjust.

Job spoke rightly about God by not caving in to the simplistic arguments of the friends, and more importantly, he maintained his relationship with God in spite of the fact that he did not enjoy the benefits of that relationship. He never did what the Accuser expected and what his wife advised: to curse God and die (2:9).

But is there a difference between the Job at the beginning of the book (a man who feared God and was blameless and innocent) and at the end (a man who feared God and was blameless and innocent)? Perhaps here we should observe that one's relationship with God, one's wisdom, can deepen and mature. After all, one of the stated purposes of the book of Proverbs is to make the wise even wiser: "Let the wise hear and increase teaching; let those with understanding acquire guidance" (Prov. 1:5). In Job's final statement, he says that before he had "heard a report of God," but now he has seen him.

---

context "construes the objective of the divine speeches to be God's vindication," so I lean toward "interpretive options that stipulate Job's repentance" (183). See my treatment in *Job*, 448–50.

12. For instance, Newsom, *Book of Job*; and Zuckerman, *Job the Silent*.

His relationship with God has gone through the flames and has emerged stronger. He is now able to trust God so thoroughly that he can suffer deeply and not demand answers.

Yes, God does restore Job's good fortunes, but not at the time of his "repentance." Indeed, he has no assurance of any change to his circumstances when he chooses to suffer in silence before God—in other words, to trust him completely in spite of his suffering. Job's eventual restoration is a narrative way of saying that the test has come to a successful conclusion.

The Nature of Wisdom: Job's Contribution

In the final analysis, the book of Job supports the picture of wisdom gained from both Proverbs and Ecclesiastes.

First, we learn again that the source of wisdom is God. While all the human characters of the book make claims to their own wisdom as they grapple with the problem of Job's suffering, their diagnoses and remedies are shown to be woefully inadequate. The three friends' and Job's retribution theology are based predominantly on the tradition of the elders. While these four all believe that suffering is the result of sin, Job differs in that he knows that his suffering can't be ascribed to any wrongdoing on his part. He is right about that, but he is wrong to believe that God works through a mechanical and absolute principle of retribution, the basis on which he inappropriately accuses God of injustice. Elihu's pretentious claim to wisdom based on a spiritual inspiration turns out to be only so much hot air not even worthy of either human or divine response. Only God is wise in the book of Job. At the end, he neither explains why Job suffers nor provides a solution to his suffering; he simply asserts his sovereign power and his vast wisdom.

Second, we learn that the proper human response to God's wisdom is submission. Thus, the book of Job joins both Proverbs and Ecclesiastes in asserting that humans must fear God. As we see Job move from one level of the fear of the Lord at the beginning of the book to what we described as an even more mature expression of that fear, we note that the book of Job adds the dimension that the wise can grow even wiser. After all, as Proverbs puts it, "the fear of Yahweh is the beginning of wisdom" (Prov. 1:7).

While we are on the subject of the fear of the Lord in connection to the way the book of Job ends, we should address the tendency of some commentators to resist the message of the canonical book. Some do so by reinterpreting Job's responses not as a reverent submission but rather as a disgusted realization that he had no other recourse before such a "cosmic bully."[13] To achieve this reading, its proponents must impose meanings on Hebrew words and Job's physical gestures for which there is no significant support. Others simply express disappointment in what they consider to be a late addition to the book, preferring to read the book without reference to the divine speeches and Job's response.[14] One cannot help feeling that these readings are the result of the "spirit of the age" at the end of the twentieth and early twenty-first centuries, and a Western one at that.

Third, and finally, the book's emphasis on the idea that the fear of the Lord is the proper response to God's wisdom again demonstrates that wisdom is fundamentally the result of a relationship with God. While wisdom is on one level connected to the practical skill of living and on another level an ethical construct, the book of Job, along with Proverbs and Ecclesiastes, furthers the idea that true wisdom has a theological foundation.

13. Perdue, *Wisdom Literature*, 125–26.
14. Newsom, *Book of Job*.

PART 2

WISDOM ELSEWHERE IN THE OLD TESTAMENT

I n our study of the nature of wisdom in the OT, we began with Proverbs, Ecclesiastes, and Job because these three books are the most forward in their presentation of wisdom in the OT. In light of recent challenges, we have not insisted that these books constitute a genre of wisdom literature, nor does our study depend on such a categorization (but see appendix 2).

While it is true that wisdom permeates Proverbs, Ecclesiastes, and Job, these books do not exhaust the OT's use of the word or concept. Scholars have recognized wisdom as a category relevant to a number of other books. Indeed, the recent critique of the category of wisdom literature also worries about the ever-expanding list of books that have been added to the genre over the past decades. If eventually everything is seen as wisdom, doesn't that weaken the very idea of a distinct wisdom genre?[1]

In my opinion, such worries are overblown. Nonetheless, in light of such fears, my claim is not that the books and passages to be treated in the next three chapters are wisdom literature. My view is that they contribute to our understanding of the nature of wisdom.

Thus, in chapter 4 we turn first to nonnarrative passages in which wisdom plays a significant role. We begin with a look at Deuteronomy that brings wisdom in connection to law, an important relationship, as we will see in later chapters. We then turn to that collection of sung prayers that we know as Psalms in order to focus on a handful of psalms that share concepts, terminology, and issues with Proverbs, Ecclesiastes, and Job. Next we will consider the prophets to see what they have to say about wisdom and those who lay claim to wisdom. We finish the chapter with a consideration of the Song of Songs. The inclusion of this collection of love poems may be the most controversial since the book never mentions wisdom, but the fact that many scholars have thought to call the Song wisdom leads us to examine possible connections.

In chapters 5 and 6 we turn our attention to wisdom in the historical narratives of the OT. Over the past three decades, the question of wisdom in narrative has been a controversial one.[2] While it would be going too far to say that any historical narrative should be categorized as wisdom literature, it is nonetheless obvious that wisdom plays an important role in the characterization of certain biblical characters and in the plots of various stories of the OT. We have divided our study into two chapters. The first study will focus on Joseph and Daniel, who were recognized as wise by their contemporaries.[3] The second study examines the accounts of Adam and Solomon, two figures who were identified as wise at first but then who plummet to the depths of folly. Through this study we hope to come to a better understanding of the nature of wisdom in the OT.

1. Kynes, *Obituary*.
2. See Crenshaw, "Method in Determining Wisdom Influence."
3. We here bracket questions of historicity as not relevant to the purpose of our study. By "contemporaries," we simply mean those other characters in the stories. Those interested in issues of history as they relate to these characters may consult the relevant sections of Provan, Long, and Longman, *Biblical History of Israel*. For Adam, see my article "Adam and Eve."

4

OTHER SOURCES OF WISDOM

Deuteronomy, Psalms, Song of Songs, and Prophecy

Proverbs, Ecclesiastes, and Job are the only books in the OT that may properly be called wisdom books, in that the nature of wisdom is their primary interest and focus. Even if one does not believe that wisdom is a literary genre (but see appendix 2), the pervasive treatment of wisdom as a concept in these books earn them a special place in our discussion.

That said, wisdom plays an important role in a number of other books as well. In this chapter, we will survey the presence of wisdom theology in Deuteronomy, Psalms, and the prophets. We will finally consider the question whether and in what way the Song of Songs might be connected with wisdom, since it is a book often associated with wisdom.

Deuteronomy: "This Will Show Your Wisdom and Understanding" (Deut. 4:6)

Even if, with a flexible and fluid concept of genre, we can still speak of wisdom literature, Deuteronomy would not be included in that category. Later, we will explore Deuteronomy further in reference to the relationship between wisdom, law, and covenant, and there we will see that it would be better to speak of Deuteronomy using other generic titles like sermon or covenant renewal document.

Thus, we here introduce Deuteronomy into the discussion not because the book is wisdom but because it speaks of wisdom at a key point in the book. It's not the only place that wisdom plays a role in Deuteronomy (see also 1:13–5; 16:19; 32:29; 34:9), but we serve our present purpose by citing Deut. 4:5–8:

> See, I have taught you decrees and laws as the LORD my God commanded me, so that you may follow them in the land you are entering to take possession of it. Observe them carefully, for this will show your wisdom and understanding to the nations, who will hear about all these decrees and say, "Surely this great nation is a wise and understanding people." What other nation is so great as to have their gods near them the way the LORD our God is near us whenever we pray to him? And what other nation is so great as to have such righteous decrees and laws as this body of laws I am setting before you today?

Moses here calls on the Israelites to obey the law that God revealed to them at Mount Sinai. What is striking for our study of wisdom in the OT is the clear connection drawn between law and wisdom.[1] If the Israelites follow the law God gave them, then others will look at them and see such a well-ordered, just, and flourishing society that they will marvel at their wisdom. The decrees themselves are wise, and as the people embody these laws in their behavior and relationship toward God and toward each other, they will display this wisdom to others outside of Israel. Scholars dispute the connection between law, wisdom, and covenant. Our purpose here is simply to introduce Deuteronomy into the broader discussion of wisdom. A fuller treatment of the issue is found in chapter 10.

The Psalms and Wisdom

At the earliest stages of form-critical analysis of the book of Psalms, Gunkel described one category of psalms as wisdom.[2] However, ever since the time of Gunkel, much debate has surrounded the utility of this type in terms of whether it is a distinctive *Gattung* (genre) and, if so, who were its authors (sages, scribes?), how they were used (cultic, noncultic?), and so on.[3] Those

---

1. As Krüger ("Law and Wisdom," 35) states: "Only here are Wisdom and Torah related to each other in the Pentateuch."
2. Gunkel and Begrich, *Introduction to Cultic Poetry*, 293–305.
3. For a helpful recent statement of the issues and description of the state of the discussion, see Jacobson, "Wisdom Language in the Psalms."

who argue that there is a wisdom genre rarely agree on the particular psalms that should be included.[4]

In spite of this disagreement, few would deny that many psalms contain an instructional element and that many utilize concepts, terminology, and metaphors that invite comparison and connection to the main wisdom books.

Psalm 1 is a prime example, as it opens with a blessing formula (*ašrê*) that is known from wisdom literature (Prov. 3:13, 18; 5:18; etc.). Like the book of Proverbs, the psalmist divides humanity into two categories, the righteous and the wicked, which are ethical categories associated with the wise and the fool respectively. Further, the wise are said to prosper, while the wicked will be destroyed. The metaphor of the path as the journey of one's life is found beginning in v. 1, where the righteous person does not "walk in step with the wicked," and in v. 6, which announces that "the LORD watches over the way of the righteous, but the way of the wicked leads to destruction." That instruction is at the heart of the psalm is seen in the announcement that the "delight" of the righteous is "in the law of the LORD" and on the one "who meditates on his law day and night" (v. 2).

Later (chap. 10) we will examine the connection between wisdom and law more carefully, and we will argue that there is a connection, in spite of differences, in that both law and wisdom offer guidance for life and require obedience. Both are similar also in that they lead to instruction. Thus, it is not surprising that other psalms that focus on law (often called Torah psalms) are thought to be wisdom psalms, the three most notable being Pss. 1 (treated in the previous paragraph), 19 (at least the second part), and 119 ("Oh, how I love your law! I meditate on it all day long. Your commands are always with me and make me wiser than my enemies," vv. 97–98).[5]

Thus far we have looked at examples of psalms that reflect the concerns and language associated with Proverbs. We now turn to psalms that have affinities with Job and Ecclesiastes.

Psalm 73 begins "Surely God is good to Israel, to those who are pure in heart" (v. 1), but from there the psalmist goes back in time to consider his earlier struggles with the prosperity of the wicked. He puts his problem concisely: "I envied the arrogant when I saw the prosperity of the wicked" (v. 3). He is quite simply mystified by the lack of proper retribution for the wicked, and on the other side by his own suffering, though he was innocent:

4. Though there is a high measure of agreement on a core that includes Pss. 1, 19 (at least the second half), 37, 49, 73, 112, 119.

5. Finsterbusch ("Yahweh's Torah," 108) points out that "Psalm 119 contains twenty-five instances of the word 'Torah' and thereby a tenth of all occurrences of the word in the Hebrew Bible."

"Surely in vain I have kept my heart pure and have washed my hands in innocence. All day long I have been afflicted, and every morning brings new punishments" (vv. 13–14).

He was almost completely lost in such thinking until he "entered the sanctuary of God" (v. 17). Perhaps here too we have another parallel to Job, who, we will remember, changed his thinking once he moved beyond hearing about God to being in God's very presence (Job 42:5).

Psalm 49 is also rich with wisdom terms and ideas. Indeed, the psalmist states that "my mouth will speak words of wisdom; the meditation of my heart will give you understanding. I will turn my ear to a proverb; with the harp I will expound my riddle" (vv. 3–4). The psalmist reflects on wicked people who are wealthy and seem to have the upper hand, but he also reminds his hearers that "all can see that the wise die, that the foolish and the senseless also perish, leaving their wealth to others. Their tombs will remain their houses forever" (vv. 10–11a). While this sentiment in one sense reflects Qohelet's thoughts, it does not frustrate the psalmist as it does him. That may be because, in a rare glimpse of the afterlife in the OT, the psalmist believes that, though the righteous die, death will not have the final say in their case: "But God will redeem me from the realm of the dead; he will surely take me to himself" (v. 15).[6]

Many also see a close connection between creation theology and wisdom (see chap. 8). Woman Wisdom describes her intimate involvement with creation (Prov. 8:22–31), and the wise father announces that "Yahweh laid the foundations of the earth with Wisdom, establishing the heavens with competence. With his knowledge the deeps burst open, and the skies drop dew" (Prov. 3:19–20). Recognizing the relationship between wisdom and creation suggests that perhaps the so-called creation psalms are related to the wisdom theme as well (Pss. 8; 19:1–6).

Finally, we should mention those psalms that, along with other wisdom themes and terms, encourage the "fear of God." Proverbs, Ecclesiastes, and Job all point to this attitude as the foundation of wisdom. Psalm 111, while probably best understood as a hymn, connects to the wisdom tradition by concluding:

> The fear of the LORD is the beginning of wisdom;
>   all who follow his precepts have good understanding.
>   To him belongs eternal praise. (v. 10)

---

6. Psalm 37 also deals with the conundrum of the prosperity of the wicked and the affliction of the innocent.

The following hymn is often identified as a wisdom psalm, beginning "Praise the LORD. Blessed are those who fear the LORD, who find great delight in his commands" (112:1). The psalm goes on to describe the virtuous man in terms that are similar to those that describe the "virtuous woman" in Prov. 31:10–31.[7]

In conclusion, we should note that while there is great disagreement about how intentionally the final editors of the book of Psalms ordered the individual psalms, there is widespread agreement that Ps. 1 serves as an introduction to the book as a whole. Jacobson, building on the work of many others, is surely correct when she concludes that the effect of Ps. 1's initial position is that it "invites us to see the Psalter as more than a prayer book or a loose collection of hymns; the Psalter is also a book of instruction. Psalms are not only prayed and sung; they are also to be read and studied."[8]

True Wisdom and False Wisdom in the Prophetic Books

What can we learn about wisdom from the prophetic books?

God's Great Wisdom

First, and most importantly, the prophets, particularly Isaiah, Jeremiah, and Ezekiel, recognize and celebrate God's wisdom.

Isaiah's woe oracle against the drunken leaders of Judah and especially Ephraim concludes with the following pronouncement: "All this also comes from the LORD Almighty, whose plan is wonderful, whose wisdom is magnificent" (28:29). The most immediate antecedent of "all this" is the description of the proper way to farm and produce grain (28:23–28). The farmer must know how to use the proper implements at the proper time to produce bread. God in his wisdom set it up that way, and "God instructs him and teaches him the right way" (28:26). Farming is an analogy (a common teaching tool of wisdom thinking) of knowing how to get along in the world. One needs to know how to use the right tools in the face of threats. The way God set up the world requires trusting God, not trusting other nations by entering into treaties with them ("we have entered into a covenant with death, with the realm of the dead we have made an agreement," v. 15). Isaiah thus calls on the leaders of Israel to turn away from their trust in foreign political alliances

7. Other psalms that speak of the fear of God, some of which we would identify as wisdom psalms and others that aren't but show influence from the wisdom tradition, include Pss. 14, 19, 25, 34, 52, 127, and 128.
8. Jacobson, "Wisdom Language in the Psalms," 155.

and trust only God. This is the way God has made the world work, and it is the way of God's wisdom.

Isaiah 31 is yet another woe oracle against those who look for help by entering into alliances with foreign nations, in this case Egypt ("woe to those who go down to Egypt for help," v. 1). They do not look for help from God. In this context, Isaiah once again cites God's wisdom ("yet he too is wise," v. 2), but this time with a threat ("and can bring disaster"). Again, the implication is that wisdom is found only with God.

Yet a third woe oracle in Isaiah ("Woe, to you destroyer," 33:1) also speaks of God's wisdom, but this time the oracle addresses the enemy of God's people, not God's people themselves. The destroyer (of God's people), perhaps Assyria, will itself be destroyed.[9] God will scatter them and then will "fill Zion with his justice and righteousness" (v. 5). As a result God "will be the sure foundation for your times, a rich store of salvation and wisdom and knowledge" (v. 6). How will Israel access this "rich store"? Isaiah tells them that "the fear of the LORD is the key to this treasure" (v. 6). In other words, when Israel puts themselves in a submissive and obedient relationship to God, God will bless them with peace and stability.

Jeremiah too celebrates God's great wisdom and contrasts it with the wisdom found among the nations, particularly over against lifeless idols. In the oracle found in 10:1–16, we find God warning Israel not to follow in the idolatrous practices of the nations. He ridicules the pagan practice of worshiping objects that human beings manufacture from wood and precious metals. Over against the idols, God is great and his name is powerful. First of all, God is contrasted over against the wisdom teachers of the nations ("among all the wise leaders of the nations and in all their kingdoms, there is no one like you," v. 7). Indeed, these pagan sages are foolish since they learn their lessons from "worthless wooden idols," v. 8). God on the other hand demonstrates his wisdom and power in his creation of the cosmos ("God made the earth by his power; he founded the world by his wisdom and stretched out the heavens by his understanding," v. 12; cf. Prov. 3:19–20; 8:22–31). Interestingly, this statement is repeated in the oracle against Babylon at the end of the book (see 51:15). In this context, God's power and wisdom explains why God can easily destroy Babylon.

Criticizing the Wise

The prophets are well known for their attack on those who claim to be wise, particularly those who were in service to the king as court counselors.[10] First, they

9. Oswalt, *Isaiah*, 372.
10. McKane, *Prophets and Wise Men*, 65–91.

criticize those from pagan nations who consider themselves wise. In an oracle against Egypt (19:1–20:6), Isaiah ridicules the wisdom teachers of that nation who give bad advice to Pharaoh and who cannot stand up against the Lord:

> The officials of Zoan[11] are nothing but fools;
>> the wise counselors of Pharaoh give senseless advice.
> How can you say to Pharaoh,
>> "I am one of the wise men,
>> a disciple of the ancient kings"? (19:11)

Or consider Jeremiah's oracle against Edom, another nation known for its wisdom, as well as the oracle against Babylon:

> Is there no longer wisdom in Teman?
>> Has counsel perished from the prudent?
>> Has their wisdom decayed? (49:7; see also Obad. 8)

> "A sword against the Babylonians!"
>> declares the LORD—
> "against those who live in Babylon
>> and against her officials and wise men!" (50:35; see also v. 37)

Ezekiel has a long diatribe against the wisdom of Tyre and specifically its king (Ezek. 28).[12]

Such attacks against foreign wisdom are to be expected by Israelite prophets, but what is surprising are the criticisms of Israelite wisdom. Examples include the following:

> I am the LORD,
>> the Maker of all things,
>> who stretches out the heavens,
>> who spreads out the earth by myself,
> who foils the signs of false prophets
>> and makes fools of diviners,
> who overthrows the learning of the wise
>> and turns it into nonsense. (Isa. 44:24–25)

> How can you say, "We are wise,
>> for we have the law of the LORD,"

---

11. Another name for the Egyptian city of Tanis.
12. For a treatment of Ezek. 28, see chap. 6.

> when actually the lying pen of the scribes
>   has handled it falsely?
> The wise will be put to shame;
>   they will be dismayed and trapped.
> Since they have rejected the word of the LORD,
>   what kind of wisdom do they have? (Jer. 8:8–9)

Jeremiah reports the response that these wise men have against his criticisms: "They said, 'Come, let's make plans against Jeremiah; for the teaching of the law by the priest will not cease, nor will counsel from the wise, nor the word from the prophets. So come, let's attack him with our tongues and pay no attention to anything he says'" (18:18).

Are the prophets against the sages then? Certainly not. They are against those who falsely claim wisdom: "Woe to those who are wise in their own eyes and clever in their own sight" (Isa. 5:21). In other words, the prophets inveigh against false claimants to wisdom who pervert counsel and distort the law just as they are against corrupt priests and false prophets. True wisdom comes from centering one's thinking not in oneself, but in God:

> This is what the LORD says:
> "Let not the wise boast of their wisdom
>   or the strong boast of their strength
>   or the rich boast of their riches,
> but let the one who boasts boast about this:
>   that they have the understanding to know me,
> that I am the LORD, who exercises kindness,
>   justice and righteousness on earth,
>   for in these I delight." (Jer. 9:23–24)

The Call to Wisdom and the Prophetic Hope for a Wise King

The bulk of the prophet's comments on wisdom assert God's wisdom over against the corrupt wisdom of those humans who claim to be wise but really are not. It would be stretching the evidence to suggest that prophets believe that the wisdom enterprise is suspect in and of itself. We should not think that the prophets were against wisdom or against those who truly were wise any more than that they were against the cult or priests (as used to be thought).[13] They exalted God's wisdom over human pretense to wisdom and thus false sages.

It is not surprising at all that prophets attack sages rather than promoting them. God calls prophets to work during times of apostasy and crisis. Their

---

13. Perdue, *Wisdom and Cult.*

work begins when the people break the covenant law, and they come to confront God's people and threaten them that unless they repent, God will bring the covenant curses on them. In the words of Jeremiah as he responds to the upbeat message of Hananiah, "From early times the prophets who preceded you and me have prophesied war, disaster and plague against many countries and great kingdoms. But the prophet who prophesies peace will be recognized as one truly sent by the LORD only if his prediction comes true" (Jer. 28:8–9).

Thus, the prophets attack false sages. On rare occasions, the prophets issue a call for true wisdom and this often in the context of judgment:

> Listen! The LORD is calling to the city—
>   and to fear your name is wisdom [*tûšiyyâ*][14]—
> "Heed the rod and the One who appointed it." (Mic. 6:9)

Indeed, according to Hosea, only the wise can really understand the message of his prophecy and respond in the proper way:

> Who is wise? Let him realize these things.
>   Who is discerning? Let them understand.
> The ways of the LORD are right;
>   the righteous walk in them,
>   but the rebellious stumble in them. (Hosea 14:9)

Wisdom here is more than intellectual apprehension. It involves obedience to the ways of the Lord.

Israel's troubles resulted from the foolish behavior of God's people, most preeminently the godless, wicked, foolish behavior of its kings who did not live up to the divine standard of piety described in Deut. 17, including the provision that he was

> to write for himself on a scroll a copy of this law, taken from that of the Levitical priests. It is to be with him, and he is to read it all the days of his life so that he may learn to revere the LORD his God and follow carefully all the words of this law and these decrees and not consider himself better than his fellow Israelites and turn from the law to the right or to the left. Then he and his descendants will reign a long time over the kingdom of Israel. (Deut. 17:18–20)

The prophets warned that the king's sinful actions would bring an end to the monarchy, and Samuel–Kings cataloged those sinful actions, answering the question of why the monarchy came to an end in 586 BC.

14. A word related to wisdom (*ḥôkmâ*) in the book of Proverbs (2:7; 3:21; 8:14).

But the prophets also looked beyond the judgment to restoration. As a part of that restoration, they expected a new king in the line of David who would rule with wisdom:

> A shoot will come up from the stump of Jesse;
>   from his roots a Branch will bear fruit.
> The Spirit of the LORD will rest on him—
>   the Spirit of wisdom and of understanding,
>   the Spirit of counsel and of might,
>   the Spirit of the knowledge and fear of the LORD—
> and he will delight in the fear of the LORD.
> He will not judge by what he sees with his eyes,
>   or decide by what he hears with his ears;
> but with righteousness he will judge the needy,
>   with justice he will give decisions for the poor of the earth.
> He will strike the earth with the rod of his mouth;
>   with breath of his lips he will slay the wicked.
> Righteousness will be his belt
>   and faithfulness the sash around his waist. (Isa. 11:1–5)

This future Davidic king will have unprecedented divine wisdom thanks to an endowment of God's Spirit. He will then rule with justice and power in a way that the previous sons of David did not.

Jeremiah shared this expectation of a wise future Davidic king:

> "The days are coming," declares the LORD,
>   "when I will raise up for David a righteous Branch,
> a King who will reign wisely
>   and do what is just and right in the land.
> In his days Judah will be saved
>   and Israel will live in safety.
> That is the name by which he will be called:
>   The LORD Our Righteous Savior." (Jer. 23:5–6)

In the latter chapters of Isaiah, the expectation centers on the servant of the Lord. This future servant too will be characterized by wisdom:

> See, my servant will act wisely;
>   he will be raised and lifted up and highly exalted.
> Just as there were many who were appalled at him—
>   his appearance was so disfigured beyond that of any human being
>   and his form marred beyond human likeness—

> so he will sprinkle many nations,
>> and kings will shut their mouths because of him.
> For what they were not told, they will see,
>> and what they have not heard, they will understand. (Isa. 52:13–15)

Reading these and similar passages in the prophets makes it difficult for us to be absolutely certain about what exactly they had in mind. It seems most likely that they thought the future king would be a human descendant of David, who would be more like David himself than those who descended from him, only even better than David. Isaiah may well have thought of the servant as a metaphor for the faithful remnant of Israel itself.

But what they thought as they wrote and what the first hearers of their message may have understood is not only speculative but also not determinative of the actual fulfillment of their message of hope. For that, at least according to a Christian canonical reading of the Prophets, we must eventually turn to the NT (see chap. 15).

The Song of Songs: How to Be Sexual in the World

A number of scholars have identified the Song of Songs as a work of wisdom literature.[15] They have a variety of reasons for so arguing, but the connection that they, and others, make between the Song and wisdom merits discussion. Is there any basis for speaking about the Song as wisdom, particularly since this erotic poem never uses the term "wisdom" or related terminology?

We begin by acknowledging that there is widespread agreement that the Song is love poetry celebrating sexuality, not an allegory of the divine-human relationship.[16] In most of the poems, an unnamed man and an unnamed woman speak of their mutual desire for physical intimacy. They long to be alone with each other in the garden, a private place for love. We also hear from a chorus of women who are sometimes the cheerleaders of the relationship, demonstrating societal approval of the man and woman's relationship, and sometimes they serve as the woman's disciples in matters of love. While almost all scholars today would identify the Song as love poetry, they disagree over whether the Song tells a story about a love relationship (the dramatic approach to the

15. Childs (*Introduction to the Old Testament*, 573–75) begins by noting the ascription to Solomon (1:1), who is considered the paramount wisdom teacher. See also Landy, *Paradoxes of Paradise*, 33; Sadgrove, "Song of Songs as Wisdom Literature"; Tromp, "Wisdom and the Canticle."

16. As was almost exclusively held from the first century AD to the nineteenth century; see Longman, *Song of Songs*, 20–38.

Song) or is a collection of love poems (the anthological approach). While in my opinion the arguments favor the latter,[17] this issue is not relevant to the question of the Song's relationship with wisdom literature.

How then might the Song be associated with wisdom? One school of thought makes the connection with wisdom through a type of allegorical reading. As we have seen in chapter 1, God's wisdom is personified as a woman in the book of Proverbs (Woman Wisdom). Perhaps the woman in the Song represents Woman Wisdom. If so, then the mention of Solomon in the superscription and in a couple of the poems might be taken as an indication that the man in the Song is Solomon throughout the book. The Jewish thinker Don Isaac Abravanel (sixteenth century) represents such an approach.[18] On this reading, the Song of Songs is an allegory of Solomon, well known for his wisdom, and his pursuit of wisdom.

I find this approach unpersuasive for the same reason that I am unconvinced by any allegorical interpretation. In a word, there is nothing in the Song of Songs that leads one to understand the woman of the Song as Wisdom and precious little reason to think that the man in the Song is Solomon.

While not persuaded by this connection to wisdom literature, perhaps we can see a connection for a different reason. After all, the book of Proverbs does speak extensively of what we might call sexual ethics (throughout the book, but particularly in chaps. 5–7). While the main burden of the wise father is to warn the son about relationships with the "strange, foreign woman," there is a section that encourages a sensuous physical relationship with one's wife that uses language reminiscent of the Song of Songs:

> Drink water from your own well,
>> gushing water from your own cistern.
> Should your fountains burst forth outside,
>> streams of water in the public squares?
> They are yours alone
>> and not for strangers who are with you.
> May your spring be blessed;
>> rejoice in the wife of your youth.
> She is a deer of love and an ibex of grace.
>> Let her breasts intoxicate you all the time;
>> be continually inebriated by her love.
> Why, my son, should you be inebriated by a stranger
>> and embrace the bosom of a foreigner?

17. Ibid., 38–44.
18. Pope, *Song of Songs*, 110–11.

> For the eyes of Yahweh are on the paths of humans,
>   observing all their courses.
> The wicked will be captured by their own guilt,
>   grabbed by the cords of their own sin.
> Those without discipline will die,
>   inebriated by their own stupidity. (Prov. 5:15–23)

One familiar with the language and imagery of the Song will note many connections here. For instance, physical intimacy denoted by the language of drinking with the consequence of being inebriated by love (see Song 5:1). Note too the figurative language that connects the woman's sexual parts to a well or a fountain (Song 4:15). There is also the use of faunal imagery ("deer" and "ibex") that one finds running through the Song.

Roland Murphy helpfully points out that the Song might be read as an "explication" of Prov. 30:19: "the way of a man with a maiden."[19] It is certainly not out of keeping with the wisdom concept to note that explicit theological language is lacking in the Song. J. M. Munro may be on the right track when she notices a wisdom connection in the relationship between the young woman of the Song and the chorus, composed of other young women, whom she is instructing in the ways of love.[20]

In conclusion, the Song does not explore the nature of wisdom, but it does connect with Proverbs on a practical and ethical level.

Conclusion

Wisdom is a term not restricted to Proverbs, Ecclesiastes, and Job. Deuteronomy, Psalms, and a number of prophets speak of and about wisdom. The Song of Songs does not speak of wisdom per se, but rather, based on the similar teaching of Proverbs, helps the reader understand the wise path in matters concerning sexuality.

Even these books do not exhaust the use of wisdom in the OT. Of course, it has long been noted that certain biblical characters who play important roles in the redemptive history of the OT have been associated with wisdom. Their connection with wisdom literature, however, has not gone unchallenged. Thus, in the next two chapters we turn to consider four principle characters who are associated with wisdom in the narrative books of the OT.

---

19. Murphy, *Wisdom Literature*, 104.
20. Munro, *Spikenard and Saffron*, 146–47.

5

JOSEPH AND DANIEL

Paragons of Wisdom

We begin our study of portraits of wisdom in the OT with a look at Joseph and Daniel. As has long been noted, the stories of these two characters have much in common. They present accounts of two wise men who demonstrate their wisdom while serving in foreign courts. Although Joseph is arguably immature at the beginning of his story, both he and especially Daniel are about as consistently wise, righteous, and godly as any character in the Bible.

Treating these historical narratives in relationship to wisdom has been the subject of vigorous discussion since the time of von Rad's article "The Joseph Narrative and Ancient Wisdom."[1] Von Rad observed a number of similarities between the story and wisdom ideas, particularly those found in Proverbs, and proposed that Gen. 37–50 was wisdom literature. While many scholars followed von Rad's assessment, Crenshaw and Redford heavily criticized von Rad's assessment.[2] They, particularly Crenshaw, were largely successful in discouraging the connection between Joseph and wisdom, so that suggesting

1. Von Rad, "Joseph Narrative."
2. Crenshaw, "Method in Determining Wisdom Influence"; Redford, *Study of the Biblical Story of Joseph*, 100–105.

a link with regard to Joseph (and Daniel or any narrative text) has become controversial.[3]

In the light of the post–von Rad discussion, we should be clear. We do not agree with von Rad that either the Joseph narrative or the Daniel story are "wisdom literature" produced by sages for the purpose of training sages. Indeed, we have already made it clear that we agree with those (like Sneed and Kynes) who dispute the idea of a wisdom tradition or even professional class distinct from other traditions and professions. But no doubt can attend the idea that there is a concept of wisdom and that Joseph and Daniel are both explicitly portrayed as those who embody the idea of wisdom.

Joseph: A Hebrew Wise Man in Egypt

The Joseph narrative is not about wisdom per se. Thus, we begin with an overview of the story by identifying what we think is its main message, and then we examine the role that wisdom plays in the portrayal of Joseph's life.

"You Intended to Harm Me, but God Intended It for Good" (Gen. 50:20)

Wisdom is not a major theme of the Joseph narrative, and so before exploring the role that wisdom does play in the story, we do well to first of all explore the central message of this final section of the book of Genesis (chaps. 37–50).

In this we are helped by Joseph's own words toward the end of the account. After Jacob, his father, died, his brothers, who had so mistreated him in his youth, now fear that Joseph will finally take revenge on them. They thus come groveling to him to ask that he forgive them and not harm them but accept them as his slaves (50:15–18). To this, Joseph responds with these memorable words: "Don't be afraid. Am I in the place of God? You intended to harm me, but God intended it for good to accomplish what is now being done, the saving of many lives. So then, don't be afraid. I will provide for you and your children" (50:19–21a).

After suffering so much throughout his life, Joseph recognized that God used his pain to put him in a position of power so that he could provide for his family, the family chosen by God to bring blessing to the world (12:1–3), so

---

3. For a fuller recounting of the debate following von Rad's article, see Wilson, *Joseph Wise and Otherwise*, 6–37. My own understanding of the Joseph narrative is supported and deepened by Wilson's study of the relationship between wisdom and the Joseph narrative. He, as I, concludes that "the text as a whole is not a 'wisdom narrative,' but many 'wisdom-like elements' have been woven into it" (300).

they could survive a devastating regional famine. To be clear, Joseph believes not that God brought rescue to the family of God in spite of his suffering but rather that God used his suffering to rescue his family.

Indeed, while Joseph's brothers sold Joseph into Egyptian slavery because they hated him ("you intended to harm me"), that was how God brought Joseph to Egypt in the first place ("God intended it for good"). Upon arrival in Egypt, he served Potiphar, a high-ranking Egyptian official. Because God was with him, Potiphar's household prospered, and Joseph was given increased responsibility and freedom. Potiphar's wife wanted to sleep with him, but he rebuffed her as the later wisdom tradition would instruct (see below, "Reading the Joseph Narrative in Light of Proverbs"). His reward was imprisonment ("you intended to harm me"), but in prison he became acquainted with the chief cupbearer and the chief baker, two high-level Egyptian officials who themselves were in prison because they had fallen out of favor with Pharaoh ("God intended it for good").

At the very start of the story, Joseph showed himself to be an interpreter of dreams (37:5–11). In prison, the two Egyptian officials had dreams that Joseph accurately interpreted as indicating that the baker would lose his head while the cupbearer would be restored to the royal court. The latter promptly forgot about Joseph in prison ("you intended to harm me") until Pharaoh had a pair of disturbing dreams ("God intended it for good").

Thus, Joseph came into the presence of Pharaoh. The dreams of Pharaoh anticipated an imminent, devastating seven-year famine but also revealed that this famine would be preceded by seven years of abundance. Pharaoh responds to Joseph's interpretation by choosing him to head up the efforts that will allow Egypt to survive the famine. His elevation of Joseph to a high position within the Egyptian government is based on his assessment of Joseph's wisdom (to be discussed in the next section). Indeed, Pharaoh's confidence in Joseph is not wrongly placed. Joseph's management of the resources of Egypt not only enables the nation to survive the famine but also strengthens Pharaoh's control over the land and its people.

The role of Joseph in the survival of Egypt and in increasing the power of Pharaoh is not the main focus of the narrative.[4] After Joseph is in a place of power, his family in Canaan comes back into the story line. The famine has hit Canaan as well, and his family's lives are threatened. They hear that grain is available in Egypt, so Joseph's brothers (with the exception of

---

4. Though it does add punch to the comment at the beginning of the exodus story that "a new king, to whom Joseph meant nothing came to power in Egypt" (Exod. 1:8). After all, the very survival of Egypt and the power that that new pharaoh enjoyed was the direct result of the ancestor of the Hebrew people whom he now chooses to exploit.

Benjamin) travel to Egypt to secure provisions for the family. Their need initiates another important theme of the Joseph narrative that has implications for the future relationship between the tribes of Israel, particularly the status of Judah.

Jacob's family is what today we would call dysfunctional. At the beginning of the story, the brothers hate Joseph because he is Jacob's favorite son. He is the favorite because he is the son of Jacob and his beloved Rachel, while the other sons are offspring of Leah or one of the concubines. Jacob shows his preference by giving Joseph a special robe. Joseph intensifies his brothers' hatred by his insensitive announcement of his two dreams that highlight his chosen leadership status in his family. It appears that he does not yet understand that his chosen status is for service, not for dominance.

In any case, as we have mentioned above, the brothers take their first opportunity to rid themselves of Joseph by selling him into slavery in Egypt, thus initiating the hard course of Joseph's life in Egypt. When they show up in Egypt with the hope of securing sustenance in the famine, Joseph is understandably concerned. Are they the same selfish brothers who sold him into slavery, or have they changed?

Thus, he conceals his identity from them and devises a test that will examine their character. He accuses them of being spies. They deny this charge and in the process reveal that they have a brother left at home, Benjamin, the younger son of Jacob and Rachel, now the favorite. Joseph insists that they leave one brother behind (Simeon) as a hostage until they return with Benjamin to corroborate their story.

He gives them grain and secretly returns their silver in the grain pouches. When they return to Canaan and tell their father about Joseph's instructions, Jacob is initially reluctant to allow the brothers to go back to Egypt with Benjamin. To Jacob, all the brothers with the exception of Benjamin are expendable, but when they run out of grain again, he has no recourse but to let them go to Egypt and take Benjamin with them.

At this point we should note the role of Judah in this story. Judah is the fourth-born son of Jacob, but by the beginning of the Joseph narrative, the first three sons have disqualified themselves from leadership. Reuben slept with his father's concubines (35:21–22; 49:3–4); Simeon and Levi angered their father when they slaughtered the men of Shechem (34; 49:5–7).[5]

At the beginning of the Joseph narrative, Judah is anything but a prominent candidate for leadership in the family. His suggestion to sell Joseph into

---

5. Though the narrator of that story almost certainly agrees with Levi and Simeon rather than Jacob, who was willing to integrate his family with the Canaanites (Longman, *Genesis*, 426–35).

slavery thwarted Reuben's plan to rescue him and return him to the family.[6] Genesis 38 then narrates a story that further darkens Judah's character. He has moved away from the family and has married a Canaanite wife and allowed his son to marry a Canaanite, Tamar. Judah does not follow through on promises to allow her to marry a third son after the first two die without fathering a child. Judah also sleeps with his daughter-in-law, whom he mistakes for a prostitute. When Tamar gets pregnant, he insists she be burned, until she reveals that the son is his, convicting him of his sin.

In a word, Judah is a despicable person at the beginning of the Joseph narrative. However, by the end of the story he has achieved a remarkable transformation. Returning to the plotline, the brothers, including Benjamin, arrive in Egypt to request more grain. Joseph, continuing his test of his brothers' character, gives them grain but also plants his divining cup in Benjamin's sack of grain.

Joseph's assistant catches up to the brothers as they are returning home and "discovers" the divining cup in Benjamin's sack. Joseph, being a "fair man," says that he will imprison only Benjamin and no one else. Thus Joseph has created a situation very similar to the one that led to his own enslavement. Will the brothers again abandon the annoying favorite son and act solely out of self-interest?

Judah is the brother who steps to the fore. In one of the lengthier speeches in the OT (44:18–34), which indicates its importance, Judah recounts the situation that has led them to bring Benjamin with them and how devastating the young son's loss would be to their aged father. Thus, Judah offers himself in place of Benjamin to serve as a slave in Joseph's household.

His offer shows remarkable transformation of character since the time he so quickly suggested to his brothers that they sell Joseph to the Ishmaelites. Joseph recognizes this change and reveals his true identity to his brothers, thus initiating a reconciliation of the family. The readers of this story also recognize the change and now understand that the fourth son is the true leader of this family. No wonder that the tribe that descends from him will assume such an important role in the future of Israel.

"There Is No One So Discerning and Wise as You" (Gen. 41:39)

The previous section explored the major themes of the Joseph narrative. We have seen that the theme of wisdom is not as important as that of God's providence or of the reconciliation of a dysfunctional family with ramifications

---

6. Reuben, the firstborn, should have simply refused to throw Joseph into the pit and calmed his brothers down, but at least he had a plan to return Joseph to the family.

for the future history of Israel. We also agree with Crenshaw that virtually every narrative in the OT will provide some illustration of the principles taught in the book of Proverbs, whether by example or counterexample, since "this book [Proverbs] covers the whole gamut of human existence."[7] That said, it is Pharaoh who makes the pronouncement that there is "no one so discerning and wise" as Joseph (41:39) and attributes that to the presence of the "spirit of God" in him (41:38).

In light of Crenshaw's trenchant critique of von Rad's reading of the Joseph narrative as wisdom literature, we need to be careful to describe our meaning here. We are not arguing that the Joseph narrative is wisdom literature (even if there is such a thing; see appendix 2) or produced by sages for illustrative use in schools that train future sages. Our perspective is that Joseph provides a portrait of wisdom that is even more fulsome than the aphorisms of the book of Proverbs.

First, it might be objected that the assessment of Joseph's wisdom comes from a pagan source. Apart from any historical considerations, though, there is little doubt that the story encourages the reader to take the assessment at face value and accept the narrator's viewpoint that Joseph is wise in, shall we say, the biblical sense.

Our next observation concerns the rationale for Pharaoh's assessment. He says, "Since God has made all this known to you, there is no one so discerning and wise as you" (41:39). In other words, Pharaoh counts Joseph wise because he was able to interpret Pharaoh's two dreams.

Pharaoh had had two disturbing dreams, but "no one," which probably specifically refers to his professional advisors, "could interpret them for him" (41:8). From what we know about Egyptian (and Mesopotamian) dream interpretation, the interpreter would listen to the contents of the dream and then consult dream commentaries to wrestle out its significance.[8]

Joseph's ability to interpret dreams, and thus his wisdom, comes from another source, as he himself had earlier stated to the chief baker and chief cupbearer: "Do not interpretations belong to God?" (40:8), a point reiterated to Pharaoh when he is asked to interpret his dreams: "I cannot do it, . . . but God will give Pharaoh the answer he desires" (41:16).

Many, including Crenshaw, would use Joseph's statement here to distance him from the wisdom literature since they believe that wisdom exclusively emphasizes human reason rather than revelation, but we will later (see chap. 7)

7. Perhaps an overstatement, but the point is well taken. See Crenshaw, "Method in Determining Wisdom Influence," 138.
8. Borghouts, "Witchcraft, Magic, and Divination," 1783.

argue that this is a misunderstanding of wisdom, where "the beginning of wisdom is the fear of the Lord," and it is not uncommon to appeal to revelation as a source of true wisdom.

However, Joseph's wisdom is not exclusively connected to his ability to interpret dreams. After all, because he is wise, Pharaoh chooses him to "be in charge of my palace" (41:40). Interpreting dreams will not help him in this massive task. In other words, Joseph's wisdom identifies him as capable of competent administration that includes preparations for the coming devastating famine.

Pharaoh's choice of Joseph as the person with the skill to navigate the coming crisis proves to be well placed. He carefully collected excess grain during the seven years of plenty and then controlled the distribution of the grain during the seven years of famine. His efforts made the court rich, since he sold the grain to those who needed it, eventually even acquiring their fields in return for the needed grain.

Perhaps it is more of a stretch, but I also believe that Joseph's life decisions both before his introduction to Pharaoh and after manifest the type of behavior that the people who produced Proverbs, Ecclesiastes, and Job would deem wise. Again, this statement should not be taken to mean that the portrait of Joseph was produced by a school of wisdom or even that it was written in light of these books, but it is illuminating to read Joseph in light of these books. The following comments are not intended to be exhaustive.

Reading the Joseph Narrative in Light of Proverbs

When we are first introduced to Joseph, he does not strike us as wise, and indeed his insensitive telling of the meaning of his dreams to his family shows that he does not take into consideration how his brothers will take the claim that he will be their superior. But his administration of Potiphar's household is exemplary and implies his ability to plan and organize well. The elaborate planning involved in his test of his brothers' character also demonstrates the kind of foresight that is indicative of the wise. Crenshaw believes that this is not a sign of wisdom, arguing that the test is cruel; however, if one thinks about the past, it certainly was a wise precaution. In our opinion, von Rad was correct to see Joseph's rejection of the sexual advances of Potiphar's wife as an illustration of the admonition from Proverbs to avoid the "strange, foreign woman" (Prov. 5–7). Since "the fear of God is the beginning of wisdom," it is odd that Crenshaw bases his protest on the fact that Joseph is motivated not only by concern for the trust placed in him by Potiphar but also by concern for God. Perhaps a stronger objection, at least at first sight, is the fact that, though Proverbs encourages such behavior by suggesting a reward, Joseph gets thrown in jail. But in the final analysis, such an objection is based on the incorrect understanding that Proverbs guarantees reward (see chap. 11) and also forgets that Joseph himself at the end of his life saw "good" in his incarceration (50:19–20).

As a final comment on Crenshaw's objections to von Rad, the former points to "the failure of Joseph to control his emotions" as a sign that Joseph does not act like a sage.[9] However, Proverbs does not discourage the expression of emotion. A wise person expresses the proper emotion at the proper level depending on the situation, and we would submit that Joseph's reactions are appropriate to the situations that confronted him.[10]

Reading the Joseph Narrative in Light of Ecclesiastes

The book of Ecclesiastes (see chap. 2) declares that wisdom "under the sun" can only take one so far. Identifying the message of the book primarily through the comments of the frame narrator encourages an "above the sun" perspective, one that begins with fear of God. We have argued that the book thus advocates wisdom, not primarily through observation and rational thought, but through revelation.[11] Joseph illustrates this understanding of wisdom since he is able to interpret the dreams, not by appeal to dream commentaries, but rather because God had revealed to him their meaning.

Reading the Joseph Narrative in Light of Job

Job, like Ecclesiastes, connects true wisdom to God's revelation (see chaps. 3 and 7). Indeed, we argued earlier that the book of Job is not about suffering but about wisdom. Though we do not believe that the question of suffering is the main issue in the book, we saw that we do learn something about wise suffering in the book as we see how Job suffers.

While the book of Job (along with the Psalms) certainly allows for God's people to lament and complain, it holds up suffering in silence and with patience as the ultimate ideal. As we follow Joseph through Gen. 37–50, we see someone who suffers and wisely guards himself against further damage from his brothers, someone who does not lament and cry but rather quietly and calmly devises plans to bring himself to a better place.

---

9. Crenshaw, "Method in Determining Wisdom Influence," 137.
10. Crenshaw (ibid.) cites 45:3, 14–15; 50:1, 17.
11. Taking the advice in 12:13–14 to be a slightly veiled reference to "the Law, the Prophets, and the Writings" (so argued in chap. 2).

Daniel: A Hebrew Wise Man in the Babylonian and Persian Courts

As we turn our attention now to Daniel, we should first note the similarity between him and Joseph. Both were in a foreign land against their will, and both found themselves serving in the royal court of pagan rulers. The wisdom of both is also an important feature of their characterization. Thus, it is not surprising that the types of criticisms leveled by Crenshaw in terms of an analysis of the book as wisdom literature are also relevant for Daniel.

Thus we begin by saying that our argument is not that the book of Daniel or any part of it is wisdom literature.[12] Our attention is drawn to Daniel simply because he is called wise.

In Spite of Present Circumstances, God Is in Control

We begin our exploration of the book of Daniel, as we did the Joseph narrative, with the recognition that the book is not wisdom literature; nor is its main theme wisdom. Accordingly, in order to keep perspective we will begin with a short statement about the book's primary message.[13]

The book of Daniel has two distinct parts. The first six chapters are about Daniel and his three friends in the foreign courts of Babylon and Persia. The second six chapters contain four apocalyptic visions. In addition, the book, as it presently stands, is written in two languages. It opens in Hebrew, and then in 2:4 the narrative switches to Aramaic. The change is not surprising since the narrator announces that the characters, in this case the royal counselors, respond to the king "in Aramaic." What is surprising is that the language does not revert to Hebrew at the end of the speech but actually continues until the end of chapter 7. There has been no consensus as to why the book is written in two languages, which even cut across its generic duality (narrative and apocalyptic).

In spite of these differences, the book of Daniel has one clear theme. Each story and each vision comfort the book's readers that "in spite of present difficulties, God is in control and will have the final victory" (*BIBD* 401). We can see this theme in the first few verses of the book. The very first verse describes how Nebuchadnezzar laid siege to Jerusalem and successfully forced its king, Jehoiakim, to submit Judah to vassal status. The narrator, however, tells the reader that it only looks like Nebuchadnezzar is in control. In reality, Nebuchadnezzar was successful only because "the Lord delivered Jehoiakim of Judah into his hand" (1:2).

---

12. And this point stands even if one accepts our argument in appendix 2.
13. For a full explication of the message of the book, see Longman, *Daniel.*

This message of God's control in spite of present appearances is repeated throughout the book. In Dan. 7, for instance, the first part of Daniel's vision describes a succession of horrifying beasts arising out of a chaotic sea. Later, the interpreting angel will tell Daniel that these beasts "are four kings that will rise from the earth" (7:17). In other words, these are nations that, like Babylon, dominate Judah. The second half of the vision tells another story. Here, "one like a son of man coming with the clouds of heaven" rides into the presence of the Ancient of Days and "was given authority, glory and sovereign power; all nations and peoples of every language worshiped him. His dominion is an everlasting dominion that will not pass away, and his kingdom is one that will never be destroyed" (7:13–14). While much about this passage might be debated, the vision clearly depicts God's great victory over the beasts that represent oppressive nations.

The main message of the book is thus that God is in control and will win the final victory. Written in the context of the persecution of God's people,[14] the book intends to comfort people who are being oppressed. The message is that God's oppressed people can survive and also thrive in the context of oppression. With an understanding of the main message of the book, we turn now to a consideration of the theme of wisdom.

"He Found Them Ten Times Better" (Dan. 1:20)

Though the book of Daniel is neither wisdom literature nor about wisdom, wisdom plays a significant role in it. The narrative presents the four Hebrew captives, particularly Daniel, as exceptionally wise, especially in contrast to their Babylonian and Persian counterparts. We will focus in on Daniel as the main character.

The narrative interest in contrasting Daniel's wisdom with that of his pagan counterparts begins in chapter 1 with his training in "the language and literature of the Babylonians" (1:4). Nebuchadnezzar is interested in taking these young, noble, and handsome political hostages of Judah, which he has just subjected to vassal status, and training them for service in his rapidly expanding empire. He also desires to control their diet so that they might not only be intellectually fit but also have the right physical appearance for their service as wise men in the court.

The main focus of Dan. 1 is on physical appearance because Daniel and his friends refuse to subject themselves to Nebuchadnezzar's diet. Daniel does

---

14. True whether, as traditionally thought, the book comes from the period of the sixth century or the later second-century BC oppression of the Jews by the Seleucid king Antiochus Epiphanes.

not make a public protest but wisely (see below) navigates behind the scenes to substitute a diet of vegetables and water for the mandated rich food and wine. Ashpenaz, the main official in charge of their training, refuses to allow them to abstain from the king's mandated diet. He is afraid that they will look worse than the other men their age (1:10), but Daniel successfully convinces the person who delivers the food to bring them vegetables and water. And, contrary to Ashpenaz's expectation, they don't look worse at all but are judged the top of their class in every category.

Why Daniel and his friends refuse the king's food has been much debated. It is doubtful that their reluctance has anything to do with kosher laws, since at a later point of life Daniel seems regularly to eat this food and drink wine (10:3). It is also unlikely that they refrain from the king's food because eating it would show political allegiance. First of all, it was a private act, not public. Second, they are eating the king's vegetables, which come from his table. And last, Daniel and his friends actually cooperate extensively with the Babylonian court until doing so explicitly conflicts with their religion.

We believe the reason is to be found elsewhere. In a word, Daniel is giving God room to work. Nebuchadnezzar feels that he is in control, and he is providing a diet that will lead to the desired physique of a Babylonian sage. If we examine contemporary pictorial representations of wise men of the ancient Near East (such as those on low reliefs found during archaeological excavations), the look is not lean but rather pudgy. The diet of rich food and wine would lead to the desired appearance. If this is true, then Daniel's diet of vegetables and water is not the best route to the desired end. But, as mentioned, at the end of the chapter they are pronounced the best, which implies that they have achieved the proper look. If their diet didn't produce it, then God must have done it.

Though Dan. 1 does not focus on their study of Babylonian language and literature, the narrator clearly announces that at the end of their study they were "in every matter of wisdom and understanding about which the king questioned them, he found them ten times better than all the magicians and enchanters in his whole kingdom" (v. 20). This statement is interesting considering what they almost certainly studied in Nebuchadnezzar's school. We have a good idea from extrabiblical sources of the curriculum used for the training of sages in the neo-Babylonian court. They would have learned to write Akkadian, and they probably already knew Aramaic, two important languages of the world at that time. Their study would have exposed them deeply to the pagan mythology of Babylon that would have been toxic to their faith. But most interesting would have been the course of divination, where they would have learned such skills as reading the liver of a sheep to determine the course of the future as well as dream interpretation. The latter plays a key role in the next chapter, to which we now turn.

In Dan. 2 the king has a disturbing dream. He calls his "magicians, enchanters, sorcerers and astrologers to tell him what he had dreamed" (2:2). He wants them to tell him not only what his dreams signified but also the content of the dream, a request to which they respond with shocked protest: "There is no one on earth who can do what the king asks! No king, however great and mighty, has ever asked such a thing of any magician or enchanter or astrologer. What the king asks is too difficult. No one can reveal it to the king except the gods, and they do not live among humans" (2:10–11).

The modern reader needs a little background here. In Mesopotamia dream interpretation worked in the following way.[15] The dreamer would describe the dream to the interpreter, who would then go to the dream commentaries to determine its significance. In other words, interpreters never claimed that they could inform the dreamer of the *content* of the dream.

We do not know why Nebuchadnezzar was unwilling to tell them the content of his dream, but it sets up a situation where the wisdom of Daniel can be contrasted with the wisdom of the Mesopotamian sages. Or to put it another way, Daniel's true wisdom will be contrasted with the wisdom he was taught in his course of study mentioned in Dan. 1. Thus, we will see that not only did Daniel and his friends owe their physique to God in spite of the food they were eating; their wisdom came not from their training but rather from God.

When the Mesopotamian wise men could not tell the king his dream, he issued a decree to "put the wise men to death" (2:13). Thus Arioch, the commander of the king's guard, went looking for Daniel and his friends. When Arioch approached him, Daniel "spoke to him with wisdom and tact" (2:14; see comments below). He asked for some time, and once it was granted, he and his friends turned to God in prayer. God responded to his prayer by informing him of the content and significance of the dream.

Thus, Daniel reveals that his wisdom is true and superior to the wisdom of the Babylonian court because it comes directly from God. After being informed by God about the dream, he praised him by acknowledging that "wisdom and power are his" (2:20) and that he was the one who "gives wisdom to the wise and knowledge to the discerning" (2:21). He made sure to tell Nebuchadnezzar that "no wise man, enchanter, magician or diviner can explain to the king the mystery he has asked about, but there is a God in heaven who reveals mysteries" (2:27–28).

---

15. Information about omens and dream interpretation in Mesopotamia is helpfully summarized in Farber, "Witchcraft, Magic, and Divination."

Thus, like Joseph, Daniel's wisdom is connected to dream interpretation. Like Joseph, he acknowledges that this wisdom comes only from God. Indeed, later when Belshazzar, a later Babylonian king, sees mysterious writing on the wall, he eventually calls Daniel, about whom he has heard "that the spirit of the gods is in you and that you have insight, intelligence and outstanding wisdom" (5:14). But, also like Joseph, the portrait of Daniel as a wise man extends beyond dream interpretation to include outstanding administrative skill and the ability to navigate life successfully even in the midst of trouble.

"Daniel Spoke to Him with Wisdom and Tact" (Dan. 2:14)

Like Joseph, Daniel's wisdom is related to his ability to interpret dreams. As we have seen, Daniel makes it extremely clear that his skill is God given, and thus it is appropriate to say that his wisdom is the result of revelation, not of learning.

However, his wisdom is not exclusively tied to dream interpretation, but it is also manifest in practical, day-to-day interchanges. The narrator points this out when Arioch, the commander of the king's guard, shows up at Daniel's residence to carry out the king's decree that all the wise men of Babylon be put to death. Rather than panic and flee or plead for his life, Daniel spoke to him in a way that gave him the opportunity to appeal to God and receive the answer that saved their lives.

Whether it is this particular episode or any of the six stories concerning Daniel and the three friends in the first six chapters of the book, we see Daniel acting with the type of care around the king (or their representatives) that the book of Proverbs advocates:

> The anger of the king is a messenger of death;
>   the wise will appease it. (16:14)

> Those who love a pure heart—
>   their lips are gracious; the king is their friend. (22:11)

> A military commander is persuaded by patience,
>   and a tender tongue breaks bone. (25:15)

Indeed, Daniel's cool head prevails in even tense situations. The following proverbs are well illustrated by his interaction with Ashpenaz in the first chapter. Daniel does not want to eat the food provided by the king, but Ashpenaz refuses to cooperate. Again, Daniel does not protest or demand, but he patiently works out another strategy to get to his desired end.

> Patience brings much competence,
>> but impatience promotes stupidity. (14:29)

> The short-tempered act stupidly,
>> and people who scheme are hated. (14:17)

> A patient person is better than a warrior,
>> and those who control their emotions than those who can capture a
>> city. (16:32)

> Those who hold back their speech know wisdom,
>> and those who are coolheaded are people of understanding. (17:27)

In our study of Proverbs, we noted that the sages often contrasted wisdom/righteousness/godliness with folly/wickedness/ungodliness. Though the terms are not used in Dan. 6, the earlier depiction of Daniel as a godly wise man encourages us to look at the chapter through the prism of wisdom and folly. Daniel 6, like Dan. 3, describes a court conflict.[16] The story pits Daniel against other "administrators and the satraps" (6:3). Daniel had so distinguished himself as a successful administrator that the king determined to promote him over his peers. Thus, the successful wise man would get his proper reward:

> Do you see people who do their work with diligence?
>> They will stand before kings;
>> they will not stand before the obscure. (22:29)

Out of jealousy his rivals then sought to slander him.

> Wrath is cruel, and anger is a flood,
>> and who can stand up in the face of jealousy. (27:4)

> The perverse produce conflict,
>> and gossips separate intimate friends. (16:28)

> Without wood, a fire is extinguished.
>> When there are no gossips, conflict calms down. (26:20)

16. The term comes from Humphreys, "Life-Style for the Diaspora."

In frustration, "they could find no corruption in him, because he was trust-worthy and neither corrupt nor negligent" (6:4). The wise Daniel isn't lazy but works hard (6:6–11; 10:4, 5; 12:11, 24, 27, etc.), nor was he ethically compromised but rather was characterized by "righteousness, justice, and virtue" (Prov. 1:3b).

The administrators and satraps therefore plotted against Daniel by convincing the king to issue a decree that would only allow prayers to be directed to the king.[17]

> A ruler who pays attention to a false word—
> All those who serve him are wicked. (29:12)

> Look, there are six things Yahweh hates,
> and seven that are an abomination to his soul:
> haughty yes, a lying tongue,
> and hands that spill the blood of the innocent,
> a heart set on iniquitous plans,
> feet hurrying to run to evil. (6:16–18)

Though they had short-term success in getting Daniel thrown into the lions' den, God preserved him, and then the accusers suffered the fate that they intended for Daniel.

> False witnesses will not escape punishment,
> and those who proclaim lies will not escape. (19:5)

> For there will be no future for evil;
> the lamp of the wicked will be extinguished. (24:20)

> For the righteous may fall seven times, but get up,
> but the wicked will stumble in evil. (24:16)

Conclusion

We have treated Joseph and Daniel together because their stories have so many similarities. They both were forced against their will to work in the

17. This decree is odd at first glance since Persian kings were not considered gods. Perhaps the point is that prayers should be directed through the king. According to Walton ("Decree of Darius," 280), the decree does not actually "deify the king but designates him as the only legitimate representative of deity for the stated time." What likely appealed to the king was that such a decree would serve as a loyalty test.

toxic environment of a foreign court. They both experienced dreams and visions and manifested their wisdom in the interpretation of the same. They both attributed their wisdom to God. Further, both men put their wisdom to practical work in helping guide their royal overlords.

The biblical narrative presents both of them as consistently displaying wisdom in their lives and in their interactions with others. This consistency contrasts with two other biblical characters well recognized for their wisdom but also for their fall into utter folly. In the next chapter, we turn to the stories of Adam and Solomon.

6

ADAM AND SOLOMON

From the Heights of Wisdom to the Depths of Folly

O f wisdom figures in the OT, none is better known than Solomon.
Among the kings of Israel and later Judah, none surpass him. We
have already seen his name associated with three books connected
to wisdom: Proverbs, Ecclesiastes, and Song of Songs. However, Solomon is
well known in the book of Kings not only for his wisdom but also for his
precipitous collapse into folly. Adam, on the other hand, might not at first
thought be considered a candidate for inclusion in our portraits of wisdom.
In the opening chapters of Genesis it is surprising that the serpent, not Adam
(or Eve), is associated with a word connected to wisdom (*ʿārûm*, in Gen. 3:1).
Wisdom, however, is clearly at play in the story of Adam and Eve's rebellion
against God, particularly with the role played by the tree that is associated
with the knowledge of good and evil. But it is especially because of a later
Adam tradition that we find in Ezek. 28 that we include Adam here as an
example of a biblical character who starts wise but ends a fool.

Adam

Wanting to Be Wise (Gen. 3)

The very first words of the story of Adam and Eve's rebellion introduce
the theme of wisdom. Here the serpent is described as "more crafty [*ʿārûm*]

than any of the wild animals the LORD God had made" (Gen. 3:1). The word
"crafty" is well known from the book of Proverbs (1:4; 8:5, 12; 12:16, 23; 13:16;
14:8, 18; 15:5; 19:25; 22:3; 27:12), where it has a decidedly positive meaning
along the lines of "prudence," "sound judgment," or "resourcefulness."

In the context of Gen. 3, however, there is no doubt about the negative
connotations of the word as applied to the serpent, who is symbolic of evil
and who shows itself to be manipulative toward harmful ends as it tries to
persuade Eve and through Eve Adam to violate the one command given to
them not to eat of a certain tree in the middle of the garden.

Indeed, the name of the tree also reveals the motif of wisdom in the telling
of the story of the rebellion of the first human beings. It is the "tree of the
knowledge (hadda'at) of good and evil" (2:17), and, as the serpent coaxes
Eve to eat its fruit, it claims that "when you eat from it your eyes will be
opened, and you will be like God, knowing good and evil" (3:5).[1] We know
that "knowledge" is something promised from study of the book of Proverbs
according to the preface of that book (Prov. 1:4b).

But God has forbidden the "knowledge" symbolized by the tree from his
human creatures, showing that "knowledge" (da'at) like "prudence" ('ārûm)
is not always beneficial. Indeed, we must ask, what is the knowledge that the
tree promises to deliver if the fruit is eaten? From the name of the tree, we
can surmise that it is knowledge of "good" and "evil"—ethical categories. Of
course, in the most fundamental sense Adam and Eve already know "good"
and "evil." They know, in the sense of being aware, what is right and what
is wrong. It is wrong to eat the fruit of the tree. At this point we need to
remember that knowledge is more than intellectual apprehension; it involves
experience.[2] By eating the fruit of the tree, Adam and Eve are not gaining
new information; they rather arrogate to themselves rather than to God the
right to define moral categories. God has told them it was wrong to eat of the
fruit, but in the act of eating it, they reject God's authority and assert their
own right to determine what is right and what is wrong.

The serpent successfully persuaded Eve to eat the fruit of the forbidden
tree. She was motivated by the hope to gain wisdom. She saw that the fruit was
"desirable for gaining wisdom" (3:6; from the hiphil of skl, a root also found
in the book of Proverbs in a positive meaning).[3] She gave some to Adam, who
also ate the fruit, and immediately they had a new awareness about themselves.
However, their new insight was detrimental in that it introduced shame into

1. For the interesting parallels between Gen. 3 and Mesopotamian rituals that "open the
eyes" of images of their gods, see McDowell, "Image of God" in the Garden of Eden.
2. See Fretheim, "yd'," NIDOTTE 2:410.
3. See Prov. 1:3; 3:4; 10:19; 12:8; 13:15; 21:11, 12; 23:12.

their lives, as illustrated by the fact that they could no longer stand naked and vulnerable before each other but had to seek cover from each other's gaze.

Thus, the Bible's first foray into the subject of wisdom at the beginning of the historical narrative reports a negative experience. We see humans grasping for wisdom on their own terms with negative consequences. Their grasping for wisdom apart from God leads to the first sin and the introduction not only of difficulties in relationships (3:16) and work (3:17–19) but also of death, spiritual (alienation from God) at first and then eventually physical. Adam and Eve's rebellion has lasting implications for human experiences thereafter, according to Paul (Rom. 5:12–21).[4]

Adam: "The Seal of Perfection, Full of Wisdom and Perfect in Beauty" (Ezek. 28:12b)

Before leaving the subject of Adam, we point with interest to Ezekiel's oracle against the king of Tyre (Ezek. 28). The prophet speaks on behalf of God and announces the doom of that powerful ruler, who has great commercial success and, as a result, tremendous pride ("In the pride of your heart you say, 'I am a god; I sit on the throne of a god in the heart of the seas,'" 28:2). Ezekiel attacks the king's pride by attacking his wisdom, presumably because it is his wisdom (understood on a practical level) that has led to his tremendous wealth: "By your wisdom and understanding you have gained wealth for yourself and amassed gold and silver in your treasuries. By your great skill in trading you have increased your wealth, and because of your wealth your heart has grown proud" (28:4–5). Though Ezekiel recognizes that the king has a certain type of wisdom that has resulted in his success, he lambasts his prideful self-understanding: "But you are a mere mortal and not a god, though you think you are as wise as a god" (28:2). He mockingly asks, "Are you wiser than Daniel? Is no secret hidden from you?" (28:3). Daniel was exceedingly wise (see previous chapter),[5] but his humility and submission to God contrast with the king of Tyre's hubris.

---

4. This is true whether Adam and Eve are the first human couple or stand for an original population of humans who were created by God, who used evolution (see Longman, *Genesis*, 82–84). The exact relationship between human sin and Adam and Eve's first sin is debated, but Paul makes it clear that their act introduced sin and death into the world. For a survey of the various views (e.g., inheritance, representative example, imputation), see Madueme and Reeves, *Adam, the Fall, and Original Sin*; and Barrett and Caneday, *Four Views on the Historical Adam*.

5. Agreeing with Dressler ("Identification of the Ugaritic Dnil") over against Day ("Daniel of Ugarit") that the Daniel mentioned in Ezekiel is the same as the biblical character, not the king known from the Ugaritic texts.

These reflections lead to God's remarkable indictment of and judgment on the king of Tyre in 28:12–19, in which he draws an analogy between the king and one who dwelt in the garden of Eden:

> You were the seal of perfection,
>> full of wisdom and perfect in beauty.
> You were in Eden,
>> the garden of God;
> every precious stone adorned you:
>> carnelian, chrysolite and emerald,
>> topaz, onyx and jasper,
>> lapis lazuli, turquoise and beryl.
> Your settings and mountings were made of gold;
>> on the day you were created they were prepared.
> You were anointed as a guardian cherub,
>> for so I ordained you.
> You were on the holy mount of God;
>> you walked among the fiery stones.
> You were blameless in your ways
>> from the day you were created
>> till wickedness was found in you.
> Through your widespread trade
>> you were filled with violence,
>> and you sinned.
> So I drove you in disgrace from the mount of God,
>> and I expelled you, guardian cherub,
>> from among the fiery stones.
> Your heart became proud
>> on account of your beauty,
> and you corrupted your wisdom
>> because of your splendor.
> So I threw you to the earth;
>> I made a spectacle of you before kings.
> By your many sins and dishonest trade
>> you have desecrated your sanctuaries.
> So I made a fire come out of you,
>> and it consumed you,
> and I reduced you to ashes on the ground
>> in the sight of all who were watching.
> All the nations who knew you
>> are appalled at you;
> you have come to a horrible end
>> and will be no more.

God is the first-person speaker in this oracle against the king of Tyre, who is directly addressed in the second-person singular ("you"). God compares the king of Tyre with someone who was "in Eden, the garden of God," which can only be Adam or the serpent. Theoretically, of course, the reference might be to Eve (or to Adam and Eve as a pair), but since the king is male, it is more likely that, unless the reference is to the serpent, God had Adam in mind.

But is it Adam or the serpent? It is very difficult to be absolutely certain, though I find myself leaning toward the idea that God mocks the king by comparing him to Adam, not the serpent. Let me say that whether it is Adam or the serpent, we are not to take this passage as giving us further information about "what actually happened" in the garden. Indeed, Gen. 2–3, in my opinion, is not giving us a blow-by-blow description of what actually happened in an actual garden either; rather, it is using highly figurative language to tell us that God did create humans (though not how) and, at their creation, they were morally innocent and capable of choice. Genesis 3 then tells us that humans rebelled against their Maker, thus explaining the realities of sin and death in the world.[6]

But what indicates that God is comparing the king to Adam and not the serpent? The oracle compares the king to a person who is "in the garden." Now granted the serpent made an appearance in the garden, but that place was not its normal domicile (about which we know nothing). In addition, it seems to me that the most natural understanding of the opening description of the garden figure ("the seal of perfection, full of wisdom and perfect in beauty," v. 12) is only applicable to Adam in the garden, not the serpent in the garden. Further, this person is adorned with precious jewels, which is reminiscent of the fact that the high priest's breastpiece (or chest pendant [CEB]) was adorned by precious jewels (Exod. 28:15–21). The priestly symbolism brings out the fact that Gen. 2 uses tabernacle imagery to describe creation[7] in a way that depicts Adam as a priest in God's holy cosmic sanctuary. In addition, the command that he "work and guard [šāmar]" the garden describes a priestly task.

At first glance, that this figure is described as a "guardian cherub" might point to the serpent more than Adam, but that would be based on the idea that the serpent is Satan, a fallen angel.[8] Such a view is never developed in the OT. As far as we know, the OT reader would simply understand the serpent in the garden to be symbolic of evil, not specifically Satan. The connection

6. For a full explanation of my understanding of Gen. 2–3, see Longman, *Genesis*, 45–84.
7. Wenham, "Sanctuary Symbolism," and many others.
8. See Longman, "Serpent."

between the serpent and Satan is made only in the NT (Rom. 16:20; Rev. 12:9) and should not be read back into the OT where the figure of Satan is not developed.

In any case, in Ezekiel the figure is not said to be a guardian cherub, but to be "as a guardian cherub." In other words, it was Adam who was charged with guarding the garden, but he failed at his task and was replaced by honest-to-goodness cherubim (Gen. 3:24).

A final indication that the comparison is between the king of Tyre and Adam concerns the fate of this garden figure, which presages the fate of the king. God expels him from the garden. Of course, Gen. 3 describes the fate of the first couple in terms of removal from the garden of Eden (Gen. 3:23–24); we do not get the same language concerning the serpent.

Ezekiel 28 creatively uses the story of the garden (Gen. 2–3) in order to mock the king of Tyre. He develops the picture of Adam given there in order to highlight uncomplimentary similarities between Adam and the king.

The real concern of this oracle is the king of Tyre. The comparison with the garden figure serves to denigrate the reputation of this powerful, arrogant, and wealthy ruler. The oracle compares the two in terms of wisdom and wealth and, in a topic not yet broached, blamelessness. Of course, Adam as created was blameless.[9] The interplay between comments about Adam and the king of Tyre implies that the king at one point was wise, wealthy, and blameless, but pride caused the downfall of both Adam and the king of Tyre.

Though the concern of the oracle is the king of Tyre, for the purposes of our study of wisdom, we are more interested in the garden figure and what we learn about wisdom from this oracle. To be clear, we do not learn more about the biblical character Adam from this passage. We should not read this text back into Gen. 2–3 as if it provides us an expanded picture of the garden experience. Ezekiel 28 embellishes the garden story in order to make its devastating critique of the king of Tyre.[10]

So what does this oracle tell us about wisdom? First of all, both the king of Tyre and Adam were originally wise. The king's wisdom resulted in great wealth, and Adam lived in the garden, the holy mount of God, and thus enjoyed God's bounty.

9. And perhaps this depiction is another argument against the association with the serpent, who was not blameless in the garden, which here intriguingly is depicted as the "holy mount of God," combining the garden imagery with the ancient Near Eastern and Israelite idea of the cosmic mountain as the place where God dwells and makes his presence known. See Clifford, *Cosmic Mountain.*

10. At this point we are not interested in whether Ezekiel created this embellishment or was using an Adam legend that was already known in his contemporary culture.

However, wisdom is not permanent; one can lose it. And the trigger to the loss, at least in this case, is pride, a turning to the self. Pride attributes wisdom and its benefits to oneself: "because you think you are wise, as wise as a god" (Ezek. 28:6). We saw that Adam and Eve exercised their pride by asserting their moral autonomy in the garden. They no longer cared about what God said was right and wrong, but they arrogated to themselves the right to define moral categories.

However, the object lesson of both the king of Tyre and Adam in the garden is that wisdom comes only in submission to God. Once pride enters the picture, wisdom is lost and so, ultimately, is God's blessing. Adam was expelled from the garden, and God would bring judgment on the king of Tyre. The pattern of wisdom and its benefits forfeited because of pride and the assertion of moral autonomy will be repeated in the story of Solomon.

Solomon

"A Wise and Discerning Heart" (1 Kings 3:12)

Solomon (reigned 965–928 BC) was the third king of Israel, inheriting from his warrior father, David, a pacified and unified kingdom.[11] Indeed, his name is Hebrew for "peace," and thus he was the appropriate one to build the temple, a permanent dwelling place for God among his settled people.

For the purposes of our study, we are interested in the role wisdom plays in Solomon's life, and as we will see, at the beginning of his reign he is the epitome of wisdom, but at the end of his life he becomes folly incarnate. The following exposition of his life focuses on this trajectory from wisdom to folly to see what we can learn about the nature of wisdom.

Both Kings and Chronicles give us relatively extensive narrations of Solomon's life, though with clear differences. Kings reveals the deep flaws in Solomon's life, while Chronicles minimizes them. Our concerns do not require a full explication of the reasons for this difference,[12] but suffice it to say that the books address the concerns of their respective audiences. The negative portrayal of Kings tells the exilic audience why they suffer God's judgment, while the positive picture in Chronicles gives its postexilic audience inspiration for godly living in the future.

---

11. This book is not the place to defend the historicity of the portraits of Solomon provided by the books of Kings and/or Chronicles, nor is it necessary for the purposes of this book, which explores the theme of wisdom in the final form of Scripture. However, for a robust presentation of the historical issues involved, see Provan, Long, and Longman, *Biblical History of Israel*, 239–58.

12. See Longman and Dillard, *Introduction to the Old Testament*, 167–201.

Both Kings and Chronicles tell us that Solomon receives his vast wisdom as a gift from God while he offers sacrifices to God at Gibeon (1 Kings 3; 2 Chron. 1). At this point of his life, both Kings and Chronicles have a basically positive view of Solomon. However, the former cannot help but take a jab at Solomon for offering a sacrifice at Gibeon, which "was the most important high place" (3:4), this comment coming soon after the narrator says that Solomon was a good king "except that he offered sacrifices and burned incense on the high places" (3:3). Chronicles, on the other hand, adds positively that "God's tent of meeting was there" (2 Chron. 1:3). The law of centralization prohibits worship anywhere but the place where God "will choose as a dwelling for his Name" (Deut. 12:11), but this provision does not become operative until the construction of the temple, and so Solomon is not violating the law by going to Gibeon.

In response to his sacrifices at Gibeon, God invites Solomon to make a request of him ("Ask for whatever you want me to give you," 1 Kings 3:5), and Solomon responds by asking for wisdom: "Give your servant a discerning heart to govern your people and to distinguish between right and wrong. For who is able to govern this great people of yours?" (3:9). God is so pleased with this request that he gives Solomon wealth and honor as well as "a wise and discerning heart" (3:12–13).

Solomon requested wisdom from God specifically for the purpose of ruling the people well. The book of Proverbs, attributed in part to Solomon, contains many sayings that talk about the benefit of wise rule and the dangers inherent in foolish governance; for instance:

> The king with justice causes the land to endure,
>   but the tax man tears it down. (Prov. 29:4)
>
> A ruler who pays attention to a false word—
>   all those who serve him are wicked. (Prov. 29:12)
>
> A king who sits on his judgment throne
>   scatters all evil with his eyes. (Prov. 20:8)

Good, effective kings who benefit their people rule by wisdom. In the words of the sages, they rule well when they have a relationship with Woman Wisdom. As she states,

> By me kings reign,
>   and nobles issue just decrees.
> By me rulers rule,
>   and princes, all righteous judgments. (8:15–16)

While the Chronicler's account of Solomon moves on from Gibeon to the construction of the temple (a central concern of the book since one of the first tasks of the postexilic community was building a second temple), the narrator of Kings immediately illustrates how Solomon's wisdom helps his people through just judgment (1 Kings 3:16–28).

The case involves two prostitutes, showing the king's concern for the vulnerable of society, who gave birth to children within three days of each other, but the baby of one of the women died. The accuser claimed that the bereaved mother took possession of her child and claimed it as her own. They lived together alone, so no one could testify to the truth of the matter. It was a matter of rival claims that could not be corroborated by an outside authority.

Solomon responded by saying that the child should be cut in two and evenly distributed. His ploy allowed him to differentiate the true from the false mother, since the former was willing to give up her claim so the child could live. Solomon awarded her the child, and justice was achieved. According to the narrator, "when all Israel heard the verdict the king had given, they held the king in awe, because they saw that he had wisdom from God to administer justice" (1 Kings 3:28).

In the next chapter the narrator describes his chief officials as well as his strategy for gaining provisions for the court, which may be an implicit affirmation of his wisdom in ruling the kingdom well and efficiently. By appointing twelve district governors (4:7–19), he is intentionally undermining tribal allegiances in the interest of creating a stronger central government.

The chapter ends with an overall assessment of Solomon's profound wisdom, beginning with the general statement that "God gave Solomon wisdom and very great insight, and a breadth of understanding as measureless as the sand on the seashore" (4:29). The description goes on to compare his wisdom favorably to other well-known wisdom figures; some are named ("Ethan the Ezrahite . . . Heman, Kalkol and Darda, the sons of Mahol," v. 31), and some are named by their region ("greater than the wisdom of all the people of the East, and greater than all the wisdom of Egypt," v. 30).[13] The narrator also comments on the prodigious output of his wisdom ("He spoke three thousand proverbs and his songs number a thousand and five. He spoke about plant life, from the cedar of Lebanon to the hyssop that grows out of walls. He also spoke about animals and birds, reptiles and fish," vv. 32–33). The paragraph concludes by telling us that "from all nations people came to listen to Solomon's wisdom, sent by all the kings of the world, who had heard of his wisdom" (v. 34).

13. See chap. 9 for the significance of this comparison with pagan wisdom.

This final statement is not illustrated immediately, but after we hear about his construction and dedication of the temple (to which we will return), we get the story of the Queen of Sheba (1 Kings 10:1–13). The significance of Sheba is that it is far away from Israel, being typically identified in what today is Yemen. The place is not only distant; it is also exotic. Solomon's wisdom has reached international status.

She comes bearing gifts in order to question him. We do not know what her questions covered, but we do hear that "nothing was too hard for the king to explain to her" (10:3). Solomon's great wisdom is affirmed not just by those in Israel but those outside as well.

The main topic between the general description of Solomon's wisdom (4:29–34) and the Queen of Sheba's visit (10:1–13) is the account of his construction and dedication of the temple (1 Kings 5–8). While wisdom is not an extensive theme in these chapters, there are reasons to understand the successful building of the temple as a manifestation of Solomon's wisdom. First, it is clear that the tabernacle's earlier construction was possible because those involved had been endowed with God's wisdom to accomplish the task (Exod. 31:1–11). Then at the beginning of the account of the building of the temple, we hear that he hires Hiram the Sidonian king to provide timber. Hiram responds by exclaiming, "Praise be to the Lord today, for he has given David a wise son to rule over this great nation" (5:7), and the narrator adds, "The Lord gave Solomon wisdom, just as he had promised him" (5:12).

In a word, Solomon was a wisdom figure unsurpassed in the history of Israel and internationally. The source of his wisdom was God, who blessed his realm beyond imagining. However, he ends his life in disgrace. Why the transition from the apex of wisdom to the nadir of folly?

"King Solomon, However, Loved Many Foreign Women" (1 Kings 11:1)

Solomon starts well. He is godly, righteous, and wise. Because of his wisdom, according to the book of Kings, he leads a prosperous nation:

> King Solomon was greater in riches and wisdom than all the other kings of the earth. The whole world sought audience with Solomon to hear the wisdom God had put in his heart. Year after year, everyone who came brought a gift—articles of silver and gold, robes, weapons and spices, and horses and mules. (1 Kings 10:23–25)

However, the final chapter describing Solomon's reign pictures an unraveling nation beset by a number of strengthening adversaries. We learn first of Hadad the Edomite, who was a political refugee in Egypt since the time

David and Joab had defeated Edom (1 Kings 11:14–22). Hadad even married Pharaoh's sister, showing his popularity with Egypt. Hadad the Edomite thus becomes a threat to Solomon's Israel from the south, while another adversary, Rezon, asserting himself as leader of an Aramean state centered in Damascus, threatened Israel from the north.

But perhaps most distressing was the developing tension between Solomon and the inhabitants of the ten northern tribes. First we learn about Jeroboam, who served Solomon as the head of "the whole labor force of the tribes of Joseph" (the northern tribes; 11:28). A conflict arose between Solomon and Jeroboam, though we are not initially told of the political realities that contributed to the conflict between the two men. We just learn that God through the prophet Ahijah told Jeroboam that he would lead the ten northern tribes in a split from the southern tribe of Judah (11:29–39). Solomon came to feel the threat of Jeroboam and tried to have him killed, but Jeroboam successfully sought refuge in Egypt.

The issue that caused the hostility between Solomon and Jeroboam becomes clearer after the death of Solomon, when his son Rehoboam goes north to be acclaimed king by the northern tribes. The son of David, it appears, automatically became king of Judah, but he needed to be accepted by the inhabitants of the north. Thus he traveled to the northern city of Shechem, where he fully expected to be accepted by the north. However, the northerners sent for Jeroboam, who returned from Egypt and now represented the interests of the northern tribes.

He presents their terms, "Your father put a heavy yoke on us, but now lighten the harsh labor and the heavy yoke he put on us, and we will serve you" (12:4). Remember that the tension between Solomon and Jeroboam arose while the latter was in charge of the northern labor forces. It is now clear that the northerners felt abused and exploited by Solomon and that he must have treated his own tribe of Judah differently. Jeroboam likely resisted or protested Solomon's treatment of the north and thus had to escape to Egypt. Now that Solomon was dead, Jeroboam found himself in a position of power to negotiate better treatment. Rehoboam, however, followed the foolish advice of his younger advisers as opposed to the wisdom of the elder advisers. The north rebelled, tearing the kingdom into two parts. Though Rehoboam's actions were the immediate precipitate of the division of the kingdom, the origin of the conflict is found in Solomon's treatment of the north during his reign.

In short, Solomon's reign started well but ended horribly.

But why?

In a word, the wise Solomon turned into a fool, and the book of Kings identifies the cause of the transition in his love of foreign women, particularly the daughter of Pharaoh:

King Solomon, however, loved many foreign women besides Pharaoh's daughter—Moabites, Ammonites, Edomites, Sidonians and Hittites. They were from nations about which the LORD had told the Israelites, "You must not intermarry with them, because they will surely turn your hearts after their gods." Nevertheless, Solomon held fast to them in love. He had seven hundred wives of royal birth and three hundred concubines, and his wives led him astray. As Solomon grew old, his wives turned his heart after other gods, and his heart was not fully devoted to the LORD his God, as the heart of David his father had been. He followed Ashtoreth, the goddess of the Sidonians, and Molek the detestable god of the Ammonites. So Solomon did evil in the eyes of the LORD; he did not follow the LORD completely, as David his father had done. (11:1–6)

The Lord had told the Israelites not to intermarry with foreign, pagan women. Indeed, the Torah prohibited the king from marrying many women period ("he must not take many wives, or his heart will be led astray," Deut. 17:17).

The problem with Solomon's marriages to foreign women is twofold. The first is obvious. They worshiped other gods and goddesses, and apparently Solomon not only accommodated their religious practices but adopted them as his own. And, second, these marriages were political alliances. Marrying, say, Pharaoh's daughter created a political alliance between Israel and Egypt, something that the prophets later vociferously condemned (Jer. 2:17–19, 36; 30:12–17; Isa. 7; 30:1–5; 31) because it revealed that the king was depending not on Yahweh alone to protect them but rather on other powerful nations. Indeed, the law of kingship, quoted in part above, even forbade going to Egypt to buy horses, not to speak of marrying an Egyptian princess (Deut. 17:16).

Ironically, one of the central instructions found in the book of Proverbs, closely associated with Solomon, was to avoid entanglements with strange, foreign women (e.g., 5:1–23; 6:20–35; 7:1–27). While a good case can be made that "foreign" here should be taken to refer to women, even Israelite ones, who make themselves foreign to the customs of their people, it certainly would include women who are not Israelite and therefore by definition do not worship Yahweh.[14] Proverbs does not speak specifically about the negative effect of foreign women on the king, but it speaks more generally about how association with the wicked leads to negative consequences.

> A ruler who pays attention to a false word—
> all those who serve him are wicked. (29:12)

14. Longman, *Proverbs*, 163–65.

> Separate the dross from the silver,
>> and a vessel will come out for refining.
> Separate the wicked from the presence of the king
>> and his throne will be established in righteousness. (25:4–5)[15]

Solomon's love of foreign women thus turned his heart from exclusive worship of Yahweh to the worship of many gods and goddesses. Thus Solomon, the epitome of a wise king, became the exemplar of the foolish king. Proverbs points out that, while the former leads to a healthy nation, the latter destroys a nation:

> Doing wicked deeds is an abomination to kings,
>> for in righteousness a throne is established. (16:12)

> A growling lion and a prowling bear—
>> a wicked ruler over a poor people. (28:15)

> A prince who lacks understanding is a cruel oppressor,
>> but one who hates unjust profit will live long. (28:16)

> A king with justice causes the land to endure,
>> but the tax man tears it down. (29:4)

In regard to Prov. 29:4, while not a tax man per se, Solomon's imposition of corvée labor on the northern tribes was a prime cause of the tearing apart of the kingdom.

Lost Wisdom

The book of Kings's account of Solomon's life raises the question about how someone so wise can become so foolish. On one level, the answer to the question points to his love of foreign women, which brought him into political alliances that betrayed a lack of trust in Yahweh and ultimately into religious affections that completely undermined his relationship with the God who made him wise in the first place.

The story of Solomon contains a warning about the possibility of losing wisdom. Wisdom is not a status, like a PhD, that once achieved cannot be lost. To be wise, one must commit oneself to a course of life (the path metaphor in the book of Proverbs). Proverbs was written not just "to give the simple

---

15. This proverb implies that if the wicked aren't separated from the king, then his throne will not be established in righteousness.

prudence" (1:4a) but also to "let the wise hear and increase teaching; let those with understanding acquire guidance" (1:5). At a certain point in his life, Solomon gave up the pursuit of wisdom and therefore lost it. As a result, his life can be read as a warning to others not to seek to find the meaning of life in anything other than God. We have seen how the book of Ecclesiastes makes precisely this point by utilizing the Solomon tradition in its creation of the figure of Qohelet (see chap. 2).

PART 3

ISRAEL'S
WISDOM

Cosmopolitan or Unique?

W e have now surveyed the main sources of wisdom in the OT, both the books that put their focus on the concept of wisdom (Proverbs, Ecclesiastes, Job) and those passages within other books that make a significant contribution to our understanding of wisdom. We are now ready to address the question of the place of wisdom within the rest of biblical literature as well as in relationship to the broader ancient Near East.

These questions have occupied the discussion of wisdom over the past decades. Many have characterized wisdom as unique within the Bible and consonant with wisdom thought outside of Israel. Indeed, what some think makes wisdom unique is its cosmopolitan nature.

We begin by considering the source of wisdom. Whereas redemptive-historical, prophetic, and legal traditions claim derivation from revelation, wisdom often appeals to experience, observation, tradition, and learning from one's mistakes (correction) for its instructions. Chapter 7 thus describes

109

the sources of wisdom and raises the question of the role of revelation in biblical wisdom.

Wisdom's supposed cosmopolitan feature is related to its theological basis in creation rather than redemptive-history and also in its shared ethos and content with, particularly, Egyptian and Mesopotamian literature. Chapters 8 and 9 explore those connections.

In this section we conclude with an exploration of the relationship between wisdom, law, and covenant (chap. 10). While these three are thought to be separate in the biblical corpus, only coming together in postbiblical material (see chap. 14), we will argue in favor of a closer relationship.

7

SOURCES OF WISDOM

Experience, Observation, Tradition, Correction, and Ultimately Revelation

Where does one find wisdom? Or to put the same question in different words, what is the source of wisdom?

We ask this question at a time when many scholars believe that the source of wisdom is categorically different from that of other aspects of the OT. If one asks concerning the source of prophecy, the answer is clear. God reveals his prophetic word to his servants the prophets, so they can say: "thus says the Lord" or "decree of Yahweh." If one asks concerning the source of law, again the answer is obvious as we read about Moses ascending Mount Sinai to receive the law from God (Exod. 19–34). In a word, the source of much biblical tradition is revelation.

Many scholars remark that wisdom is different in this regard. Biblical (as opposed to postbiblical, see chap. 14) wisdom does not emanate from God directly (revelation) but rather is gained through ordinary human means of knowing: experience, observation, tradition, and learning from mistakes.

In the present chapter we will explore the question of the source of wisdom. As we do, we will see that the sages do encourage learning from our experience, from the tradition of past generations, and from heeding correction. Much of what is presented as instruction in Proverbs, for instance, comes from these sources.

At root, however, wisdom (contrary to much scholarly opinion) emanates from God and thus may ultimately be called revelatory. Indeed, the OT makes clear that the only true source of wisdom is God. We will see that when wisdom is sought from tradition, experience and observation, and so forth apart from revelation, not only is wisdom unattainable, but it becomes twisted and actually proves to be folly. In the second half of the chapter, then, we will look at specific examples of seeking wisdom apart from revelation.

Tradition

The Teaching of the Fathers

Proverbs suggests that tradition can bear insight. Listen to what the father says to the son at the beginning of his teaching in Prov. 4:

> Hear, sons, fatherly discipline,
>   and pay attention to the knowledge of understanding.
> For I will give you good teaching;
>   don't forsake my instruction.
> For I was a son to my father,
>   tender and the only one of my mother.
> He taught me and said to me . . . (Prov. 4:1–4a)

The father imparts wisdom to his son that was first passed on to him by his father, who probably received it from his father. In other words, one does not have to experience something to determine whether it constitutes wise or foolish behavior.

Indeed, the finished form of the book of Proverbs may be considered a repository of godly tradition that intends to guide its readers toward a life of wisdom. That this collection of fatherly advice is ultimately from the heavenly Father is recognized from the close connection between wisdom and law. We can see this in the connection drawn between words pertaining to the wisdom of the father and those denoting law (for full discussion, see chap. 10). One such law word is "command" (*miṣwâ*):

> My son, if you grasp my speech
>   and store up my commands [*miṣwōtay*] within you,
> bending your ear toward wisdom . . . (2:1–2a)

> My son, don't forget my instruction,
>   and let your heart protect my commands [*miṣwōtay*]. (3:1)

> Let your heart hold on to my words;
>> guard my commands [*miṣwōtay*] and live. (4:4)

> Protect, my son, the command [*miṣwat*] of your father;
>> don't abandon the instruction of your mother. (6:20)

Another foundational word found in conjunction with the wisdom of the father is "law" or "instruction" (*tôrâ*):

> Listen, my son, to the teaching of your father;
>> don't neglect the instruction [*tôrat*] of your mother. (1:8)

> The instruction [*tôrat*] of the wise is a fountain of life;
>> turning aside from death traps. (13:14)

The Tradition of the Ten Commandments

The close connection between law and wisdom leads us to reflect on the relationship between the teaching of wisdom, particularly as we find it in the book of Proverbs, and the Ten Commandments, which is an expression of God's will for how his people should live. They are expressed in the form of general ethical principles. It is particularly the final six commandments that regulate human-to-human relationships that are relevant here. We will illustrate by citing the commandment followed by a relevant proverbial saying and list other relevant references.

> Honor your father and your mother, so that you may live long in the land the LORD your God is giving you. (Exod. 20:12)

>> Listen, my son, and receive my speech,
>>> and years of life will be multiplied to you. (Prov. 4:10)[1]

> You shall not murder. (Exod. 20:13)

>> Look, there are six things Yahweh hates,
>>> and seven that are an abomination to his soul:
>> haughty eyes, a lying tongue,
>>> and *hands that spill the blood of the innocent*,
>> a heart set on iniquitous plans,
>>> feet hurrying to run to evil. (Prov. 6:16–18; see also 1:10–12)

---

1. Note the similar promise of long life added to honoring parents by listening to their wise advice. See also Prov. 1:8; 4:1; 10:1; 13:1.

You shall not commit adultery. (Exod. 20:14)

> For the commandment is a lamp, and the instruction a light,
>> and the path of life is disciplined correction
> to guard you from the evil woman,
>> from the flattering tongue of the foreign woman.
> Don't desire her beauty in your heart;
>> and don't let her absorb you with her eyelashes. (Prov. 6:23–25; see
>> the entirety of 6:20–35, as well as 2:16–19 and chaps. 5 and 7)

You shall not steal. (Exod. 20:15)

> Fraudulent scales are an abomination to Yahweh,
>> but an accurate weight brings his favor. (Prov. 11:1; see also
>> 1:13–14)

You shall not give false testimony against your neighbor. (Exod. 20:16)

> He who proclaims truth speaks justly,
>> but a false witness is fraudulent. (Prov. 12:17; 3:30; 6:18, 19; 10:18;
>> 12:19)

You shall not covet your neighbor's house. You shall not covet your neighbor's wife, or his male or female servant, his ox or donkey, or anything that belongs to your neighbor. (Exod. 20:17)

> Look, there are six things Yahweh hates,
>> and seven that are an abomination to his soul:
> haughty eyes, a lying tongue,
>> and hands that spill the blood of the innocent,
> *a heart set on iniquitous plans*,
>> feet hurrying to run to evil. (Prov. 6:16–18)[2]

The Tradition of the Ancient Near East

The evidence is persuasive that the ancient Israelite teachers who wrote about wisdom availed themselves not only of Israelite tradition but also of wisdom from the broader ancient Near East. This is particularly notable in the book of Proverbs where we can see the influence of ancient Near Eastern wisdom literature on the form and on the content of that book's teaching.

2. The italicized portions in the quotations above specifically relate to the commandments at issue.

We will only be illustrative and not exhaustive in our examples.[3] We will also return to this topic in a later chapter (see chap. 9).

The ancient Near Eastern cultures, especially Egypt, had a vibrant wisdom tradition. In Egypt, the instruction (*sby3t*) literature is known from the time of the Old Kingdom period through the Middle Kingdom (Hardjedef, Kagemni, Ptahhotep, and Merikare) down to the New Kingdom and later (Ani, Amenemope, Anksheshonqy, and Papyrus Insinger). Most of these texts, like Proverbs and Ecclesiastes (12:12), are instructions of a father (sometimes the king) to his son. Thus, the very form of the instructions in Proverbs, a father speaking to his son, is current in the broader ancient Near East.

And then there are many examples of similar teaching. Perhaps the best examples come from the Instruction of Amenemope, which contains proverbs that are strikingly similar to examples from the book of Proverbs. Two examples will make our point

> Do not wear yourself out to get rich;
>   be wise enough to desist.
> When your eyes light upon it, it is gone;
>   for suddenly it takes wings to itself,
>   flying like an eagle toward heaven. (Prov. 23:4–5 NRSV)

> Do not strain to seek excess
>   when your possessions are secure.
> If riches are brought to you by robbery,
>   they will not stay the night in your possession.
> When the day dawns they are no longer in your house.
>   Their place can be seen but they are no longer there.
> The earth opened its mouth to crush and swallow them
>   and plunged them in dust.
> They make themselves a great hole, as large as they are.
>   And sink themselves in the underworld.
> They make themselves wings like geese,
>   And fly to heaven. (Amenemope 9.14–10.5)

Both Proverbs and Amenemope warn against overanxious pursuit of wealth. They suggest that wealth gotten in such a way is fleeting, and they both use a bird analogy to make their point.

> Do not remove an ancient landmark
>   or encroach on the fields of orphans,

3. For more detail, see Longman, "Proverbs."

> for their redeemer is strong;
> he will plead their cause against you. (Prov. 23:10–11 NRSV)

> Do not remove the boundary stone on the boundaries of the cultivated
>   land,
> nor throw down the boundary of the widow. (Amenemope 7.12)

The connection between these two texts is obvious. They both warn against taking advantage of the vulnerable by trying to steal their land.

Again, these are just examples, but they raise an interesting theological question. We have seen from the first chapter that the fear of the Lord is the beginning of wisdom, but here we observe that the Israelite wisdom teachers learned from Egyptians, who do not fear God. What are we to make of this?

First, there is no doubt that Israelite sages respected ancient Near Eastern wisdom. This is seen not only in what appears to be clear influence, as illustrated above, but also in the way Solomon's wisdom is favorably compared with Eastern and Egyptian wisdom: "Solomon's wisdom was greater than the wisdom of all the people of the East, and greater than all the wisdom of Egypt" (1 Kings 4:30). For this to be a compliment, the wisdom of the East and of Egypt has to be pretty spectacular.

Again, what are we to make of this? To make sense both of the necessity of the fear of the Lord as well as the respect that the Israelite sages pay to Egyptian wisdom, we might appeal to the concept that later theologians termed common grace. That is, the Israelite sages recognized that other ancient Near Eastern people could observe what worked and what didn't work in the world and make some helpful suggestions expressed in a catchy way. The Israelites could then adapt this teaching to their own culture. In other words, "all truth is God's truth." However, my guess is that if the Israelites were asked, they would in the final analysis have to say that the Egyptians were not wise. After all, since they did not recognize the most important truth about the cosmos, they were ultimately fools.

Conclusion

Wisdom learns from tradition, insights passed down from past generations. Indeed, both Proverbs and Ecclesiastes (see Eccles. 12:12 and earlier comments)[4] are presented as fathers instructing their sons. Note all the admonitions of the father for the son to pay attention that typically begin his teaching throughout the speeches in Prov. 1–9 (1:8; 2:1; 3:1; 4:1; etc.). We have seen that this tradition

---

4. Particularly the first few pages of chap. 2.

has connections with the law and with the instructions of the broader ancient Near East. In the next section we will learn that this tradition comes also from the experience and observation of the previous generations.

Experience and Observation

What is tradition based on? In part, it is based on experience and observation. We learn by our life experience if we observe what works and what doesn't work. We learn by also observing the experience of others and seek to emulate them when their experience leads to successful living and seek to avoid their behavior and attitudes when it leads to trouble.

In the book of Proverbs, the wise even learn from observing the experience of ants:

> Go to the ant, you lazy people!
>   See its paths and grow wise.
> That one has no military commander, officer, or ruler;
>   it gets its food in summer,
>   gathers its provisions at harvest. (6:6–8)

Here the wisdom teacher cites the behavior of ants with the hope of warning lazy people that their lifestyle will lead to poverty.

In another passage the wise father appeals to the experience of a person who sleeps with a woman who is not his wife in order to warn his son:

> When from the window of my house,
>   from behind my lattice I looked down,
> I looked for a moment,
>   and I perceived among the sons a youth who lacked heart.
> He was crossing the street at the corner,
>   and he marched on the path to her house
> at the beginning of the evening of the day
>   in the middle of night and darkness.
> All of a sudden a woman propositions him,
>   in the attire of a prostitute and with guarded heart.
> She is boisterous and defiant;
>   her feet do not rest in her own house.
> A foot in the street, a foot in the public squares,
>   she lurks beside every street corner.
> She grabs him and she kisses him.
>   Her face is brazen as she speaks to him. (Prov. 7:6–13)

The father continues to relate the experience of this wayward young man that gets him into serious trouble. Again, he hopes that he will keep the son from repeating this harmful behavior.

Everyone has experiences, but not everyone is observant and self-reflective about those experiences in order to learn how to navigate life successfully. This leads us to a special case of learning from experience and observation: learning from mistakes.

Correction: Learning from Mistakes

The wise learn from their mistakes. They accept correction, and they change their attitude and behavior in order to avoid the same mistakes. Fools do not listen to those who point out their errors; indeed, they will mock those who try. Thus they are doomed to repeat those errors.

> Those who love discipline love knowledge;
>> and those who hate correction are dullards. (Prov. 12:1)

> Those who guard discipline are on the way to life,
>> and those who abandon correction wander aimlessly. (Prov. 10:17)

Thus, humility is a prime virtue of the wise person, while the fool is filled with pride. Humility begins with fear of the Lord and continues with respect for the person who tries to teach them (the father mainly in the book of Proverbs). According to Woman Wisdom:

> Those who fear Yahweh hate evil,
>> pride and arrogance, and the path of evil.
>> I hate a perverse mouth. (Prov. 8:13)

> He [God] mocks mockers,
>> but he shows favor to the humble. (Prov. 3:34)

> The fear of Yahweh is wise discipline,
>> and humility comes before glory. (Prov. 15:33)

> Pride comes before a disaster,
>> and before stumbling comes an arrogant attitude. (Prov. 16:18)

The ability to learn from one's mistakes is really a special case of learning from experience and observation. One makes mistakes in daily life, and the wise person is self-reflective and can grow from the experience.

The Wisdom of the Elders

In the light of the above, we can see why the default belief in the ancient Near East, and in Israel proper, was that the older people became, the wiser they were. After all, young people have not had much experience from which to learn about life. They may have begun to benefit from tradition, but the future would give them more opportunities to learn and apply the lessons from the past. In addition, youth are just making their first mistakes from which they will learn as their elders correct them.

Thus, under expected circumstances, youth are immature (*petî*) and the elderly have wisdom. As we will see below ("Tradition Gone Awry: Job"), the expected is not always the case.

A Final Word: Back to Revelation

As we have seen, there is no question but that those who call themselves wise learn from, and base their instruction on, what we might consider normal human investigative practices. As the father in Proverbs tells his son, becoming wise is hard work:

> My son, if you grasp my speech
> > and store up my commands within you,
> bending your ear toward wisdom,
> > extending your heart toward competence—
> indeed, if you call out for understanding,
> > shout for competence,
> if you seek it like silver
> > and search for it like hidden treasure—
> then you will understand the fear of Yahweh,
> > and you will find the knowledge of God. (Prov. 2:1–5)

The father tries to make the son realize that wisdom entails study and calls for diligence and urgency in order to achieve that goal. Certainly there is no sense given here that the son is simply to pray and wait for God to download wisdom without the son's strenuous effort.

That said, the father continues after his exhortation for his son to work hard for wisdom by saying:

> For Yahweh bestows wisdom,
> > from his mouth come knowledge and understanding.
> He stores up resourcefulness for those with integrity—
> > a shield for those who walk in innocence. (Prov. 2:6–7)

Biblical wisdom is consistent on this theme. True wisdom's ultimate source is not human intelligence or insight, but only God. In this sense, wisdom's source is divine revelation. Notice that even our very ability to learn by what we have called normal human investigative methods is only possible because God has given us that capability:

> An ear to hear and an eye to see—
>   Yahweh made both of them. (Prov. 20:12)

Thus even our capacity to reflect on our experience, learn from our mistakes, and benefit from tradition ultimately is a gift from God. That wisdom is from God is taught in many ways in the Hebrew Scriptures.

The Fear of the Lord Is the Beginning of Wisdom

In our study of Proverbs, Ecclesiastes, and Job, we have seen that they all agree that true wisdom is not possible apart from a proper relationship with God characterized by fear. Fear puts one in the proper attitude (humility) to receive instruction that ultimately comes from God, though perhaps mediated by his human agents.

The book of Job gives the most powerful expression to this idea as we see Job move to a deeper measure of wisdom through his experience of suffering. We have characterized the book as a wisdom debate (chap. 3), which God wins. All the human participants claim to be wise (see "Tradition Gone Awry: Job" below), but Job does not find wisdom in himself or in other humans, but only in God. One might respond that God does not teach him anything; he simply overpowers him with questions that he can't answer and demonstrations of his power. But that is precisely what he does teach Job. He teaches him to live with mystery and ambiguity in the midst of his suffering.

Learning from Woman Wisdom

In chapter 1 we examined the figure of Woman Wisdom, concluding that she was a metaphor—a personification, to be more exact—of Yahweh's wisdom, and, from the location of her house on the highest point of the city (Prov. 9:3), a metonymy representing God himself. She invites all the immature men to join her in a meal, an appeal to enter into an intimate relationship with her. If they do, they will gain "understanding" (9:6). If they don't and rather accept the invitation of Woman Folly, who represents the false gods and goddesses of the surrounding nations, the immature won't gain wisdom, but rather they will die (9:18). In this way too the book of Proverbs teaches that wisdom comes from God alone.

Collins insists that this is not truly revelation. As he puts it, "One might speak of a revelation of wisdom in Proverbs, chapter 8, where wisdom is said to call out 'on the heights, beside the way, at the crossroads.' This revelation, however, does not require extraordinary experiences such as visions, but rather the attentive observation of everyday experience and, above all, deference to tradition."[5] I think this is too restrictive an understanding of revelation and the claims of Proverbs and other passages that speak of wisdom. Indeed, in a moment we will be turning our attention to Ecclesiastes and its critique of learning from experience apart from revelation.

Learning from the Tanak

Below ("Experience and Observation apart from Revelation: Ecclesiastes") we will recall that Qohelet represents one who does not understand that wisdom comes ultimately from God.

On the positive side, it is appropriate to remind ourselves of our earlier conclusion concerning the interpretation of the final admonition of the frame narrator to his son:

> The end of the matter. All has been heard. Fear God and keep his commandments, for this is the whole duty of humanity. For God will bring every deed into judgment, including every hidden thing, whether good or evil. (12:13–14)

In our close look at this passage, we suggested that there is here, in this book written very late in the postexilic period, an allusion to the three-part Hebrew canon: the Torah/Law (obey the commandments), the Nebi'im/Prophets (live in the expectation of judgment), and the Ketubim/Writings (fear God). In this way the frame narrator urges his son to turn away from trying to find meaning in the world "under the sun," which we understand to mean "apart from God and his revelation."[6] Rather, the son (who is the implied reader with whom we should identify) can only find meaning in God's revelation (the Tanak).

Law and Wisdom

We argue for a closer connection between law and wisdom than is normally accepted by scholars today.[7] However, there is no doubt about the close

---

5. Collins, *Jewish Wisdom in the Hellenistic Age*, 2–3.
6. Longman, *Ecclesiastes*, 66.
7. See chap. 10.

connection between the two found in Deut. 4:5–8. What demonstrates Israel's wisdom to the nations? None other than their obedience to God's law revealed to them on Mount Sinai: "See, I have taught you decrees and laws as the LORD my God commanded me, so that you may follow them into the land you are entering to take possession of it. Observe them carefully, for this will show your wisdom and understanding to the nations, who will hear about all these decrees and say, 'Surely this great nation is a wise and understanding people'" (Deut. 4:5–6).

Dreams and Visions as Wisdom

One might say that, though wisdom comes ultimately from God, it comes in a different way than, say, in the Prophets and the Law. Perhaps so as we consider the material as presented so far. We grant that we are using "revelation" in a broad sense. However, it has not been uncommon for scholars to speak of wisdom in a way that sounds like a secular humanistic discipline.[8] And we present the above to counteract that tendency.

Further, one often hears that the connection between wisdom and revelation in the narrow sense is a phenomenon only found in postbiblical books.[9] In this regard, we simply draw attention again to the accounts of Joseph and Daniel, whose wisdom is presented as the result of dreams and visions sent to them by God.

Conclusion

We have now explored and examined the sources of wisdom as described in the biblical text, and the message has been consistent. While wisdom entails study, hard work, and practice to implement, the ultimate source is God. In that sense, wisdom is revelatory. Apart from God there is no true wisdom.

Seeking and Claiming Wisdom apart from God

Our point is illustrated also by negative examples. The message of Scripture is also consistent that seeking and claiming wisdom apart from God is actually dangerous folly. This point is true even if that supposed wisdom is sought in tradition, experience and observation, and learning from our mistakes.

8. See "Wisdom versus the Rest of the Old Testament" in chap. 8.
9. See chap. 14.

Experience and Observation apart from Revelation: Ecclesiastes

A full exposition of Ecclesiastes is found in chapter 2. For now, suffice it to say that in the main body of the book (1:12–12:7), Qohelet attempts to find the meaning of life "under the sun" (*taḥat hašemeš*)—that is, apart from revelation. He looks for meaning in areas like work, money, pleasure, even wisdom, but he always concludes "meaningless, meaningless" (*hăbēl hăbālîm*). In terms of our present interest, we should note how often Qohelet uses the verb "to look/see/observe" (*rā'ah*; 1:14, 16; 2:12, 13; 3:10; etc.). Qohelet exemplifies the person who tries to learn through experience and observation apart from the framework of revelation, and thus he ends up frustrated. Bartholomew and O'Dowd rightly note, "When [Qohelet] depends on reason and observation alone, Qohelet despairs over ever being able to discern the appropriate time for anything . . . committed as he is to his autonomous epistemology, he cannot solve the tension between these views."[10] Thus not all experience, not even experience that is observed and evaluated, leads to wisdom, but only that wisdom that is viewed through the larger perspective of revelation.[11]

Tradition Gone Awry: Job

As we argued in chapter 3, the book of Job is a wisdom debate. Who is wise, and where can we find wisdom? The focus of the debate is Job's suffering. Who has the right interpretation of the reason for Job's suffering, and who can offer him a way out?

The conflict begins when Job complains about his suffering in the presence of his three friends, Elihu, Bildad, and Zophar. They respond with righteous indignation, arguing that there is one and only one possible reason why he is in emotional and physical pain—sin.

How do they come to their conclusion? In large part, they argue that "sinners suffer and therefore sufferers are sinners" based on the traditions of those who came before them. Bildad cites the fathers as authorities in his first speech:

> For ask now the former generations,
>> and focus on the discoveries of their fathers.
> For we are yesterday and do not know,
>> for our days are a shadow on earth. (8:8–9)

---

10. Bartholomew and O'Dowd, *Old Testament Wisdom Literature*, 223.

11. As Shields (*End of Wisdom*, 239) states it: "In contrast to Qoheleth, the epilogist briefly, but conclusively points to an alternative form of wisdom—wisdom founded in the fear of God and obedience to God's commandments."

Our own experience is too brief to be authoritative, so we should turn to the teaching of the past. And when we do, according to Bildad, we will conclude that only sinners suffer and therefore Job is a sinner.

After insulting Job's claim to wisdom (15:1–10), Elihu too invokes the wisdom of tradition to support his claim that sin is the only reason why people suffer: "The gray-haired and elderly are with us, much older than your father" (15:10). A little later in this same speech he tells Job: "I will show you; listen to me. What I have seen, I will recount to you, things sages have declared and their fathers have not hidden" (15:17–18).

There is no question but that the wisdom of the three friends is really folly. God announces this when he says to Elihu, "you did not speak what is correct about me" (42:8). Thus, their appeal to tradition was not thoughtful. Sometimes tradition misleads.

Revelation Falsely Asserted: Eliphaz and Elihu

Above we suggested that at the bottom of all true wisdom is revelation from God. The fear of the Lord is the beginning of wisdom. A relationship with Woman Wisdom is mandatory for a true sage. Even the ability to learn from experience and observation, from our mistakes, and from tradition is a gift of God (Prov. 20:12).

But not all claims to revelation or divine inspiration are valid. Eliphaz and Elihu from the book of Job provide examples.

In Eliphaz's opening speech, he tells Job:

> A word stole over to me;
>   my ears took a whisper of it.
> In anxious thoughts of night visions,
>   when deep sleep falls on people,
> fear and trembling called to me;
>   my bones trembled mightily with fear.
> A spirit passed my face;
>   the hair on my skin stood on end.
> It stood there, but I could not recognize its appearance.
>   A form was before my eyes.
>   Silence, but I heard a voice:
> Can mortals be righteous before God?
>   Can a man be pure before his Maker? (Job 4:12–17)

In his first speech Eliphaz begins the attack of the three friends on Job's integrity. He is suggesting, with a modicum of civility in this first speech, that

Job's suffering is a result of his sin. Typically, the three friends appeal to tradition and experience to support their claims, but this is a rare, indeed unique, instance when one of the friends appeals to a kind of spiritual authority.

The exact nature of this spiritual authority is a bit unclear. Elihu is a bit indirect as he describes this experience to Job. Is the spirit an angel or perhaps even a reference to God himself?[12] Whichever it is, Eliphaz is suggesting that this spirit is not of this world and thus is invested with authority. After all, whatever the precise identification of the spirit, it is an otherworldly presence.

In the silence, he heard only a voice. The voice speaks a word that at first is hard to penetrate. The claim is that no one can be righteous before God. And if no one can be perfectly righteous, then Job is not either and deserves the suffering that is coming his way.

In a subtle, secretive, yet bold way, Eliphaz is enlisting divine support for his contention that Job is a sinner in need of repentance. But, as we concluded above in regard to the three friends' appeal to tradition, their argument is bogus, and therefore this claim to divine revelation is false.

Eliphaz is not the only one to claim a supernatural origin for his wisdom. Elihu makes it his central claim as well. Indeed, Elihu makes a big point of claiming that spiritual inspiration lies behind his argument. He contrasts it with the wisdom of experience, based on the long life of the three friends, and tradition that is the primary source of the wisdom of the three friends, which he rightly sees has failed miserably:

> So Elihu the son of Barakel the Buzite answered and said:
> "I am young,
>   and you are aged.
> Therefore, I was very afraid
>   to express my opinion to you.
> I said, 'Let days speak,
>   and an abundance of years make wisdom known.'
> However, it is the spirit in a person,
>   the breath of Shaddai, that gives them understanding.
> The many are not wise;
>   the elders do not understand justice.
> So I say, 'Listen to me!
>   I will show you my opinion.'" (Job 32:6–9)

Elihu's appearance at this point is something of a surprise. Whether or not his speech is a later addition to the book, in terms of its final form, we

---

12. So Clines, *Job 1–20*, 131, who points out that "form" is typically used of God.

should assume that he has been standing by silently as the three friends have engaged Job in a debate over the reason for and the solution of his suffering.

Here he states that he remained quiet out of respect for his elders. Their miserable failure, however, has forced him to speak. Here he claims divine (spiritual) inspiration for what follows. But in the end, what follows is nothing new. Though he may put a bigger emphasis on the disciplinary nature of suffering (Job 33, but see Eliphaz in Job 5:17), in the end he too asserts a retribution theology. If you sin, then you suffer; conversely, if you are suffering, then you are a sinner. Job is suffering; therefore, he is a sinner (see chap. 3).

When Elihu stops speaking, no one responds to him, not Job and not God. The best understanding of this silence is that it is the ultimate insult. Elihu is an arrogant person, claiming divine authority that he does not have. He is not even worth answering.

Conclusion

What is the source of wisdom according to those books that speak of wisdom? God. Thus, no one is wise unless they fear him. No one is wise unless they have an intimate relationship with Woman Wisdom, who stands for God himself.

God gives his creatures the ability to learn from their mistakes, experience and observation, and tradition. However, unless one has a proper relationship with God, these potential sources of wisdom can lead to folly and destruction, not to wisdom and success. Indeed, claims to divine inspiration can be misleading as well, as we learn from the examples of Eliphaz and Elihu.

8

WISDOM, CREATION, AND (DIS)ORDER

Wisdom thinks resolutely within the framework of a theology of creation.[1]

In perhaps the most quoted single sentence concerning wisdom literature over the past forty years, Zimmerli pronounces that creation theology is the basis of wisdom thinking. As we examine his thesis in this chapter, we will observe that the connection he draws between wisdom and creation has less to do with wisdom's explicit interaction with creation (though there is some of that) and more to do with a perceived absence of connection to the major themes of the redemptive history (including not only the history of Israel but also covenant, law, and cult). The present chapter will describe and interact with the viewpoint of Zimmerli and his followers concerning the relationship between wisdom and creation. The following chapters will ask whether the perceived absence of the major themes of the rest of the OT are as absolute as thought by many scholars of wisdom. While we will question the supposed absence of redemptive history, law, covenant, and cult in later chapters, we must begin with a description of their perceived absence since this absence plays a significant role in driving the Zimmerli school to its conclusion that wisdom thinking is based on creation theology.

1. Zimmerli, "Place and Limit of Wisdom," 316.

Wisdom versus the Rest of the Old Testament

There is no denying that biblical writings connected to wisdom, particularly Proverbs, Ecclesiastes, and Job, are different than other books of the OT. We look in vain for any reference to the patriarchs and the promises given to them or the exodus from Egypt, arguably the paradigmatic redemptive event in the OT. The same may be said for the conquest and settlement, the monarchy (though, of course, Proverbs, Ecclesiastes, and Song of Songs has a connection with Solomon),[2] the exile, or the events of the restoration. Thus, wisdom literature lacks explicit interaction with the contents of Gen. 12 through Esther. In this, wisdom also differs significantly from the prophets, who do look back to the past. The prophets often evoke memory of God's promises to the patriarchs and the exodus, as well as the sad history of disobedience that stretched down to the time in which God called them to bear witness to the coming judgment due to their sin.

Wisdom also lacks extensive, explicit reference to the covenants that God established with his people. The historical books narrate the moments that God instituted covenants with his people through Abraham, Moses, and David.[3] In this wisdom also differs from the prophets. Indeed, the prophets can be called lawyers of the covenant. After all, the threats of judgment are based on the blessings and curses of the covenant (e.g., Deut. 27–28) that would come into effect if Israel broke the covenant law.

And speaking of law, again unlike the books of theological history and the prophets, there is no explicit mention of the Ten Commandments or the case law that flows from them. We will address the possible connection between wisdom, law, and covenant in chapter 10, but the perceived absence of law and covenant in wisdom is yet another significant reason why Zimmerli and others move away from redemptive history and toward creation as the foundation of wisdom.

Finally, in terms of differences from the rest of the OT, scholars in the Zimmerli school draw attention to the lack of reference to the cult,[4] or religious rituals, of Israel. The rest of the OT is full of descriptions of and interactions with priests, sacrifices, religious festivals, Sabbath, and sanctuary, but such mentions are absent from wisdom literature, according to those who want to highlight the differences between wisdom and the rest of the OT.

2. See Schultz, "Unity or Diversity in Wisdom Theology?"
3. Omitting reference to the Noachian covenant, which was a covenant between God and all of creation, not specifically his people.
4. In 1977 Perdue (*Wisdom and Cult*) showed that interest in the cult was not completely missing in wisdom.

In its most extreme form, some scholars, particularly of the previous generation, have argued that God himself plays a secondary role in wisdom literature
and that it emphasizes humanity and not the God of Israel. Some even go so
far as to suggest that wisdom is secular in orientation, at least as compared
to the rest of the OT. Consider the following representative quotations from
Gerhard von Rad and the early work of Walter Brueggemann:

> Since the objects of this search for knowledge were of a secular kind, questions
> about man's daily life, systematic reflection on them was held to be a secular
> occupation.

> I believe it is much more plausible to suggest that in the wisdom tradition of
> Israel we have a visible expression of secularization as it has been character-
> ized in the current discussions. Wisdom teaching is profoundly secular in that
> it presents life and history as a human enterprise.[5]

One more observation leads Zimmerli and others to their conclusions regarding the uniqueness of wisdom literature in the biblical corpus. The wisdom
literature of Israel and the wisdom literature of the surrounding cultures,
particularly Egypt and Mesopotamia, share many features and much specific
content, leading to the idea that wisdom literature is universalistic in its appeal
(and thus based on creation) rather than particular to Israel and its unique
redemptive history. We will devote a later chapter (chap. 9) to describing and
evaluating the connection between Israelite and ancient Near Eastern wisdom.
Our point in this chapter is served simply by noting that the undeniable connections are influential in the thinking of the Zimmerli school. After all, if Israel
shares these ideas with other non-Yahwistic cultures, wisdom must be based
on creation, available to all, rather than redemptive history unique to Israel.

According to the Zimmerli school, wisdom is a secular concept, but it
became a component of both Testaments of the Bible because it is inherent
in creation—specifically, human creation.[6]

Creation in Wisdom

What is the actual connection between wisdom and creation? Unlike the
exodus, for instance, wisdom literature explicitly evokes creation theology,

---

5. From von Rad, *Wisdom in Israel*, 57–58; and Brueggemann, *In Man We Trust*, 81–82;
both quoted from Z. Schwáb, *Toward an Interpretation*, 48–49. For Schwáb's longer survey of
scholars who describe wisdom as secular, see ibid., 162–74.
6. Westermann, *Roots of Wisdom*, 1.

though perhaps not as frequently as one might expect from the role given to it by the Zimmerli school. We begin with an examination of specific texts in the biblical wisdom books.

Creation in Proverbs

In terms of creation theology in wisdom, Prov. 8 plays a pivotal role, and that is where our emphasis will be. However, before turning our attention to chapter 8, we take note of Prov. 3:19–20, which provides a succinct statement by the sages as to the relationship of God's wisdom and creation.

> Yahweh laid the foundations of the earth with Wisdom,
>   establishing the heavens with competence.
> With his knowledge the deeps burst open,
>   and skies drop dew.

In this passage the sages assert that God created the cosmos ("earth" and "heavens" constitute a merismus indicating every created things) using wisdom. The second parallelism announces that the precious waters from below ("the deeps") and above (the "dew" from the skies) also are the result of God's wisdom/knowledge.

This passage informs us that the cosmos is made not by chance but by God's wisdom, implying order. The implication is clear for those who want to know how the world works. To navigate life well, it is important to have a relationship with Yahweh who created the cosmos with his wisdom, and as we learned at the beginning (1:7) and throughout the book of Proverbs, that relationship is cultivated by an attitude of fear toward God.

It is interesting to note the similarities between 3:19–20 and 24:3–4, where the latter is rendered:

> With wisdom a house is built;
>   with competence it is established.
> With knowledge rooms are filled
>   with all precious and pleasant wealth.

Perhaps we are to think of Yahweh's construction of the cosmos as building a house. Indeed, that is the conclusion of Van Leeuwen, who also provocatively suggests further connections between 3:19–20 and other passages in the OT. He does this on the basis of the concurrence of the three words that we have translated "wisdom," "competence," and "knowledge."[7] First, he points to

---

7. Van Leeuwen, "Building God's House."

the use of these words in conjunction with the building of the tabernacle in Exod. 31:1–3, noting that it is now a scholarly commonplace to comment on the connection between God's cosmos building and the construction of the tabernacle. Next, he points to the use of the three words in relationship to Solomon's construction of the temple, which replaced the tabernacle (see 1 Kings 7:14).

Proverbs 3:19–20 clearly makes a connection between God's wisdom and creation. This connection is elaborated in a fascinating manner in Prov. 8, particularly 8:22–31, the autobiography of Woman Wisdom. Since Prov. 8 plays a key role in the theology of wisdom found in Proverbs, we examined it in an earlier chapter (chap. 1). There we also argued that Woman Wisdom, the firstborn of creation and the observer and participant in creation, stands for none other than Yahweh himself, who created the cosmos. While some may challenge the bold identification of Yahweh as Woman Wisdom, there is no doubt here that this passage describes the creation as the result of divine wisdom. God's wisdom was present and participating in the creation of the world. Wisdom mediates the relationship between God and humanity. Wisdom, as crafter of creation, plays and laughs before God as well as with humanity. Again, the message is that if one wants to know how the world works, how to navigate life, then one must have wisdom.[8]

Creation in Job

Earlier we described the book of Job as a debate over the source of wisdom. While each of the human participants in the book claims wisdom, they each, including Job himself, are utterly inadequate to deal with the issue of Job's suffering. They neither understand its causes, nor can they prescribe a remedy.

God himself makes his fearsome presence known to Job at the end of the book. Job, who apparently affirms retribution theology, accuses God of injustice since he knows that he does not deserve his pain. In response, God does not offer any explanations but simply asserts his power and his wisdom. He puts Job in his place by pummeling him with questions. Among other things, his questions communicate to Job (and the reader) that he, God, is the Creator and he, Job, is the creature:

> Where were you when I founded the earth?
> Tell me, if you have understanding.

8. Bostrom (*God of the Sages*, 59–67) also briefly discusses a handful of passages that speak of God as the Maker of humanity (14:31; 16:4, 11; 17:5; 20:2; 22:2; 29:13), though these do not materially change the fact that the creation motif is not a pervasive theme of the book.

Who set its measurements? Surely you know.
    Or who extended the line on it?
On what are its bases sunk?
    Or who set the cornerstone,
when the stars of the morning sang for joy
    and all the sons of God shouted gleefully?
Who shut the Sea with doors,
    and who brought it out bursting forth from the womb,
when I made the clouds its clothes,
    and deep darkness its swaddling clothes?
I prescribed my boundary on it;
    I set up bar and doors,
and I said, "You will go this far and no more,
    and here your proud waves will stop." (38:4–11)

God, the God of wisdom, here puts Job in his place by telling him that he is the creature and not the Creator. What is particularly interesting here is the description of the creation process not as bringing about the material world through the power of God's word (Gen. 1:1–2:4a) but rather as bringing order to chaos. The Sea is here personified and represents the power of chaos, which God controls by shutting it in and giving it a boundary that God commands it not to transgress. The Sea is pictured as a baby that bursts forth from the womb of its mother, and then God clothes it and controls it.

Creation in Ecclesiastes

In the book of Ecclesiastes, neither Qohelet nor the second wise man commenting on Qohelet's thinking speak as directly about God as Creator or the creation as either the books of Proverbs or Job in the examples cited above. However, neither is the creation theme entirely absent. The following passages illustrate Qohelet's reflections on God the Creator.

Perhaps the most memorable is also the most tenuous reference. In his last comment, Qohelet begins his reflection on death[9] by encouraging the reader to "remember your creator in the days of your youth" (12:1), or at least that is an example of a common translation of the verse. The Hebrew actually has "your creators" (*bôre'êkā*), raising the possibility that there is a problem with the Hebrew text. Crenshaw, for instance, repoints the consonants to read *bə'ērêkā*, "your well," a metaphorical reference to "your wife."[10] That said, the ancient witnesses, including the Septuagint (*ktsias*)

9. See discussion in chap. 2.
10. Crenshaw, *Ecclesiastes*, 185.

and the Vulgate (*creatoris*), support a simple emendation of the Hebrew to a singular "your creator."

In Eccles. 3:1 Qohelet asserts "for everything there is a season, and a time for every activity under heaven" and follows this with a listing of examples beginning with "a time to be born and a time to die" and ending with "a time of war and a time of peace" (3:2, 8). In 3:11 Qohelet attributes this state of affairs to God himself: "He makes everything appropriate in its time." There is some question as to whether Qohelet is speaking of God at the time of creation. Most commentators and versions understand the use of the perfect aspect of the verb here as a past-tense reference back to creation, but others support Whybray's position that "it is more probably that the perfect tense is used here in the Hebrew to express a general truth and should be rendered by the present tense in English."[11] At the time of my writing my commentary on the book, I supported Whybray's view,[12] but I have since changed my mind toward the majority opinion, though it is impossible to be absolutely certain about it.

I have found that God made people upright. (Eccles. 7:29)

Though there are some naysayers,[13] Qohelet's statement appears to be a reflection of the story of the creation of humanity particularly in Gen. 1. There we read that God created the cosmos and humanity and then pronounced them "very good" (Gen. 1:31). There is ancient precedence for this understanding, particularly in the explicit connection drawn by the Targum to Ecclesiastes.[14]

We turn finally to two passages in Qohelet's speech in the book of Ecclesiastes that reflect the language of Gen. 2:7 ("Then the LORD God formed a man from the dust of the ground and breathed into his nostrils the breath of life, and the man became a living being"). The first is found in chapter 3, where Qohelet is questioning the idea that humans are different from animals by stating, "All go to the same place. All come from the dust, and all return to the dust" (3:20). The second passage is even clearer in its connection to the Genesis creation account when Qohelet concludes his reflection on death by indicating that at the end "the dust returns to the earth as it was, and the spirit returned to God, who gave it" (12:7).

That Qohelet situates his thinking in the context of creation seems clear even when there is not the same explicit description of the creation itself as

---

11. See Whybray, *Ecclesiastes*, 72.
12. Longman, *Ecclesiastes*, 112.
13. Ogden, *Qoheleth*, 124–25.
14. See Levine, *Aramaic Version of Qohelet*, 40.

we saw in Proverbs and Job. At this point, though, we have purposefully not interpreted these statements in their broader context. We will do so below.

Creation in the Wisdom Psalms

Many psalms reflect on the creation. Not every psalm that speaks of God's creation can be considered a wisdom psalm. Psalm 24 is best considered a hymn that opens with an affirmation that God owns everything and everyone because he created the earth. Psalm 136 is a liturgical psalm that celebrates God's creation (vv. 5–6) and moves on to speak of God's great acts in history, most notably the exodus.

Three psalms that are commonly identified as wisdom psalms marvel in God's creation of humanity (Ps. 8), the heavens (Ps. 19), and the cosmos including the earth and its inhabitants (Ps. 104). For the first two, it must be admitted, the identification as wisdom is based on their creation theology. Psalm 104 brings the wisdom theme to explicit reflection when the psalmist pronounces:

> How many are your works, LORD!
>   In wisdom you made them all;
>   the earth is full of your creatures. (Ps. 104:24)

In this way the psalmist joins the chorus of other wisdom texts that ascribe the creation of the world to God's wisdom.

Creation in the Song of Songs

The Song of Songs is a love poem or, better, an anthology of closely related love poems (see chap. 4). One would not expect to find any reflection of creation theology in a book filled with expressions of desire and erotic play.

Phyllis Trible, however, made a compelling case that the Song's garden imagery, read in the context of the canon as a whole, evokes memory of the garden of Eden.[15] In Gen. 2 Adam and Eve are in the garden; they are naked and they feel no shame as they enjoy their "one flesh" union (Gen. 2:24–25).

This blissful intimacy is short lived, though, and comes to an end in Gen. 3. There we learn of their rebellion against God and the disruption of the divine-human relationship, which impacts the human-to-human relationship. We observed the latter in that Adam and Eve can no longer stand naked and unashamed, but rather seek to cover themselves first with fig leaves and then with "garments of skin" (3:21) that God provides for them.

---

15. Trible, *God and the Rhetoric of Sexuality*.

Reading the Song of Songs against the background of the accounts of the creation and fall draws out the significance of the garden imagery in the former. This is particularly the case when the garden is the setting of the physical intimacy between the man and the woman, as exemplified by Song 2:8–17:[16]

The Woman

The sound of my lover!
    See, he is coming,
    leaping over mountains,
    bounding over hills!
My lover is like a gazelle
    or a young stag.
He is now standing behind our wall,
    staring through the window,
    peeking through the lattice.
My lover responded and said to me,
    "Rise up, my darling,
    my beautiful one, and come, . . .
For now the winter has passed,
    the rains have come, gone.
Blossoms appear in the land.
    A time of singing has arrived,
    and the sound of turtledoves is heard in our land.
The fig tree ripens its fruit,
    and the vines, in blossom, spread their fragrance.
Rise up, O my darling,
    my beautiful one, and come. . . .
My dove, in the crevices of the rock,
    in the hiding place in the cliff,
Let me see your form!
    Let me hear your voice!
For your voice is agreeable,
    and your form is pleasant."
"Grab the foxes,
    the little foxes!
They are ruining the vineyards,
    our vineyards in bloom."

16. Falk (*Love Lyrics*, 139–43) draws the contrast between the countryside (including garden settings) and the city in the poems of the Song. The former is a place of privacy and intimacy; the latter is hostile to love.

>My lover is mine and I am his;
>   he grazes among the lilies.[17]

This poem is a striking example of what Trible had in mind when she spoke of the Song of Songs as a poetic account of the redemption of sexuality after the story of its rupture in Gen. 3. In this way Trible, who does not make the connection herself, contributes to our understanding of the relationship between wisdom and creation theology. The Song with its pervasive garden imagery evokes a picture of sexual desire that reflects the order established by God at the creation. The unnamed man and woman of the Song are no one in particular—that is, the Song is not a historical reminiscence of an actual relationship but rather stands for everyone. The message is that a relationship of mutuality, intense passion, exclusive love, and intimacy is a possibility in spite of the damage done by human rebellion against God.

Conclusion

We have examined five of our main sources for wisdom (Proverbs, Job, Ecclesiastes, Psalms, and Song of Songs) and have seen that each, to various degrees and in various ways, has exhibited an interest in creation. Proverbs is clearest in its assertion that God created through his wisdom, though even here Bostrom is right to say that "the notion of creation cannot be said to play a dominant role in the book."[18]

Wisdom's recognition that God created the cosmos by his wisdom also leads to the belief that the creation will be ordered and not chaotic. The sages thus teach their disciples how to navigate life in light of creation order. But are the sages really so confident that their advice based on their understanding of how the world works will really lead to successful results defined as a flourishing life? As we take a closer look in the next part of the chapter, we will see that things may not be as simple as we might think at first glance.

Wisdom and Creation Order: The Right Time

As mentioned in the previous section, that God created the cosmos through his wisdom implies that the cosmos, far from being chaotic, is ordered and predictable. That, at least, is the conclusion drawn by many students of wisdom in the past decades. If the cosmos is ordered and predictable, then it ought to

---

17. Translations of Song of Songs come from Longman, *Song of Songs*.
18. Bostrom, *God of the Sages*, 80.

be possible to live life in such a way that maximizes success and minimizes pitfalls. And that does seem to be a fair assessment of the type of instruction that Proverbs proposes to give. Wisdom instruction intends to help people do the right thing at the right time, say the right thing at the right time, and express emotions that are appropriate to the situation. In a phrase, timing is everything when it comes to living by wisdom.

Above we commented on Qohelet's assertion that "for everything there is a season, and a time for every activity under heaven" (3:1). The book of Proverbs famously highlights the importance of timing in one's speech and actions as in the following proverbs:

> It is a joy to a person to give an answer!
> How good a word at the right time! (15:23)
>
> Apples of gold in a silver setting
> is a word spoken in its right timing. (25:11)

Proverbs 15:23 is fairly straightforward. Proverbs 25:11 is also clear in its main message, which is that a word spoken at the right time is of great value. The words may have some inherent worth (they are "apples of gold" [perhaps some kind of ornament]), but spoken at the right time their value is greatly enhanced (set in silver).

But these proverbs are simply making explicit what is implicit in the proverb as a literary form or genre. Proverbs, as proverbs, make no universal truth claim; they are only true if applied to the right situation. That is why, after all, there are "contradictory proverbs." Before turning to biblical examples, consider first the following proverbial pairs in the English tradition:

Haste makes waste.
The early bird catches the worm.

Too many cooks spoil the broth.
Many hands make light work.

Actions speak louder than words.
The pen is mightier than the sword.

Look before you leap.
Strike while the iron is hot.

In terms of biblical wisdom, we go right to the most famous of the "contradictory proverbs"—namely, Prov. 26:4–5:

> Don't answer fools according to their stupidity;
>   otherwise, you will become like them yourself.
> Answer fools according to their stupidity;
>   otherwise, they will become wise in their own eyes.

Those who did not understand the nature of the proverb as only true when applied in the right situation (at the right time) go back at least to the time of Jamnia (AD 90), where a group of rabbis gathered in the aftermath of the destruction of the temple to discuss the future of Judaism. Among many other concerns the rabbis affirmed the authority of the Proverbs over against a few voices that argued that Proverbs contradicted itself so it could not possibly be authoritative (that is, "make the hands unclean").[19]

But the point is that wisdom involves more than learning the proverbs by rote; one must also learn how to apply them to the right situation. Fools can know the proverbs, but if they don't know how to apply them correctly, then the proverbs are useless to them, as Prov. 26:7 warns:

> The legs of a lame person dangle,
>   and a proverb in the mouth of fools.

Just like the legs of a lame person cannot help them walk, so are proverbs known by those who don't know how to use them. Proverbs 26:9 has an even more dire warning:

> A thorn bush in the hand of a drunk,
>   and a proverb in the mouth of fools.

A proverb invoked by someone who does not know how to apply it correctly is not only useless but potentially dangerous. The image is of a drunk person madly waving a thorn bush, blood rushing down the arm and occasionally and randomly striking others.

Proverbs 26:4–5 is just the most obvious example of proverbs that, when placed side by side, would upend each other if applied as if they were universally true statements. Other examples are more subtle and not placed together. But consider the following advice concerning wealth.

First, Proverbs is often cited (by those who don't know the book well) as a guide to prosperity. Isolated statements can be (incorrectly) used as proof texts for such a viewpoint. An example is Prov. 3:9–10:

---

19. Beckwith, *Old Testament Canon*, 278–81. The language of "unclean hands" sounds strange to our ears but is based on the idea that one becomes unclean if one comes into contact with something holy.

> Honor Yahweh with your wealth
>   and from the first of your produce.
> And your barns will be filled with plenty,
>   and your vats will burst with wine.

But it takes more than simply "faith" to get rich; one also has to work hard:

> A slack palm makes poverty;
>   a determined hand makes rich. (Prov. 10:4)

Honor God, and you will get rich; work hard, and get rich. But is this the whole truth or even the epitome of what the book of Proverbs teaches about wealth? Absolutely not.

The sages of Proverbs know full well that someone can be faithful and work hard but still, through no fault of their own, be poor: "Much food comes from the arable soil of the poor, but it is swept away because of a lack of justice" (Prov. 13:23). The sages do not specify the nature of the "lack of justice," because there are a number of possibilities (an oppressive landlord or bureaucrat, excessive taxes, even a destructive weather event).

However, as demonstrated by Van Leeuwen, the most compelling argument against using passages like Prov. 3:9–10 as if they are always true are the so-called better-than proverbs.[20] Here are only two of multiple examples:

> Getting wisdom is much better than gold,
>   and getting understanding is to be preferred over silver. (Prov. 16:16)

> It is better to be a poor person and walk blamelessly,
>   than one with crooked paths and wealthy. (Prov. 28:6)

These better-than proverbs talk about relative values and make the point that wisdom, righteousness, and godliness are what is important in comparison to wealth. These proverbs are far from commending poverty or denigrating wealth, but they are admitting that sometimes a decision must be made between a life of wisdom and a life of wealth, and when a person is confronted with such a choice, the answer is clear: wisdom with poverty is much better than folly with wealth.

Our purpose here is not to give a well-rounded picture of the teaching on wealth and poverty in the book of Proverbs.[21] There are additional nuances.

---

20. Van Leeuwen, "Wealth and Poverty."

21. For such a picture, see Whybray, *Wealth and Poverty*; Washington, *Wealth and Poverty*; Longman, *Proverbs*, 573–76; Longman, *How to Read Proverbs*, 117–30.

However, enough has been said to indicate that it is useless and dangerous to quote any one passage and hold it up as the universally true teaching on a subject.

As David Bland reiterates in his helpful recent book, "if you know only one proverb, you know none."[22] He also goes on to say that not only must a proverb be applied to the correct situation for it to be true, but "the situational nature of the proverb manifests itself in the way in which the same proverb can have an indeterminate number of meanings based on the context in which it is used."[23]

Bland takes a look at the English proverb "silence is golden" to make his point. There are actually different "right" times to apply this aphorism. A parent might appropriately say this to a child who is being noisy in a library. Or one might say this to encourage a shy person not to be self-conscious about the awkward gaps in conversation. Or one might utter this to oneself or another to express contentment in a beautiful wilderness setting.

The bottom line, again, is that proverbs embed instruction that takes great skill, wisdom, to use correctly. We must be aware that no single proverb expresses the whole truth about a matter and that proverbs may have multiple meanings depending on the context. While this sounds complex, it is also true that when someone utters a proverb that is right for the situation, it is immediately recognized as true.

My grandmother was adept at English proverbs and provides a good example of timely use of proverbs. I have vivid memories of her on one Thanksgiving telling my mother and my aunt that "too many cooks spoil the broth," which they understood immediately and left the kitchen so my grandmother could prepare the turkey the way that she wanted. After dinner, though, I have an even more vivid memory of her coming into the TV room where my cousins and I were watching football and telling us that "many hands make light work." While the principles in these two proverbs are clearly opposed to each other, we knew immediately the "rightness" of the proverb as we got up to help her wash the innumerable dirty dishes.

Proverbs intend to bring order to disorder, thus in this sense wisdom assumes an ordered world based on God's creation of the world through his wisdom. So why doesn't wisdom always work?

The World Isn't So Perfectly Ordered after All

Proverbs does urge its readers to live wisely by saying the right thing at the right time and doing the right thing at the right time in order to achieve a

---

22. Bland, *Proverbs and the Formation of Character*, 77–78.
23. Ibid., 106.

desired and beneficial result. That said, we have also demonstrated above that Proverbs does not claim that such words and actions will always achieve the desired result. Sometimes the lazy are rich and the hard worker is poor even though God created the world so that the hard worker would get rewarded. Indeed, the better-than proverbs tell us that the sages understood that there are times when a person has to make a choice between, say, wisdom and wealth. Proverbs, we have suggested, point to the best strategy to achieve a desired result all other things being equal. But often things are not equal.

As we saw in chapter 3, the book of Job presents a thought experiment that illustrates that wisdom does not always lead to a tranquil or successful life. The same is true for the book of Ecclesiastes, where we saw in chapter 2 that Qohelet, while acknowledging a limited benefit to wisdom, ultimately felt that death rendered wisdom no better than folly (2:12–17). Indeed, the fact that God made the world so that there was a right season for everything under the sun just led to increased frustration on Qohelet's part since he felt that God did not give his human creatures the ability to discern the proper time (3:1–15). While the frame narrator points his son to what we called an "above the sun" perspective (fear God, obey his commandments, and live in light of the future judgment), he does not challenge Qohelet's view that "under the sun" life is meaningless.[24]

All this is a selective review of our earlier studies of Proverbs, Job, and Ecclesiastes. Contra many depictions of the relationship between these three books, Job and Ecclesiastes are not criticizing the message of Proverbs; they rather are a canonical corrective to an overreading of the book that apparently was an ancient error as well as a modern one (e.g., the prosperity gospel).[25]

Further illumination of the relationship between wisdom, creation, and order is provided by an examination of Paul's allusion to the book of Ecclesiastes in Rom. 8:

> I consider that our present sufferings are not worth comparing with the glory that will be revealed in us. For the creation waits in eager expectation for the children of God to be revealed. For the creation was subjected to *frustration*, not by its own choice, but by the will of the one who subjected it. (8:18–20a, emphasis added)

24. Indeed, in 12:10 the frame narrator tells his son that Qohelet "wrote honest words of truth." That is, life is difficult and then you die as long as you stay "under the sun."

25. My view is only slightly different from that presented by Enns, *Inspiration and Incarnation*, 63–72, though he puts more emphasis on diversity than I would. However, he is correct to say that while there is diversity of message, the books don't subvert each other.

The word "frustration" (*mataiotes*) connects his comment here with the book of Ecclesiastes since it is the Greek translation of the Hebrew word translated "meaningless" (*hebel*) in the Greek OT. Paul, however, reveals why the creation is meaningless—"it was subjected to frustration, not by its own choice, but by the will of the one who subjected it." Paul here clearly alludes to the account of the fall in Gen. 3. God subjected the creation to frustration in response to the rebellion of Adam and Eve.[26]

Thus, when we think of wisdom's connection to creation theology, it is wrong-minded to think only of Gen. 1–2. To the extent that wisdom is related to creation theology, it does not return us to Eden but recognizes that we live in a troubled, disordered world.

In chapter 6 ("Wanting to Be Wise [Gen. 3]") we noted that while not making the case that Gen. 3 is wisdom literature, we can't read the account of humanity's rebellion there without noticing the language and concepts related to wisdom. In this tragic account of the fall, we see that Adam and Eve's acquisition of "wisdom" backfires on them. Their eyes are opened, but what they now see is not pretty because of their rebellion. Thus, they can no longer stand naked and without shame, and they take steps to cover themselves up. They are finally ejected from the garden into the broader world, which Paul has told us is now subjected to frustration. The world is warped; we are warped. No wonder that Qohelet could not find meaning "under the sun." No wonder wisdom only goes so far in bringing order to a disordered world.

Paul does not end his reflections with a disordered world, however. Below we will see that God subjected the world to frustration "in hope." But before we move to Paul's redemptive message, we need to consider how the books of Job and the Song of Songs also acknowledge that creation is disordered.

When God speaks from the whirlwind, he peppers Job with questions, the first ones concerning the creation. Here we see creation theology playing its most explicit role in the book. God puts the accusing Job in his place by reminding him that he was the Creator and not Job himself.

The presentation of the creation story, however, takes a fascinating twist when compared with the account in Gen. 1–2. Though debated, many scholars, including myself, see an absence of the so-called combat motif in Genesis.[27] In Mesopotamian and probably Canaanite accounts of creation, the creator god (Marduk and Baal) forms the cosmos after defeating the gods representing

26. It is widely recognized that Paul here is using the divine passive and thus referring to God as the one who subjected the creation to frustration.
27. Longman, *Genesis*, 3, contra Levenson, *Creation and the Persistence of Evil*.

the waters (Tiamat and Yam). In Genesis, the Spirit of God hovers over the waters but does not fight the waters.

However, when God talks about his creation of the world in Job, the waters are personified and God claims not so much to create the waters but to control the waters like a parent controls a rambunctious child:

> Who shut the Sea with doors,
>   and who brought it out bursting forth from the womb,
> when I made the clouds it clothes,
>   and deep darkness its swaddling clothes?
> I prescribed my boundary for it;
>   I set up a bar and doors.
> And I said, "You will go this far and no more,
>   and here your proud waves will stop." (38:8–11)

In other words, God's description of creation in Job presumes a measure of chaos that needs controlling.

Job has wanted to meet with God in order to confront him about his suffering. He believes that God is unjust and that a wise, God-fearing, pious person of integrity like himself does not deserve to suffer. In essence, God responds here by saying that the world that he created does not work as neatly as Job assumes by his charge of injustice. God does not eradicate chaos and evil, but he does control it in a way that Job, or for that matter any human, could not possibly do. In the very next section, he goes on to challenge Job by saying:

> In your days, have you commanded the morning?
>   Can you inform the dawn of its place
> so it grabs the edges of the earth,
>   so the wicked can be shaken out of it?
> The earth is transformed like clay by a seal impression,
>   and its features stand out like a garment.
> Light is held back from the wicked,
>   and their upheld arm is broken. (38:12–15)

God, not Job, commands the morning, and in this way he controls but does not remove evil. The earth here is likened to a seal impression on soft clay. When a seal is stamped on or rolled across the clay, it produces depressions and raised areas similar to the hills and valleys of the surface of the earth. As the light dawns from the edge of the earth, it sheds its light across the surface of the earth, and then, using another analogy, God shakes evildoers out of commission (at least until the next night) like a person shakes the dirt off a garment.

The relevant point for our discussion is that the connection between wisdom and creation and order is not as simple as some would make it out to be. It is not simply a matter of if one is wise, then one knows how the creation works, since God created the world ordered. The wise understand that creation order has been disturbed, and therefore it does not always work as one might expect.

Even the Song of Songs recognizes that the type of intimacy celebrated in its beautiful poems is not easily achieved. Trible was right to say that the garden theme in the Song, when read canonically, tells the story of the redemption of sexuality (see "Creation in the Song of Songs" earlier in this chapter).[28] To review, Gen. 2 depicts Adam and Eve in the garden of Eden, naked and unashamed, but in Gen. 3, because of sin, they cover themselves up. In the Song of Songs, a man and woman are back in the garden enjoying themselves. To this important point we would add only one caveat—enjoying themselves most of the time.

George Schwab has highlighted themes and even whole poems that indicate the poet's awareness that the redemption of sexuality is not completely ac-complished.[29] Intimacy between the man and the woman is often threatened, as signaled by the man's warning of the threat of the foxes in the garden of love (2:15). Not only that, but love is not easily achieved, as we learn from the disturbing but powerful poem describing how the man approaches the woman for intimacy only to be refused entry (5:2–6:3). But then once she is aroused, she opens the door for him and sees that he is not there. Thus, she goes on a harrowing search for him in anticipation of union in the garden. In addition, the woman who instructs the women of Jerusalem in matters of love has to warn them that no matter how desirable intimacy is, it is a powerful and dangerous emotion that should not be prematurely incited: "I adjure you, daughters of Jerusalem, by the gazelles or the deer of the field, not to awaken or arouse love until it desires" (2:7; 3:5; 8:4).

As we noted above, Paul tells the Roman church that the creation was subjected to frustration, and those who speak about wisdom in the OT know this. It is not that the world is so disturbed that God's creation is totally distorted. It often functions as it should but not exactly as it was intended, thanks to human rebellion.

Finally, we return once again to Paul's comments in Rom. 8 in which he recognizes, as did Qohelet, that the world is *mataiotes/hebel*. Though

28. Trible, *God and the Rhetoric of Sexuality*.
29. G. Schwab, *Song of Songs' Cautionary Message*.

Qohelet does not progress beyond this sad observation, the frame narrator urges his son not to get mired in Qohelet's true and honest conclusion but rather to cultivate an "above the sun" perspective. In the same way, Paul does not stop where Qohelet does. Yes, the world was "subjected to frustration, not by its own choice, but by the will of the one who subjected it," but he continues, "in hope that the creation itself will be liberated from its bondage to decay and brought into the freedom and glory of the children of God" (Rom. 8:20b–21). Paul speaks of the redemption of a world made meaningless by human sin and death. The message of the NT is that the person and work of Jesus Christ has won that redemption. As we consider the gospel of redemption, we realize that Jesus redeems us by subjecting himself to the suffering of the fallen world. He experienced *hebel* like Qohelet could not even imagine.

Conclusion

We began this chapter with Zimmerli's famous quotation, "Wisdom thinks resolutely within the framework of a theology of creation." We noted that though the sages spoke sparingly of creation directly, it was indeed crucial to their worldview. God created the cosmos by his wisdom, which presumes that the world is organized in a harmonious manner. Thus, the appeal of wisdom is that it puts one in touch with the way the world works so that the wise can flourish and bring benefits to themselves and to their families and to their communities. To act contrary to the way God made the cosmos is to act foolishly and bring harm on oneself and others.

Wisdom, however, does not naively assert that wisdom will always work. To act wisely does not automatically bring reward. In the second half of the chapter, we observed that the sages were well aware that the world was broken. However, the world's brokenness does not bring chaos, so there is still great benefit to the "way of wisdom."

A comment by Oliver O'Donovan captures well the perspective of the OT sages:

> The universe, though fractured and broken, displays the fact that its brokenness is the brokenness of order and not merely of unordered chaos. Thus it remains accessible to knowledge in part. It requires no revelation to observe the various forms of generic and teleological order which belong to it. An unbeliever or a non-christian culture does not have to be ignorant about the structure of the family, the virtue of mercy, the vice of cowardice, or the duty of justice. Nor

does such a one have to fail entirely to respond to this knowledge in action, disposition or institution.[30]

It is important to affirm with O'Donovan that one does not have to be a believer to see how the world works to at least some extent. The world, though broken, is not shattered beyond recognition, and God's human creatures, though deeply flawed, are not insane. Wisdom remains accessible to all, at least to a certain point. That certain point, though, falls short of theological wisdom. The unbeliever does not, in the words of O'Donovan, have to be "ignorant about the structure of the family, the virtue of mercy, the vice of cowardice, or the duty of justice," but by definition the unbeliever remains ignorant of what is the most fundamental and essential truth of the cosmos— that God created it and that everything is dependent on him. While one can live with wisdom on a practical and perhaps even on an ethical level, without fear of the Lord there is, in the final analysis, no foundation to that wisdom.[31]

30. O'Donovan, *Resurrection and Moral Order*, 88, quoted in Treier, *Virtue and the Voice of God*, 46.
31. "Proverbs actually mainly encourages the reader to listen to instruction rather than to explore reality with an open mind; that besides listening to the fathers' teaching, the key to wisdom is the fear of the Lord and not a search for natural regularities" (Z. Schwáb, *Toward an Interpretation*, 63).

9

ISRAELITE WISDOM
IN ITS ANCIENT NEAR
EASTERN SETTING

I srael was far from a people sealed off from its neighbors, and thus the Bible was not written in a cultural vacuum. The rediscovery of ancient Near Eastern cultures over the past two centuries[1] has provided archaeological and literary resources that have enriched our understanding of the "cognitive environment"[2] of Israel and the OT. At least since the publication and study of the Instruction of Amenemope in 1923,[3] which bears significant similarity to some of the contents of the book of Proverbs, there has been great interest in the relationship between biblical wisdom materials and counterparts in the ancient Near East. Indeed, the similarities between Israelite and ancient Near Eastern wisdom have been used as evidence that wisdom speaks to universal concerns rather than concerns that are particular to Israel. That said, there are a number of deeply contested issues associated with the relationship between and the significance of the comparison of biblical and ancient Near Eastern wisdom.

1. The modern period of the study of the ancient Near East started in earnest when Europeans came back into sustained contact with the Middle East starting with Napoleon's invasion of Egypt around 1800 AD.
2. I borrow the term from Walton, *Genesis 1 as Ancient Cosmology*.
3. Budge, *Facsimiles*; and Budge, *Teaching of Amen-Em-Apt*.

The following chapter will only hint at the extensive number of ancient Near Eastern texts that have been brought into this discussion. We will not provide an exhaustive survey of Sumerian, Egyptian, Akkadian, Hittite, and Aramaic literature associated with wisdom.[4] Our interest addresses the following questions:

> Is there ancient Near Eastern wisdom?
>
> What is the relationship between biblical and ancient Near Eastern wisdom?
>
> Is biblical wisdom particular to Israel, or is it universal?

Is There Ancient Near Eastern Wisdom?

> "Wisdom" is strictly a misnomer as applied to Babylonian literature.

W. G. Lambert's discouraging statement, at least when first read, is actually the opening line of his important book *Babylonian Wisdom Literature*.[5] He, of course, recognizes that Akkadian has a word for wisdom (*nemequ*) but points out that it is most often associated with mantic practices like divination. Lambert, nonetheless, allows for the use of "wisdom" as a reference to a number of Babylonian texts because of their similarity to biblical wisdom texts like, especially, Proverbs, Job, and Ecclesiastes, and for some, also the Song of Songs and others.

To scholars like Kynes, as one might suspect, this smacks of circular reasoning because he questions the identification of a separate wisdom genre in the Bible, and he would go beyond Lambert and dispute the presence of any wisdom genre in the ancient Near East, believing that it is an imposition of a foreign category.[6] We have agreed that he is correct as regards a kind of rigid, realistic understanding of genre, but we have found utility with the category as long as our understanding of genre is much more flexible and admitting of fuzzy edges. What cannot be denied, in our opinion, is that there are many texts that have interesting similarities with books that focus on wisdom in the OT, particularly Proverbs, Job, and Ecclesiastes, but also the Song of Songs. To give the reader a sense of the resources available in the different cultures of the ancient Near East, we provide the following overview.[7]

---

4. See Sparks, *Ancient Texts*, 56–83, and associated bibliographies; also see Walton, *Zondervan Illustrated Bible Backgrounds Commentary*, vol. 5.

5. Lambert, *Babylonian Wisdom Literature*, 1.

6. Kynes, *Obituary*.

7. For a more optimistic approach to the question of Mesopotamian wisdom, see Cohen, *Wisdom from the Late Bronze Age*; as well as the work of Beaulieu cited below.

Mesopotamian Wisdom

History dawns with the advent of writing (ca. 3100 BC) in Mesopotamia. A people we know as the Sumerians lived in what is today southern Iraq, between the Tigris and the Euphrates Rivers. By the end of the third millennium, they were eventually displaced by a Semitic people who spoke and wrote Akkadian and who formed two power centers, one in the south centered around the city of Babylon and the second in the north centered around the city of Asshur. Over the next millennium and a half, there were swings of power between the Babylonian and Assyrian kingdoms.

Sumerian culture, religion, writing, and literature exercised a huge influence on the Babylonians and Assyrians. The Babylonians and Assyrians also preserved much earlier Sumerian literature. Thus, though we can draw distinctions, we present Sumerian, Babylonian, and Assyrian wisdom under the rubric of Mesopotamian wisdom.

In terms of the religion of Mesopotamia, wisdom is associated with certain gods. In Sumer, Enki was the god of wisdom. According to certain myths, Enki (Ea in Akkadian) possessed the ME's (*parsu* in Akkadian), which are the principles of the cosmos or perhaps "traditional rules" of civilization.[8] In the description by Averbeck, they "were the offices, arts, and crafts with their associated functional powers that shaped and tooled Sumerian culture and society so that it worked for both gods and people."[9]

In "Enki and the World Order," Enki has the ME's, given to him by the god Enlil, as well as the ability to determine destinies (NAM-TAR), and he sets out on a journey to distribute the ME's throughout civilization. At the end of the text as we have it, the goddess Inanna complains that Enki did not distribute any of the ME's to her. The topic of the ME's and the relationship between Enki and Inanna is the subject of another Sumerian myth, "Inanna and Enki." Here Enki gives Inanna the ME's while he is drunk. He tries to get them back before she deposits them in her temple in Uruk, but the text is broken off so we don't know its resolution.

These texts associate the ME's that order the world with Enki, the god of wisdom. But "order" may be the wrong word if it is taken to imply, like biblical wisdom, only what we would recognize as virtues that lead to harmony between people and creation. In the list of ME's given in "Inanna and Enki," we find not only things like heroism and righteousness but also dishonesty, the plundering of cities, and the singing of lamentations. These too are considered divinely instituted norms.

8. Wiggermann, "Theologies, Priests, and Worship," 1865.
9. Averbeck, "Myth, Ritual, and Order."

But back to Enki and wisdom. "In Mesopotamia, the god Ea (Enki in Sumerian), in his role as bringer of the arts of civilization to the human race, was the god of wisdom par excellence and the craftsman God."[10] From "Enki and the World Order" and "Enki and Inanna" we have seen how he distributed the ME's throughout the land, but we have seen nothing explicit about bringing wisdom to humanity.

Here we will briefly mention the tradition of the seven preflood sages, beginning with Oannes (Adapa), whose account is most fully known through the third-century-BC author Berossus, whose writings are known from much later sources. However, the tradition of the seven sages, fish-men, is known at least as early as the "Erra Epic" (no later than the eighth century BC), which speaks of "the Seven Sages of the Apsu, the holy carp, who are perfect in lofty wisdom like Ea (Enki) their lord" (1.163).[11] The idea seems to be that Enki/Ea imparted wisdom to humanity through these seven preflood sages.

One of those seven preflood sages was named Ziusudra (also known as Atrahasis or Utnapishtim) in various legends concerning the flood. He is often referred to as the Babylonian Noah. In the Sumerian creation text known as the "Eridu Genesis"[12] we learn that Ziusudra, son of Shuruppak (see below), was the one whom Enki/Ea warned about the coming flood. In the Sumerian "Death of Gilgamesh" we learn that Gilgamesh traveled to meet with the flood hero and there learned of certain rituals that he then imparted to his city of Uruk. This king of Uruk is best known today in the Babylonian tale called the "Gilgamesh Epic." The narrator begins the epic by introducing Gilgamesh as "he who has seen everything. . . . Anu granted him the totality of knowledge of all. He saw the Secret, discovered the Hidden, he brought information of (the time) before the Flood."[13] Thus the Gilgamesh Epic may be read as a "quest for wisdom and antediluvian knowledge."[14]

The idea of wisdom is very important to Mesopotamian thought. Originating with the gods, particularly Enki/Ea, it comes to humanity through the vehicle of the seven preflood sages. Wisdom involves knowing how the world (civilization) works. It is thus a practical category, but more than that, it involves religious ritual and also becomes connected with divination. "It [wisdom] included not only all skills required to lead a proper life but also ritual prescriptions and a number of arcane disciplines and esoteric arts accessible

10. Beaulieu, "Social and Intellectual Setting," 4.
11. Translation by S. Dalley in COS 1:408.
12. Translation by T. Jacobsen in COS 1:513–15.
13. Kovacs, Epic of Gilgamesh, 3.
14. Beaulieu, "Social and Intellectual Setting," 5.

to a restricted elite of specialists who acted as mediators between the divine and human worlds."[15]

Thus wisdom finds a place within the Mesopotamian mythic tradition, but further we find compositions that bear resemblance to the biblical books that we have identified as wisdom. Here we will give a brief accounting of what we know. Mesopotamian literature includes "instructions, proverbs, fables, and disputations" that are often counted as part of the wisdom tradition.[16] In this chapter we will give only a taste of the specific texts that fit this categorization.

Among the earliest wisdom writings are proverb collections from ancient Sumer. Indeed, we have twenty-eight proverb collections, some of which are as old as the Early Dynastic III period (2600–2550 BC) and continue in use well after Sumerian ceased as a spoken language.[17] Yet another important wisdom text originally written in Sumerian, but having a later Akkadian translation, is known as the "Instructions of Shuruppak." Shuruppak is a prediluvian king who is speaking to his son Ziusudra (the flood hero; see above). He gives him instructions "relating to secular life, that is, the management of a household, animal husbandry, agricultural work, and social behavior in general."[18] Notice that the form of this instruction being a father speaking to a son will be seen both in Egyptian and also Israelite wisdom (Proverbs, Ecclesiastes). We also observe a father instructing his son in the Babylonian text known as the "Counsels of Wisdom."[19]

Another group of wisdom compositions in Akkadian, often overlooked, are three texts that are found within the broader genre of what I have elsewhere called fictional Akkadian autobiography.[20] The genre of fictional autobiography has a basic three-part structure, the first two parts being shared by all the texts—namely, (1) a first-person introduction followed by (2) a first-person narrative history. The third part divides the fictional autobiographies into four subcategories: those that end (1) with blessings and curses ("Sargon Birth Legend," "Idrimi"), (2) with prophecy ("Marduk Prophecy," "Shulgi Prophecy," "Uruk Prophecy," "Dynastic Prophecy," "Text A"), (3) with a donation to the religious establishment ("Cruciform Monument of Manishtushu," "Agum-kakrime Inscription," the "Autobiography of Kurigalzu"), and (4) with

---

15. Ibid., 18. Van der Toorn ("Why Wisdom Became a Secret") argues that wisdom shifts from "wisdom by experience" to "wisdom by revelation" as we move from the second to the first millennium.

16. Beaulieu, "Social and Intellectual Setting," 8.

17. The most recent edition may be found in Alster, *Proverbs of Ancient Sumer*. See the review article by Veldhuis, "Sumerian Proverbs."

18. B. Alster in COS 1:569.

19. See *ANET* 425–27; and Foster, *Before the Muses*, 1:328–31.

20. Longman, *Fictional Akkadian Autobiography*.

some form of instruction ("Cuthaean Legend of Naram-Sin," "Adad-guppi Inscription," and the "Sennacherib Autobiography"). The latter is the group associated with wisdom, since after giving an account of their life, the putative speakers (Naram-Sin, Adad-guppi, and Sennacherib) give advice based on their life. A little later in this chapter we will see the relevance of this group of texts to the book of Ecclesiastes.

Thus far we have surveyed texts that form a cultural background for the book of Proverbs. We also have texts in both Sumerian and especially Akkadian that address the issue of an innocent sufferer and thus are similar to the book of Job. While it would be impossible to prove, it appears to me that these compositions, particularly the "Babylonian Theodicy" with its interchange between a sufferer and a friend, may have provided the literary vehicle for the biblical author of Job to explore questions concerning suffering and wisdom.

The issue of innocent suffering appears first, at least according to our present knowledge, with a Sumerian composition referred to as "Man and His God."[21] We know this text from tablets that are from the Old Babylonian period (eighteenth and seventeenth centuries BC), but it originated at some unknown earlier time. It is a prayer of a sufferer to his god, who hears him and restores him.

Closer to home in terms of similarities with Job are two Akkadian works, the first of which is known as "*Ludlul Bel Nemeqi*": "I will praise the Lord of wisdom." The Lord of wisdom is Marduk, who is Enki/Ea's son, who is also connected with wisdom and is the king of the Babylonian pantheon. This text is a monologue by a sufferer who describes his horrible pain. He appeals to Marduk, who eventually restores him. While there are some hints that his suffering is the result of some kind of ritual offense, one oft-quoted section makes it clear that at least in the Babylonian tradition, one cannot know what the gods like and what they do not:

What seems good to one's self could be an offense to a god,
What in one's own heart seems abominable could be good to one's god.
Who could learn the reasoning of the gods in heaven?
Who could grasp the intentions of the gods of the depths?
Where might human beings have learned the way of a god?

Yet another text, known as the "Babylonian Theodicy," also deals with the issue of the innocent sufferer and the justice of the gods. This text, which

21. Kramer, "'Man and His God.'"

like "*Ludlul*" is attested by seventh-century-BC tablets, is in the form of a dialogue or debate between two men, one a sufferer and the other his friend. Like Job, the sufferer questions the justice of the gods while the friends defend it. Unlike the book of Job, however, the friend comes around to the sufferer's perspective at the very end.

Egyptian Wisdom

Writing in Egypt started soon after writing appeared in Mesopotamia, though there is no connection between the two writing systems. Thus, it appears writing started independently. Instructional literature comparable to the book of Proverbs is among the earliest attested texts in Egyptian literary history.

Though, as with Mesopotamia, some scholars question the existence of wisdom literature in Egypt,[22] there is no doubting that there are a plethora of texts that are didactic in nature and that even share insights similar to those we find in the book of Proverbs.[23] The primary type of writing that can be associated with wisdom is called *sbȝyt* in Egyptian, a word that may be translated "teaching" or "instruction."[24]

The similarity with Proverbs (and also Ecclesiastes [see 12:12]) is that the instructional literature of Egypt takes the form of a father who teaches his son. The father is typically a high official, or even the king, who wants to form his son for future life and service. These texts typically, but not always, are set within the upper levels of Egyptian society. There are a number of these texts, appearing for the first time at the earliest stages of Egyptian history (Old Kingdom, ca. 2715–2170 BC) and extending all the way down to the latest periods. Some of the best-known examples include the instructions of Ptahhotep, Merikare, Amenemope, Anksheshonqy, and Papyrus Insinger.

While there is not a term in these texts that could be translated "wise" or "wisdom," the instructions that the father gives to his son in large measure intend to inculcate attitudes and habits that are similar to what we find in Proverbs and that also promise the same results. We can see this particularly as the father tries to keep the son from being a hothead and instead to react to life with maturity.

22. Lichtheim, *Maat*. She bases her doubt on the lack of a word in Egyptian that can clearly be translated "wise/wisdom" before the Late Period of Egyptian history.
23. For specific parallels between proverbs in the Bible and ancient Egyptian instructional sayings, see Longman, "Proverbs."
24. Ray ("Egyptian Wisdom Literature," 18) prefers "enlightenment."

And even though there is not a word exactly comparable to wisdom, there is a concept, *ma'at*, that comes close. *Ma'at* is a difficult word to translate but seems to point to the idea that there is an order to the world, and if one behaves in a manner befitting that order, then life will work out in a positive way. One might think of *ma'at* as referring to the harmony, justice, and truth of the created order.

Not only is there a vibrant genre of instructional literature from Egypt,[25] but we also have texts that we might term speculative or pessimistic that fit in more with Job and Ecclesiastes. Five texts are typically discussed in this regard: The "Admonitions of Ipuwer" describe a period of time when society is deeply disrupted and expresses hope for a good king.[26] The "Eloquent Peasant" tells the story of a poor man, Khu-n-Anup, who is exploited by a wealthy landowner. The peasant seeks, and eventually gets, justice.[27] The "Complaints of Khakheperre-Sonb" contain proverbs that describe an upside-down society:

> Right is cast outside,
> Wrong is in the council hall;
> The plans of the gods are violated,
> Their ordinances neglected,
> The land is in turmoil.[28]

The fourth text, the "Protocol of Neferti," is similar to the preceding in that it too describes a world in turmoil and expresses hope for a future king who will set things to order. It is unclear whether this is a prophetic vision or a text that is simply "anticipating developments."[29]

Perhaps the most interesting of the pessimistic texts from Egypt is the "Dispute over Suicide," which is also called a "Dialogue of a Man with His *Ba*," which comes from the twelfth dynasty during the Middle Kingdom period (ca. 2133–1670 BC).[30] The Egyptian term *ba* is difficult to understand and to translate, but it comes close to the idea of one's soul or inner self. In a sense, the composition is a self-dialogue. Both the man and his *ba* recognize how difficult and full of disappointment life is. It is not really clear that they

25. For instance, we should take note of the genre of autobiographies, commonly written on tomb walls, that speak of a person's life "in order to present their personal experiences as food for thought for their peers." So Perdu, "Ancient Egyptian Autobiographies," 2243.

26. Translation by N. Shupak in *COS* 1:93–98.

27. Ibid., 1:98–104.

28. Ibid., 1:104–6.

29. Goedicke, *Protocol of Neferyt*, 3.

30. Translations may be found in J. A. Wilson, *ANET* 405–7; and Lichtheim, *Ancient Egyptian Literature*, 1:163–69.

actually contemplate suicide, but in any case the *ba* urges the man to accept a difficult life rather than to live with disappointment. In his classic study, Goedicke argues that the text is "the promulgation of an idealistic philosophy within which the goal is to master the shortcomings of the mundane world by knowledge of the fleetingness of corporeal existence and of a true eternal home in transcendence."[31]

While there seems to be a close relationship between Egyptian and Hebrew instructional literature, the connection between Egyptian pessimistic literature and, say, Job and Ecclesiastes, is not strong. Yes, both traditions struggle with injustice and the difficulties of life, but that is only to be expected considering the human condition.

Aramaic Wisdom

We do not have much by way of non-Hebrew Northwest Semitic literature, but we have one important example, known as the "Instructions of Ahiqar,"[32] written originally in Aramaic, as we know from a version found at the Egyptian site of Elephantine.[33] The papyrus comes from the fifth century BC, though it was likely composed earlier. The plot is set during the reigns of the Assyrian kings Sennacherib (704–681 BC) and his son Esarhaddon (680–669 BC). The main character is Ahiqar, who serves these kings as their advisor.

Ahiqar has no sons, so he raises his nephew Nadin as his apprentice. Ahiqar serves Sennacherib and his son Esarhaddon well, but during the latter's reign Nadin betrayed his uncle and spread lies about him so that the king sentenced him to death. Fortunately for Ahiqar, the officer sent to execute him owed the sage his life. Thus, Ahiqar devised a plan and they kill another person and burn his body and pass the corpse off as that of Ahiqar, who then escapes and seeks refuge away from the king. After some time passes, the Egyptians approach Esarhaddon for help planning a major building project, and the king expresses regret about the loss of Ahiqar. The general then admits to the king that Ahiqar was still alive and thus the sage was restored to the court.

On this background, the composition shifts to instructions that the restored Ahiqar gives to his nephew Nadin. In this teaching of an older figure to a younger one, in this case an uncle to a nephew, and in the didactic form of the material, we see similarities to the wisdom traditions of both Israel and

31. Goedicke, *Report*, 58.
32. Lindenberger, *Aramaic Proverbs*; Greenfield, "Wisdom of Ahiqar."
33. According to Parker ("Literatures of Canaan," 2400), Aramaic speakers who emigrated to Egypt took it with them.

Egypt. In addition, a number of Ahiqar's admonitions to Nadin bear similarity to what we find in Proverbs, most notably saying 3, "Spare not your son from the rod; otherwise, can you save him [from wickedness]?" with which we can compare Prov. 23:13–14: "Don't withhold discipline from young people. If you strike them with a rod, they will not die. Strike them with a rod, and you will extricate their lives from Sheol."

What Is the Relationship between Biblical and Ancient Near Eastern Wisdom?

In our above survey of ancient Near Eastern texts, we have discussed compositions in Sumerian, Akkadian, Egyptian, and Aramaic that bear resemblances to biblical books that teach about wisdom. As we have gathered these texts, we have hinted at resemblances. In this section, we summarize these similarities of form and content in regard to specific books, focusing on the core three texts: Proverbs, Job, and Ecclesiastes.

Proverbs

The connection between the book of Proverbs and the instructional or didactic literature is strong in both form and content.

In terms of form, the proverb, which is the staple particularly of the second part of the book of Proverbs (chaps. 10–31), is common in early Sumerian, Akkadian, Aramaic, and especially Egyptian literature. On the level of the whole book, probably the closest parallel is with the instructional literature of Egypt. As mentioned above, we have about a couple dozen texts that stretch from the Old Kingdom period down to the Ptolomaic period that have similarities with the book of Proverbs. The best-known example and probably the instructional text that has the most similarity to Proverbs in terms of form and content is the Instruction of Amenemope. Many believe it originates in the thirteenth century BC, centuries before Solomon, the purported author of (parts of) the book of Proverbs.

In terms of form, Amenemope opens with a prologue that, like the prologue of Proverbs (1:1–7), provides information about the speaker (Amenemope, a functionary in the Egyptian court) and his intended recipient (his son, Hor-em-maakher), and most importantly the prologue also states the purpose of the composition. As has long been noticed, there is a particularly striking formal relationship between Amenemope and a section of Proverbs called the "Sayings of the Wise" (22:17–24:34) in that the former has thirty chapters and the latter announces in its prologue:

Have I not written for you thirty[34] sayings
with advice and knowledge? (Prov. 22:20)

Amenemope also is a particularly good example of the common advice that
one hears in both Egypt and Israel. We do not have the contrast between the
wise and the fool that we see in Proverbs, but we have an analogous contrast
between the "silent person" and the "heated person." We also have frequent
exhortations to heed the advice of the speaker with the added incentive of
success that we often see in the book of Proverbs.

Just to highlight a few examples of the similarities between the advice of
Proverbs and of Amenemope, we cite the following similar pairs.

Pair 1

Beware of robbing a wretch. (Amenemope 4.4)[35]

Don't steal from the poor, because they are poor,
    and don't oppress the needy in the gate.
For Yahweh will accuse their accusers,
    and he will press the life out of those who oppress them. (Prov.
    22:22–23)

Pair 2

Better is poverty in the hand of the god,
Than wealth in the storehouse;
Better is bread with a happy heart
Than wealth with vexation. (Amenemope 9.5–9)

Getting wisdom is much better than gold,
    and getting understanding is to be preferred over silver. (Prov. 16:16)

It is better to be a poor person and walk blamelessly,
    than one with crooked paths and wealthy. (Prov. 28:6)

The saying of Amenemope compares not only formally with the better-than
statements from Proverbs but also with the values expressed, in that both the
Egyptian and the Israelite texts prize piety and happiness over wealth.

The following example illustrates that both Amenemope and Proverbs
disdain unjust and unfair business practices:

---

34. This involves a slight emendation, widely accepted, of the Hebrew *šilšôm* to *šəlōšîm*.
35. Translations of Amenemope are from M. Lichtheim in COS 1:116–22.

Pair 3

Do not remove the scales nor alter the weights
Nor diminish the fractions of the measure;
Do not desire a measure of the fields,
Nor neglect those of the treasury. (Amenemope 17.18–21)

Fraudulent scales are an abomination to Yahweh,
    but an accurate weight brings his favor. (Prov. 11:1)

As a reminder, we cite examples of the formal and topical similarities between Proverbs and Amenemope to illustrate the similarities found between Israelite and Egyptian wisdom and also other ancient Near Eastern wisdom traditions.[36] Little doubt exists that the Israelite sages who produced proverbs benefitted from their knowledge of the wisdom of the broader ancient Near East.

Job

In the case of Job, we have, as described above, a number of Mesopotamian and Egyptian texts that grapple with the issue of undeserved suffering. Of course, this issue is not unique to Israel or to the ancient Near East for that matter. Indeed, it is not restricted to ancient people, since even today people continue to struggle with the question of why they experience pain in life, as shown by the large number of books on the topic even today.

Undeserved suffering is thus a human question, not an Israelite or ancient Near Eastern question. Thus, unlike Proverbs, we cannot be certain that the anonymous author(s) of Job had any knowledge of the ancient Near Eastern texts that we discussed above. At best, perhaps the "Babylonian Theodicy" suggested the format of a discussion or debate as a way to handle the issue, but not even this is certain.

If we are correct in our interpretation (see chap. 3), then the book of Job differs more from its ancient Near Eastern counterparts than is usually appreciated. We have argued that Job is not fundamentally about suffering at all. Suffering is the question that wisdom must address. Thus, Job is a debate about the nature and origin of wisdom. We have nothing like this in ancient Near Eastern literature.

Ecclesiastes

The form of Ecclesiastes looks very similar to the genre of Akkadian fictional autobiography described above, particularly the fourth subgenre, which

---

36. For a full survey, see Longman, "Proverbs."

ends with instructions based on the life experience of the speakers. More specifically, Ecclesiastes, as we described above (chap. 2), contains two voices, not just one. Qohelet is the speaker in the body of the book (1:12–12:7), and his words are framed by that of a second unnamed wise man who reflects on Qohelet's speech as he teaches his son about life "under the sun" (1:1–11; 12:8–14).

Qohelet's speech is the one that follows the pattern of the fictional Akkadian autobiographies in that it has three parts:

First-person introduction ("I, Qohelet, have been king over Israel in Jerusalem" 1:12),

followed by his first-person account of his question from the meaning of life (1:13–6:9),

after which he offers wise advice based on his sad experience (6:10–12:7).

Thus, Ecclesiastes shares formal similarities with certain ancient Near Eastern texts, and it would not be at all surprising, though certainly not provable, that the author of Qohelet's speech knew this genre.

In terms of content, however, these Akkadian texts really are nothing like Qohelet's rather depressing speech. That said, the attitude he expresses is not at all unprecedented in the ancient Near East. It is not uncommon for commentaries to turn to the Gilgamesh Epic for a like-minded thinker.

Above we described the Gilgamesh Epic as a journey for wisdom. In the process of the search, Gilgamesh stops at an inn and tells the proprietor his hope to find everlasting life, to which she responds with a skeptical attitude that sounds similar to Qohelet's thinking:

> Gilgamesh, whither rovest thou?
> The life thou pursuest thou shalt not find.
> When the gods created mankind they set aside,
> Life in their own hands retaining.
> Thou, Gilgamesh, let full be thy belly,
> Make thou merry by day and by night.
> Of each day make thou a feast of rejoicing,
> Day and night dance thou and play!
> Let thy garments be sparkling fresh,
> Thy head be washed; bathe thou in water.
> Pay heed to the little one that holds onto thy hand,

Let thy spouse delight in thy bosom!
For this is the task of [mankind]! (tablet X)[37]

However, the similar attitude tells us nothing about whether the author of Ecclesiastes has any knowledge of the Gilgamesh Epic. Indeed, such a skeptical attitude can be found in any age, including our own.[38]

Is Biblical Wisdom Particular to Israel or Is It Universal?

Our survey of ancient Near Eastern wisdom and its comparison with the three core wisdom texts of the OT all lead up to the question of whether the similarities and openness to foreign wisdom is unique to this part of the canon. Is biblical wisdom universal or particular? And is wisdom literature unique in this regard in relationship to other portions of the OT?

In terms of form, the answer to the second question is negative. Ancient Near Eastern literature shares interesting formal connections with all genres of biblical literature.[39]

However, there does seem to be a special openness among Israel's sages to learn from the wisdom of the surrounding foreign nations. They gained insight from the wisdom thinkers of Egypt in particular, but also other nations. They appreciated their insights. Otherwise how can one make sense of the appraisal of Solomon's wisdom in the book of Kings?

God gave Solomon wisdom and very great insight, and a breadth of understanding as measureless as the sand on the seashore. Solomon's wisdom was greater than the wisdom of all the people of the East, and greater than all the wisdom of Egypt. (1 Kings 4:29–30)

As we mentioned earlier, his statement works as a compliment only if the writer believes that Egyptian wisdom is profound. One cannot even imagine a comparable statement about an Israelite prophet ("Elijah was a wonderful

---

37. E. A. Speiser in *ANET* 90.

38. This throws doubt on attempts to date the book by finding similar attitudes. While it is almost certain that Ecclesiastes was written in the postexilic period, it is a weak argument that the book is more specifically to be situated in the Hellenistic period, which is proposed by Perdue, "Book of Qohelet," 103–16. Samet ("Religious Redaction in Qohelet") refers to a number of lesser-known literary texts that share Qohelet's attitude toward life and what she sees as later conservative redactions of that attitude.

39. See Sparks, *Ancient Texts*. Of course there are similarities and differences, but the point is that ancient Near Eastern literature evidences historical literature, law, and even prophecy from Mari and the neo-Assyrian period.

prophet, even better than the prophets of Baal"; for the Deuteronomist's assessment of the prophets of Baal in relationship to Elijah, see 1 Kings 18).

One cannot doubt that the faithful in Israel had a different attitude toward foreign wisdom than toward other elements of their culture. This awareness leads some scholars to suggest that Israel's wisdom is universal and not particular. A recent example comes from William Brown, rightly regarded as one of the best interpreters of biblical wisdom:

> Ancient Israel's sages had no qualms incorporating the wisdom of other cultures. Biblical wisdom seeks the common good along with the common God. Wisdom's international, indeed universal appeal constitutes its canonical uniqueness. The Bible's wisdom corpus is the open door in an otherwise closed canon.[40]

One can understand where Brown is coming from in this statement, but is this the whole story? Would the Israelite sages have embraced their Egyptian, Babylonian, Assyrian, and Aramean counterparts with open arms as collaborators in the search for truth ("the common good along with the common God")? In my opinion, absolutely not.

Let's begin with the obvious. We have seen that the central theme of wisdom repeated over and over again with slight variations and taught in a multitude of ways is "the fear of the Lord is the beginning of wisdom." This is the fundamental lesson of Proverbs, Job, Ecclesiastes, the wisdom psalms, and Deuteronomy.

The fear of the Lord is the *beginning* of wisdom. Whether beginning is taken temporally or foundationally, the clear point is that unless one fears the Lord, there is no wisdom. And it is the Lord, Yahweh, Israel's deity, not the "common God," who is to be feared.

There is, accordingly, no way that the Israelite sages who produced Proverbs, Job, and Ecclesiastes would think that ancient Near Eastern wisdom teachers were wise in the most important sense of the word. After all, the latter are ignorant of the most important and basic truth of the cosmos. But why would Israelite sages study their writings and incorporate some of their ideas into their own wisdom collections?

At this point a theologian might start talking about "common grace." Those who do not worship the true God are not stupid, totally immoral, or insane. They live in the world, and some observe and learn from their experiences. They see what works in the world and what is fair, and they

40. Brown, *Wisdom's Wonder*, 3.

write about it. The biblical sages know this and are open to learning from them, but they place their knowledge on its proper foundation, a proper relationship with Yahweh. People of faith today can learn an important lesson from Israel's interaction with pagan thought, and we will be turning to that subject in appendix 1.

10

WISDOM, COVENANT, AND LAW

S cholars commonly characterize wisdom as independent of the main theological themes of the rest of the OT and thus more universal in its appeal than other parts of Scripture. While there is some truth in this assertion, the universality of wisdom is often overplayed. As we have already seen, the fear of the Lord is at the center of wisdom, and that imparts a distinctive particularity in and of itself. Apparently, one cannot be truly wise without a proper relationship with Yahweh, Israel's sole and distinctive God.

The more universal appeal of wisdom is often located positively in the relationship between Israelite wisdom and the wisdom of the broader ancient Near East (see chap. 9), and negatively in the absence of references to redemptive history in favor of a creation theology (see chap. 8) as well as an absence of priestly theology. In addition, some scholars posit a distance from the important concept of the covenant and the legal component within it. Brown, for instance, asserts that "whether apart or together, the wisdom books cannot be shoehorned into Israel's . . . covenantal traditions."[1] The present chapter will explore the relationship between wisdom, covenant, and law in order to test this assertion.

1. Brown, *Wisdom's Wonder*, 3.

Covenant in the Old Testament

Covenant is one of the most pervasive topics in the OT and has been the subject of extensive scholarly discussion and debate.[2] We serve our purposes, however, by presenting an overall description of the nature of covenant and its scope in the OT rather than delving into the details of those debates.

While the covenant concept cannot be limited to the occurrence of the word "covenant" (an important point, as we will see for our study of covenant and Proverbs), we begin by pointing to the story of Noah as the first place where we encounter the word (*bǝrît* in Hebrew). God announces that he will establish a covenant with Noah in Gen. 6:18 and does so after the flood (9:8–17). Noah is the representative not only of his family and future descendants but also of "every living creature on earth" (9:10). In this covenant, God promises stability in the creation and points to the rainbow as the sign of the covenant. The sign is a symbol that represents the covenant and reminds the covenant partners of the terms and obligations of the relationship. The rainbow is an appropriate sign for this covenant not only because a rainbow comes out after rain but also because the Hebrew word (*qešet*) is used for bow as a weapon. Thus, God hangs up his bow after waging war against his human creatures.

A close reading of Gen. 9 highlights some intertextual echoes with the creation story (blessing [9:1], command to "be fruitful and multiply" [9:1, 7], image of God [9:6]). Furthermore, as we mentioned, the heart of the Noachian covenant assures the stability of the creation order that had been violently disrupted by the flood. Genesis 9 thus provides a re-creation narrative that puts back into place the creation order established in Gen. 1–2. In addition, some scholars argue that the relationship between God and Adam and Eve has all the earmarks of a covenant (most importantly a law supported by sanctions) and thus, even though the word *bǝrît* is not found in Gen. 1–2, the idea is. If so, then the Noachian covenant ought to be thought of as a re-creation covenant after the Adamic covenant, the original creation covenant.[3] A clear decision on this question is not necessary for our purposes.

After the Noachian covenant, God makes the next explicit covenant in the Bible with Abraham. The word *bǝrît* occurs for the first time in the Abraham narrative at Gen. 15:18 and then is pervasive in Gen. 17 (see vv. 2, 4, 7, 9, 10, 11, 13, 14, 19, 21). These chapters describe two moments in Abraham's life when he finds himself doubting God's intention or ability to fulfill the promises made to him in Gen. 12:1–3:

2. For an excellent summary and bibliography up to the date of publication (2003), see Williamson, "Covenant."
3. Beeke, "Christ, the Second Adam."

The LORD had said to Abram, "Go from your country, your people and your father's household to the land I will show you.

> "I will make you into a great nation,
>   and I will bless you;
> I will make your name great,
>   and you will be a blessing.
> I will bless those who bless you,
>   and whoever curses you I will curse;
> and all peoples on earth
>   will be blessed through you."

The crises of Gen. 15 and 17 arise because Abraham and Sarah have been unable to have children, and if they cannot have a child, then there will be no future great nation that God will bless and use as a blessing to the world. God responds to Abraham's doubts by coming and reaffirming his intention to fulfill the promises given in Gen. 12:1–3.

Thus, the covenant with Abraham is often characterized as a covenant of promise, and circumcision is the sign of this arrangement (Gen. 17:9–14).[4] While some want to say that God's arrangement with Abraham is only formalized as a covenant beginning with Gen. 15, it is likely better to think that the covenant was established at Gen. 12 and that Gen. 15 and 17 are better viewed as renewals of an already established covenant. In this covenant again we see a connection between obligation ("Go from your country") and reward ("I will make you into a great nation").

There is no missing the relationship between law, on the one hand, and reward and punishment, on the other, in the next covenant that is sometimes called the Mosaic covenant or the Sinai covenant. We read the account of the establishment of this covenant in Exod. 19–24. In this covenant, God gives Israel the law, Ten Commandments, and case law, which are sanctioned by penalties if not observed. The sign of the Mosaic covenant is the Sabbath (Exod. 31:12–18). Below we will analyze the structure of the book of Deuteronomy, which is a renewal of the Sinai covenant just before the death of Moses, and again see the connection between law and reward and punishment. Deuteronomy is the first of a number of the renewals of the Mosaic covenant found in later Israelite history (see Josh. 24; 1 Sam. 12; Neh. 9–10).

The final OT covenant is the one God made with David that establishes a dynasty of kings (2 Sam. 7; 1 Chron. 17). At the beginning of 2 Sam. 7 David expresses his desire to build God a "house" (temple; Heb. *bayit*). After all, he

---

4. See Robertson, *Christ of the Covenants*, 127–46.

has a nice cedar house, so why should God's dwelling continue to be a tent? God, however, does not want David to build him a house, but rather God will build a "house" (dynasty; Heb. *bayit*) for David. In other words, God tells David that his descendants will succeed him on the throne "forever" (2 Sam. 7:16), though there is a note of conditionality in God's statement that "when he [the royal Davidic descendant] does wrong, I will punish him with a rod wielded by men, with floggings inflicted by human hands" (2 Sam. 7:14). Unlike the earlier covenants, there is no sign mentioned in connection with the Davidic covenant.

The development of OT covenants may thus be summarized in the following way:

Name	Reference	Focus	Sign
Adamic (?)	Gen. 1–2	creation	none
Noachian	Gen. 9	re-creation	rainbow
Abrahamic	Gen. 12:1–3 (renewals: chaps. 15 and 17)	promise	circumcision
Mosaic	Exod. 19–24 (renewals: Deut.; Josh. 24; 1 Sam. 12; Neh. 9–10)	law	Sabbath law
Davidic	2 Sam. 7 (1 Chron. 17)	kingship	none

These are the five covenants of the OT, but before the end of the OT time period, Jeremiah speaks of a future new covenant. Most of Jeremiah's oracles are announcements of the future punishment on Judah, but Jer. 30–33 is a collection of salvation oracles that look beyond the judgment to restoration. At the heart of this so-called Book of Comfort (or Consolation) stands the announcement of a future new covenant:

> "The days are coming," declares the LORD,
>   "when I will make a new covenant
> with the people of Israel
>   and with the people of Judah.
> It will not be like the covenant
>   I made with their ancestors
> when I took them by the hand
>   to lead them out of Egypt,
> because they broke my covenant,
>   though I was a husband to them,"
>   declares the LORD.
> "This is the covenant I will make with the people of Israel
>   after that time," declares the LORD.
> "I will put my law in their minds
>   and write it on their hearts.

I will be their God,
and they will be my people.
No longer will they teach their neighbor,
or say to one another, 'Know the LORD,'
because they will all know me,
from the least of them to the greatest,"
declares the LORD.
"For I will forgive their wickedness
and will remember their sins no more." (Jer. 31:31–34)

Again our purpose, which is simply to survey the development and general nature of the covenant idea in the Hebrew, does not permit us to go into great detail or discuss differences of opinion concerning the new covenant. However, Jeremiah describes this new covenant as different from the old covenant (particularly the Mosaic covenant), which the people had broken. This future new covenant will be more intense, more intimate, more internal, and more immediate than the old covenant.

The NT understands that Jesus is the one who initiates the new covenant. Jesus announces this at his last supper ("this cup is the new covenant in my blood, which is poured out for you," Luke 22:20). The author of Hebrews cites Jeremiah's new covenant oracle twice to make this point clear (Heb. 8:7–13; 10).

It is not that the new covenant replaces the old covenant, but rather the new covenant fulfills the purposes of the old covenants. Jesus is, after all, the Messiah (anointed king) who fulfills the promise that David would have a descendant who would rule as king forever. Jesus is the perfect keeper of the law and also the one who bore its penalty on our behalf. He is the ultimate seed of Abraham (Gal. 3:16). Christ's relationship to the Noachian covenant is not as clear as these others. However, if we do think of the Noachian covenant as a re-creation covenant in connection with the creation covenant of Adam, then perhaps we are to see the connection in the NT language of Jesus as the "second Adam" (e.g., Rom. 5:12–21).

Covenant and Treaty

Our survey has followed the development of covenant in the OT and into the NT as it relates to the relationship between God and his people. The word *bərît* is also used in regard to the formalization between two different groups of humans. In such contexts, the Hebrew word is often translated "treaty" (e.g., Gen. 21:27, 32; 26:28). Recognizing this, we come to realize that the covenant between God and his people is more specifically described as a treaty.

This insight has been highlighted by studies over the past three quarters of a century that have noted the parallels between certain biblical covenantal texts and ancient Near Eastern treaties.[5] Such study has focused on, but not been limited to, the book of Deuteronomy, which shares a similar structure with ancient Near Eastern treaties. We know the latter from two groups of treaties that are known today: Hittite treaties from the mid-second millennium BC and neo-Assyrian treaties from the seventh century BC. Scholars have debated about which of these two corpora Deuteronomy is closest to because the conclusion would support differing views over when the biblical book was composed, but again our interest is not in such matters. These ancient treaties, though, can be divided into two types: parity treaties between states that are nearly equal in power and vassal treaties in which a powerful state (a sovereign) enters into relationship with a weaker state (a vassal). The biblical covenants between God (the sovereign) and his people (the vassal) naturally take the form of a vassal treaty. For our purpose, we note that ancient Near Eastern vassal treaties, whether early or late, consistently display five parts:

Introduction of the Parties (typically the kings of the sovereign and the vassal nations)

Historical Prologue (the history of the relationship between the two parties up to the present day)

Law (obligations imposed by the sovereign on the vassal)

Rewards and Punishments (consequences for obedience or disobedience to the law)

Witnesses (as a legal document witnesses were necessary; in the ancient Near Eastern treaties, the witnesses were the deities of both nations)

With this background, we turn to the book of Deuteronomy as our example and note a similar structure:

Introduction (1:1–5)

Historical Review (1:9–3:27)

Law (4–26)

Rewards and Punishments (27–28)

Witnesses (30:19–20)

5. For a magisterial study, see Kitchen and Lawrence, *Treaty, Law and Covenant*.

The book of Deuteronomy is set at the end of Moses's life, after he had led Israel out of Egypt and through the wilderness for forty years. Due to his own rebellion (Num. 20:1–13), Moses was not allowed to enter the promised land. Thus, before the Israelites—the second generation born in the wilderness— entered the land, he gave them a last sermon on the plains of Moab, after which he would ascend Mount Nebo to die.

The purpose of the sermon was to remind them of their relationship with God, established at Mount Sinai, where they entered into a covenant/treaty with God and committed themselves to obey the law, which was given on that occasion (Exod. 19–24). Their parents' generation had betrayed that commitment, and now Moses led the next generation in a covenant/treaty renewal ritual.

For our purpose, what is of interest is the relationship between covenant and law and between law and the rewards and punishments, as these will bear on our understanding of the relationship between wisdom and law and covenant.

Law is consistently embedded in a covenant context in the Bible. Law follows historical prologue, which emphasizes all the wonderful acts that the sovereign accomplished on behalf of the vassal. In the ancient Near Eastern treaties, the historical prologue was likely just so much political propaganda, but in the Bible God has graciously acted on behalf of his people, most notably by freeing them from their Egyptian bondage. In the law God places obligation on Israel, the vassal, based on the gracious deliverance he provided in the past. And from the law flows the rewards and punishments dependent on the vassal's obedience or disobedience.

Wisdom and Law

Before considering the possibility that wisdom finds a place within the covenantal arrangement of the relationship between God and humans in the Bible, we first reflect on the relationship of wisdom and law. The law of the OT expresses God's will for how his people who love him should live. The Ten Commandments, of course, are the foundation of the law of God, which regulates how his people should relate to him and to other people. "You shall have no other gods before me" (Exod. 20:3), the first commandment, and "you shall not murder" (Exod. 20:13), the sixth commandment, are well-known examples.

When we turn to the book of Proverbs, we again have material that expresses God's will for how his people who love him should live. Consider the following:

Stay away from a foolish person,
>   for you will not know knowledgeable lips. (14:7)

Commit your acts to Yahweh,
>   and your plans will be established. (16:3)

Listen to advice and receive discipline
>   so you might grow wise in your future days. (19:20)

These proverbs begin with an imperative, instructing, even commanding, the listener to adopt a certain attitude or behavior, similar to the intention of the law. Here we begin to see a connection between wisdom and law; they are not foreign entities but serve similar purposes.

However, while there are a number of proverbs that begin with an imperative, many are simply observations. Can they have a relationship to law as well? Here are some examples:

Wine is a mocker; strong drink a carouser.
>   Those it leads astray will not become wise.
The dread of a king growls like a lion;
>   those who infuriate him lose their lives.
The glory of a person is to back away from an accusation,
>   but every stupid person lets it break out.
During winter, the lazy do not plow;
>   at harvest, they will ask, but nothing! (20:1–4)

While these observations are not explicit commands, they certainly and very clearly imply certain behaviors and attitudes. The first proverb discourages drunkenness, the second warns against angering the king, the third advises to hold back on accusations, and the final proverb urges hard work.

Wisdom, at least proverbial wisdom, has overlapping interests and purposes with law. They both encourage certain behaviors and attitudes and discourage or prohibit other attitudes. We should not fail to see that there are differences as well.

The biblical law comes directly from God. In Exodus the Ten Commandments are introduced with "and God spoke all these words" (20:1). The first case laws that follow the Ten Commandments (20:22–26) also come directly from God to Moses, who relates them to the people ("Then the Lord said to Moses," 20:22), and God continues the case laws by telling Moses, "These are the laws you are to set before them" (21:1; with the laws given in 21:2–23:19).

In the book of Proverbs wisdom comes most often from the father to his son, as is seen particularly in the first part of the book (chaps. 1–9) with the repeated address to "my son" (beginning at 1:8). It is true that the father is not the only one to address the young men who are the recipients of the instruction. Woman Wisdom, who at least represents by way of personification God's wisdom if not God himself (see chap. 1), also imparts instruction to the young men. Still, the instruction often comes from a human father to a son, and this provides a difference with biblical law.

However, one must question whether this is much of a difference in the final analysis. The father is not God, of course, but clearly presents himself as God's proxy. While the father learns wisdom that he imparts to his son through experience, observation, learning from mistakes, and tradition, ultimately Proverbs (and wisdom generally) asserts that all true wisdom derives from God himself (see chap. 7).

For this reason, biblical legal terms can be used to refer to the teaching of the father. The father begins his lengthy speech exhorting the son to pay attention to his teaching with the following:

> My son, if you grasp my speech
>   and store up my *commands* within you,
> bending your ear toward wisdom,
>   extending your heart toward competence. (2:1–2)

Or consider the very next speech, which begins:

> My son, don't forget my *instruction*,
>   and let your heart protect my *commands*. (3:1)

The words "command" (*miṣwâ*) and "instruction" (*tôrâ*) are associated with the legal tradition and are found throughout the book of Proverbs.[6]

There is yet another difference between wisdom and law that we need to take into account. As we described proverbial wisdom earlier, we noted that proverbs are "not always true," or more positively, proverbs are always true when applied to the right situation. One cannot both "not answer" (26:4) and "answer" (26:5) at the same time, so both proverbs cannot always be true. It depends on the fool and the situation. That is not the case with law. "You shall not commit adultery" (Exod. 20:14) is always true no matter what the circumstance.

---

6. For *miṣwâ*, see also 4:4; 6:20, 23; 7:1, 2; 13:13; 19:16. For *tôrâ*, see also 1:8; 6:20, 23; 7:2; 13:14; 28:4, 7, 9; 29:18; 31:26.

We have again found a trait that shows that law and wisdom are two different things; we do not deny that. However, our point is that they are closely related—maybe not siblings, but close cousins. After all, when the situation is "right" for a proverb, then it becomes "law" for that situation. If you do not answer a fool when you should have answered a fool, then you fall short of what God wants for that situation.[7]

Law and wisdom are closely tied in yet another way. Obeying the law and living according to wisdom leads to reward, and disobedience to law leads to punishment. This point brings us to consider the relationship between wisdom and covenant.

Wisdom as Covenantal

We begin with the often-recognized fact that covenant (bərît) is not a pervasive or even common word found in wisdom literature, though we have seen it is a significant one in other biblical literature. Covenant (bərît) occurs only one time in Proverbs, twice in Job, and never in Ecclesiastes.

In Proverbs the word occurs in reference to the strange, foreign woman who tempts men into an illicit relationship. The father urges his son to turn to wisdom, who will extricate "you [the son] from the strange woman, from the foreign woman with her flattering speech, abandoning the intimate relationship of her youth, forgetting the covenant [bərît] of her God" (Prov. 2:16–17).[8] Proverbs also refers to qualities that are closely connected to the covenant in particular "covenant love and faithfulness" (ḥesed and 'emet). An example is found in Prov. 3, where the father instructs the son not to let "covenant love and faithfulness abandon you; bind them on your neck; write them on the tablet of your heart" (3:3; see also 14:22; 16:6; 20:28).[9]

Job explicitly mentions covenant twice. The first occurrence is found in Eliphaz's opening speech when he refers to the blessed state of one whom God reproves or disciplines. If Job embraces God's discipline, then he says to him, "You will have an alliance [bərît] with the stones of the field, and the wild animals

7. Estes ("Wisdom and Biblical Theology," 855) notes that "even a casual reading of the wisdom books reveals that the actions and attitudes that are condemned as folly and wickedness are the same kind as those that are prohibited in the law and denounced by the prophets." See also Overland, "Did the Sage Draw from the Shema?"

8. Kidner (Proverbs, 62) argues that this is a reference to the Sinai covenant, while Hugenberger (Marriage as a Covenant) sees a connection with Mal. 2:14 and the marriage covenant.

9. As Grant ("'When the Friendship of God Was upon My Tent,'" 330) points out, "the collocation of the language of covenant alongside other word groups that pervade the OT/HB . . . is another indication of the significance of the covenant concept in the mentality of the biblical authors."

of the field will make peace with you" (5:23). The word I have translated "alliance" could have been translated "covenant" or "treaty," but the reference does not appear to be one of the historical covenants mentioned above (though the Noachian would be closest), but rather a way to refer to the fact that the happily disciplined person will live at harmony with creation. The second occurrence of *bǝrît* is found in Job 31:1, where, in the context of his final protest of innocence, Job claims that he "cut a covenant with my eyes; so how could I leer at a virgin?" Again, this reference does not appear to be to one of the historical covenants but an agreement that he made with himself not to lust after women.

However, the word "covenant" does not have to be present for the concept to be relevant. Indeed, in our survey above we noted that neither Gen. 12:1–3 nor 2 Sam. 7 use the term "covenant," though the term is found in later reflections on the relationship between Abraham and David respectively (Gen. 15 and 17; Pss. 89 and 132). Thus, we need to look beyond the word to see if wisdom connects to covenant in other ways.

In noting the connection of law/wisdom with covenant, we follow in the footsteps of Meredith Kline, who argued that the whole of Scripture, all its parts, relate to the covenant between God and his people. In regard to wisdom he states, "The central thesis of the wisdom books is that wisdom begins with the fear of Yahweh, which is to say that the way of wisdom is the way of the covenant."[10] By noting a connection between "fear of the Lord" in wisdom and covenant, Kline makes a connection with not only proverbial wisdom but also the wisdom of Job and Ecclesiastes, where we have seen that the "fear of the Lord" is also the central concept.[11]

He further states, in conformity with our comments in the previous section, "One way it [wisdom] performs this [the explication of the covenant] is by translating the covenant stipulations into maxims and instructions regulative of conduct in different areas of life and under its varying conditions. But the wisdom books are equally concerned with the outworking of the covenant sanctions in human experience."[12]

The close relationship between law and wisdom in connection to covenant may be seen in the book of Deuteronomy, which we have already identified as having the same structure as a covenant/treaty renewal text. In Deut. 4:5–8 Moses speaks:

> See, I have taught you decrees and laws as the LORD my God commanded me, so that you may follow them in the land you are entering to take possession of

10. Kline, *Structure of Biblical Authority*, 64.
11. Also Grant, "Wisdom and Covenant."
12. Kline, *Structure of Biblical Authority*, 65.

it. Observe them carefully, for this will show your wisdom and understanding to the nations, who will hear about all these decrees and say, "Surely this great nation is a wise and understanding people." What other nation is so great as to have their gods near them the way the LORD our God is near us whenever we pray to him? And what other nation is so great as to have such righteous decrees and laws as this body of laws I am setting before you today?

God calls on Israel to obey his law, and in their obedience they will demonstrate their wisdom to the world (see treatment of this passage in chap. 4).

According to the treaty form of the covenant, Israel's obedience to the law will lead to the blessing that is described in Deut. 27 and 28 and thus earn the attention and holy envy of the surrounding nations. That envy will be holy because it will lead the surrounding nations to recognize that a righteous God is with Israel.

In the OT, law is embedded in a covenant/treaty context, as are the rewards and punishments that flow from obedience or disobedience. Proverbial wisdom is like law in that it also can be considered stipulations of the covenant/treaty that also has sanctions.

Job, Lament, and Covenant

While our study of law, covenant, and wisdom has focused on Proverbs, Jamie Grant has argued persuasively that the very dynamic of the book of Job depends on a kind of covenant consciousness. In the first place, the "fear of the Lord" is prominent in the book, which is inherently covenantal (Deut. 10:12–13).[13]

Covenant/treaty, as we have seen above, notes a connection between obedience to law and blessing and disobedience and curse, and the same is true, as explicated above, about the relationship between wisdom and folly and reward and punishment. Job's laments are fueled by the realization that though he is righteous and wise, he suffers. Thus, the ground of Job's lament is rooted in a covenantal understanding of Job's relationship with God.[14] Grant identifies the center of Job's lament in Job's belief that the covenantal God who has promised to be with his people has withdrawn that presence, and thus he sadly remembers the now-gone past when "friendship with God was over my tent; when Shaddai was still with me" (Job 29:4–5).

13. As developed in chap. 3.
14. Grant makes a helpful distinction between the historical covenants and the concept of covenant ("'When the Friendship of God Was upon My Tent,'" 337).

Conclusion

We must grant that the relationship between wisdom and law and covenant is not a major theme in the canonical books. There are rare exceptions, such as the passage in Deut. 4 cited above.

That acknowledged, this chapter has argued that there is an implicit connection between wisdom and law and covenant that expresses itself in a number of subtle ways. In conclusion, we will add one more argued by Van Leeuwen, who points to the way the book of Proverbs refers to God consistently by his particular covenant name, Yahweh ("the Lord"), rather than by a more generic term like ʾĕlōhîm (God). Thus he in our opinion rightly concludes:

> The editors of Proverbs are very consistent in avoiding the suggestion that the God of the sages is any other than Israel's covenant God, Yahweh. . . . Proverbs has profound similarities to ancient Near Eastern wisdom. Perhaps the consistent use of "Yahweh" was meant to forestall the idea that the God of Proverbs was not Israel's covenant God.[15]

15. Van Leeuwen, "Proverbs," 33, quoted in Grant, "Wisdom and Covenant: Revisiting Zimmerli," 107.

PART **4**

FURTHER
REFINING OUR
UNDERSTANDING
OF WISDOM

I n the first two parts of this book, we explored wisdom by examining a
number of biblical texts in which wisdom plays a leading role. From this
study we attempted to gain an understanding of wisdom. We saw that
wisdom was more than a skill of living (the practical level). It also encouraged righteous behavior (the ethical level) and most fundamentally a right
relationship with God characterized by fear (the theological level).

We then turned our attention to the question of how Israelite wisdom fit
into the rest of the canon, as well as how it related to wisdom in the broader
ancient Near East. We concluded that, while wisdom had a distinctive character compared to other parts of the OT, it certainly was not an outlier but
related well with law, covenant, and redemptive history, as well as having a
special relationship with creation theology. In terms of the broader ancient

Near East, while Israelite wisdom had a more comfortable relationship with its counterparts in neighboring cultures, we saw that, in the final analysis, OT wisdom was particular to Israel, not cosmopolitan or universal. After all, "the fear of Yahweh is the beginning of wisdom" (Prov. 9:10). Nothing could be more particular than this conception of wisdom.

Before turning to postbiblical wisdom (in part 5), we want to first examine three topics, among the many we could have chosen, that have been controversial in recent years in the academy and the church. The first has to do with retribution. Does the book of Proverbs, does wisdom, promise too much? A surface reading might lead one—and indeed in the case of advocates of what has become known as the "prosperity gospel" has led people—to believe that if you are wise, you will be happy, wealthy, and healthy. Others read a book like Proverbs and think it is just unrealistic. In chapter 11 we will take up the question of retribution in wisdom. The second issue concerns the social setting of wisdom. Where was wisdom to be found in Israelite society? Was there a class of sages distinct from prophets, priests, government officials, or others? And were there schools that propagated wisdom ideas to students? Third, and finally, we look at the issue of gender in wisdom. Fathers teach sons in Proverbs and Ecclesiastes. The teaching of Proverbs in particular seems specifically addressed to young men, as it warns about consorting with promiscuous women and living in an attic rather than in a house with an irritating woman. How is a woman to read the book of Proverbs? On the other hand, Proverbs presents wisdom as a woman. Indeed, we have argued (chap. 1) that Woman Wisdom stands for God himself. Does such a striking image of God make up for the male-oriented teaching of the book?

11

THE CONSEQUENCES OF WISE AND FOOLISH BEHAVIOR

The Issue of Retribution Theology

Wisdom in the OT is often associated, for good reason, with the topic of retribution. As we will see below, Proverbs connects wisdom with reward. Wise behavior leads to wealth, health, longer life, good relationships, and other benefits. In a word, wisdom leads to life in the fullest sense. By contrast, foolish behavior leads to the opposite consequences, including poverty, sickness, and troubled relationships. In short, folly leads to death.

Job, however, casts a cloud of suspicion on this idea of retribution. As a wise and God-fearing man, Job seems the perfect candidate for blessing, and at first his life seems to confirm the strong connection between good behavior and good results. God, however, decides to test the motivations of Job's piety, and this good man suddenly experiences the most profound suffering, raising questions over the easy relationship between behavior and quality of life.

In the book of Ecclesiastes (see chap. 2), Qohelet comes to see that reward does not always accompany right behavior. He asserted that rather than blessing, the righteous often experienced injustice, rendering life meaningless.

This chapter explores the large topic of retribution in wisdom beginning with these three core books. Do they send mixed messages? What do they intend to teach their readers about reward and punishment?

Retribution in Proverbs

The book of Proverbs frequently draws a connection between wise behavior and reward and foolish behavior and punishment. While there are countless examples, here are a handful of relevant passages:

> Don't be wise in your own eyes.
>   Fear Yahweh and turn away from evil.
> This will bring health to your body
>   and refreshment to your bones.
> Honor Yahweh with your wealth,
>   and from the first of your produce.
> And your barns will be filled with plenty,
>   and your vats will burst with wine. (Prov. 3:7–10)

> The righteous person is delivered from distress,
>   but the wicked will take his place. (Prov. 11:8)

> Those who curse their father and their mother—
>   their lamp will be extinguished in the middle of the dark. (Prov. 20:20)

> Those who dig a pit will fall into it;
>   those who roll a stone will have it turn back on them. (Prov. 26:27)

These passages illustrate the pervasive teaching of the book of Proverbs that there is a connection between wise and righteous acts and good benefits and between foolish and wicked ones and negative consequences. Indeed, the last quoted proverb implies that the bad act will bring its own negative consequences on the perpetrator.[1]

---

1. The idea that foolish acts have the seed of their own negative consequences within them was highlighted by Koch (*Um das Prinzip der Vergeltung*), who argued for an "act-consequence" nexus in wisdom. Most scholars today believe that this view is too simple to explain the nature of proverbial thinking and prefer to speak of a "character-consequence relationship." Wisdom does not simply try to get people to act wisely but rather encourages behaviors that will transform character that leads to good results (Bostrom, *God of the Sages*, 91–92).

The Prosperity Gospel

The teaching of Proverbs often convinces people even today to believe that good behavior automatically leads to good results and leads some people to affirm what is popularly known as the "prosperity gospel." Many churches in the United States as well as globally teach the prosperity gospel today. Church historian Philip Jenkins has reported its popularity in the Global South, particularly Africa and South America.[2] To others who have tried to live wisely but have not experienced success in life, the book of Proverbs and its retribution theology lead to skepticism and rejection. Indeed, for most the idea that good behavior, even that described by the book of Proverbs, guarantees good results and bad behavior leads to negative consequences just does not ring true to life. Too many good people suffer, and many wicked people thrive. It all leads us to question what we are to make of this teaching found in biblical wisdom. Can wisdom, and in particular the book of Proverbs, really be used to support a strict retribution theology, which can contribute to a kind of prosperity gospel? Or to put it a little less strongly, can wisdom literature lead to the expectation of benefits for wise behavior and punishments for foolish behavior?

We will address these questions first by looking at the message of the book of Job and then also of Ecclesiastes. We begin here out of recognition that, while individual biblical books have their own integrity, the church recognizes that any individual book of the Bible is a component part of the Scripture as canon. This commitment to the Scripture as canon warrants reading any part within the context of the whole. In other words, here and throughout this present book, we engage in what has been called canonical interpretation.[3] Indeed, we believe that the books of Job and Ecclesiastes are particularly important to a canonical reading of Proverbs on the issue of retribution theology in order to prevent what we will come to see as an over-reading of Proverbs on the subject.

After looking at the contribution of Job and Ecclesiastes to the issue of retribution, we will then return to Proverbs in order to demonstrate that the idea that Proverbs guarantees reward and punishment is unfounded. That said, the nexus of wisdom and positive outcomes, and foolishness and negative ones, must have some meaning, so we will conclude the chapter with

2. Jenkins, *New Faces of Christianity*.
3. Childs is commonly recognized as the one who encouraged the interpreters of the church and academy to regain a canonical perspective in interpretation. Among his many works that forwarded canonical criticism is *Biblical Theology*. Throughout the 1980s many other interpreters, far too many to name, followed Childs's lead.

a consideration of that question along with a reflection on the question of retribution throughout the Bible, including the NT.

Retribution in Job

In chapter 3 we presented Job as a book about wisdom, and the following comments are informed by that interpretive approach. We observed that the main subject of the book is wisdom and its ultimate source in God. The author of Job in its final form created a thought experiment to explore the subject of wisdom. Job's suffering was the problem that required wisdom to diagnose and to resolve.

While the book does not purport to answer the question of why humans suffer, it nonetheless completely undermines belief in mechanical and absolute retribution theology. After all, the book of Job describes its main human character as blameless. He fears God, turns away from evil, and is called "innocent and virtuous" (1:1, 8; 2:3). He is wise, righteous, and godly. In addition, he is rich and has a happy and large family. Even so, in response to the Accuser's suspicion that Job only acts to get the benefits for himself, God allows him to remove the benefits, which include his wealth, his family, and also his health.

There is no need here to rehearse in any detail the debate that ensues, since we covered it sufficiently in chapter 3, except to remember that all the human participants without exception embraced a mechanical understanding of retribution theology. "If you sin, then you suffer; therefore, if you are suffering, then you are a sinner." Job differs only in knowing that he is innocent, though his retribution theology leads him to accuse God of injustice. The conclusion of the book of Job serves to repudiate this crude, naive way of thinking about retribution. To suppose that a person suffers because they are a sinner (or that they live well because they are wise, godly, and righteous) is not only wrong-minded but cruel.

Retribution in Ecclesiastes

As with Job, our reflection on retribution in Ecclesiastes follows the interpretation of that book presented in an earlier chapter (chap. 2). There we observed that the book contains two voices, that of Qohelet and that of a second wise man we referred to as the frame narrator.

Qohelet's ultimate conclusion was that life is meaningless, and one of the principle reasons he gave for that sad conclusion was the injustice that permeates the human experience. For the world to be just, according to Qohelet, retribution theology should work. After all, since death is the end of the story for humans, according to Qohelet, then for life to be fair, the wise person should enjoy the benefits of having wisdom in the here and now.

In the earlier chapter we interpreted two key texts in Qohelet's speech that express this sentiment, 7:15–18 and 8:10–14, as well as selections from chapter 9. Among these examples was the following, which clearly captures Qohelet's frustration at discovering a just world as he looked for meaning "under the sun":

> Then I turned and observed something else under the sun. That is, the race is not to the swift, the battle not to the mighty, nor is food for the wise, nor wealth to the clever, nor favor to the intelligent, but time and chance happen to all of them. Indeed, no one knows his time. Like fish that are entangled in an evil net and like birds caught in a snare, so people are ensnared in an evil time, when it suddenly falls on them. (9:11–12)

We can also observe his thinking in the following passage not cited in the earlier chapter:

> Furthermore I observed under the sun:
> The place of judgment—injustice was there!
> The place of righteousness—injustice was there!
>
> I said to myself, "God will judge the righteous and the unjust, for there is a time for every activity and for every deed too." I said to myself concerning the human race, "God tests them so that they may see that they are like animals." For the fate of human beings and the fate of animals are the same fate. One dies like the other. There is one breath for all. Human beings have no advantage over the animals, for everything is meaningless. All go to the same place. All come from the dust, and all return to the dust. Who knows whether the breath of humans goes up above and the breath of animals goes down to the depths of the earth? (3:16–21)

Qohelet here begins with a simple observation. As he looked at places where one might expect justice (the court perhaps), there was none to be found. Justice would acquit and reward the innocent and righteous and declare guilty and punish the wicked. But apparently Qohelet witnessed the opposite. Even so, one might reason, if there isn't human justice, perhaps we can count on divine justice. Qohelet thus quotes to himself what I would take was a theological truism of his day ("God will judge the righteous and the unjust, for there is a time for every activity and for every deed too," 3:17), that God would ultimately see that the righteous and the wicked get what is coming to them.

But, in a style of arguing typical of Qohelet, he ultimately undermines what at first might seem a hopeful thought. Qohelet's second utterance to himself conflicts with the first: "God tests them so that they may see that they are like animals." He then goes on to explain that humans are like animals in that they die, and, as one who does not have confidence in the afterlife, he must reckon that death brings the end of everything ("All come from the dust, and all return to the dust," 3:20). But here is the rub. If there is no justice in this life and there is no (certain) life after death, then where is justice to be found? Nowhere for sure. Thus, according to Qohelet, one cannot count on proper retribution in this life or the next.

That is Qohelet's perspective, but as we saw in chapter 2, Qohelet's voice is framed by a second wise man who is interacting with his son concerning Qohelet. Thus, the second wise man's opinion represents the perspective of the book. Qohelet does not think there is justice on earth or in heaven, but what does the frame narrator say about the retribution principle?

We again will not repeat our analysis of the frame narrator's speech (12:8–14) found in chapter 2. Our conclusion was that the frame narrator affirmed Qohelet's speech was true given the stated context. That is, he is right that the righteous/wise/godly are not always rewarded and the wicked/foolish/ungodly do not always suffer in this life ("under the sun"). Thus, those who presume that they will be rewarded for good behavior (the prosperity gospel) are much mistaken. That said, the frame narrator has a different perspective on divine judgment. Indeed, the very last thing he tells his son, and the final statement of the book, is "for God will bring every deed into judgment, including every hidden thing, whether good or evil" (12:14). Thus the conclusion of the book of Ecclesiastes is that, while retribution may not work out in this life, there is a future judgment.

Beyond a Superficial Understanding of Proverbs

Job and Ecclesiastes are clear in the message that retribution theology is wrong-minded and, when applied to a person who suffers, quite cruel. But now it is important to return to Proverbs and ask whether that book really teaches retribution theology as is popularly thought and, perhaps surprisingly, believed by some scholars who want to pit the message of Proverbs against that of Job and Ecclesiastes. Against this idea, we present two considerations. First, the better-than proverbs demonstrate that, in the mind of the sages who produced Proverbs, people sometimes or perhaps frequently have to choose between wisdom and wealth, and when such a situation arises, there is no doubt about which to choose. The second consideration will lead us back to the question of the proverb as a genre, where we will see that, as Bruce Waltke put it, proverbs don't make promises.[4]

Better-Than Proverbs

As the name suggests, better-than proverbs compare two things and assign them relative value. The first colon of the parallelism begins with "better" (*tôb*), and then the second colon begins with "than" (the comparative *min*). What is named in the second colon is not necessarily bad or undesirable, but the value of what is named in the first colon is so vastly superior that if a choice must be made between A and B, the wisdom teacher proclaims that a person should choose A. Here are some examples of better-than proverbs in the book of Proverbs:

> Better a little with fear of Yahweh
>   than great treasure and turmoil with it. (15:16)

> Better a little bit with righteousness
>   than a large yield without justice. (16:8)

> Better to be a humble spirit with the needy
>   than dividing plunder with the proud. (16:19)

> Better a dry crust with peace and quiet
>   than a house full of contentious feasting. (17:1)

> Better to be poor and walking in innocence
>   than have crooked lips and be a fool. (19:1)

Raymond Van Leeuwen identified these proverbs as indicative of the fact that the sages did not intend to make wealth an automatic and guaranteed consequence of wisdom, or poverty a consequence of folly.[5] After all, these proverbs clearly show that qualities like the fear of the Lord, innocence, peace and quiet, and humility are to be preferred over wealth. No doubt it is best to be wise and rich, but sometimes (maybe even often) one must make a choice between the two, and in those circumstances, wisdom should be chosen over money.

Proverbs Are Not Promises

One of the most tempting misuses of a proverb is to treat it as if it is making a promise. If one does X, then Y will be the result. A classic example is Prov. 22:6:

4. Waltke, "Does Proverbs Promise Too Much?"
5. Van Leeuwen, "Wealth and Poverty." For more indications within Proverbs that "seem to undermine the idea of a deed-consequence-nexus both from a sceptical or critical angle," see Loader, "Bipolarity of Sapiential Theology" (quotation on 366).

> Train up youths in their path;
>> then when they age, they will not depart from it.

My translation preserves the ambiguity of the Hebrew, where it is not immediately clear who "their" refers to in the first colon. The most immediate
antecedent is "youths," and the argument can be made that we should translate
"train up youths in their path" and understand this to be an admonition to find
out the natural bent of the child, the pedagogical approach that is most appropriate to the child's personality. Or, as is more likely since "path" is typically
associated with God's path, the wisdom teacher could be encouraging parents
to raise children in God's way. The latter gives rise to traditional interpretations
like that we find in the NIV: "Start children off on the way they should go."

However, whichever of these two interpretive directions we might choose, a
superficial reading treats this proverb as giving a promise. If someone does X
(raise a child in a certain way), then Y will be the result (as they grow older they
will not depart from it). It is a mistake, though, to treat the proverb as a type of
guarantee. That is not what proverbs do. Again, it is a genre issue. Proverbs are
not in the business of giving promises. Rather, they encourage people toward
attitudes and actions that will lead toward a desired goal, all other things being
equal. It is more likely that a child will grow up to be wise if their parents train
them in the Lord's way. But perhaps that child will come under the negative
influence of his or her peers (see, for instance, the advice given in 1:8–19).

Thus, again, we should not consider Proverbs as providing fodder for a
prosperity gospel. With their examples and statements showing that the wise
do not always prosper and the wicked do not always languish, Job and Ecclesiastes are not providing counterexamples to Proverbs but are instead offering
a corrective to a misreading of Proverbs.

Wisdom provides a realistic picture of life, though it can easily be miscon-
strued as has been from ancient times to modern. Psalm 73, a wisdom psalm,
is the testimony of a person who had misunderstood wisdom.

Coming to Terms with the Unfairness of Life (Ps. 73)

The composer of Ps. 73, a wisdom psalm, struggled with the issue of retribution. He recounts his anguish after he had found resolution. The movement
of the psalmist's thought bears resemblance to that of Job, but goes further.

The psalmist begins his poem reflecting his mood after his struggle: "Surely
God is good to Israel, to those who are pure in heart" (Ps. 73:1), but then he
plunges into the darkness of his past despair:

> But as for me, my feet had almost slipped;
> I had nearly lost my foothold.
> For I envied the arrogant
> when I saw the prosperity of the wicked. (73:2–3)

The next stanza describes the wicked rich as having no concerns, though they are proud and insulting toward God (73:4–12). The psalmist sums up his description by saying, "This is what the wicked are like—always free of care, they go on amassing wealth" (v. 12). Here the psalmist shares his sincere impressions of the rich, though it may be warped by his envy. To him, they seemed like they had no cares, though it may be that they are simply putting up a façade.

To the psalmist, however, the apparent ease of the wicked person's life contrasted with the difficulties that he, an innocent person, experienced:

> Surely in vain I have kept my heart pure
> and have washed my hands in innocence.
> All day long I have been afflicted,
> and every morning brings new punishments. (73:13–14)

Thus the psalmist shares his exasperation and frustration that the world did not work as his theology informed him it would. The wicked should suffer and the righteous should flourish, but he was experiencing the exact opposite of his expectations.

He confesses that at this point he was "senseless and ignorant; I was a brute beast before you" (73:22). However, his thinking experienced a radical transformation when he "entered the sanctuary of God" (73:17). The sanctuary was the holy place, likely the temple, where God made his presence manifest to his people. Here is an important similarity to Job's experience. Job's moment of transformation came when he had a more personal experience of God's presence ("My ear had received a report of you, but now my eyes have seen you," Job 42:5).

The psalmist's experience of God opened his eyes to the reality that stood behind the surface. Previously, he saw the wicked living a life of wealth and ease, but now he realized that their good life would not last. Rather, they were on "slippery ground" and would be suddenly destroyed. The psalmist also came to realize that he was the one who had the true riches, a vibrant relationship with God. "Yet I am always with you; you hold me by my right hand" (73:23). But when will this reversal of fortune happen?

> You guide me with your counsel,
>   and afterward you will take me into glory.
> Whom have I in heaven but you?
>   And earth has nothing I desire besides you.
> My flesh and my heart may fail,
>   but God is the strength of my heart
>   and my portion forever. (73:24–26)

Reading these verses in light of the fuller revelation of the afterlife that we have in the NT, many Christian readers have no doubt that these verses point to the heavenly realities. However, the Hebrew does not have to be read that way, and the vast majority of scholars would say that the psalmist did not intend his words to have that meaning and that his OT readers would not have understood him to refer to an afterlife.[6]

In the final analysis, we cannot be absolutely certain. However, while it is true that many biblical authors are not aware of the afterlife, and some even imply a disbelief in the possibility, in my opinion scholars are too quick to deny that some places in the OT provide glimpses of this teaching that are more fully developed in the NT. To read the psalmist as simply saying that sometime in the indeterminate future in this life he can be assured that his lot and the lot of the wealthy wicked will change is simply banal and out of accord with reality. Certainly, like Qohelet, he knew wicked people who were praised through their lives and even given an honorable burial (Eccles. 8:10–15). Again, while we cannot be certain, it seems to me that the psalmist is alluding to the idea that he will find his reward and the wicked will find their punishment, perhaps in this life, but certainly in the afterlife.

Conclusion

At first glance Proverbs seems to support a type of retribution theology where the wise prosper and the foolish languish. Indeed, much teaching in the OT appears to support such ideas.[7] For instance, in the Torah, blessings and curses follow the law in keeping with its covenant structure:[8]

> If you fully obey the Lord your God and carefully follow all his commands I give you today, the Lord your God will set you high above all the nations on

6. Johnston, *Shades of Sheol* (see 204–6 for his treatment of Ps. 73).
7. Longman, "Why Do Bad Things Happen to Good People?"
8. See chap. 10.

earth. All these blessings will come on you and accompany you if you obey the LORD your God. (Deut. 28:1–2)

However, if you do not obey the LORD your God and do not carefully follow all his commands and decrees I am giving you today, all these curses will come on you and overtake you. (Deut. 28:15)

The law connects disobedience to punishment, so when Israel broke the covenant and rebelled against the law, the prophets came and threatened Israel with the covenant curses if they did not repent. Jeremiah is a case in point. Israel has broken the law by its idolatrous behavior and many other sins (Jer. 10:1–22; 11:1–17). The people and their leaders have broken the law and thus deserve to suffer the curses.

The people did not respond favorably to Jeremiah and the other prophets' message, and thus the punishment came on them in the form of the Babylonian destruction of Jerusalem and the deportation of its leading citizens. In the midst of the exile, the author(s) of Samuel–Kings wrote a history answering the question, "Why are we in exile?" Their answer was that they had sinned and thus deserved the punishment that came on them. Specifically, they rehearsed Israel's past by examining how well they kept the Deuteronomic law. Thus, particularly when compared with the more positive remembrance of the past by the Chronicler, Samuel–Kings gives a rendition of the many and grave sins of Israel, telling its exilic audience that God's retribution on them was well deserved.

Any of these many parts of the OT, when isolated from the rest of the canon, could be used to support a retribution theology. Thus it is not surprising that such ideas persist even today. It is no wonder that people read Proverbs quickly and conclude that it teaches a simplistic notion of reward and punishment. Indeed, even Jesus's disciples held such notions. When they came across a man born blind, their question to Jesus was telling: "Rabbi, who sinned, this man or his parents, that he was born blind?" (John 9:1). Jesus's response debunks their prejudices: "Neither this man nor his parents sinned, but this happened so that the works of God might be displayed in him" (9:3). In other words, while sin can lead to suffering, that is not the only explanation for the pain of the world.

But the point of this chapter is that such a naive notion of retribution is not the message of the canon; it's not even the message of the book of Proverbs. Job and Ecclesiastes in particular prevent us from reading Proverbs in that way. In the final analysis, while Proverbs may emphasize rewards and punishments in order to motivate wise behavior, and Job and Ecclesiastes raise questions for those who might take such a view mechanistically as guarantees, they are "not opposing factions, but rather different appropriations under different conditions of the deeply elemental polarity of understanding and its limits."[9]

We might ask why a mechanistic notion of retribution persists among those who turn to the Bible, which, when read as a canonical whole, so clearly does not teach it. We can only speculate here, but the thought that the success or failure of our lives is ultimately beyond our control is distressing to say the least. It is frightening to know that we can do our best to follow the way of wisdom and still end up suffering—even though wisdom is the best route to a desired conclusion, all other things being equal. Thus, even when we understand the whole biblical teaching on retribution, we may still find ourselves asking "What did I do to deserve this?" when trouble comes, because to think otherwise is unsettling.

But the book of Job, in particular, urges its readers to move beyond the questions of whether we deserve what life brings us. Yes, as the lament psalms and the book of Lamentations demonstrate, God invites his people to express their pain to him, including their anger directed at God. However, the story does not end there. Ultimately, according to the picture of suffering developed in the book of Job, God desires our silent trust in spite of the pain of life.[10]

9. Loader, "Bipolarity of Sapiential Theology," 381. See also the helpful study by Schultz, "Unity or Diversity in Wisdom Theology?"

10. So too in Lamentations, the man of affliction affirms "it is good for a man to bear the yoke while he is young. Let him sit alone in silence, for the LORD has laid it on him. Let him bury his face in the dust—there may yet be hope. Let him offer his cheek to one who would strike him, and let him be filled with disgrace" (Lam. 3:27–30). In terms of the lament psalms, Brueggemann (Psalms and the Life of Faith, 3–32) helpfully points out that once God answered these prayers of disorientation, the faithful would respond with psalms of thanksgiving. Pemberton (After Lament) completes the picture, though, by asking, what if God does not answer the lament and the pain continues? He then points to psalms of confidence (Pss. 23; 131; etc.), prayers that are sung to express trust in God in the midst of pain.

12

THE SOCIAL SETTING
OF WISDOM

In this chapter we will consider whether we can pinpoint a social locale for the development of wisdom thinking. We have already conceded that recent studies have correctly questioned whether there was a distinct genre of wisdom literature that would have been clearly recognized in ancient Israelite circles, but we have insisted and demonstrated that there was a known category of wisdom. In this chapter we will examine what we can know about wisdom's place in Israelite culture and society.

First, we will explore the question of schools in ancient Israel and whether they were incubators of wisdom ideas. If there were schools, in what sector(s) of ancient Israel did they appear? Possibilities include the temple, the court, or both. If not schools, did families pass down wisdom from father to son, parents to children? Second, we will address the status of the sage in ancient Israel. Was there a distinct profession that differed, say, from priests, prophets, kings, and other royal officials? If so, where did they fit into Israelite society, and how did they interact with other societal leaders? Third, and connected to the first two issues, we will look into the question of the origins of wisdom ideas and the development of wisdom forms such as the proverb. Should we locate wisdom with the court, the temple, the village, the elders, fathers, or elsewhere?

As we will soon see, answering these questions is not an easy task, and they do not lead to definite and certain answers. Nonetheless, it is still interesting to evaluate the evidence that we have to move toward tentative conclusions. We must also acknowledge that the answers to our questions might be different depending on the period of Israelite history we are considering. Unfortunately, we will have to live with some uncertainty due to debates over when certain relevant and cited passages were written.

Were There Schools in Ancient Israel?

We begin with the question of schools in ancient Israel. If there were schools, then they could be the place where wisdom was incubated and professional sages were trained. We recognize that schools are nowhere mentioned in the OT. That, of course, does not settle the question, but it renders the answer to our question more difficult. Joshua ben Sira is the first to mention a school at the end of Sirach (second century BC, see chap. 14), where he appeals to the reader to "draw near to me, you who lack education, and stay in my school [*bet midrash*, "house of study"]" (51:23 CEB). Thus, our conclusions on the subject of schools must be based on indirect evidence and are, therefore, necessarily tentative and speculative.

What is the indirect evidence in favor of the presence of schools in Israel during the OT period, and how strong is it? First, there is indisputable evidence for schools before and during the OT period in Mesopotamia and Egypt. In the third millennium BC, the *E.DUB.BA.A* (Sumerian, "House of the Tablets," Akkadian, *bit tuppi*) was an institution for the purpose of training professional scribes who could write and read and who would then go on and serve in various parts of society, particularly the royal court and temple. Scribal training continued after the Sumerian period and into the Babylonian and Assyrian periods. We have a rough idea of the curriculum of such schools and even some fascinating literary compositions that give a personal and at times humorous look at the education of young scribes.[1] In these *edubbas* the students would learn how to write Sumerian and, in the second millennium BC, Akkadian, prepare various documents, and learn mathematics and other topics.[2]

Wisdom forms such as proverbs were collected and composed by *edubba*-trained scribes. Indeed, some proverbs comment on scribal training: "A scribe who does not know Sumerian, what kind of scribe is he?"[3] While we

---

1. For example, see H. L. J. Vanstiphout's translation of "The Dialogue between Two Scribes," "The Dialogue between a Supervisor and a Scribe," and "The Dialogue between an Examiner and a Student" in *COS* 1:588–93.

2. Pearce, "Scribes and Scholars." See also Sneed, *Social World of the Sages*, 73–75.

3. Alster, *Proverbs of Ancient Sumer*.

know the names of precious few ancient Akkadian authors, the scribe Saggil-kinam-ubbib, who wrote the Job-like text known as the "Babylonian Theodicy" (see chap. 9) made his presence known by embedding his name by means of an acrostic. Thus we know that school-trained scribes/sages produced compositions similar to those that contain biblical wisdom.

In Old Kingdom Egypt (ca. 2686–2180 BC) education took place through apprenticeship of a father with a son or a mentor with a student who would eventually enter the profession of the instructor. As time went on, more formal schools were developed, beginning in the First Intermediate Period (ca. 2189–2133 BC), during a time when the central government was weak and local regions needed to train their own scribes. By the time of the New Kingdom (ca. 1550–1070 BC), we have a pretty good understanding of the basic education of scribes as they learned the complicated hieratic script (which came in more than one form) from the age of ten, their instruction becoming increasingly difficult and specialized depending on whether they were going to serve in the royal court, the temple, or the military. Eventually, after mastering hieratic script, some would learn hieroglyphs. For our purposes, the details of Egyptian school education are less important than the mere fact that schools existed in the country during the biblical period.[4]

That there were certainly schools in Mesopotamia and Egypt during the biblical period has led some to argue that it is highly likely that there were also such institutions in biblical Israel.[5] However, differences between Israel and these two other cultures could make us hesitant to draw such a conclusion. Probably the major such consideration is that Hebrew is a much easier language to learn than the complicated scripts of ancient Sumer, Babylon and Assyria, and Egypt. Of these only Hebrew is alphabetic, having only twenty-two letters as opposed to hundreds of signs that represent either morphemes or syllables. There had to be some form of education in Hebrew, but it could be educated fathers instructing their sons at home or something much more informal than an institutional educational facility.[6]

There is other indirect evidence that supports the idea of education in ancient Israel, but once again, it does not necessarily point to schools as there

4. For a nice overview of education in Egypt, see Wente, "Scribes of Ancient Egypt."
5. The strongest advocate for the presence of schools during the biblical period in Israel is Lemaire, "Sage in School and Temple"; Lemaire, "Sagesse et ecoles." Sneed (*Social World*, 152–56) has argued for a view close to Lemaire's based on the work of Rollston, *Writing and Literacy*.
6. Sneed (*Social World*, 179–82) suggests that learning Hebrew beyond the rudiments would have been more rigorous and involved more training than we might imagine, but even so there is no question that an alphabetic system is easier than syllabic or logographic writing systems.

were in other regions of the ancient Near East. The other indirect evidence appeals to biblical texts that seem to suggest the payment of tuition money:

> Why is it that the price is in the hand of the fool
> to acquire wisdom with an empty heart? (Prov. 17:16)

> Acquire truth, and don't sell
> wisdom and discipline and understanding. (Prov. 23:23)

However, rather than pointing to literal tuition, these passages may simply be based on a commercial metaphor and, as has been pointed out, the second passage is found in the Words of the Wise (Prov. 22:17–24:22), a section of Proverbs thought to be heavily influenced by Egyptian wisdom. The latter might explain that though the proverb was originally literal in reference to tuition, when brought over to Israelite society it could have been understood metaphorically.

Some have also pointed to Prov. 5:13 in reference to the presence of schools with teachers ("I did not listen to the voice of the one who instructed me; I did not extend my ear to my teacher"), but the question is not whether there were those who taught others, but whether this instruction took place in a formal institution that could be called a school.

Finally, as Stuart Weeks points out, "the very existence of written documents indicates that some sort of education must have been available in Israel," as does the existence of certain types of epigraphic materials such as abecedaries and other types of school exercises.[7] But surveying the indirect evidence, Weeks rightly concludes, as do we, that the presence of formal schools can be neither proved nor disproved since this evidence points to education that "might have taken one or more of various forms, from parental teaching or apprenticeship through to an established system of schools, and might have included anything from basic literacy through to professional training and familiarization with classic literature."[8]

Were There (Professional) Sages in Ancient Israel?

Our second question concerns the presence of a group of people who might be identified as sages or wisdom figures in ancient Israelite society. We begin

---

7. Weeks, *Early Israelite Wisdom*, 132–56 (quotation on 132).

8. Ibid., 132. The oldest abecedary is dated to the late tenth century BC from Tell Zayit (Tappy and McCarter, *Literate Culture*). See also the classic study by Crenshaw ("Education in Ancient Israel"), who states, "Evidence for the Hebrew Bible is largely circumstantial, and some texts say more about literacy in general than about how that ability to read and write was acquired" (602).

with the acknowledgment that the OT represents a lengthy period of time. The existence and status of "sage" would likely be different in the various time periods of ancient Israel. As stated earlier in this study, the question of the history of the composition of the various books of the OT has been and continues to be seriously contested among scholars. If traditional views identifying Moses as the first writer of Scripture are correct, then the OT begins in the second half of the second millennium BC and continues to the second half of the first millennium. Many scholars today situate the composition of Scripture mainly to the postexilic period. In any case, for the purposes of this study, we will continue to stay away from the unavoidable speculation involved in determining the date of composition of texts and approach our question by looking at the Bible as a whole.

We begin with what we believe is an obvious statement. The OT identifies people as wise (*ḥākām*). The question, though, is whether this label is simply highlighting a personal trait or whether it is a professional designation. Solomon, for example, is called wise, but he was not a sage. He was a king, a wise king (at least early in his reign) to be sure. But are there some people who are sages? That is, are there professional wise men and women?

Are there passages that refer to professional sages in Israel?[9] The following are some possibilities:

The wise woman of Tekoa. After Absalom killed his half-brother Amnon to avenge the rape of his sister Tamar, he fled from his father David to the land of Geshur (2 Sam. 13:23–39). David mourned the absence of his son but refused to call him back because of his crime. Joab, desiring the return of Absalom, then enlisted a woman identified only as a "wise woman" (*'iššâ ḥăkāmâ*), whom he used to present a fictional scenario to the king that persuaded David to change his mind and allow Absalom to return (2 Sam. 14).

The wise woman of Abel Beth Maakah. Later in his reign, David faced a rebellion led by Sheba son of Bikri (2 Sam. 20). Eventually, Joab besieged the city of Abel Beth Maakah where Sheba sought refuge. The tense situation reached resolution when a wise woman (*'iššâ ḥăkāmâ*) presented herself to Joab and deftly negotiated an end to the scheme by providing him with the rebel's head.

Court counselors. Perhaps the most famous court counselors in the OT are Ahithophel and Hushai, who play an important role during Absalom's rebellion against his father David (2 Sam. 15–16). They are never called wise men or sages, but they are clearly portrayed as counselors who give "advice"

9. Other cultures such as those in Egypt and Mesopotamia did have professional sages, and the Bible mentions them (e.g., Gen. 41:8; Dan. 2:12–14).

(*'ēṣâ*) within the court. Indeed, Ahithophel is introduced as an "advisor" (*yô'ēṣ*, the root from which *'ēṣâ* originates; 2 Sam. 15:12 CEB). At first both men are advisors to David, but when the civil war breaks out, Ahithophel goes with Absalom. David instructs Hushai to feign support for Absalom in order to subvert Ahithophel's counsel, a plan that works very well. While it is true that these men are not called *ḥākām*, the term *yô'ēṣ* may be a designation that also indicates the professional sage.[10] After all, the wise person, though not necessarily a professional, is one who gives advice (*'ēṣâ*) according to Proverbs (1:25; 19:20; in addition, see the comments on Jer. 18:18 below).

Jonadab is yet another example of a court counselor. In this case, he is called a "very wise man" (*'îš ḥākām mə'od*), which is usually translated "a very shrewd man," since his advice to prince Amnon leads to the rape of his half-sister Tamar (2 Sam. 13:3).

This survey of passages intends to be illustrative not exhaustive. They serve to show that there were people, men and women, who were recognized as particularly wise and from whom people sought advice. Some, such as Jonadab and Ahithophel, were thought wise, though they used their wisdom for bad ends.

Perhaps the fact that the biblical narrator associates doubtful characters with wisdom is evidence that the term is being used as a professional designation. It makes a difference if one is called wise in Proverbs. Advice in Proverbs is always righteous and godly and effective, but this is not necessarily so outside Proverbs. Indeed, in chapter 2 we argued that when the frame narrator called Qohelet wise (*ḥākām*), it did not put an imprimatur on his words. Indeed, the description of his activities as a *ḥākām* ("he heard, investigated, and put in good order many proverbs," Eccles. 12:9) sounds like a professional description.

Perhaps the strongest case for the presence of a professional class of sages in the OT may be drawn from Jeremiah. Jeremiah cites his critics as saying: "Come, let's make plans against Jeremiah; for the preaching of the law by the priest will not cease, nor will counsel from the wise, nor the word from the prophets" (18:18). Here the wise person (*ḥākām*) associated with counsel (*'ēṣâ*) appears with two groups—priests and prophets—that are distinct professional categories in the OT.

In the final analysis, however, we cannot be absolutely certain. The textual evidence appears to support the idea of a distinct professional group known as sages, and the presence of professional sages in neighboring cultures supports the idea.

10. For others designated as *yô'ēṣ*, see 1 Chron. 26:14; 27:33; 2 Chron. 22:4; 25:16; Ezra 7:18.

What Is the Social Setting of Wisdom Forms?

Until recently, scholars spoke confidently about a distinct genre of wisdom literature that had at its core Proverbs, Ecclesiastes, and Job. The presumption was that this literature was produced by a distinct group of sages within Israelite society who were trained in some sort of school. We have already remarked that recent studies have cast doubts on all aspects of this picture, beginning with the idea that there was a distinct genre of wisdom literature.[11]

That said, we have argued that there is a concept of wisdom that recurs throughout the OT that we can explore. There are also certain literary forms that are associated with wisdom, preeminently the proverb. While there are other forms that we might legitimately also connect with the concept of wisdom (the reflection, disputation, riddle, etc.), we will focus here specifically on the proverb to ask if there is a specific sector of Israelite society from which the proverb originated and in which the proverb was applied.

This question has been discussed and debated in previous modern scholarship. Von Rad in his groundbreaking study of wisdom connected the collection of wisdom forms firmly within the context of the royal court based on analogy with ancient Egyptian wisdom texts, as well as the mention of Solomon.[12] That said, he also admitted that wisdom figures associated with the court "functioned as collectors of non-courtly teaching material and that wisdom was not by any means located only at court."[13] Over against the idea that proverbs stem from the court is the recent work of Westermann and Golka, who examine proverbs in modern tribal societies and who conclude that proverbs are the product of a society of small Israelite farmers.[14]

In the final analysis, however, it appears that the origin, development, collection, and use of the proverb does not have a single setting but rather comes from all sectors of the society. This conclusion in particular pertains to the production and use of proverbs.

In the book of Proverbs, the superscription ("The proverbs of Solomon, the son of David, king of Israel," 1:1) connects the book to the royal court, as does the role given to the "men of Hezekiah" (25:1) and even the mention of Lemuel, who is identified as the "king of Massa" (31:1). And some, though not many, find their primary if not their only application in the upper classes of the court. For instance, though the following proverb may have a secondary application to any situation in which one is in the presence of the powerful,

11. Kynes, *Obituary*.
12. Von Rad, *Wisdom in Israel*.
13. Ibid., 17.
14. Westermann, *Wurzeln der Weisheit* (ET: *Roots of Wisdom*); and Golka, *Leopard's Spots*.

it would find direct application only in the court, and it almost certainly emerged from a courtly setting:

> When you sit down to dine with a ruler,
>> carefully consider what is in front of you.
> Place a knife at your gullet
>> to control your appetite.
> Don't long for his delicacies,
>> for they are false food. (23:1–3)

While other proverbs also come from the court and find their primary use there (16:10–15; 25:1–7), most are almost certainly not from the court but, as Westermann and Golka suggest, from a village farming setting:

> An insightful son harvests in the summer;
>> a disgraceful son sleeps during harvest. (10:5)

And still others could be from nonroyal, yet urban, settings:

> Fraudulent scales are an abomination to the Lord,
>> but an accurate weight brings his favor. (11:1)

> Poverty and wealth don't give to me!
>> Allow me to devour my regular allotment of bread, . . .
> lest I don't have much and I steal,
>> and I profane the name of my God. (30:8b–9)

Conclusion

Now that we have surveyed the evidence available to us regarding the existence of schools, a professional class of sages, and the social location of wisdom, we can see that there is not enough there for us to be certain on any of these questions.

Certainly education existed in ancient Israel, probably taking different forms in different time periods and different regions. We cannot, however, assert that there were schools as such, since training may well have taken place in family situations or through a mentor-apprentice system. It is equally difficult to be certain about the existence of a professional class of sages during the OT period. Calling someone a wise person (*ḥākām*) may simply be a description of their character. Some passages, though, seem to reach further, particularly when it comes to court officials who served as advisors to the government. In terms of the social location of wisdom, the evidence suggests multiple settings. The content of proverbial instruction seems to emanate from all levels of society.

13

WISDOM AND GENDER

For readers in the twenty-first-century Western world in particular, wisdom raises questions concerning gender. Feminist scholars have rightly raised questions about the attitude toward women found in OT wisdom that all readers, male and female, should consider. Wisdom often takes the form of a father's instruction to a son, and a significant amount of the teaching seems to marginalize women's interests. In Proverbs, Ecclesiastes, and to a lesser extent Job, women come across as more of a problem than anything else. Proverbs, though, also speaks of a woman whose name is Wisdom. Does the figure of Woman Wisdom show that the ancient Israelite sages have a positive view of women, or is she a literary creation that serves the interest of male readers?

Wisdom's Patriarchal Perspective

One can understand why women readers of biblical wisdom might be put off by the rhetoric of books like Proverbs, Job, and Ecclesiastes. Take the book of Proverbs. It presents itself largely as the discourse of a father to a son.

> Listen, my son, to the teaching of your father. (1:8a)

> My son, if you grasp my speech
>   and store up my commands within you. (2:1)

> My son, don't forget my instruction. (3:1a)[1]

1. See also 1:10, 15; 3:11, 21; 4:10, 20; 5:1, 20; 6:1, 3, 20; etc.

Nowhere in the book does the father speak to his daughters or, for that matter, does a mother speak to her children, male or female. For this reason, the instructions of the book of Proverbs are male oriented.

We can detect this masculine focus in two areas. First, in the discourse section of Proverbs (chaps. 1–9), the father warns his son about the strange/foreign woman:

> My son, to my wisdom pay attention;
>   to my competence, extend your ear,
> so you might guard discretion,
>   and your lips might protect knowledge.
> For the lips of a strange woman drip honey,
>   and her palate is smoother than oil.
> But in the end she is bitter as wormwood,
>   sharp as a two-edged sword.
> Her feet go down to death;
>   her step grabs on to Sheol.
> She refuses to observe the way of life.
>   Her paths wander, but she does not know it. (5:1–6)[2]

What exactly is meant by the strange/foreign woman can be debated. Perhaps the reference is literally to foreign women who might lead Israel astray as foreign women led Solomon to worship false gods (see chap. 6). Or perhaps, and I think this is more likely,[3] these are Israelite women who act in ways that are foreign and strange to the customs and laws of Israel by desiring sex outside the bounds of marriage.

Which of these two interpretations is correct is less important to our present concerns than that the book focuses on the danger of predatory women and ignores the danger of predatory men. Indeed, a modern reader may with good reason respond to this strand of teaching in Proverbs by saying that the problem of male predators is a more pressing concern than female predators.[4] After all, while females can abuse and exploit males in our day, the number of females who are raped and abused far exceeds the number of males who are raped and abused. But Proverbs speaks only about the threat certain women pose to men and not the threat certain men pose to women.

---

2. This passage begins a lengthy section that includes chaps. 5–7, which is largely focused on warning the son to stay away from dangerous women.

3. Longman, *Proverbs*, 163–65.

4. Fontaine (*Smooth Words*, 156) rightly says, "Were we to consider the actual axes of power and abuse in ancient societies of the biblical world, only the most biased observer would not conclude that the *real* proverbial truth to be learned there should be directed at young girls and women: *Beware the man!*"

A second example of the male-focused teaching of Proverbs can be observed in its advice concerning cohabiting with an irritating woman:

> It is better to live in the corner of a roof
>   than with a contentious woman in a shared house. (Prov. 21:9)[5]

Again, we have no comparable teaching concerning the irritating male. Nowhere in Proverbs do we read anything like:

> It is better to live in the corner of a roof
>   than with a contentious man in a shared house.

The father-son discourse seen in Proverbs is also found in a more subtle form in Ecclesiastes. As explained in chapter 2, the book of Ecclesiastes contains two voices, that of Qohelet (the Preacher/Teacher) and that of the unnamed second wise man (or frame narrator). As Eccles. 12:12 makes clear, Qohelet's speech, though dominating the book (1:12–12:7), is the subject of discussion between the frame narrator and his son. Like Proverbs, in other words, this book presents the instruction of a father, not a mother, to a son, not a daughter.

Also as explained in the chapter on Ecclesiastes (chap. 2), while Qohelet's opinions do not express the message of the book, one can understand why his speech is unsettling to women readers. Indeed, his view can be rightly categorized as misogynistic. Consider the following:

> I began to devote myself to understand and to explore and to seek wisdom and the sum of things, and to understand the evil of foolishness and the folly of madness. And I was finding: More bitter than death is the woman who is a snare, whose heart is a trap and whose hands are chains. The one who pleases God will escape her, but the one who is offensive will be captured by her. "Observe, this I have found": Qohelet said, "one thing to another to find the sum of things, which I am still seeking but not finding, I found one man out of a thousand, but I did not find a woman among all these. Only observe this: I have found that God made people upright, but they have sought out many devices." (Eccles. 7:25–29)

Job too is a male-dominated book. The major human characters of the story are all male: Job, the three friends, and Elihu. The only female character is Job's wife, who plays what looks to be a negative role in the book, urging

---

5. Similar statements may be found in 21:19; 25:24; 27:15–16.

Job to "curse God and die" (2:9). Indeed, this brief appearance of Job's unnamed wife is suggestive enough that in the history of interpretation she assumes a major role as a shrew to an extent that is out of proportion to the amount she actually appears in the book.[6]

An honest assessment of the role of women in Proverbs, Ecclesiastes, and Job, books that we have identified as focused on wisdom, leads us to conclude that the books are clearly patriarchal. One cannot deny that they are male oriented. This is true even though it is also the case that some elements within these books empower women. Modern readers, especially in the West, must address this question.

Positive Depictions of Women in Wisdom

To ensure that we are being fair to the ancient literature in its ancient context, we should also highlight biblical wisdom's positive depictions of women. We agree with Fontaine's general assessment that "the wisdom tradition of ancient Israel allowed both private and public expressions of women's competence and contribution to the world of the wise."[7]

First, we note the role of mothers in the book of Proverbs. In the discourse, the father is the speaker, but he appeals to the mother's wisdom and draws his son's attention to it:

> Listen, my son, to the teaching of your father;
>> don't neglect the instruction of your mother. (Prov. 1:8; see also
>> 6:20)

While the mention of the mother's wisdom may appear minor, it should be pointed out that it is rare, but not unprecedented, in the ancient Near East.[8]

Proverbs also shows its interest in mothers in addition to fathers in passages that put a premium on bringing joy to one's mother as well as having the utmost respect for her:

> A wise son makes a father glad,
>> and a foolish son is the sorrow of his mother. (Prov. 10:1)

> A wise son brings joy to a father,
>> but a foolish person despises his mother. (Prov. 15:20)

6. Balentine, *Have You Considered My Servant Job?*, 77–110.
7. Fontaine, *Smooth Words*, 88.
8. Fox, *Proverbs 1–9*, 82–83.

We should also note that on at least one occasion a mother provides instruction. In the final chapter of the book, an otherwise unknown king of a non-Israelite kingdom, Lemuel king of Massa, reports the teaching he received from his mother:

> What, my son?
>> What, son of my womb?
>> What, son of my vow?
> Don't give your strength to women,
>> your ways to that which wipes out kings. (Prov. 31:2–3)[9]

The book ends with a picture of the "noble woman" (31:10, see vv. 10–31), which, among many other wonderful qualities, also highlights her sagacious teaching (v. 26, "She opens her mouth in wisdom, and covenantal instruction is on her lips").[10] In this regard as well, we draw our attention again to women who are depicted as wise in the historical books. See chapter 12 for a brief discussion of the wise woman of Tekoa and the wise woman of Abel Beth Maakah.

Last, we will mention the Song of Songs, which we have suggested does have a connection to wisdom (though it is not wisdom literature as such; see chap. 4). Surprisingly, at least in its ancient context, the woman's voice is slightly more dominant than the man's. Brenner points out that out of the one hundred and seventeen verses of the Song, the woman speaks sixty-one and a half of them.[11] Not only does she speak, but she speaks freely about her most intimate desires. The picture of the woman is extremely positive and, as Exum points out, "the attention the woman receives is unique in the Bible and so too is her characterization."[12]

Women in Wisdom: A Redemptive-Ethical Reading

We should not deny the obvious: from a twenty-first-century perspective, wisdom in the OT is couched in patriarchal language. Proverbs and Ecclesiastes, in particular, are discourses in which a father instructs a son in ways that are often specifically shaped to male concerns. What are modern readers, particularly women readers, to make of this?

In the first place, we must recognize that wisdom is no different from the rest of the OT. While books connected with wisdom, in my opinion, raise

9. Her teaching extends through v. 9.
10. For a stimulating study of this poem, see Wolters, *Song of the Valiant Woman*.
11. Brenner, "Women Poets and Authors," 88.
12. Exum, *Song of Songs*, 25.

the question of patriarchy in a special way, the rest of the OT too, as far as such matters are explicit, are the writings of male writers to a male audience. From what we know, and it is true that much of the OT is anonymous, there are no female authors or redactors, or books that are addressed specifically to a female audience.[13]

In response, we begin by stating that, for those of us who affirm the sacred status of Scripture, we must realize that while the Bible was written *for* us, it was not written *to* us. Contemporary readers are not the implied readers, so for every book of the Bible we must first read it as written to the original audience, whom we are not, and then ask how the message of the text we are studying is relevant for us today. For instance, the history presented in Samuel–Kings was shaped for an audience living during the exile that was interested in finding out why they were suffering the depravations of the conquest of Jerusalem. The NT epistles are not timeless writings but are focused on the concerns of their first readers. Thus, with every biblical book, we engage in a process of taking the message that was directed to the original audience and applying it for us today.

Indeed, we can already see an interest in expanding the audience for the book of Proverbs in the preface to the book. While the book, particularly Prov. 1:8–9:18, contains a father's instruction to his son in the interest of making his immature son wise, the book is also addressed to the wise to make them even wiser:

> to give to the simple prudence,
>> to the young knowledge and discretion.
> Let the wise hear and increase teaching;
>> let those with understanding acquire guidance. (1:4–5)

Of course, while the prologue expands the audience of the final form of the book, there is no reason to think that even the editor who added the prologue thought to include women readers in the expansion.

As I have thought about this question, I have been greatly helped by the work of William Webb, who describes what he calls a "redemptive-movement hermeneutic."[14] I believe he has rightly captured the idea that on some topics,

---

13. There are the occasional arguments in favor of female authorship, such as those who believe that Song of Songs was written by a female poet (Brenner, "Women Poets and Authors," 88). LaCocque (*Romance, She Wrote*, xi) believes "the author of the Song was a female poet who intended to 'cock a snook' [i.e., thumb her nose] at all Puritans." There is an extensive biblical tradition of women who sang songs; see Bekkenkamp and van Dijk, "Canon of the Old Testament," 79.

14. Webb, *Slaves, Women and Homosexuals*, 52.

but not all, Scripture does not present a static "utopian" ethic but rather takes people where they are in their cultural moment and moves them toward what I would call the "Edenic ideal."

After all, consider Jesus's comments concerning divorce (Matt. 19:1–12). When Jesus informs his disciples that divorce would only be permissible if there were sexual infidelity, they immediately recognized that the Mosaic law (Deut. 24:1–4) had a much more open policy on divorce, at least for the man. For our purposes, we should especially note Jesus's justification both for the Mosaic provision as well as for his statement: "Moses permitted you to divorce your wives because your hearts were hard. But it was not this way from the beginning. I tell you that anyone who divorces his wife, except for sexual immorality, and marries another woman commits adultery" (Matt. 19:8–9). The Mosaic law did not promote the Edenic ideal, but now Jesus pushes his followers closer toward the ethic of "the beginning."

Webb's understanding[15] is motivated by the following basic observations:

1. The OT law does not legislate the ultimate divine ethic but rather takes God's people where they are and pushes them toward the Edenic ideal.
2. Though not the ideal, the OT law, when judged against the standards of the broader Near East, is closer to the ideal.
3. The NT moves closer to the ideal, but even then ethics have not moved fully toward the ultimate goal.
4. In spite of its less-than-full implementation of Edenic ethics, the NT often expresses theological principles that will lead to further developments toward the ideal.

Before turning to the subject of women, we might briefly consider the Bible's teaching concerning slavery to illustrate a redemptive-ethical trajectory. In reading the Eden story, one cannot even imagine the institution of slavery (see below on the equality of male and female in Gen. 1–2). The OT law does not abrogate slavery but rather regulates slavery to minimize the abuses in a way that contrasts with other ancient Near Eastern legislation concerning slavery. Turning to the NT, we are initially shocked to understand that slavery persists beyond the time of the coming of Christ. Paul does not advocate for the abolishment of slavery. Indeed, in the book of Philemon, Paul instructs the runaway slave Onesimus to return to Philemon, his owner. Indeed, the epistles give instructions to Christian slaves to be obedient to their owners.

---

15. While Webb has stimulated my thinking on this subject, the following formulation represents my thinking and does not necessarily reflect his approach in every detail.

However, in Paul's exhortation to Philemon to treat Onesimus "no longer as a slave, but better than a slave, as a dear brother," v. 16) and elsewhere (see below on Gal. 3:18), we have the theological seeds for the abolition of slavery and thus a move even closer to the Edenic ideal.

But what about the Bible's teaching about women and, in particular, the patriarchy of the OT as we have seen displayed in wisdom? For this subject, we will begin with the Edenic ideal. Genesis 1–2 presents a picture of men and women as equal in every sense. God created both men and women in his image and charged them both with the task of ruling the earth in his name (Gen. 1:27–28). In the picture image given in the second creation account (2:4b–25), God created the woman from the man's side, clearly indicating their equality. The woman is not created from Adam's head as if she is superior or from Adam's feet as if she were inferior, but from his side, showing mutuality and equality. Nothing points to her subordination, including the statement that she is to be the man's "helper" (2:18). The Hebrew word (*'ezer*) does not denote an inferior status, since it is the word used to describe God's relationship to Israel (Pss. 33:20; 89:18–19; see also Deut. 33:39). Indeed, a good argument could be made that the word should be translated "ally" in reference to their joint task of guarding the garden.

The fall, as narrated in Gen. 3, had many negative ramifications on God's good creation including on the relationship between men and women. This disruption is best expressed by the punishment levied by God on the woman: "To the woman he said, '. . . Your desire will be for your husband, and he will rule over you'" (Gen. 3:16).

My own view, in agreement with many others, is that the woman's "desire" is not a romantic desire but rather a desire to control.[16] This desire to control is met by the male intent to dominate. Whatever one's view on the specific meaning of desire, however, the message of Gen. 3 is that a new power struggle has entered the realm of human relationships. I would suggest that it is in Gen. 3, not in Gen. 1–2, that we have roots of the patriarchy that we see in the OT.[17]

The OT law does not legislate God's final word for the relationship between men and women but rather curbs the most egregious abuses that might arise and, as it does so, distances itself from the ethic of the surrounding cultures. As Webb compares the OT with the surrounding ancient Near Eastern cultures, he notes that the former has better rights for women slaves and concubines, protections for wives from physical punishment, inheritance rights in certain circumstances, the right to initiate divorce, and much more. We will cite one

16. Foh, "What Is the Woman's Desire?"
17. A fuller discussion of my comments on Gen. 1–3 may be found in Longman, *Genesis*.

specific example. The Mosaic law, which allows for polygamy, nonetheless by regulating it protects the multiple wives from the type of abuse that might otherwise be common (Exod. 21:7–11).

Turning to the NT, a restoration of Edenic relationships between men and women moves even closer, but it is not there yet. Take polygamy for instance. Polygamy is not abrogated, but the requirement that elders and deacons must be the husband of one wife (and only one; see 1 Tim. 3:2, 12) indicates that at least leaders of the church must reflect the Edenic ideal of monogamy. But even so, we are not there yet. Pivotal passages in the NT express principles that will and can be developed further even beyond the NT period. Pride of place can be given to Gal. 3:28: "There is neither Jew nor Gentile, neither slave nor free, nor is there male and female, for you are all one in Christ Jesus."[18]

Implications for Reading Old Testament Wisdom

How, then, does the redemptive-ethical trajectory affect our reading of the books that speak of wisdom?

The issue really focuses on two books, Proverbs and Ecclesiastes, both of which adopt the ancient Near Eastern practice of fathers instructing their sons. We will thus illustrate the impact of a redemptive-ethical trajectory reading of these two books in particular, since women readers find them particularly troubling. After all, these books intend the actual reader (us) to identify with the implied reader (the son) in order to receive the teaching of the authoritative speaker of the book (the father). What is a woman reader[19] to do?

To summarize the salient points from above, while God's Edenic ideal was gender equality, human sin led to patriarchy, an imbalance of power between the genders. During the OT period, God did not legislate his ideal but rather pushed his human creatures toward it, differentiating Israel from the surrounding cultures. Proverbs and Ecclesiastes nonetheless reflect the patriarchy of this redemptive-historical time period. Readers in the twenty-first century AD, however, live in a different redemptive-historical moment. We live in the aftermath of the coming of Christ, which moves us closer to the Edenic ideal. In other words, we move closer to and work toward the ideal expressed in Gal. 3:28 that there is neither male nor female. We read Ecclesiastes and Proverbs accordingly.

18. Webb (*Slaves, Women and Homosexuals*) argues that "in Christ texts," though not specifically mentioning men and women, are relevant when read in the light of Gal. 3:28. He cites 1 Cor. 12:13; Eph. 2:15; 4:22–24; Col. 3:11.

19. Or, for that matter, an older male reader.

In one sense the issue is most pressing with Proverbs, a book whose express purpose is to impart wisdom, since in Ecclesiastes the gender of the recipient of the father's instruction does not influence the content of the teaching in any significant way.

After all, we are speaking here of the shape of the book where a father addresses a son in order to evaluate Qohelet's thinking (see chap. 2). The son is indeed the implied reader with whom the actual readers must identify, but here the twenty-first-century reading is as easy as imagining a parent, even specifically a mother, evaluating Qohelet's thought to a daughter, with whom the female reader identifies. Granted, Qohelet himself makes remarks and imparts misogynic advice (see 7:27–29), but we have seen (chap. 2) that the status of Qohelet's speech in the book of Ecclesiastes is equivalent to that of the three friends in Job. Both Qohelet and the three friends present perspectives that are deeply critiqued, not affirmed, by the canonical book.

But what about Proverbs, where not only is the trope the instruction of a father to a son but the very content of the instruction is often male oriented? We have seen that the preamble already expands the audience beyond immature male readers to the wise (1:5), but a redemptive-ethical trajectory encourages women readers to take the teaching of Proverbs and shape it to their situation. Such a reading means that women readers should make appropriate changes, in other words reading mutatis mutandis,[20] before applying the teaching to themselves. Thus women readers should read exhortations like those cited above:

> Listen, my son, to the teaching of your father (1:8a).

And read them as:

> Listen, my daughter, to the teaching of your mother.

Indeed, the awareness of this issue fuels gender-neutral translations of the book of Proverbs today that allow this type of mutatis mutandis reading to happen more naturally. The NLT, for instance (see also NRSV, NJB), renders Prov. 1:8a in the following manner: "my child, listen . . ." The NLT is a functional equivalent translation[21] that intends to engender the intended meaning of the ancient text in a modern vernacular equivalent so that the English translation communicates the same thought to the modern reader that was meant for the ancient reader.

---

20. I would like to thank Amy Felt, a graduate student at Covenant Theological Seminary, for suggesting the phrase mutatis mutandis to me.

21. See Longman, "Accuracy and Readability."

But a redemptive-ethical reading of Proverbs goes beyond what a translation can easily produce.[22] Even so, when a woman reads a proverb like Prov. 21:9 ("It is better to live in the corner of a roof than with a contentious woman in a shared house"), she should naturally simply substitute "man" for "woman." In the same way, in regard to the rather extensive teaching of the father that the son should avoid the promiscuous woman in order to continue on the path of wisdom (see 5:1–6 above), a woman reader should take the advice to avoid men who seek to lure her into bed.

When it comes to the figure of Woman Wisdom in the book of Proverbs, the issue becomes more complicated. After all, as we observed earlier, this female portrait of God as a strong, powerful, assertive woman rightly appeals to many women today. On the other hand, the author of Proverbs uses the figure in a way that appeals to male desires. The father urges the son to enter into an intimate, even erotic, relationship with this woman (see 4:8–9; 9:1–6). In these instances, perhaps a woman reader will choose to imagine the appeal to intimacy from Male Wisdom. The choice is hers.[23]

In terms of the teaching on the "noble woman" that ends the book (31:20–31), women have mixed reactions.[24] On the one hand, like Woman Wisdom herself, the noble woman pictures a strong woman who greatly benefits her family and her community in a way that brings her public praise. On the other hand, it at least implicitly puts incredible expectations on women and in a way that appears to benefit her husband, who occupies a position of authority in the public sphere. There is no comparable description of the "noble man" whose gifts benefit the woman. That acknowledged in this patriarchal book, the twenty-first-century woman reader should read this passage mutatis mutandis, and in this case Ps. 112 helps because this psalm pronounces a blessing on the man[25] who acts comparably to the noble woman in Prov. 31.

The bottom line to this discussion is that wisdom, including the teaching of the book of Proverbs, is meant for the whole people of God. Immature and wise, male and female, young and old can learn from the teaching concerning wisdom and grow in skill of living, ethical choices, and godliness.

22. Though it may call for, and certainly allows for, translations of Proverbs that are specifically meant for female readers.

23. Let me at this point say that in one sense I don't think that a redemptive-ethical reading of Proverbs is different in principle from how it was likely used during the OT time period. Certainly parents wanted their daughters to be wise and to live with wisdom, righteousness, and godliness. Indeed, we have seen that the historical books speak of wise women (see chap. 12). It is likely that parents took the content of the teaching of Proverbs and taught it to their daughters.

24. Based on my experience teaching on the book of Proverbs for the last four decades.

25. In this case obscured by gender-neutral translations.

Excursus: The Worship of the Goddess

In this chapter we have explored issues connected with gender and wisdom. We have acknowledged that OT wisdom has a patriarchal shape to its teaching compared to modern twenty-first-century Western ideas. We developed our understanding of Webb's redemptive-movement ethic as it impacts how we read this literature today. In our opinion, it does not help to deny OT patriarchal structures or to argue that those structures ought to be ours. A canonical reading of Scripture points first to Eden to see God's creative purposes, and in particular his desire for the equality of men and women, who are both created in his image. We don't cave in to the punishment of the curse on women any more than we do to the fact that God cursed the ground with weeds. We work to restore the Edenic ideal. We pull up weeds, and we work toward gender equality.

Second, Scripture encourages us in terms of its message of redemption. In Paul's words, "the creation waits in eager expectation for the children of God to be revealed. For the creation was subjected to frustration, not by its own choice, but by the will of the one who subjected it, in hope that the creation itself will be liberated from its bondage to decay and brought into the freedom and glory of the children of God" (Rom. 8:19–21).

Unfortunately, not everyone recognizes the redemptive-ethical trajectory (as signaled by Jesus's words on divorce and so much more), and so they freeze patriarchy as the biblical norm that remains relevant for today. Because of this, I, for one, can understand the frustration of many Christian women who feel that the Bible is an instrument of abuse, as it is used as an excuse for men to dominate women. However, though sympathetic, I cannot agree with the direction taken by some Christian feminists, and in particular those connected with the so-called Sophia movement. I feel compelled to speak about the Sophia movement in a book about biblical wisdom because, as the name implies, it roots its ideology in the wisdom traditions of the Bible. I also feel that it is appropriate to speak about this movement since I am writing this book on the occasion of the publication of a reprint edition of *Wisdom's Feast* (1st ed., 1986; 2nd ed., 1996) in 2016.[26] This book is at the center of a movement within mainline churches and provides both the theological rationale and the liturgical practice of Sophia.

---

26. Cole (née Cady), Ronan, and Taussig, *Wisdom's Feast*. Until the recent reprinting of this work, I thought that the Sophia movement had dissipated or been radically marginalized in the aftermath of the criticism that arose following the Reimagining Conference held in Minneapolis in 1993. Although the movement has not been much in the public eye since that time, this reprint edition may signal an attempt to reassert its influence.

The name Sophia is the Greek equivalent to the Hebrew word *ḥokmâ*, or "wisdom." But, as mentioned, advocates of the Sophia movement begin their reflections on OT texts that speak about wisdom, in particular the figure of Woman Wisdom. Of course, they are attracted to Woman Wisdom because she appeals to "those who seek models of powerful womanhood."[27] And there is no question that she provides those models. They rightly describe Woman Wisdom as "proud, assertive, angry and threatening, creative, and energetic."[28]

In their study of Woman Wisdom in the OT, they include healthy doses of intertestamental, apocryphal books (see chap. 14) that witness to further developments of this figure. Much of their depiction of Woman Wisdom for contemporary appropriation comes from these books, particularly as they explore the divine status of Woman Wisdom. Since Protestants—and most advocates of Sophia theology are Protestants—don't recognize the Apocrypha as canonical, this inclusion deserves at least some justification, which they do not provide.

But inclusion or not, it is their reflection on the divine status of the OT figure that bears scrutiny. In the first place, the discussion seems murky (perhaps intentionally so) and secondly does not seem justified by the biblical material itself. When I say that their description of the divine status of Woman Wisdom (Sophia) seems murky, what I mean is that it is not at all clear whether they think that Sophia is a separate god or not. The following statements suggest that they believe Sophia is a different god from Yahweh. In the preface to the 1986 edition of the book, for instance, they say: "This book is an invitation to the reader to begin living with this amazing rediscovered goddess of the Bible."[29] Then we read, "Sophia is a female goddess-figure appearing clearly in the scriptures of the Hebrew tradition, and less directly in the Christian Gospels and Epistles."[30] On the next page is an even stronger statement that there is a difference between Yahweh and Sophia: "She [Sophia] even begins to rival Yahweh's power, in her demands for people to follow her and her promise of salvation to those who do."[31]

In an interesting and telling passage, we learn that the sages of Israel themselves were careful (and purposefully murky) on the subject of the divine status of the goddess:

> The dogmatic status of the biblical Sophia then is clear. She is to all intents and purposes divine, creating, judging, and ruling just as God is. If the sages, however,

27. Ibid., xxiii.
28. Ibid., 41–42.
29. Ibid., xxiii.
30. Ibid., 10.
31. Ibid., 11.

were asked directly whether Sophia was God, they would wisely sidestep the question in order to avoid conflict with those in Hebrew theological circles who insisted on God's uniqueness. They would avoid an unequivocal answer by using metaphors like "the breath of the power of God" or "the consort of the throne." This would in no way detract from their imaginative introduction of a new divine figure. It would only signal their political shrewdness."[32]

Of course, their imaginative speculation of the political motivations of the ancient sages is pure fiction with no justification in the text itself. Indeed, it is much more likely an expression of the "political shrewdness" of their own intentionally murky assertions of the divine status of Sophia, particularly in light of the criticism that they have received even from within their own rather mainline, progressive denominations (more on this below).

To think of Woman Wisdom in the book of Proverbs as a separate divine figure is preposterous on exegetical grounds, and certainly this conclusion is confirmed when reading, as one should, in a canonical context that insists that there is only one God, named Yahweh (see chap. 1). That said, the use of such a powerful woman figure as a metaphor for God, who is neither male nor female, should nonetheless be emphasized these days by women who want to push against the patriarchalism that remains in the church. God does not privilege his precious male creatures any more than his precious female creatures.

But does the NT lend support to today's advocates of the worship of Sophia? In the quotation above they acknowledge that the NT mutes the presence of Sophia. After all, the NT centers on a male mediator between God and humanity—namely, Jesus. How does Jesus relate to Sophia? Although the authors of *Wisdom's Feast* acknowledge that Sophia does not play a significant role in the NT,[33] they present two reasons for this. The first is that gnostics "developed a special liking for the Jesus-Sophia association."[34] Thus, the NT authors played down the connection for fear of being thought to support gnostic ideas.

Second, they detect an insidious move in the writings of the NT. Citing approvingly the work of Engelsman,[35] they see a tendency in the NT to reassert patriarchy by subsuming Sophia to the male Jesus. Jesus hijacks (my word) Sophia's qualities and characteristics and turns the worship of the goddess into the worship of a male deity. However, a new day dawns, and the

---

32. Ibid., 29.

33. Indeed, probably even less a role than they believe, since they have a tendency to detect Sophia in passages that most naturally read as referring to the concept of wisdom with no hint of personification. See their treatment of 1 Cor. 1 (ibid., 33–34).

34. Ibid., 44.

35. Engelsman, *Feminine Dimension*, 119.

advocates of the worship of Sophia aim to complete what the NT started but also consciously repressed. After all, while "the Christ-figure . . . has served as a primary heroic symbol within the Church and western culture, placing progress, transcendence and domination close to the heart of classical western spirituality,"[36] it is time, according to *Wisdom's Feast*, to reassert the worship of the goddess. Thus the book concludes with multiple chapters presenting new rituals for the church that focus not on Jesus but on Sophia.

There have been many critiques of the Sophia movement, even within the mainline, more theologically liberal traditions in which its advocates work.[37] For those of us who prize the Scriptures as the Word of God, it is evident on the surface of it that the Bible itself does not bear the weight that their theology puts on it.[38] It is more than a matter of believing that the Bible does not complete the task of describing the goddess; it is that there is nothing—beginning with the fact that Woman Wisdom in the OT is a metaphor for God's wisdom and represents God himself (chap. 1)—that would suggest a trajectory leading to the worship of a Sophia figure.

36. Cole, Ronan, and Taussig, *Wisdom's Feast*, 7.
37. I found it telling that in the most recent edition of *Wisdom's Feast* the authors acknowledge the criticism but do not meaningfully interact with it. Rather, they express outrage and offense and accuse their critics of reactionary ideas.
38. See the powerful critique provided by Jobes, "Sophia Christology."

PART 5

THE AFTERLIFE
OF ISRAEL'S
WISDOM

O ur survey of Hebrew wisdom now completed, we turn our attention to what we are calling its aftermath. We do not know (and it
is much debated) when the various books of the OT were written
and reached their final form. The same is true for the collection of books that
the Jewish community calls the Tanak and Christians the Old Testament.

That said, even before these writings reached a stable form, they were read
and studied by the Jewish community of the Restoration and the Diaspora.
Thus we begin our look at the aftermath of Hebrew wisdom by studying wisdom in the so-called Apocrypha (particularly Sirach and Wisdom of Solomon
but also Baruch), *1 Enoch*, and a handful of Dead Sea Scrolls. We then turn
our attention to the NT. A Christian theology of wisdom must continue into
the NT. Indeed, as the Jewish scholar John Levenson recognized, "Christian
exegesis requires that the Hebrew Bible be read ultimately in a literary context

that includes the New Testament. To read it only on its own would be like reading the first three acts of Hamlet as if the last two had never been written."[1]

Such study begins by exploring just how the OT wisdom traditions might point to the coming of Jesus Christ. At the end of his work on earth, he told his disciples that his coming had been anticipated by all Scripture, presumably including the wisdom literature:

> "How foolish you are, and how slow to believe all that the prophets have spoken! Did not the Messiah have to suffer these things and then enter his glory?" And beginning with Moses and all the Prophets, he explained to them what was said in all the Scriptures concerning himself. (Luke 24:25–27)

> "This is what I told you while I was still with you: Everything must be fulfilled that is written about me in the Law of Moses, the Prophets and the Psalms." Then he opened their minds so they could understand the Scriptures. (Luke 24:44–45)

Earlier in his ministry, he chastised those who avidly read Scripture but rejected his message because, after all, "these are the very Scriptures that testify about me" (John 5:39). Thus, Jesus himself warranted the study of the Hebrew Scriptures in a way that testified to his coming. Needless to say, Jesus's words can be both misunderstood and misapplied, leading to a gross distortion of the biblical message.

We might, for instance, too quickly read the OT from a NT perspective and lose what Childs calls the "discrete voice" or "discrete witness" of the OT.[2] We must first read any passage of the OT from the vantage point of its original authors as they address the first intended audience, also known as the implied readers. Here we see the benefits of what we might call a historical-grammatical, or historical-critical, approach.

Nevertheless, to stop with a historical-grammatical reading falls short of a full understanding of the text from a Christian perspective. Christological readings of the OT were commonplace among the church's earliest interpreters. They read the text in the spirit of Augustine, who famously claimed that the NT was in the OT concealed, and the OT was in the NT revealed.

Of course, if the OT meaning of the text is not appreciated, then such Christian readings can and did lead to all kinds of extravagant claims about how the OT revealed Christ. Indeed, some christological readings appear quite arbitrary in their assignment of symbolic meaning to a text. The Song

1. Levenson, *Hebrew Bible*, 9.
2. Childs, *Biblical Theology*, 76.

of Songs might be cited as a case in point where the human dimension of this erotic love poem was overlooked in favor of an exclusively allegorical reading that even assigned christological significance to the details of the text.[3]

That admitted, the solution is not to reject christological readings of the OT as a foreign reading of the NT back into the OT but to practice such readings with restraint, guided by the way the NT itself appropriates the OT.

Thus in this chapter we will see how the NT authors themselves used the wisdom traditions of the OT to describe Jesus as a sage. Here we will observe that Jesus is not only the epitome of God's wisdom, but he is also associated with Woman Wisdom herself.

But not even this christological use of the wisdom literature exhausts the wisdom theme in the NT. Many NT authors, but perhaps particularly James, urge their Christian readers to turn from the folly of this world and embrace wisdom. Therefore, after looking at Jesus as the ultimate sage, we will turn our attention in chapter 15 to the presentation of Christian wisdom in order to explore continuity and discontinuity between the meaning of wisdom in the OT and in the NT.

---

3. See Longman, *Song of Songs*, 20–48, for a history of interpretation. A well-known example for using the details of the text in an illegitimate christological sense may be seen in the common ancient interpretation of 1:13, where the woman describes the man as a sachet of myrrh lodged between her breasts, which is seen as a reference to Jesus, who spanned both the OT and NT.

14

INTERTESTAMENTAL WISDOM FROM THE APOCRYPHA TO THE DEAD SEA SCROLLS

Before following the trajectory of the concept of wisdom into the NT, we pause in this chapter to examine its development in the so-called intertestamental period. Pride of place belongs to two books that the Roman Catholic Church considers canonical: Sirach (Ecclesiasticus) and the Wisdom of Solomon. They are part of the OT Apocrypha, a group of books also referred to as the Deuterocanonicals (not a "secondary canon," but rather as belonging to the second canon). Protestant Christians, like the present author, while not considering these books canonical, do believe, at least historically, that they should be read as edifying literature.[1] We will take a briefer look at a third book of the Apocrypha—namely, Baruch—that has a significant statement about wisdom as well.

After exploring these apocryphal books, we will then consider the significance of wisdom in scrolls from the corpus from the Dead Sea. While this does not exhaust the occurrence of wisdom during this time period even among

---

1. For an excellent presentation of the evidence in favor of the "narrower" Protestant canon, see Beckwith, *Old Testament Canon*.

the writings that are extant today, they will serve to represent the nature of wisdom during the period between the two Testaments.[2]

In this chapter, we intend to keep our focus on the concept of wisdom in these intertestamental writings. Rather than any kind of full survey, our interest in these books is primarily threefold. First, from them we can learn how the wisdom concept was appropriated from the canonical books and further developed during this time period. Second, related to the first, we believe that this development brings out themes and concerns that are implicit in the canonical books as related to wisdom. Third, these books also provide a bridge to the NT teaching on wisdom that will be the focus of the next two chapters.

Sirach

The first book we will analyze goes by different names among different groups. Ben Sira, or the longer title the Wisdom of Joshua Ben Sira, is the Hebrew title of the book named after the author of the book (Joshua ben Sira), and Ecclesiasticus is the Latin name used in the Vulgate. We will refer to the book by its Greek name, Sirach, which is the name found in the Septuagint.

We have a Greek translation of the Hebrew composition of the original book.[3] The translation was done by the author's grandson, not named, who also provided a prologue to the book. He refers to his grandfather Joshua's (Jesus in Greek) goal in the book: "that lovers of learning who were committed to education and wisdom should gain much more by living according to the Law" (prologue 13–14).

Joshua's grandson interestingly reflects on the difficulty of translation: "what was originally expressed in Hebrew does not have the same power when translated into another language" (prologue 21–22). He also references previous sacred writings in the standard three-part form ("the Law, the Prophets, and the other writings that followed them," v. 1–2; "the Law, the Prophets, and the other ancestral scrolls," vv. 8–10; "the Law, the Prophets, and the rest

2. I am using "intertestamental" in a loose manner, since the final editing of OT volumes probably overlaps with the writing of some of these books, and then others, like the Wisdom of Solomon, may have been written at the time when early NT books were being composed.

3. The Hebrew version of Sirach was lost from about AD 400 to 1900. In the twentieth century there were fragmentary Hebrew manuscripts of the book found at Masada, among the Dead Sea Scrolls (2Q18 and 11QPsa), and from the Cairo Geniza. They cover about two-thirds of the book. For a good summary of the text-critical issues associated with the book, see Murphy, *Tree of Life*, 67–69. Sirach quotations in this chapter are from the CEB, which translates the Greek version of the book. For a scholarly edition, see Wright's translation in Pietersma and Wright, *New English Translation of the Septuagint*, 715–65.

of the scrolls," vv. 24–25). These references indicate that the OT has come or is coming to final form before or at this time. Joshua, according to his grandson, was steeped in this literature.

The clearest evidence of when the translation was done is also seen in the prologue, when Joshua's grandson notes that he began his work of translation after arriving in Egypt "in the thirty-eighth year of the rule of King Euergetes" (v. 27). There are two kings from the Ptolomaic period who have the cognomen Euergetes ("Benefactor"), but the only one of these two who is appropriately associated with Sirach is Ptolomy VIII, who started his reign in 170 BC. That would put the translator's arrival in Egypt in 132 BC. Joshua's work would be two generations before this date (ca. 200 BC).

The book bears most similarity with Proverbs in its exaltation of wisdom, development of the metaphor of Woman Wisdom, and practical and ethical advice. There are also some psalm-like prayers in the book (see 23:1–6; 36:1–22).

Wisdom according to Sirach

Like Proverbs, the purpose of Sirach is to impart wisdom to its readers.[4] Ben Sira thinks of himself as a latecomer to the wisdom task, completing the already-extensive work accomplished by his predecessors in books like Proverbs: "I was the last to keep vigil, as one who gathered the leftovers after the grape pickers" (33:16).[5] As we explore the concept of wisdom in this intertestamental book, we will quickly see that Joshua ben Sira's understanding of wisdom is very similar to that of Proverbs, making explicit themes that are implicit in the earlier book.[6]

Fear of the Lord and the Law

In earlier chapters we noted the theological nature of wisdom in the book of Proverbs first becomes evident in 1:7 with the statement that "the fear of Yahweh is the beginning of knowledge." The idea that the fear of the Lord is fundamental to wisdom is often repeated in Proverbs (1:29; 2:5; 3:7; 8:13; 9:10; 10:27; 14:2, 26, 27; 15:16, 33; 16:6; 19:23; 22:4; 23:17;

4. It also intended to show "the superiority of Jewish wisdom and encourages its readers to keep its traditions" in the context of an increasingly Hellenizing culture (Phua, "Sirach, Book of," 720).
5. Cited by Snaith, "Ecclesiasticus," 170.
6. Some scholars believe that these themes are not implicit in Proverbs but are an extension of ideas found in Proverbs.

24:21; 28:14; 29:25; 31:10) as well as in Job (28:28), Ecclesiastes (see esp. 12:13–14), and elsewhere. According to Sirach, "all wisdom comes from the Lord. It lives with him forever" (1:1). Thus for humans to be wise they must fear the Lord. Like Proverbs, Sirach emphasizes the necessity of such a relationship with God pervasively throughout the book. Since there are too many references to cite, we give just a few examples beginning with the first mention of the phrase:

> Fear of the Lord is a person's glory, boasting, gladness,
>   and crown of rejoicing.
> Fear of the Lord will cheer the heart,
>   and it will give gladness, joy,
>   and a long life.
> Things will go well at the end
> for those who fear the Lord.
>   They will be blessed
>   at the time of death. (Sir. 1:11–13)

To get his readers to adopt the proper attitude toward wisdom, Ben Sira appeals to their self-interest, a rhetorical strategy used in book of Proverbs as well. Why should someone fear the Lord? Because those who fear God live long and happy lives and will even have a good ending when they die.

In our earlier study of the fear of the Lord, we noted that this fear does not make a person run away but leads to obedience. The same notion is found in Sirach, with an important twist that brings an implicit theme clearly into focus. While the relationship between wisdom and law is debated when it comes to the book of Proverbs, there is no question about the relationship in Sirach. The wise person fears God and obeys the Torah, as Sir. 19:20 puts so succinctly: "Fearing the Lord is the whole of wisdom, and all wisdom involves doing the Law." Other relevant passages that connect wisdom, the fear of God, and the law include:

> Those who keep the Law
> become masters of their thoughts;
>   fearing the Lord
>   leads ultimately to wisdom. (21:11)

> Whoever fears the Lord
> will do these things,
>   and whoever has a firm hold
>   on the Law will possess Wisdom. (15:1)

Of course, Ben Sira is not the first to make an explicit connection between wisdom, the fear of the Lord, and Torah obedience. We noted this in our earlier study of Deuteronomy (chap. 4). Thus, even if one hesitates to see the connection in Proverbs, which in our opinion one shouldn't, it is wrong to see the connection as an intertestamental development.

We should note that there is a debate over what "the Law" refers to in Sirach. Is it a universal law grounded in creation (as might be suggested by 1:8–9), or is it the Mosaic law (as might be suggested by 1:26–27)?[7] We believe, along with Wright[8] and Schnabel,[9] that it is the latter, though Wright raises questions over whether it is the Pentateuch as we know it in final form today.

It has commonly been stated that Joshua ben Sira, despite his references to law, does not cite specific Pentateuchal legislation. However, as Wright points out, "we encounter possible allusions to specific legal texts in the sage's instruction on respect for parents (3:1–6), on the poor and marginalized (4:1–10), and on reproaching a neighbor or friend (19:13–17). Ben Sira specifically refers to the Law in one passage where he discusses the treatment of an adulteress (23:16–26)."[10]

Before moving on to the next topic, we should note that there is also an explicit connection between wisdom and covenant, a category we argued was also relevant for a proper understanding of Proverbs, though the theme was not explicit. We note, for instance:

> God placed knowledge before them,
>   and he gave them a code for living.
> God established an eternal covenant with them,
>   and he showed them his decrees. (17:11–12)

> All these things are in the covenant scroll of the Most High God,
>   the Law that Moses commanded us,
>   the inheritance of the congregations of Jacob. (24:23)

Of course, the larger role of covenant in Sirach should not be surprising. Biblical law, as we have seen, is always embedded in a covenantal context.

Woman Wisdom

Another important theme in the book of Proverbs that highlights its theological nature is Woman Wisdom. In our earlier study we noted that Woman

---

7. A helpful discussion of this question can be found in Wright, "Torah and Sapiential Pedagogy," 160–65.

8. Ibid.

9. Schnabel, *Law and Wisdom*.

10. Wright, "Torah and Sapiential Pedagogy," 173.

Wisdom was commonly recognized as a personification of God's wisdom, and we went on to argue that the location of her house on the highest point of the city meant that she stood for God himself over against Woman Folly, who represented all the false gods and goddesses that tempted Israel to follow them (see chap. 1).

Woman Wisdom also plays an important role in Sirach, again promoting the theological nature of wisdom. As we will see, the way Sirach presents her only confirms the close relationship between wisdom, fear of God, and the law. We will begin with the passage in Sir. 15 that we cited above that ended with "whoever has a firm hold on the Law will possess Wisdom" and then continues:

> She will come to meet them like a mother,
>   and she will await them like a young bride.
> She will feed them bread of understanding,
>   and will give them water of wisdom to drink. (15:2–3)

We will stop here, though the description of Woman Wisdom continues in this passage. Here Woman Wisdom, like a mother and young bride, provides sustenance for her children/groom, who represents the wise. This picture is reminiscent of Prov. 9:1–6 when Woman Wisdom prepares a sumptuous meal for those who elect to partake in it.

As in Proverbs 8:22–31, Woman Wisdom is the first of God's creations: "Wisdom was created before everything else. Right understanding is as old as eternity" (Sir. 1:4). In what may be the most powerful depiction of Woman Wisdom in the book, we see how wisdom is associated with creation, and thus universal, but also particular to God's chosen people Israel. In chapter 24 she is depicted as speaking "in the midst of her people" and "in the assembly of the Most High":

> I came from the mouth
> of the Most High,
>   and I covered the earth like a mist.
> I lived in the heights,
>   and my throne was in a pillar of cloud.
> I alone encircled the vault of heaven
>   and walked in the depths of abysses.
> In the waves of the sea and in every land,
>   and among every people and nation,
>   I led the way.
> I sought a resting place

among all these.
    In whose allotted territory
    should I make my home?
Then the creator of all things
gave me a command;
    the one who created me pitched my tent
    and said, "Make your dwelling in Jacob,
    and let Israel receive your inheritance." (24:3–8)

Thus again, as in the book of Proverbs, the figure of Woman Wisdom attests to the theological nature of Israel's wisdom. Unless one has a relationship with the God of Israel that is characterized by fear and leads to obedience to the law of Israel as presented by the covenant God made with Israel, one does not have wisdom.

The Ethical and Practical Nature of Wisdom

As we have seen in our earlier study, wisdom has a practical side, teaching people how to live life in an appropriate way. As in Proverbs, wisdom is more than just a guide to successful living; it also is a guide to living a life of virtue. The connection we observed above between wisdom, law, and covenant makes that point already since the law was seen as guiding people to good living in every sense of that word.

Again as in Proverbs, the teaching of parents, particularly the father, plays an important place in the instruction of the book:

Listen to a father's warning, children,
    and act accordingly
    so that you may be safe.
The Lord gives pride of place
to a father above his children
and establishes a mother's judgment
above that of her offspring. (3:1–2)

We are thus not surprised to find that the book contains a great deal of guidance for everyday living:

Don't be timid in your prayer,
    and don't neglect caring for those in need. (7:10)

This proverb also illustrates the fact that Sirach gives advice in the areas of prayer, sacrifice, and holy days, subjects not lacking in Proverbs but not as frequently mentioned. Other examples of practical/ethical advice that sound similar to what we find in Proverbs include the following:

> Run away from sin
> like you would from a snake. (21:2)

> Ill-timed talk is like party music
> during mourning. (22:6)

> Many have refused to make a loan,
> not because they were vicious
>   but because they were cautious
>   about being needlessly cheated. (29:7)

> If you have household slaves,
> treat them like yourself,
>   because you purchased them with blood. (33:31)

There is also a lot of teaching about family, especially wives and children. It has often been pointed out that, from a modern perspective, Sirach might be considered demeaning and oppressive of women. However, it is more correct to say that Ben Sira was demeaning of ungodly women (and the same can be true of males). We see this in such passages as:

> An uneducated son is a disgrace
> to a father,
>   and a daughter's birth is a liability.
> A prudent daughter
> will get a husband of her own. (22:3–4)

However, it must be said in the final analysis that Sirach indeed was a misogynist with such statements as:

> Sin began with a woman,
>   and because of her all of us die.
> Don't allow an outlet for water,
>   and don't give a wicked wife
>   freedom to speak.
> If she doesn't do as you say,
>   divorce her. (25:24–26)

That said, he also appreciates a godly woman, as he acknowledges, "A good wife is a great blessing. The one who fears the Lord will receive her as part of his God-given portion" (26:3).

Wisdom and History

We have already argued that wisdom does have some connection with re-demptive history in Proverbs, Ecclesiastes, and Job, though it is not a major, explicit theme. That wisdom is inherently at odds with history is disproved by Sirach, which more frequently connects with redemptive history. Sirach 16:7–9 is an example:

> The Lord didn't seek reconciliation
> with the ancient giants
>   who rebelled in their might.
> He didn't spare Lot's neighbors,
>   whom he detested
>   because of their arrogance.
> He showed no mercy on a nation
> doomed to destruction,
>   on people who were driven off
>   because of their sins.

In this regard, we should take special note of the conclusion of the book, where Ben Sira praises "famous people and our ancestors" (44:1) and tells of "their wisdom" (44:15). The list includes Enoch, Noah, Abraham, Isaac, Jacob, Moses, Aaron, Phinehas, Joshua, Caleb, the judges, Samuel, Nathan, David, Solomon, Elijah, Elisha, Hezekiah, Isaiah, Josiah, Ezekiel, Zerubba-bel, Joshua, Nehemiah, and the postbiblical priest, Simon the son of Onias.

Conclusion

The book of Sirach continues and expands on many themes found in the book of Proverbs. Here again we encounter a concept of wisdom that is practical (skill of living), ethical, and theological. The practical interest of the book may be seen in its everyday advice, especially regarding family life. The ethical nature of wisdom becomes explicit in what is implicit in Proverbs— namely, the connection between wisdom and Torah. The theological nature of wisdom continues in the concept of the fear of God and the presentation of the figure of Woman Wisdom. As in Proverbs, wisdom is a universal feature connected to how God created the world but is also particularistic in that God gave wisdom to Israel in a special way. In this regard, Schnabel refers to "Ben Sira's wisdom conception with its twofold character as a cosmological entity and as the salvation-historical possession of Israel" and goes on to conclude that "wisdom links the two areas of creation and history."[11] Again,

---

11. Schnabel, *Law and Wisdom*, 28.

the connection to Israel's particular redemptive history (and covenant) is something that Sirach brings out much more clearly than the book of Proverbs, where it is an implicit feature.

The Wisdom of Solomon

We here refer to the book as it is known in the Greek; the Latin tradition titles it the Book of Wisdom. As the Greek name implies, the book presents itself as the words of Solomon, who speaks in the first person, to those "who judge the earth" (1:1),[12] that is, other rulers. Solomon's main interest is to persuade rulers to live with wisdom. After all, "the more wise people there are in the world, the more likely it is that the world will be saved. A sensible ruler gives stability to his people. So it will do you good to be instructed by my words" (6:24–25). Rulers better heed Solomon's advice: "if you don't keep the Law, or if you don't act according to God's plan, then he'll fall upon you very suddenly and very terribly. Judgment falls hard on those in high places" (6:4–5). To further his appeal, Solomon tells the story of his own discovery of wisdom. He sought wisdom ("from my youth, I loved her and sought her out. I sought to make her my bride," 8:2), and he recounts his prayer to God that he grant him wisdom ("give me Wisdom, who sits enthroned beside you," chap. 9, esp. v. 4). God granted him wisdom even though he was "just a human like everyone else" (7:1).

While the author presents his thoughts in the voice of Solomon, that tenth-century-BC king did not write or contribute to the book. It shows awareness of the Septuagint, which means that it cannot be older than the second century BC, and most feel that the latest we can date its composition is AD 50. The book was originally written in Greek, almost certainly by a Jew[13] who may have lived in Alexandria. While rooted in the message of the OT, "the influence of Hellenism is striking."[14]

Woman Wisdom

We have seen the important figure of Woman Wisdom already in Proverbs and Sirach. She continues to play a central role in the Wisdom of Solomon.

12. All quotations of the Wisdom of Solomon in this chapter are from the CEB. For a scholarly edition, see Wright's translation in Pietersma and Wright, *New English Translation of the Septuagint*, 697–714.
13. Schaper ("*Nomos* and *Nomoi*," 293) points out that "there is no trace whatsoever in the book of Wisdom of specifically Christian *theologoumena*."
14. Murphy, *Tree of Life*, 85.

As in the previous books, at a minimum she is a personification of God's wisdom and, in our opinion, by metonymy represents God himself. To be in relationship with Woman Wisdom is to be in relationship with God himself.

As mentioned, the Wisdom of Solomon purports to be the words of King Solomon and bears testimony to his relationship with Woman Wisdom. In Proverbs the father calls on his son to make Wisdom his sister, a term with clear romantic/sexual overtones (Prov. 7:4; see Song 4:10). In addition, Prov. 9:1–6 depicts Woman Wisdom calling men to come to her house for dinner, a clear invitation to intimate relationship. Solomon, in the Wisdom of Solomon, makes this romantic/sexual metaphor explicit when he claims "from my youth, I loved her and sought her out. I sought to make her my bride" (8:2). Wisdom of Solomon even cites Solomon's prayer requesting wisdom ("Give me Wisdom, who sits enthroned beside you," 9:4). And since he seeks her, Solomon finds her because "Wisdom is bright and unfading. She readily appears to those who love her. She's found by those who keep seeking after her. She makes herself known even in advance to those who desire her with all their hearts. Someone who awakens before dawn to look for her will find her already sitting at the door" (6:12–14).

He desires this relationship because "she knows God's secret ways and is a partner in God's works" (8:4), a statement again reminiscent of Proverbs, where such is implied since she was the firstborn of creation and thus observed and perhaps participated in God's work of creation (8:22–31). In his prayer, Solomon said to God, "You have Wisdom with you. She knows all your works. She was present with you when you were making the world" (9:9). Thus, as a result of his relationship with Woman Wisdom, the Solomon persona boldly claims, "I now know everything, visible and hidden" (7:21). After all, he has access to such deep and extensive knowledge because he knows the One who knows everything.

The Wisdom of Solomon describes Woman Wisdom as a spirit "that wants only what is best for humans" (1:6). That Wisdom is a spirit is reminiscent of Proverbs, when she says, "I will pour forth my spirit to you; I will make known to you my words" (Prov. 1:23). Here the spirit refers to God's spirit, though not specifically in this OT context the Third Person of the Trinity.[15] Wisdom's spirit is further described as "insightful, holy, unique, diverse, refined, kinetic, pure, spotless, transparent, harmless, delighting in what is good, sharp, unstoppable, overflowing with kindness, delighting in humans, steadfast, secure, not anxious, all-powerful, and all-seeing" (Wis. 7:22–23). Here we may likely see the fusion of Hebrew wisdom theology and Greek

15. Longman, "Spirit and Wisdom," 97–98.

thought since she is "here described in a series of twenty-one (7×3) epithets, borrowed largely from Greek philosophy."[16]

As a holy spirit, Wisdom will not have anything to do with the wicked (1:4–6). Thus, only the righteous possess wisdom. A relationship with Woman Wisdom is both earned and a gift, just as in the book of Proverbs. It is earned by study and obedience: "The real beginning of wisdom is to desire instruction with all your heart. Love for instruction expresses itself in careful reflection. If you love Wisdom, you will keep her laws. If you are attentive to her laws, you can be assured that you will live forever" (6:17–18). Even so, it is also a gift of God. For this reason, Solomon says to God: "Who's ever known your counsel, unless you gave them wisdom and sent down your Holy Spirit from on high?" (9:17). Wisdom of Solomon 6:17–18, along with other passages (2:11–12; 6:3–5; 9:5; 16:7; 18:4, 9), again illustrates the explicit interconnection between wisdom and law in the intertestamental period. That said, the connection is not as pervasive as we saw in Sirach, perhaps because of a new emphasis on the relationship between wisdom and spirit (see above).[17]

Wisdom and History

Canonical wisdom literature has often been characterized as not interested in the history of Israel. While it is true that redemptive history is not a major topic in Proverbs, Ecclesiastes, and Job, we have argued that by connecting Proverbs and Ecclesiastes to Solomon, wisdom literature is connected to the history of Israel.

That the concept of wisdom is not inherently at odds with history can also be seen in the Joseph and Daniel narratives. We have already seen a more explicit relationship between history and wisdom in Sirach, and now we can add the other major intertestamental wisdom book, since the Wisdom of Solomon also interweaves wisdom and history.

Beginning in chapter 10, the author of the Wisdom of Solomon speaks of seven examples of wisdom from biblical history and usually contrasts them with examples of wicked godlessness. These seven are not named, but they are easily identified by their description. The first is Adam: "wisdom gave him the strength to have dominion over everything" (10:2).[18] He contrasts this with the story of Cain before moving on to the story of Noah, whom Wisdom rescued

16. Winston, *Wisdom of Solomon*, 178.

17. There are some who would argue that law in the book is not to be "identified with the *nomos*/Torah" but rather with the "'standards' of wisdom itself" (Schaper, "*Nomos* and *Nomoi*," 297).

18. See Ezek. 28 for an earlier tradition linking Adam and wisdom. Our treatment of this passage may be found in chap. 6.

when the flood waters came. As for Abraham, "Wisdom found [him] . . . and kept him pure before God" (10:5). Wisdom then saved Lot from "the fire that descended on the five cities" (10:6). Wisdom also rescued Joseph (10:13–14). The seventh and final example of Wisdom's rescue of his people is the story of the exodus, which is the historical moment most extensively discussed in the book (10:15–21; 19:1–9). The exodus may have played a particularly important role in the book because of the oppression that the Alexandrian Jewish community was experiencing. For Jews living in Egypt, the story of the exodus would resonate in important ways.[19]

Wisdom and Idolatry

In our study of Proverbs we argued that Woman Wisdom represented Yahweh's wisdom by way of personification and by metonymy Yahweh himself. Thus Woman Folly in Prov. 9 represents the false gods and goddesses of the nations by virtue of the location of her house on the highest point of the city. In this sense, Proverbs criticizes false religion and the idolatry associated with it.

Thus, the book of Wisdom's intense diatribe against idolatry is not foreign to literature that concerns itself with the topic of wisdom. If, as is taught in a number of books, the fear of the Lord is the beginning of wisdom, then the worship of false gods is the height of folly. The likelihood that the Wisdom of Solomon was written in Egypt in the first half of the first century AD renders it probable that the author's readers live in a society permeated with the practice of idolatry. It is particularly in chaps. 13 and 14 that we hear his anti-idol invective. Idolatry results from the foolish confusion of the creation with the Creator. Rather than worshiping the "maker of everything" (13:1), "they thought that all these things—fire or wind or quickly moving air or a constellation of stars or rippling water or the sky's bright lights that govern the world—were all gods" (13:2).

Like Isaiah (see 40:12–25; 44:9–22), the author of the Wisdom of Solomon shakes his head at how ridiculous it is that people would fashion an image with their own hands and then worship it (13:11–16). He wonders "how much more miserable . . . are those people who put their trust in things that are dead?" (13:10). He feels so strongly about it because "the worship of nameless idols is the origin of all evil—its cause as well as its result" (14:27).

Wisdom, the Ungodly, Death, and the Afterlife

As suggested above, the Wisdom of Solomon was likely written during a period when the people of God experienced persecution at the hands of the

---

19. Enns, "Wisdom of Solomon." See also his longer study, *Exodus Retold*.

ungodly. It looked like the latter were winning, but the Wisdom of Solomon suggests that death is the consequence of ungodliness and life the result of wisdom and righteousness. These connections, of course, find an earlier echo in Proverbs, but here the author takes the long view.

Even if the godly suffer and die in this life and the ungodly seem to thrive, that is not the end of the story. While "doing what is right means living forever" (1:15), the ungodly "made a treaty with death" (1:16). Thus, while it appears that God's people lose, in reality "their leaving us [their death] seemed to be their destruction, but in reality they are at peace. It may look to others as if they have been punished, but they have the hope of living forever" (3:3–4). The godly eventually "will burst forth and run about like fiery sparks among dry straw" (3:7). On the other hand, "the ungodly will get what their evil thinking deserves" (3:10). Interestingly, despite the influence of Hellenism on the author, the book's perspective comports with the biblical idea that the afterlife results from one's relationship with God rather than any inherent quality of the human soul as in Hellenistic thought.

Conclusion

Wisdom of Solomon, like Sirach, presents similarities and differences with the book of Proverbs. The persona of Solomon hovers in the latter, whereas his role becomes central in what is rightly called the Wisdom of Solomon. Wisdom is practical, ethical, and definitely theological here. The practical seems more subdued in the apocryphal book, but certainly the ethical is found in wisdom's relationship with law, and the figure of Woman Wisdom plays a major role, indicating its theological significance in the book. Wisdom again interplays with history and also warns against idolatry in this fascinating example of intertestamental wisdom.

Baruch and 1 Enoch

Before leaving the OT Apocrypha, we will look briefly at the powerful poem concerning wisdom that is found in the book of Baruch. The opening of the book attributes the writing to Baruch, Jeremiah's associate (Jer. 32:10–16; 36:1–31), who is speaking to the exiles in 582 BC, five years after the start of the exile. After a confession of guilt that led to the exile (Bar. 1:10–2:10) and prayer for deliverance (2:11–3:8), Baruch then speaks of wisdom (3:9–4:1).

Baruch begins with an appeal, much like we find in the book of Proverbs, for Israel to pay attention to wisdom: "Hear the commandments of life,

O Israel; give ear, and learn wisdom!" (3:9).[20] We should take note how here wisdom is parallel to "the commandments of life," which could be a reference to the law. The connection between wisdom and law, common in the intertestamental period, is made explicit at the end of the poem, where Woman Wisdom "is the book of the commandments of God, the law that endures forever" (4:1). The exhortation that Israel attend to wisdom is urgent because they "have forsaken the fountain of wisdom" (3:12) and thus languish under oppression. If they would just turn to wisdom, then their lives would be much better.

But Woman Wisdom is not at all easy to find. In language similar to that found in Job 28, Baruch asks "Who has found her place? And who has entered her storehouses?" (3:15, cf. Job 28:12, 20). Unfortunately, "no one knows the way to her or is concerned about the path to her" (3:31). No human being, that is. God, on the other hand, "knows her, he found her by his understanding" (3:32). And God has given her to "Israel, whom he loved" (3:36). And it is through Israel that wisdom becomes available to the whole world: "Afterward she appeared on earth and lived with humankind" (3:37). The poem concludes as it started with an appeal that God's people grasp the gift of wisdom ("Turn, O Jacob, and take her; walk toward the shining of her light," 4:2).

Baruch thus exemplifies an understanding of wisdom that we have also seen in Sirach and Wisdom of Solomon. He speaks about wisdom through the figure of Woman Wisdom and sees a connection between her and the Torah. In addition, Baruch sees wisdom as the special possession of Israel, but through Israel wisdom becomes available to the whole world.

First Enoch is not found in the OT Apocrypha but is considered a pseudepigraphal book (i.e., a book falsely claiming to have been written by a notable biblical personage). Woman Wisdom is the subject of the brief chapter 42, from a part of *1 Enoch* referred to as Similitudes (chaps. 37–71). The dating of Similitudes is debated, particularly since this is the only part of *1 Enoch* not found at Qumran. Apart from attempts to date Similitudes as a late Christian addition,[21] most scholars believe that it is a Jewish work dating to the first century BC and no later than the first century AD. In Baruch, Woman Wisdom settled in Israel before becoming available to the world. *First Enoch* 42 has a quite different perspective:

> Wisdom could not find a place in which she could dwell;
> but a place was found (for her) in the heavens.

20. Throughout this chapter, all quotations of the book of Baruch are from the NRSV.
21. Milik, "Problemes."

Then Wisdom went out to dwell with the children of the people,
but she found no dwelling place.
(So) Wisdom returned to her place
and she settled permanently among the angels.
Then Iniquity went out of her rooms,
and found whom she did not expect.
And she dwelt with them,
like rain in a desert,
like dew on a thirsty land.[22]

According to *1 Enoch*, Woman Wisdom wanted to dwell with humanity but found no place to settle. Thus she returned to heaven, while Iniquity (Woman Folly) found herself at home on the earth.

The *Testament of Job*

The exact date of the composition of the *Testament of Job* cannot be determined, but most scholars would place it sometime between 100 BC and AD 200. It is most likely written by a Jewish author who was familiar with the Septuagint version of the book of Job, which differs significantly from the Masoretic Text. It indeed shares many ideas with the Septuagint.

Like the Septuagint, it identifies Job with Jobab (*T. Job* 1.1; 2.1). The transformation of Job into a patient man, observed in the Septuagint, is complete in the *Testament of Job*. In response to his first wife, Sitis, who wants him to curse God and die, Job exhorts her to be "patient till the Lord, in pity, shows us mercy" (*T. Job* 26.5).[23] He tells his children, based on his experience, "You also must be patient in everything that happens to you. For patience is better than anything" (27.6–7).

Job's suffering is directly the result of the devil, who is angry because Job destroyed an idol (*T. Job* 6–8, though the devil does go to God to get permission). Job did this knowing that suffering would be a result. In a reversal of the biblical book, it is the three friends (called "kings") who lament Job's fate and express confusion, while Job maintains a strong confidence in God. Elihu is portrayed as an enemy of Job "inspired by Satan" (41.5). Job is eventually restored.[24]

The *Testament of Job* is even further removed from the Hebrew version of the biblical book than the Septuagint version. The origin of many ideas

22. Isaac, "1 (Ethiopic Apocalypse of) Enoch," 1:33.
23. Translations of the *Testament of Job* are from Spittler, "Testament of Job."
24. Besserman, *Legend of Job*, 41.

that become commonplace about Job during the Middle Ages are found in both the Septuagint and the *Testament of Job*.

Wisdom at Qumran

Besides intertestamental, apocryphal books like Sirach, Wisdom of Solomon, *1 Enoch*, and Baruch, documents from the Dead Sea community also demonstrate an interest in wisdom. Few, if any, of these texts were composed by the circles around the Teacher of Righteousness, but the community there (the *yaḥad*) nonetheless studied and learned from several wisdom texts besides the canonical and apocryphal books (copies of Sirach were also found at Qumran).

We will take a short look at eight examples of wisdom compositions found at Qumran, emphasizing the two largest, 4QInstruction and 1/4QMysteries. After our survey, we will offer some summarizing comments about how these texts relate to biblical and apocryphal wisdom.

4QInstruction

The best-known composition commonly identified as wisdom at Qumran is 4QInstruction[25] (1Q26; 4Q415–18, 423). It was first published in 1999,[26] and since then 4QInstruction has occupied a prime place in the discussion of wisdom in Second Temple Jewish literature. Most scholars believe that 4QInstruction was written in the second century BC, but Kampen argues that it could have been composed as early as the late third century BC.[27] While the text was obviously widely used by the Dead Sea community, it is unlikely to have been composed by the sect.

The addressee of 4QInstruction is called the *mēbîn*, which can be translated "man of discernment/understanding." The addressee or student is most often referred to in the singular, but occasionally in the plural. It was probably meant for a community of learners, but the singular addressee makes the teaching more personal and intimate.[28] From the way the speaker addresses the *mēbîn*, it is clear that he/they are poor. In an instruction concerning the *mēbîn*'s relationship to his/their parents, the teacher says: "Honor your father in your poverty and your mother in your lowly state, for as God is to

---

25. Also known as *mûsār lǝ-mēbîn*.
26. Strugnell and Harrington, *Qumran Cave 4.XXIV*.
27. Kampen, *Wisdom Literature*, 43–44.
28. Goff, *4QInstruction*, 12.

man so is his father, and as the Lord is to a person so is his mother" (4Q416 2 iii 15–16).[29]

Like the book of Proverbs, 4QInstruction seeks to impart practical advice to its readers. There is practical instruction on marriage, relationships, self-control about food consumption, and debt management. That said, perhaps the most interesting aspect of 4QInstruction is connected to the commonly occurring phrase *rāz nihyeh*, which most experts translate something like "mystery that is to be."[30] Nothing like this concept occurs in Proverbs, Ecclesiastes, or Job, but Aramaic *rāz* ("mystery") is found in Dan. 2 (vv. 18, 19, 27, 30, 47), where it refers to the message of Nebuchadnezzar's dream that portends the future.[31]

According to the teacher, the *mēbîn* must study the *rāz nihyeh* in order to understand and to gain wisdom, particularly in terms of the unfolding of history and especially the future judgment. As many interpreters have pointed out, 4QInstruction has an apocalyptic worldview in which "the dominion of God is manifested in a deterministic divine place according to which reality unfolds."[32]

1/4QMysteries

The second most well-known wisdom text from Qumran goes by the name the Book of Mysteries (1QMysteries 27 and 4QMysteries 299–301). The title derives from the appearance of the phrase *rāz nihyeh*, shared with 4QInstruction, that is typically translated "mystery that is to be." The *rāz* points to the eschatological vision of the total destruction of the wicked. The following passage catches the heart of the instruction of the Book of Mysteries:

> Just as smoke vanishes and is no more, so wickedness will vanish forever and righteousness will be revealed like the sun, the plan of the world. All who hold on to the mysteries of transgression will no longer be. Knowledge will fill the world and there is no folly any longer. That which is to come is determined, the prediction is true.[33]

The quotation also illustrates the deterministic viewpoint held by the author(s). God is in control from creation to judgment, and nothing can thwart his will, which will assure the ultimate victory of those who seek knowledge over the wicked.

29. Translations of 4QInstruction come from ibid.

30. Kampen (*Wisdom Literature*) offers a minority view with his translation "mystery of existence," which he uses throughout his translations of the relevant texts.

31. See discussion of Dan. 2 in chap. 5.

32. Goff, *Discerning Wisdom*, 16.

33. Translation from Kampen, *Wisdom Literature*, 197.

In an intriguing but fragmentary passage, the Book of Mysteries mentions "the diviners [*ḥartummîm*] who teach transgression" and who "speak the parable and relate the riddle before it is discussed."[34] Kister believes that the composition as a whole is addressed to these diviners, but Kampen rightly argues that there is no evidence of this.[35] That said, they are likely rivals to those responsible for the writing of the Book of Mysteries. In this we have a dynamic similar to that in Dan. 2, where Daniel and his three friends are able to interpret Nebuchadnezzar's dream after the failure of the Babylonian diviners.[36]

The Book of Mysteries, like 4QInstruction, provides an example of the fusion of wisdom such as we have in Proverbs and an apocalyptic vision of the future. The division with the diviners and the assertion of a group of elect individuals may well place this text at the end of the third or early second centuries BC, at the time of the rise of different parties in Judaism. However, there seems to be unanimity among specialists that the passage, though respected among the community at the Dead Sea (the *yaḥad*), was not produced by the circle associated with the Teacher of Righteousness.

4QThe Evil Seductress (4Q184)[37]

This fascinating composition found at Qumran describes a woman who lures men from their path into death ("her gates are gates of death. When entering her house she steps into Sheol").[38] She seduces the righteous by her sexual charms and leads them to destruction.

Some of the language and certainly the portrait of this woman derive from the picture of the strange woman of Prov. 7. The latter is a married woman who seduces men while her husband is away. Both women lead men to their death. While there are similarities that demonstrate that the author of the Dead Sea text writes with awareness of Prov. 7, Goff rightly notes the differences: "4Q184 transforms the Strange Woman of Prov. 7 from an alluring but dangerous married woman into a mythological figure of evil."[39] In my opinion the latter may result from a further development of the relationship that Proverbs develops between the picture of the strange woman and the picture of evil as Woman Folly in Prov. 9.

34. Kampen, *Wisdom Literature*, 202.
35. Kister, "Wisdom Literature," 23, 46. See Kampen, *Wisdom Literature*, 195.
36. So Kampen, *Wisdom Literature*, 196.
37. This text also goes by the name Wiles of the Wicked Woman.
38. Translations are those of Kampen, *Wisdom Literature*, 238.
39. Goff, *Discerning Wisdom*, 121.

4QSapiential Work (4Q185)

This text does not contain the noun "wisdom" but does use a verbal form of the root (*ḥkm*) to encourage readers to "gain wisdom." Plus, most interpreters understand the third-person feminine suffix to refer to wisdom.[40]

Like 4QInstruction and 1/4QMysteries, this text may have an apocalyptic edge to it, since the fragmentary introduction mentions angels and judgment. But 4QSapiential Work has greater similarity to Proverbs and Sirach in that the text is filled with exhortations to pay attention and to hear the teaching and promises a blessing on those who do. The composition also speaks of the Torah as a source of wisdom.

4QWords of the Maskîl to All Sons of Dawn (4Q298)

This fascinating composition is written in a script that has become known as CryptA, a cipher where each symbol represents a letter in the Hebrew language. Its purpose must have been to keep the contents of the text available only to the *Maskîl* or "sage." There are a handful of other texts from Qumran that are written in this script, and they all clearly originate within the sect at Qumran itself. If this is true of 4QWords of the *Maskîl* to All Sons of Dawn, then this text is the only wisdom composition that has a definite sectarian origin.

The name of this fragmentary composition comes from the introduction, which identifies the message as one from the *Maskîl* ("sage") to the sons of the dawn. The identity of the latter is disputed. Some believe that it refers to novices of the sect (as opposed to the "sons of light"), while others dispute this identification and argue that it is just another name for members of the sect.[41]

The small portion of text that has survived does say that the *Maskîl* hopes that his hearers will "gain understanding of the end of the ages" as they grow in virtues like justice, righteousness, humility, meekness, and strength.[42]

4QWays of Righteousness (4Q420–21)

This fragmentary composition presents some problems and ambiguities of generic identification. There is no denying the wisdom elements in the text, including a reference to the "yoke of wisdom," which is also found in Sir. 51:25–26 (see also Matt. 11:25–20). There are also halakhic statements ("legislation relating to the temple")[43] that make some believe it is not wisdom

40. So, e.g., Kampen, *Wisdom Literature*, 252–53.
41. Ibid., 272–73.
42. Ibid., 275–76.
43. Ibid., 284.

but a sectarian rulebook.[44] However, most Dead Sea Scrolls scholars would place this writing among the wisdom texts.[45]

Instruction-Like Composition B (4Q424)

While this text wins the award for the least interesting and imaginative title given to it by modern scholars, it is clearly a wisdom text that has echoes of Proverbs and Deuteronomy (showing again the interplay of law and wisdom in these texts). The fragments we have advise distancing oneself from certain types of people with bad character traits; for example, "Do not send a man dull of heart to come up with thoughtful plans, for the wisdom of his heart is hidden and he has not mastered [it . . .] he has not found the skill of his hands."[46]

4QBeatitudes (4Q525)

Since macarisms play an important role in the text as we have it in fragmentary form, the composition goes by the name Beatitudes though it is not at all clear that this names its most important feature. Besides the macarisms, this text is also related to previous wisdom compositions through the personification of wisdom as a woman (see Prov. 1; 8–9; Sir. 24; Bar. 3:9–4:4; Wis. 7:7–9:18). We also find in 4QBeatitudes considerable interplay between wisdom and Torah. The fragmentary conclusion looks forward to the destruction of the wicked, a fate avoided by those who listen to the teaching of this text.

Conclusion to the Dead Sea Scrolls

These eight compositions are the most distinctive wisdom compositions known from Qumran. We should add that the presence of fragments of Sirach at Qumran signals an interest in this intertestamental wisdom book.[47] In addition, we have wisdom psalms in the Psalms scroll found at Qumran (11QPs[a]).

The various sapiential texts at Qumran show roots back into biblical wisdom, particularly Proverbs.[48] Many of the texts offer practical advice concerning various topics that concern the nitty-gritty of life, as well as ethical guidance that would lead to righteous behavior. In several texts, a teacher

44. E.g., Tigchelaar, "Sabbath Halakha."
45. So Goff, *Discerning Wisdom*, 160–61.
46. Kampen, *Wisdom Literature*, 305.
47. Ibid., 341–64.
48. There is nothing like Job or Ecclesiastes among the nonbiblical texts at Qumran.

instructs students.[49] Wisdom also has a theological dimension similar to biblical wisdom in that true wisdom comes from God. Though the distinctive phrase "the fear of the Lord" is not found, we do get glimpses of Woman Wisdom (as well as Woman Folly).[50]

Our survey has also revealed developments since the biblical period. For instance, as we saw with Sirach and Wisdom of Solomon, the connection between wisdom and law is much more explicit than in the book of Proverbs. Contrary to many scholars, we have suggested that wisdom and law are implicit in Proverbs, and everyone recognizes that wisdom and law are connected in Deuteronomy, though the dating of that book is disputed and thus also the date of this connection.

In addition, and connected to the above, is the more explicit idea that wisdom is revealed by God. Again, we argued that revealed wisdom is found in biblical wisdom (unarguably in Dan. 2; see chap. 5), but there is no dispute about the revelation of wisdom in Qumran texts.[51]

Perhaps the most fascinating development in Qumran wisdom is the connection with apocalyptic, particularly in the concept of the *rāz nihyeh* ("mystery that is to be"). Again, we can find the roots of this connection in the Bible (Daniel) and intertestamental literature (*1 Enoch*), but it reaches its fullest development in Qumran literature. Von Rad,[52] before the recent close study of Dead Sea wisdom, argued that apocalyptic was a development of wisdom. It is more likely the fact that apocalyptic ideas influenced wisdom and vice versa; or in the words of Collins, "wisdom instruction was not inherently wedded to the kind of worldview that we find in Proverbs, but could just as well be used in the service of an apocalyptic worldview."[53]

Second Temple Wisdom: Conclusions

This chapter treats several wisdom compositions written during the Second Temple period, most of which were written during the Hellenistic period. For that reason, it is appropriate to call these books representative of the Second Temple period. What might be misleading is to use this label to differentiate

49. Missing is the language of father instructing son that is so familiar from Proverbs and found also in Ecclesiastes.
50. Particularly in The Evil Seductress (4Q184), Sapiential Work (4Q185), and Beautitudes (4Q525); see Crawford, "Lady Wisdom and Dame Folly."
51. E.g., Rofé ("Revealed Wisdom," 1) states "a characteristic of Qumran theology is the notion of revealed wisdom, i.e., the idea that humanity receives wisdom by revelation."
52. Von Rad, *Old Testament Theology*, 2:306.
53. Collins, *Jewish Wisdom*, 229.

them from books that speak of wisdom found in the Bible, since it is likely that Job and Ecclesiastes are also Second Temple literature, and the final form of Proverbs was probably reached around the same time.

Bracketing the question of relative dates of books and their constituent parts, we will now make some concluding observations concerning the relationship between biblical and nonbiblical wisdom compositions.

1. The most salient similarities may be found between Second Temple literature and Proverbs rather than with Job or Ecclesiastes. The kind of practical, ethical, and theological expression of wisdom found in the biblical book continues in Sirach, Wisdom of Solomon, and most of the Qumran texts. The *Testament of Job* appears to be an exception to this statement, but only in name. By turning Job into a paradigm of patience right from the start of his story, the *Testament of Job* presents Job as a model of virtues more in keeping with Proverbs than either the canonical Job or Ecclesiastes.[54]

2. We argued earlier that there is an implicit connection between wisdom and law in Proverbs, and thus we are not surprised that many but not all the later nonbiblical texts make explicit the connection between wisdom and Torah. Kister's comments are helpful here in terms of the relationship between wisdom and Torah in these texts: "The Second Temple period was, above all, the period of interpretation, and its major project was amalgamating, through interpretation, concepts from diverse biblical strata in a Hellenistic environment. It is true, for instance, that 'wisdom functions for post-exilic writers as a hermeneutical construct to interpret the Torah,' but it is equally true that the Torah functioned as a hermeneutical construct to interpret wisdom, and probably to a larger extent."[55]

3. In the same way, rather than seeing the connection between wisdom and revelation as an entirely new phenomenon, we rather believe it is a further development of a connection found in the biblical books. True, in much of its teaching Proverbs appeals to experience, observation, tradition, and learning from one's mistakes. But even these avenues of wisdom are ultimately revelatory (Prov. 20:12). After all, one cannot be wise unless one fears God and has an intimate relationship with Woman Wisdom, ultimately representing God, who instructs her disciples. The father in

---

54. Later we will see that the Epistle of James will utilize this picture of a patient Job from the Septuagint/*Testament of Job* tradition (see chap. 15).

55. Kister, "Wisdom Literature," 19.

Proverbs is a proxy for God. In any case, Dan. 2 seems to prefigure the idea that true wisdom comes not from observation and tradition (so the Babylonian wisdom teachers) but rather from revelation by God.

4. In many ways, the most surprising development in nonbiblical wisdom during the Second Temple period is the connection with apocalyptic, particularly in the concept of the *rāz nihyeh* ("mystery that is to be") and the teaching about the judgment that is coming against the wicked. Daniel 2 may provide a helpful analogy within biblical books, since God reveals to Daniel the meaning of Nebuchadnezzar's dream that anticipates God's coming judgment against the wicked nations that seek to oppress God. In terms of the relationship between wisdom and apocalyptic, perhaps Kister's statement about the relationship between wisdom and Torah is also appropriate here in the sense that we might say that "wisdom functions for post-exilic writers as a hermeneutical construct to interpret *apocalyptic*," and "*apocalyptic* functioned as a hermeneutical construct to interpret wisdom."[56]

---

56. Ibid. For the continuation of the integration of apocalyptic and wisdom ideas in later Judaism, see 2 Baruch, composed after the destruction of the second temple by the Romans. Kim, "Wisdom and Apocalyptic in 2 Baruch."

15

NEW TESTAMENT WISDOM

I n this chapter, we move from Jewish appropriation of Hebrew wisdom
to Christian reception. New Testament writers understood that Jesus
was a teacher so sagacious that he was considered the ultimate wisdom
teacher, but even more tellingly, they associated him with Woman Wisdom.[1]
We will then move on to the expectation that Jesus's followers themselves
will reflect his wisdom.

Jesus the Sage

The Gospels and the Epistles bear witness to the deep wisdom of the Messiah.
First-century AD Judea had its scribes, teachers, and sages, but none were
like Jesus. We first explore the Gospels' presentation of the life of Jesus and
then turn to the Epistles' reflections on his life and ministry.

The Gospels

CONFOUNDING THE TEACHERS IN THE TEMPLE (LUKE 2:40–52)

The Gospels provide very little information about Jesus after his birth and
before the start of his public ministry. Luke, though, relates a story that serves
to demonstrate that even at a young age Jesus demonstrated great wisdom.

---

1. Witherington, *Jesus the Sage*.

The story is bounded by similar statements that create an inclusion and frame the story of Jesus in the temple:

> And the child grew and became strong; he was filled with wisdom, and the grace of God was on him. (2:40)

> And Jesus grew in wisdom and stature, and in favor with God and man. (2:52)

The proof of his wisdom is given in 2:41–51. Jesus and his parents traveled to celebrate the Passover in Jerusalem. Upon their return, his parents realized that Jesus was not with them, probably because they traveled in a group and assumed that their twelve-year-old was safe in the group. Of course, once they knew he was not with them, they went back to Jerusalem and after three anxious days found him at the temple. While there is much more to make of this episode, the description of his activities and the reaction of onlookers is of most interest: "they found him in the temple courts, sitting among the teachers, listening to them and asking them questions. Everyone who heard him was amazed at his understanding and his answers" (2:46–47). The amazed reaction of the audience is the first of many such accounts.

THE REACTION TO HIS TEACHING

When Jesus began his ministry many years later, he taught with such power and wisdom that he set himself apart from all others. The people in his hometown commented on his wisdom and power but then ultimately rejected him because they thought they knew his origins:

> Coming to his hometown, he began teaching the people in their synagogue, and they were amazed. "Where did this man get this wisdom and these miraculous powers?" they asked. "Isn't this the carpenter's son? Isn't his mother's name Mary, and aren't his brothers James, Joseph, Simon and Judas? Aren't all his sisters with us? Where then did this man get all these things?" And they took offense at him. (Matt. 13:54–57; see also Mark 6:2–4)

Not only in his hometown but also throughout the land Jesus became known for the insight of his teaching, which came with demonstrations of power. On one Sabbath, while he was in Capernaum, he taught in a synagogue with great effect on those who heard him: "The people were amazed at his teaching, because he taught them as one who had authority, not as the teachers of the law" (Mark 1:22).

Not everyone, of course, was convinced by Jesus's wisdom. On one occasion, some "Pharisees and teachers of the law" challenged him to produce a sign (Matt. 12:38). Jesus rejects their request on the grounds that they have seen enough. In this context he asserts that his wisdom is such that they should recognize who he is. He mocks them for their ignorance by saying, "The Queen of the South will rise at the judgment with this generation and condemn it; for she came from the ends of the earth to listen to Solomon's wisdom, and now something greater than Solomon is here" (Matt. 12:42). Of course, Jesus here refers to the story of the Queen of Sheba (1 Kings 10:1–3), who stood amazed at Solomon's great wisdom. But Jesus's wisdom far surpasses that of Solomon.[2]

Jesus taught using the parable. His choice of the parable as the vehicle of teaching also underlines his role as the ultimate sage. Of course, Jesus did not invent the parable; it was the common form of instruction by other wisdom teachers of his day. The connection between the parable and OT wisdom can be seen in the very word. "Parable" in Greek is *parabolē*, which is the word used in the Septuagint to translate the Hebrew word *māšāl*, or "proverb."

The Epistles

Not surprisingly, Paul attests to Jesus's wisdom as described in the Gospels. Indeed, for Paul, Jesus is the very embodiment of God's wisdom. He tells the Colossians, "My goal is that they may be encouraged in heart and united in love, so that they may have the full riches of complete understanding, in order that they may know the mystery of God, namely, Christ, in whom are hidden all the treasures of wisdom and knowledge" (Col. 2:2–3). Christ makes manifest the mystery of God, and specifically he abounds in the wisdom and knowledge of God.

In perhaps the longest reflection on wisdom, Paul speaks about wisdom and folly at the beginning of his Corinthian correspondence (1 Cor. 1:18–2:16). Later we will cite a portion of this passage (1 Cor. 2:10–12) regarding Christian wisdom. Here we will focus on what Paul says in this passage about Christ.

In the context of contrasting the wisdom of this world and the wisdom of God, Paul explains why the focus of his proclamation is the crucified Christ, who is "the power of God and the wisdom of God" (1 Cor. 1:24). A little later, he assures the Christians in Corinth that they "are in Christ Jesus, who has become for us wisdom from God—that is, our righteousness, holiness and

2. Ford, *Christian Wisdom*, 27.

redemption" (1 Cor. 1:30). Paul exalts in declaring God's wisdom, a mystery, which is none other than Christ (1 Cor. 2:7).

Thus, the Gospels and Paul make it abundantly clear that Jesus is wise, even preternaturally so. He is the very wisdom of God. Accordingly, we are not surprised to see that the NT authors on occasion associate Jesus with Woman Wisdom herself.

Jesus as Woman Wisdom

The New Testament Testimony

The witness of the Gospels and Paul join to proclaim Jesus a person of unprecedented wisdom. He embodies the wisdom described in the OT. He is indeed the ultimate sage. But Jesus is more than the ultimate sage. By associating him with Woman Wisdom, the NT authors announce that Jesus surpasses normal human wisdom. In our earlier study, we observed that Woman Wisdom at a minimum is the personification of Yahweh's wisdom, but we went on to argue that Woman Wisdom, by virtue of the location of her house on the highest point of the city, is none other than Yahweh himself.[3]

We turn first to the Gospel of Matthew, which depicts Jesus as claiming this relationship with Woman Wisdom. In response to the Jewish leaders who complained about his rather celebratory lifestyle, he reminded them that they were also critical of John the Baptist, who led an ascetic life:

> For John came neither eating nor drinking, and they say, "He has a demon."
> The Son of Man came eating and drinking, and they say, "Here is a glutton
> and a drunkard, a friend of tax collectors and sinners." But wisdom is proved
> right by her deeds. (Matt. 11:18–19)

"But wisdom is proved right by *her* deeds." The Greek is clear; Jesus is not speaking about wisdom in the abstract or as a concept. He is connecting himself and his actions with those of Woman Wisdom.

Next we turn to the prologue to the Gospel of John, which begins with words that echo Prov. 8:

> In the beginning was the Word, and the Word was with God, and the Word was
> God. He was with God in the beginning. Through him all things were made;
> without him nothing was made that has been made. In him was life, and that

---

3. See chap. 1.

life was the light of all mankind. The light shines in the darkness, and the darkness has not overcome it. (John 1:1–5)

Of course, John's prologue reflects the opening of the book of Genesis: "In the beginning God created the heavens and the earth" (1:1), but Johannine scholars are quick to recognize the echoes from Prov. 8, which describes Woman Wisdom's role in creation (Prov. 8:22–31).

Our third example is even more to the point. In Colossians we hear Paul's triumphant proclamation that:

The Son is the image of the invisible God, the firstborn over all creation. For in him all things were created: things in heaven and on earth, visible and invisible, whether thrones or powers or rulers or authorities; all things have been created through him and for him. He is before all things, and in him all things hold together. (Col. 1:15–17)

The language of "firstborn over all creation" certainly reminds us of Woman Wisdom, whom "Yahweh begot . . . at the beginning of his paths, before his works of antiquity. From of old I was formed, from the beginning, from before the earth. When there were no deeps, I was brought forth, when there were no springs, heavy with water" (Prov. 8:22–25). In addition, Paul's reference to "thrones or powers or rulers or authorities" evokes Prov. 8:15–16, in which Woman Wisdom makes the claim that

> by me kings reign,
>   and nobles issue just decrees.
> By me rulers rule,
>   and princes, all righteous judgments. (Prov. 8:15–16)

Finally, we turn to Rev. 3:14. Here John records in the letter to the church in Laodicea that "these are the words of the Amen, the faithful and true witness, the *ruler* of God's creation." Reading in English, it is difficult to see the connection back to Woman Wisdom of Prov. 8. However, the Greek word translated "ruler" is *archē*, which is the word used in the Old Greek translation for the rare Hebrew word that occurs only in Prov. 8:30 (*'āmôn*). The Greek-reading author and readers of Revelation would have seen the connection to Woman Wisdom.

The NT testimony is that Jesus is associated with Woman Wisdom. He is her very embodiment. Notice that we have been very careful to say that Jesus is associated with Woman Wisdom. We have avoided words like identification. We turn now to consider why.

Association, Not Identification

The NT on at least four occasions (Matt. 11:18–19; John 1:1–5; Col. 1:15–17; Rev. 3:14) describes Jesus in language reminiscent of Woman Wisdom. That is clear. What has been disputed through the centuries is the precise nature of that relationship. As it turns out, the question of the nature of the relationship between Jesus and Wisdom is the center of crucial christological controversies.

The roots of the controversy go back to the controversial teachings of Arius (AD 250–336), who was an influential Christian presbyter in Alexandria, Egypt. He taught that Jesus was subordinate to God, being the firstborn of creation (Prov. 8:22–25; John 1:1–5; Col. 1:15–17). He took other passages to mean that God (the Father) was superior to the son ("the Father is greater than I," John 14:28). Arius's intellectual followers are referred to as Arians and his system of thought as Arianism. Arius was declared a heretic at the First Council of Nicea in AD 325, a pronouncement that was reaffirmed by the First Council of Constantinople in AD 381. Under the influence of Arius's main theological opponent, Athanasius, the creed that emanated from Nicea proclaimed rather that Jesus was "God from God, Light from Light, true God from true God." According to the Constantinopolitan Creed, Jesus was "begotten, not made." Indeed, he was eternally begotten since the Father was always the Father.

Regarding Woman Wisdom, Arius's problem is that he treated Prov. 8 and its uses in the NT (1) as a literal statement and not as a poem and (2) as a prophetic statement about Jesus. Thus, he and his followers identified Jesus and Woman Wisdom rather than recognizing that the NT authors were making an association between the two.

That Prov. 8 is a poem is an obvious point that needs no elaborate defense. At the center of the poem is the personification of Woman Wisdom. While we can debate the precise nature of the personification—Does she represent God's attribute of wisdom or, ultimately, God himself? (see chap. 1)—there is no doubt that Woman Wisdom is a personification. Proverbs 8 has all the other characteristics of Hebrew poetry (esp. parallelism and figurative language). To treat the language (such as the description of her as the first act of God's creation) as literal is a category mistake.

A second type of category mistake is to treat this profound and powerful poem as a prophecy that Jesus fulfills. Again, Woman Wisdom is not a description of the later incarnate Jesus. The association that the NT draws makes an important point—that Jesus is the very embodiment of God's wisdom—but the text is not claiming that Jesus is like Woman Wisdom in all the details given by the wisdom teacher in Prov. 8.

Though he lived over a millennium and a half ago, Arius's influence continues today among those who would use passages like Prov. 8 and its NT echoes to argue that Jesus is not equal to the Father. The Church of Jesus Christ of Latter-day Saints (Mormonism) is a prime example. Thus, a consideration of this misreading of Prov. 8 is still germane.

Indeed, there are other recent mistreatments of Prov. 8 that lead to theological controversies. Perhaps most notable among these is the so-called Sophia movement among certain extreme feminist theologians and church leaders. Disdaining a male mediator between God and humans who accomplishes redemption through an act of violence, advocates of Sophia theology substitute the veneration of a female mediator (Sophia, the Greek word for wisdom) for that of Jesus. They also reject the Lord's Supper, believing it to be a ritual that underscores the violence of traditional Christianity (the bread and wine representing the body and blood of the Savior). In its place, they substitute a ritual that uses honey and milk. This group expressed its beliefs most publicly at a worship service in Minneapolis in 1993. Even relatively permissive denominations distanced themselves from this group and censured clergy who participated at that time.[4]

From these historical and contemporary examples of misuse of the imagery of Woman Wisdom in Prov. 8, we understand the importance of careful interpretation of this important passage.

A Christian Reading of Proverbs 9

Proverbs 9 confronts the reader with a choice at a pivotal place in the book (see detailed treatment in chap. 1). Proverbs 9 brings the first part of the book, composed of discourses or speeches, to a close before giving way to the second part, which is composed of proverbs per se. In the discourses, the young men who are addressed are described as walking on a path, which stands for the journey of life. In chapter 9, the path comes to a mountain on which sits Woman Wisdom's magnificent seven-columned house. From there she invites the young men to join her for a sumptuous meal. The meal represents an invitation to an intimate and deep relationship. At the end of the chapter, the young men receive a second invitation from a woman named Folly. She too wants a relationship with the young men, but her intentions are evil and lead to death, as opposed to the life-giving intentions of Woman Wisdom. The narrator thus warns the young men to reject Folly's invitation.

4. See my excursus on the Sophia movement at the end of chap. 13.

The young men are the implied addressees of the book's instruction, and all subsequent actual readers stand in their place and are thus confronted with the choice of dining with Woman Wisdom or with Woman Folly. In our earlier, more detailed examination of this chapter in its OT context, we argued that Woman Wisdom stands for Yahweh's wisdom, indeed for Yahweh himself. After all, her house is on the highest point of the city (9:3), the place of the temple. Woman Folly's house is also on the heights of the city (9:14), so she too represents deity, in her case the false gods and goddesses who stand as rivals to the worship of the true God Yahweh, gods like Baal, Asherah, Anat, Marduk, Ishtar, and the like.

The Christian reader thus understands the choice between a relationship with the true God or the false gods of the nations. But in light of the NT's association between Woman Wisdom and Christ, and the further revelation about the triune nature of the biblical God, the Christian reads Prov. 9 as a choice between a deep, life-giving relationship with Jesus and anything or anyone that would rival our relationship with God through Jesus.

Conclusion

As is well known, the NT presents Jesus as the ultimate king (Messiah/Christ), the ultimate prophet (Acts 3:22), and the ultimate priest (in the "order of Melchizedek," Heb. 6:13–7:17). Through description in the Gospels and assertion in the Epistles, as well as association with Woman Wisdom, Jesus was also seen as the ultimate sage. The Christian reading Prov. 9 understands that the decision is whether to dine with Jesus, Woman Wisdom, or any other thing or person that takes the place of Christ as the center of our lives. For the Christian, living wisely entails listening to the voice of Christ as he speaks through Scripture.

Christian Wisdom in the New Testament

In the first part of this chapter we focused on how the NT presents Jesus Christ as the ultimate sage and associates him with Woman Wisdom herself. The message is clear to the NT's Christian audience: to be wise means being in relationship with God as he made himself manifest in the incarnation. We will also see that the NT continues the close association between wisdom and the spirit of God, who in the NT is the Third Person of the Trinity, the Holy Spirit. In the remainder of the chapter, we explore the nature of wisdom as presented by the NT. What is Christian wisdom? How do the authors of the NT describe Christian wisdom? As we will see, perhaps not surprisingly, NT wisdom continues the themes of OT wisdom that begin with a relationship with God—Father, Son, and Holy Spirit—characterized by fear.

Working Out Our Salvation with Fear and Trembling

In a bid to make faith in the biblical God palatable and attractive, many Christian leaders today put a premium on God's love and on the NT presentation of Jesus as our friend. He loves us, and we should respond to his sacrificial love with affection of our own toward him. And, the argument typically continues, if we love God, then we have no reason to fear anything. Indeed, 1 John 4:18 can even be cited as something of a proof text for this view of God: "There is no fear in love. But perfect love drives out fear, because fear has to do with punishment. The one who fears is not made perfect in love." Thus, it appears that if a person has fear, then their love has not yet been perfected.

Of course, this understanding of the gospel is true, but it is a partial and significantly misunderstood truth. Our view is corrected by noting the robust NT instruction that Christians must fear God. During his earthly ministry Jesus instructed those who listened to him to "not be afraid of those who kill the body and after that can do no more. But I will show you whom you should fear: Fear him who, after your body has been killed, has authority to throw you into hell. Yes, I tell you, fear him" (Luke 12:4–5).

We also learn from the Gospel of Luke that God blesses those who fear him. Mary's song sung before the birth of Christ proclaims "His mercy extends to those who fear him, from generation to generation" (Luke 1:50). Or we can think of Peter speaking to Cornelius concerning his realization that God loves not only Jews but also gentiles: "I now realize how true it is that God does not show favoritism but accepts from every nation the one who fears him and does what is right" (Acts 10:34–35).

The early church was described as those who feared God: "Then the church throughout Judea, Galilee and Samaria enjoyed a time of peace and was strengthened. Living in the fear of the Lord and encouraged by the Holy Spirit, it increased in numbers" (Acts 9:31). Paul ascribes his motivation to spread the gospel to his fear of God: "Since, then, we know what it is to fear the Lord, we try to persuade others" (2 Cor. 5:11).

That the NT fear of God is more than respect is clear from Paul's statement that Titus's "affection for you is all the greater when he remembers that you were all obedient, receiving him with fear and trembling" (2 Cor. 7:15) and from his exhortation to the Philippian church, saying, "continue to work out your salvation with fear and trembling" (Phil. 2:12).

These and numerous other passages make clear that Christian faith is characterized by the fear of the Lord, a fear that causes us to tremble before the holiness of an awesome and glorious God, a fear that leads to obedience. The fear that perfect love casts out is the fear of other people or circumstances. If we love God perfectly, then that love is combined with fear of God, leaving no space for fear of anyone or anything else.

The New Testament Wisdom Book: The Book of James

James, likely the brother of Jesus, begins the book named after him with what looks to be an epistolary greeting to the recipients of his writing, "To the twelve tribes scattered among the nations: Greetings" (1:1). While this looks like the opening of a letter, it lacks the familiar salutations at the end. The "twelve tribes scattered among the nations" is an allusion to the Diaspora of the Jews, but in this case it may well simply be a way to address all Christians, whether of Jewish or gentile background, since Christians were indeed scattered throughout the nations.

Wisdom comes up in the very first paragraph following the superscription. In the midst of encouraging his readers who face persecution, he advises, "If any of you lacks wisdom, you should ask God, who gives generously to all without finding fault, and it will be given to you" (1:5). Here James affirms the strong OT teaching that God is the sole source of wisdom. In the same way that Woman Wisdom offers wisdom to those who ask her (Prov. 1:20–33), so he encourages them to ask God, who will give to those who ask.[5] Wisdom is a quality that would help the fledging church navigate the turbulent waters of persecution.

James is also sensitive to the transience of life and applies it to the struggles of the poor and the pride of the wealthy: "But the rich should take pride in their humiliation—since they will pass away like a wild flower. For the sun rises with scorching heat and withers the plant; its blossom falls and its beauty is destroyed. In the same way, the rich will fade away even while they go about their business" (1:10–11). Here we think immediately of Ps. 73, a wisdom psalm whose author finds solace in the fact that the wicked rich will not last long, or Ps. 49, which states that all die, including the wealthy. In Ecclesiastes, Qohelet also reflects on the transience of life.

James speaks to the nitty-gritty issues of wisdom, such as proper speech and control of one's emotional expression. Consider for instance the advice

5. God will give wisdom to those who ask, but such a divine response does not mean that the recipient moves to a fully mature wisdom. Asking God for wisdom places one on the right path of an ever-growing wisdom that leads to life.

found in 1:19–20: "My dear brothers and sisters, take note of this: Everyone should be quick to listen, slow to speak and slow to become angry, because human anger does not produce the righteousness that God desires" (cf. Prov. 8:32–34; 11:16; 15:31; 17:18; 27:2; 30:33). James's wisdom on proper speech is found also in his statement that "those who consider themselves religious and yet do not keep a tight rein on their tongues deceive themselves and their religion is worthless" (1:26) and in his teaching about the power of the tongue, which can both "praise our Lord and Father" and "curse human beings, who have been made in God's likeness" (3:9; see all of 3:1–12). In 4:1–3 he further analyzes the roots of anger that issues forth in fights and quarrels.

James 3 ends with a reflection on two types of wisdom when it asks, "Who is wise and understanding among you?" (3:13). James begins his answer by describing "wisdom that comes from heaven," which is "pure; then peace-loving, considerate, submissive, full of mercy and good fruit, impartial and sincere. Peacemakers who sow in peace reap a harvest of righteousness" (3:17–18). He contrasts this with wisdom that "does not come down from heaven but is earthly, unspiritual, demonic. For where you have envy and selfish ambition, there you find disorder and every evil practice" (3:15–16).

Another connection between James and the instructions of the sages who produced the book of Proverbs appears in James's ridicule of those who make plans without taking into consideration the will of God and, once again, the transience of life:

> Now listen, you who say, "Today or tomorrow we will go to this or that city, spend a year there, carry on business and make money." Why, you do not even know what will happen tomorrow. What is your life? You are a mist that appears for a little while and then vanishes. Instead, you ought to say, "If it is the Lord's will, we will live and do this or that." As it is, you boast in your arrogant schemes. All such boasting is evil. If anyone, then, knows the good they ought to do and doesn't do it, it is sin for them. (4:13–17)

To this we might compare:

> To humans belong the plans of the heart,
> but from Yahweh comes a responding tongue. (Prov. 16:1)

> Commit your acts to Yahweh,
> and your plans will be established. (Prov. 16:3)

> Human hearts plan their path,
> but Yahweh establishes their step. (Prov. 16:9)

James 5 ends with additional themes familiar from OT wisdom literature. The first paragraph (vv. 1–6) condemns the rich for exploiting the poor (Prov. 28:27; 29:7) and warns them that their wealth will soon disappear (Pss. 49; 73; Prov. 11:18).

In the next paragraph James admonishes his readers to be patient in suffering. The Lord is indeed coming and will rescue them from their persecution, but in the meantime they need to "be patient and stand firm" (5:8). This context includes an explicit appeal to Job as an example of the type of attitude suffering Christians should adopt. Most modern translations of James opt for a rendering along the lines of the NIV: "As you know, we count as blessed those who have persevered. You have heard of Job's perseverance and have seen what the Lord finally brought about. The Lord is full of compassion and mercy" (James 5:11; cf. NRSV, which uses "endurance" rather than "perseverance"). The translation "perseverance" for Greek *hypomonē* differs from the traditional rendering "the patience of Job" (see KJV). While modern translations almost always improve on traditional renderings when they differ, I do not believe that is the case here.

Patience is a passive waiting for a desired goal, whereas perseverance or endurance allows for complaint or fight while holding on till the goal is achieved. The modern translation of 5:11 is driven by the fact that the biblical Job is anything but patient. However, the question arises whether James is appealing directly back to the biblical Job or looking at Job through the prism of the *Testament of Job* (see above, chap. 14), popular when the book of James was written. In the *Testament of Job* the main character is the epitome of patience.[6] However one translates *hypomonē*, James's mention of Job again highlights the influence of OT wisdom literature on his thinking and writing.

The Spirit and Wisdom in the Old and New Testaments

Our study of Jesus as the ultimate sage should not lead us to neglect the close connection between wisdom and the spirit (Spirit) of God in the Scriptures. The role of the Spirit in the OT is not easy to determine, since the biblical teaching of the Trinity really only begins to take shape in the NT. To be sure, the OT speaks of the spirit of God, but likely not in the fully developed understanding of the Holy Spirit as a person within the Godhead (Father, Son, and

---

6. Balentine (*Have You Considered My Servant Job?*, 15–49) traces the development of the character of Job as an exemplar of patience from the biblical book through the Septuagint, the *Testament of Job*, the NT Epistle of James, and into the Middle Ages (Gregory the Great's *Moralia in Job* [sixth century]).

Holy Spirit). God, after all, is a spiritual being, and the spirit (of God) may
be roughly synonymous with God, and we should not read the OT as if they
had insight into the trinitarian nature of God.[7]

Nevertheless, there is continuity between how the OT speaks of the spirit of
God and how the NT speaks of the Holy Spirit.[8] The OT testifies to the close
connection between the Spirit and wisdom in several interesting passages. In
Exod. 31 God tells Moses that he has filled Bezalel the master craftsman "with
the Spirit of God, with wisdom, with understanding, with knowledge and
with all kinds of skills" (v. 3) for the purpose of constructing the tabernacle.
Here wisdom, conferred by the Spirit of God, is connected with technical
skill.[9] In Genesis, Pharaoh acknowledges that Joseph's wisdom in interpreting his dreams and planning for the famine comes from the spirit of God:
"'Can we find anyone else like this man—one in whom is the spirit of God?'
Then Pharaoh said to Joseph, 'Since God has made all this known to you,
there is no one so discerning and wise as you'" (41:38–39). The same connection between spirit and wisdom is made by the narrator of Deuteronomy
in speaking of Joshua, who was full "of the spirit of wisdom" (Deut. 34:9).

In Proverbs, Woman Wisdom appeals to her potential disciples by promising
them that she will "pour forth my spirit to you; I will make known to you my
words" (1:23).[10] Significantly binding spirit, Messiah, and wisdom together is
Isaiah's anticipation that:

> A shoot will come up from the stump of Jesse;
>   from his roots a Branch will bear fruit.
> The Spirit of the LORD will rest on him—
>   the Spirit of wisdom and of understanding,
>   the Spirit of counsel and of might,
>   the Spirit of knowledge and fear of the LORD—
> and he will delight in the fear of the LORD. (Isa. 11:1–3a)

Jesus again is the epitome of God's wisdom. He is the one on whom the
Spirit descended like a dove at his baptism and sent him out to the wilderness
(Mark 1:9–13). Paul reflects the spiritual nature of Jesus's wisdom:

7. Walton, "Ancient Near Eastern Background," 66–67.
8. E.g., Acts 2:16–18 cites Joel 2:28 when the Holy Spirit descends on the disciples on the
day of Pentecost.
9. Van Leeuwen ("Cosmos, Temple, House") has pointed out the interesting analogy between
the temple-like cosmos created by God by his wisdom (Prov. 3:19–20; 8:22–31), the cosmos-like
temple constructed by divine wisdom (Exod. 31), and a house constructed by the wisdom of
a wise woman (Prov. 14:1).
10. Longman, "Spirit and Wisdom."

The Spirit searches all things, even the deep things of God. For who knows a person's thoughts except their own spirit within them? In the same way no one knows the thoughts of God except the Spirit of God. What we have received is not the spirit of the world, but the Spirit who is from God, so that we may understand what God has freely given us (1 Cor. 2:10–12).

Conclusion

Our survey of wisdom in the NT sees significant continuity with the OT. Jesus is the epitome of God's wisdom, or, perhaps better, the very incarnation of God's wisdom. He is the one on whom the Spirit of the Lord rests. His delight is in the fear of the Lord.

Thus, the church is called to relationship with him and to inculcate and demonstrate the same fear that is the beginning of wisdom. Christians are God-fearers who submit to the instruction of Christ. The book of James urges Christians to seek the wisdom from above (from God) and to demonstrate that wisdom in their speech, their relationships with others, their planning, their handing of money—indeed, in all of life.

APPENDIX 1

WISDOM IN THE TWENTY-FIRST CENTURY

Our study has focused on OT wisdom. The subtitle of this book speaks of "Wisdom in Israel" because we contend that, though OT wisdom has a different stance toward its pagan counterparts than, say, the prophets have toward the surrounding cultures and religions, Israelite wisdom is nonetheless distinct (particular) from other contemporary wisdom as opposed to just another manifestation of a worldwide phenomenon. After all, Israelite wisdom starts with the claim that "the fear of the Lord [Yahweh] is the beginning of wisdom." There is no true wisdom apart from a proper relationship with the God of Israel.

When we turned our attention to the NT, we were struck by the presentation of Jesus as the epitome of divine wisdom, Woman Wisdom herself, and the call that his followers become God-fearers who, filled with the Spirit, are wise. The implication, then, is that to be wise means to be in a relationship with Jesus.

But what does it mean to be wise in the twenty-first century? As recently as 2007, theologian David Ford started his stimulating book on Christian wisdom by saying, "Wisdom has on the whole not had an easy time in recent centuries in the West. It has often been associated with old people, the premodern, tradition and conservative caution in a culture of youth, modernization, innovation and risky exploration." He goes on to say "it may be making a comeback."[1] The last ten years have more than confirmed his prediction.

Wisdom is a term that is back in vogue, not just in the church but in the broader culture. A recent example is the work of Krista Tippett, the host of NPR's *On Being* and a Peabody award winner and recipient of the National Humanities Medal, who in 2016 published *Becoming Wise: An Inquiry into the Mystery and Art of Living.* This insightful book explores topics like speech, body, love, faith, and hope in ways that are reminiscent of themes in the book of Proverbs from a perspective of what, we must admit, is a kind of amorphous spirituality. While not hostile to her rather rigid Southern Baptist upbringing and appreciative of certain Christian leaders like Shane Claiborne, Miroslav Volf, and Walter Brueggemann, she likely would not want to be pigeonholed in a narrow religious category. But still, the helpful nature of her writing reminds us that wisdom on the practical and ethical levels is not restricted to those who embrace orthodox Christian theology.

So again we ask the question, what does wisdom look like in the twenty-first century? We will answer this question in two parts, corresponding to our earlier analysis of biblical wisdom having three levels or components: practical, ethical, and theological. We will begin by exploring twenty-first-century wisdom on the practical and ethical levels. Then we will go on to discuss twenty-first-century wisdom that includes the theological dimension.

Navigating Life with Wisdom in the Twenty-First Century and Beyond

We have covered much territory up to this point as we have moved from wisdom in the OT and through the intertestamental period into the NT. We now take a huge leap forward to the present day, skipping the interesting question of the reception of these ideas from the first century AD until now.[2]

Our interest is whether and how the ancient biblical concept of wisdom might have continuing relevance in our contemporary society. Surprisingly, wisdom has experienced a bit of a revival not only in ecclesiastical circles but also in society at large. Of course, the understanding of wisdom's continuing relevance will differ, though overlap, among and between people of faith and others.

As mentioned above, the distinction we made early in this book between the practical, ethical, and theological dimensions of biblical wisdom will be

1. Ford, *Christian Wisdom*, 1.
2. The history of interpretation of specific books associated with wisdom may be found in Longman and Enns, *Dictionary of the Old Testament.*

useful at this point. Western society at large speaks of wisdom according to the first two levels, but not the third, while people of faith might insist that unless the third dimension is present we are not really talking about biblical wisdom ("the fear of Yahweh is the beginning of knowledge," Prov. 1:7). In addition, we should also realize that there is more than one ancient tradition of wisdom, whether we are talking about Aristotle's concept of practical wisdom or reason (*phronēsis*), Confucius's *Analects*, any number of ancient proverb collections, and more. While Christians will focus, sometimes exclusively, on canonical wisdom, others treat biblical wisdom as one of any number of sources of insight into living life today.

People of faith should take their cue from those who wrote, collected, and edited the biblical book of Proverbs. Earlier we observed that Proverbs is a collection of wise sayings that originated not only in Israel but from outside Israel, particularly Egypt, as well. Throughout Proverbs, but particularly in the Words of the Wise (Prov. 22:17–24:34), we find proverbs that seem inspired by Egyptian instruction texts such as that of Amenemope but have been adapted and contextualized.[3] Though not regarded as wise in the most profound and foundational sense, the Egyptian sages still had value in the eyes of the Israelite sages.

This appendix is suggestive, not exhaustive, as we consider wisdom's continuing relevance. We provide examples of the utility of wisdom in different areas of life and survey some of the literature of the past couple of decades that seeks to present wisdom, whether specifically under that name or not, as a means of living life well in the twenty-first century.

Living Life Wisely

Though not viewed specifically in the biblical sense, the idea of wisdom entered again into the public arena with the publication of Dan Goleman's influential book *Emotional Intelligence*. With a PhD in psychology, Goleman is a science journalist who has brought the work of psychologists and neuroscientists to a broader audience in order to debunk the common idea that one's IQ is the most important predictor, if not the only predictor, of life success. In the generation before his book, there was little scientific study of emotions, but in the decade before his book and certainly since its publication, human emotion has been the subject of intense scrutiny.

IQ measures one's ability to master facts and solve problems (a kind of "knowing that"), whereas emotional intelligence measures skill of living,

---

3. See chap. 9 and Longman, "Proverbs."

knowing when to say or do the right thing at the right time and expressing the proper emotion at the level appropriate for the situation (a kind of "knowing how"). Take anger, for instance. Goleman points out that someone who is emotionally intelligent is "able, for example, to rein in emotional impulse, to read another's inmost feeling; to handle relationships smoothly—as Aristotle put it, the rare skill 'to be angry with the right person, to the right degree, at the right time, for the right purpose, and in the right way.'"[4] His quotation from Aristotle shows that he is not basing his comments exclusively on biblical wisdom. Indeed, he nowhere shows any awareness of biblical wisdom at the time of writing this book. Nonetheless, anyone who knows the book of Proverbs knows that his description of emotional intelligence largely matches the practical level of the biblical wisdom tradition.

What is success in life anyway? Again, Goleman's description of emotional intelligence resonates with the types of goals that the sages in Proverbs hoped to achieve. They include healthy and happy relationships with friends and family, being able to earn a living by having and keeping a job or career, and living a healthy life. While emotional intelligence does not guarantee such success, it is, as we said regarding biblical wisdom earlier (see chap. 11), the best route to a desired conclusion.

Thus, the research he presents that shows the correlation between life success and emotional intelligence also supports the contemporary benefits of the wisdom presented by the ancient biblical sages. In the past, people believed, and many still do today, that the key to success in life is a high IQ, perhaps measured by good grades in school. Many parents put pressure on their children to get good grades in high school in order to get into a top-rated liberal arts college with the hope that they will have successful careers. These hopes are sometimes realized, but perhaps not as consistently as one might think. After all, there is some truth to the adage that "A students teach B students who work for C students." The idea is that C students did not spend all their time in the library but were out interacting with people and learning the skills associated with what we call emotional intelligence or wisdom.

The qualities associated with emotional intelligence (wisdom) make the connection with success obvious. While this list from Goleman's book is not exhaustive, from it we can see again how closely it reflects what the Bible teaches about wisdom. Emotional intelligence includes "self-control, zeal and persistence, the ability to motivate oneself."[5] It also includes "abilities such as being able to motivate oneself and persist in the face of frustrations; to control

4. Goleman, *Emotional Intelligence*, xiii.
5. Ibid., xii.

impulse and delay gratification; to regulate one's mood and keep distress from swamping the ability to think; to empathize and to hope."[6] In other words, someone who is emotionally intelligent has the type of character that is able to weather "the turmoil—or opportunity—life's vicissitudes bring."[7]

Again, emotional intelligence is no guarantee of success in life, but it is a typical route to success. Perhaps before closing our discussion of Goleman's analysis of emotional intelligence, we should point out that while the same cannot be said of those with only a high IQ, people can have both intellectual intelligence and emotional intelligence.

Goleman's work has stimulated others to write about emotional intelligence, though possibly under a different label.[8] Though not directly flowing from biblical teaching on wisdom from the Bible, these public examinations of wise living bear great similarities to what we have called the practical and ethical dimensions of wisdom. Though lacking the theological dimension, they retain their value for us in a way similar to how the Israelite sages who wrote about biblical wisdom were surely enamored with and learned from their Egyptian and other ancient Near Eastern counterparts. While Christians should always remember that their wisdom should be firmly founded on the right relationship with the true God, we can still learn from those who have made helpful observations about how humans flourish well in the world.

Leading with Wisdom

The book of Proverbs makes it very clear that wisdom is an essential requirement for leaders. A wise leader creates a flourishing community, while a foolish leader destroys community. Woman Wisdom proclaims:

> By me kings reign,
> and nobles issue just decrees.
> By me rulers rule,
> and princes, all righteous judgments. (Prov. 8:15–16)

Many of the proverbs about a king presuppose a godly, wise king like Solomon in his youth. The wise king promotes ethical behavior and undermines and removes wickedness to the benefit of the community at large.

---

6. Ibid., 34.
7. Ibid., 36.
8. Besides Tippett, mentioned in the introduction to this chapter, see the reference to the work of David Brooks below.

> A king who sits on his judgment throne
> scatters all evil with his eyes. (20:8)

> A wise king scatters wicked people,
> and he rolls the wheel over them. (20:26)

> A king with justice causes the land to endure. (29:4a)

The proverbs warn of a foolish wicked king and compare the damage he causes to that of a predatory animal:

> A growling lion and a prowling bear—
> a wicked ruler over a poor people. (28:15)

In earlier chapters (5 and 6) we examined the wise leadership of Solomon (in his early phase), Joseph, and Daniel—all of whom through their wise actions, decisions, and behavior brought positive benefit to the communities in which they found themselves.

In a recent book, Mark Strom examines the importance of wisdom for leaders in business, politics, the military, and throughout twenty-first-century society.[9] The premise of his book is that "leading well is bringing wisdom to life."[10] Strom, while trained in biblical studies, cites not only canonical wisdom but wisdom from the ages and across cultures. "It's [wisdom] an old idea found in traditions from the ancient Near East to the First Peoples in America."[11]

Strom approaches wisdom primarily on what we have called the practical level, the skill of living. He teaches the importance of discovering patterns of life ("I view wisdom as reading the patterns of life with discernment and applying your insights with integrity and care. I then look at leadership as a pattern of human experience").[12] Much like the sages of the book of Proverbs, he advises leaders to be attentive and present to their experiences in order to read patterns and then to live into them. In the context of wise leadership, he encourages careful naming and conversation. Words, he rightly says, shape reality, and it is important to say the right word at the right time to the right person, accentuating the wise-timing aspect of biblical wisdom. He exposits the importance of wise influence ("relationships make or break change").[13]

9. Strom, *Lead with Wisdom*.
10. Ibid., 27.
11. Ibid.
12. Ibid., xi.
13. Ibid., 49.

While much of the emphasis stays on the practical level of wisdom, the ethical level is not neglected. He understands that "wisdom is not an accumulation of knowledge but springs from a deep orientation of the heart."[14] Indeed, a leader with practical wisdom but without ethical wisdom is not wise at all. "Someone may read life well and have a fine sense of judgement. But if her personal integrity is questionable, we might call her clever or astute, but never wise. Wise leadership needs integrity."[15]

Strom's promotion of wise leadership is in keeping with biblical teaching as we have seen it in earlier chapters. While, as we mentioned, he draws on many different wisdom traditions, at every point but one they cohere with the core of biblical teaching on practical and ethical wisdom. The departure, of course, comes in the omission of the fundamental theological dimension of biblical wisdom. Strom is writing for a general audience and does good service in so doing, and I suspect that he personally knows that in one sense wisdom on the practical and ethical levels without the theological foundation is rather anemic. Nonetheless, his important and insightful study demonstrates the continuing relevance of biblical wisdom for leadership today.

Wisdom and Education

Education in the West is in crisis on all levels, from preschool to graduate school, for a host of reasons too numerous to even list. Not all are relevant in a book on wisdom, but I would suggest that part of the problem is that the emphasis in education in the past couple centuries has been on the cultivation of IQ and not wisdom. For this reason, schools that go against this trend are noteworthy. I simply give two examples. The first concerns the training of engineers at Northwestern University in Chicago.

From an outsider's perspective, engineering seems like the last place where wisdom would be required or even necessary. We want our engineers to know a lot about mathematics, physics, metallurgy, and other subjects that require a high IQ. However, a recent article in the *Wall Street Journal* makes clear that wisdom indeed is an essential component of being a good engineer. The engineering school of Northwestern University has devised a course in order to encourage its students toward the types of qualities that create effective engineers. While the article (and most likely the school) does not use the term wisdom, as we list the qualities that the school cultivates in its students, we can see that they are indeed the same qualities that biblical wisdom seeks to inculcate in people in general.

14. Ibid.
15. Ibid., 23.

The school assigns the students a task that does not have an easy solution and may be insoluble. The article then lists the strategy with the intended goal as follows:[16]

Listen to and understand the people you're trying to help	Empathy
Be open to alternative ways of thinking	Creativity
Get help from others	Teamwork
Try many ideas, even strange-sounding ones	Brainstorming
Adopt an entrepreneurial attitude	Risk-taking
Accept the inevitable failures	Humility
Try and try again	Resiliency

Of course, this type of wise character development can be put to good use in every profession. A common complaint about doctors is that, though they are good at their specialty, they don't have a good "bedside manner." A bedside manner refers to the ability to communicate well with patients, nurses, and fellow doctors. It includes the proper type of empathy, particularly when speaking with very ill patients. Of course, by now we recognize these and other qualities necessary to have a good bedside manner as the traits of a wise person. Imagine medical schools including these types of skills as a requirement of their curriculum.[17]

Though we could comment on all the professions,[18] I will speak of only one more: professional Christian ministry. I taught in a seminary for the first two decades of my career and continue to teach at a number of different schools that are preparing men and women for ministry. The school where I started my teaching career is representative of typical seminary education and its almost exclusive emphasis on developing only the mind. Students succeed if they have a high IQ, but having good character that is appropriate for the ministry typically counts for little.

There are some notable exceptions to this, though. I have had the privilege, for example, to teach at the Seattle School of Theology and Psychology since its founding in the late 1990s. No institution is perfect, but the Seattle School is exceptional for its emphasis not only on its students' intellectual development in theology and related areas but also for its cultivation of their character and ability to understand their social context. This spirit is captured

16. The list and the article about the school are found in S. Shellenbarger, "Why Solve the Unsolvable?," *Wall Street Journal*, February 24, 2016, D1–2.

17. Fiddes (*Seeing the World and Knowing God*, 5) notes "there has been an increasing volume of voices in healthcare circles about the need for 'wisdom' in medicine" and gives bibliography.

18. See below for some comments on law and legal professionals.

by a statement highlighted on its web page (http://www.theseattleschool
.edu): "Our mission is to train people to be competent in the study of the text,
soul, and culture in order to serve God and neighbor through transforming
relationships." Again, I would call this training in wisdom for the ministry.
The ability not only to know theology and the Bible but to know oneself as
well as others in the context of our society is critical to effective ministry.[19]

Spiritual Formation and Wisdom

The types of skills that are developed by the curriculum at the Seattle School
are also important for those who become spiritual directors—those who provide guidance to others concerning their spiritual formation. Being a spiritual
director involves much more than learning a formulaic curriculum and applying it uniformly to all people or approaching every person in the same way.

Because of the need for wisdom in spiritual formation, I was struck by the
helpful approach taken in a recent book titled *Spiritual Companioning*, as
exemplified by the following two quotations:

> Spiritual direction is not primarily about problem solving or becoming directly
> involved in finding solutions to situations. However, at times a director may
> choose to address emotional pain, frustration, fear, or a need for clarity in a
> particular situation by engaging the directee in more intense dialogue or dis-
> cussion about what is happening and what interventions may be needed. The
> spiritual director does not propose answers, but works with the person to clarify
> the situation and find best practices.

> We would be remiss not to address the importance of artfulness more fully.
> Creativity is absolutely critical to any spiritual direction relationship.[20]

Creativity, artfulness, working individually with each person to help them
find direction for their life rather than giving them a set of rules—these are
all qualities of the wise spiritual director.

Wisdom in the Courtroom?

Can wisdom inform the practice and execution of law in the courtroom?
The book of Kings provides an example that answers this question affirma-
tively. Solomon's divinely given wisdom finds expression in a judicial ruling

---

19. For a stimulating attempt to recover a sense of theology and the study of theology as
wisdom, see Treier, *Virtue and the Voice of God*.
20. Both quotes are from Reed, Osmer, and Smucker, *Spiritual Companioning*, 68–69.

in 1 Kings 3:16–28.[21] The case involves two prostitutes, both of whom claim to be the mother of the baby. Solomon discovers the truth of the matter by announcing that the child will be divided so that each woman can have half. When the true mother ("the woman whose son was alive," 3:26) immediately gives up her claim in order to save the child's life, Solomon grants her custody of the child. The narrative ends by saying that this decision demonstrated that Solomon "had wisdom from God to administer justice" (3:28).

Of course, it's one thing to see that wisdom plays a role during the biblical period, but can wisdom inform the practice and execution of law in the twenty-first century? Interestingly, the question occupies an important discussion among legal theorists where there is a robust literature discussing the place of wisdom in the courtroom. The discussion of wisdom here does not necessarily or even usually flow directly out of the full biblical conception of wisdom (as we saw earlier in this appendix with the idea of emotional intelligence), but neither is it completely unrelated, as we can see in the study of Brett Scharffs titled "The Role of Humility in Exercising Practical Wisdom," which focuses on the importance of wisdom in judges.

Scharffs begins not with biblical wisdom but with Aristotle's concept of *phronēsis*,[22] practical wisdom or practical reason, which bears close resemblance to what we have called the practical and ethical levels of biblical wisdom. As Richard Posner defines it, "Practical reason . . . is not a single analytical method or even a set of related methods but a grab bag of methods, both of investigation and of persuasion. It includes anecdote, introspection, imagination, common sense, intuition . . . , empathy, imputation of motives, speaker's authority, metaphor, analogy, precedent, custom, memory, 'induction' (the expectation of regularities, related both to intuition and to analogy), 'experience.'"[23]

Scharffs's exploration of the role of wisdom in a judicial setting takes a decidedly biblical turn when he discusses the interplay of sympathy and detachment with the biblical concepts of mercy and justice and asks how these two oftentimes conflicting virtues can be mediated with one another. His answer, based on Mic. 6:1–8, is humility, a virtue that, along with mercy and justice, is promoted in biblical wisdom literature.

Scharffs's and others' advocacy for wisdom in the twenty-first-century courtroom is to be applauded and encouraged. In our democratic society, with its emphasis on the separation of church and state, it is not surprising

21. Earlier considered in chap. 6.
22. Particularly relevant is Aristotle, *Nicomachean Ethics*, book 6, chap. 5; see Ackrill, *New Aristotle Reader*.
23. Posner, "Jurisprudence of Skepticism," 838; cited also in Scharffs, "Role of Humility," 133.

(or even regrettable) that the theological dimension of wisdom does not enter into the discussion. However, certainly Christian lawyers and judges will find impetus for exercising wisdom in their work in their fear of God.

Living Wisely in the Fear of God in the Twenty-First Century and Beyond

In the first part of this appendix we considered living with wisdom in the twenty-first century on the practical and ethical levels. The Bible recognizes the value of such wisdom to be sure, but it is not the Bible's final word on wisdom. To be truly and fully wise, one must embrace God. Thus, in the second part of this appendix we put forward the following description of the twenty-first-century Christian sage.

The Wise Person Fears God

Again, the beginning or foundation of wisdom in the Bible, OT and NT, is the fear of God. There is no wisdom apart from a relationship with God that submits to the one and true God, whom Christians know as the Father, Son, and Holy Spirit. The Triune God is the Creator and Sustainer of the cosmos. If our knees don't knock as we consider with whom we have a personal relationship, then our conception of God is too small and we cannot claim to be wise in the biblical sense. Yes, God loves us, but that does not diminish his sovereignty and authority in our lives. Our fear cannot be terror, however, but rather should compel us to bow in his presence. From this attitude of worship, we humble ourselves to hear his voice and follow his guidance. Indeed, as we saw in the book of Ecclesiastes, there is a fear of God that does not lead to obedience (that expressed by Qohelet) and is not wisdom. Again, authentic fear of God makes us attentive to God's voice. But where do we hear him?

The Wise Person Knows Scripture

In the book of Proverbs the wise son hears God's voice when the father speaks. He hears and responds when Woman Wisdom calls him. The father is none other than God's proxy, and Woman Wisdom is an image of God himself. The wise follow the advice of the instructions provided by the father and Woman Wisdom. We have argued above that the biblical wisdom teachers understood that there was a connection between proverb and law and that the wise person obeyed Torah (as the frame narrator instructed, "Fear God and keep his commandments," Eccles. 12:13). The intertestamental books made this connection between wisdom and law explicit. Woman Wisdom speaks Torah (see also Deut. 4:4–9).

Since the beginning of its history, the church has recognized that Scripture as a whole is canon, the standard of faith and practice. To cite an oft-quoted passage, "All Scripture is God-breathed and is useful for teaching, rebuking, correcting and training in righteousness, so that the servant of God may be thoroughly equipped for every good work" (2 Tim. 3:16–17). Thus, to hear God's voice, we turn first to Scripture.

The Wise Person Is Hermeneutically Savvy

But is it enough just to learn Scripture? In the first place, hearing God's voice in Scripture is more than simply memorizing Scripture. It is possible to know the Bible well but use it foolishly. One must study the Bible carefully to hear God's voice well. Some people have a misconception of the Bible—and that is, to put it bluntly, that it is easy to understand. This view is a particular misconception of Protestant Christianity. Over against certain medieval Catholic views, Protestant theology urged that everyone can read the Bible on their own and didn't need a priest to read it and interpret it for them. Much good came out of this emphasis on the priesthood of all believers and the clarity of Scripture. After all, the Bible is clear—on its main and essential teachings. But, though the main and essential teachings of Scripture are perspicuous, to use the technical theological term, the entire teaching of Scripture is not clear by any account. To read Scripture well in order to hear the voice of God takes study, and not just individual study. It takes a community to read Scripture well and to keep us from our own idiosyncratic readings.

Thus, the twenty-first-century Christian sage is an adept interpreter of the Bible, which requires much study of ancient genres, literary conventions, and history. The sage knows that the Bible is written *for* us but not *to* us. The various books of the Bible were written to their original audiences, and we need first of all to ask what God was saying through the human authors of Scripture to their original audiences before asking what God is saying to us today. The twenty-first-century sage understands that we read the Bible from a limited perspective constricted by our economic status, gender, ethnicity, educational level, and so forth. Thus, we need to listen to (and read) interpretations from people who share our faith but who are different from us. Much more could be said here, of course, but the point is clear: the sage is hermeneutically savvy.[24]

24. Ford (*Christian Wisdom*, 52–89) presents a stimulating argument for "a wisdom interpretation of Scripture."

The Wise Person Learns about God's World from All Sources

The wisdom tradition of the OT also encourages learning from a wide variety of sources and not just the Bible (see chap. 7). This perspective goes against certain Christian traditions that wrongly, in my opinion, understand *sola scriptura* as meaning that we learn about ourselves and our world only from the Bible and that other, secular sources of knowledge are so corrupted that they are of no use.

In response to this latter view, we first of all note that the sages of Proverbs learned from their experience. They observed what worked and what did not work as they walked the path of life and as they advised others as to the best route to their flourishing. They also learned from their mistakes. Granted, all wisdom, even that derived most directly from experience and observation, comes ultimately from God, and in this regard we cite again Prov. 20:12: "An ear to hear and an eye to see—Yahweh made both of them."

In the second place, in response to the idea that the only worthwhile truth is that found in Scripture, we point again to the Israelite sages' appreciation and utilization of the wisdom of the broader ancient Near East (chap. 9). The evidence indicates that they were astute students of the instructional literature of Egypt and Mesopotamia. Since the "fear of the Lord is the beginning of knowledge," the sages of Israel would have recognized the ultimate failure of foreign wisdom, but that did not stop them from appropriating its good insights, insights based on experience and observation. This has tremendous implications for Christian thinking. Let me give just two examples based on contemporary inter-Christian (particularly evangelical Protestant) debates.

The first has to do with current debates in the realm of science and Christianity, particularly as it relates to the creation-evolution debate.[25] Many people believe that the Bible gives a literal account of how God created the world and that this account differs dramatically from that of science. One response is to regard science, if one may generalize, as godless or secular and therefore distorted. Accordingly, some Christians reject science as secular and therefore discount its conclusions on that a priori basis. However, scientists, when they are doing good science and not engaging in discussions of metaphysics, are basing their theoretical conclusions on observation of God's creation. Indeed, it is possible that science in this regard can help us read the Bible better—that is, according to its original intention. As Pope John Paul II put it, "science can purify religion" just as religion "can purify science from idolatry and

25. Charles, *Reading Genesis 1–2*.

false absolutes. Each can draw the other into a wider world; a world in which both can flourish."[26]

Our second example comes from discipline of psychology and its clinical practice, counseling. In 1970 Jay Adams published a groundbreaking book, *Competent to Counsel*,[27] which initiated a revival of biblical counseling. Until that time, it was typical for pastors and other Christian counselors to seek insights from non-Christian sources like Sigmund Freud, Carl Rogers, and many others. Adams and his school of thought eschewed the dependence on secular theory and proposed that our understanding of human behavior be based solely on the Bible.

Adams should be commended for his recovery of the Bible as the foundation of our thinking about ourselves as psychological/emotional/cognitive persons, but if we listen to the Israelite sages and attend to their humility as they learned from their pagan counterparts, we will not reject out of hand the insights of nonreligious thinkers. We will, like the Israelite sages, need to subject the latter's thinking to critique, questioning whether or how their insights fit in with our Christian worldview, but we will continue to learn from many different sources.

With this example, and before moving on to our next proposition, I wish to suggest that the Christian counselor is about as close as we get today to the ancient sage. The task of the Christian counselor is to help clients understand themselves in their context and to guide them. To be a Christian counselor, one must obviously be in a vibrant relationship with God, listening to his Word, living and thinking within the framework of a Christian worldview formed by Scripture, and guiding a person from that perspective. To learn how to understand people takes insight and practice, not only listening to what they say but also watching their body language and picking up on subtle clues. A counselor needs to know how to ask the right questions and to maintain a proper and helpful relationship with the counselee. These are all the qualities and skills of the wise person.

In the final analysis, sages in the twenty-first century will not only be avid students of Scripture but will also learn from many other sources. They will learn as they observe and reflect on their own life experiences. What worked and what didn't (and why)? They will learn from their own mistakes.

They will also learn from others, from other Christians and those of other religions, as well as from nonreligious people. They will learn from

---

26. Quoted in Cunningham, *Darwin's Pious Idea*, 284.
27. First published by Presbyterian and Reformed Publishing Company, Phillipsburg, NJ, and later reprinted by numerous others.

conversations with others who share their life experiences and their insights. They will learn from reading the thinking of others. This may include simply practical insights about life or may be more academic in nature. In terms of the latter, I find the writing of David Brooks insightful, particularly his book *The Social Animal*.[28] Here Brooks describes human development in an anecdotal and personal style that captures great insights from the best work done in sociology, psychology, neuroscience, and more.

The Wise Person Knows How to Read Text, Circumstances, and People

In the previous section we argued that it was not sufficient simply to know Scripture to be wise. As we noted earlier (see chap. 8), it is not enough simply to know the proverbs; one must know how to use them. Indeed, according to Prov. 26:7, 9, knowledge of the proverb alone is useless and even dangerous:

> The legs of a lame person dangle,
>   and a proverb in the mouth of fools.
> A thorn bush in the hand of a drunk,
>   and a proverb in the mouth of fools.

One needs to know the proper time to apply the proverbs since they are not universal truths but rather are true only if applied at the right time. But how does one know whether or not it is the right time to apply a proverb? The short answer is that the sage, both ancient and twenty-first century, needs to be able to read the circumstances. This involves, of course, also reading the people involved in the situation. But how does one do that?

The wise person learns how to read people by attending closely to what they say and the circumstances in which they say it. The wise person also looks beyond the words to bodily gestures that may indicate more than the words show at face value. If the wise person has a history of relationship with someone, then the wise person draws on that history, perhaps in terms of mistakes in interactions from which something was learned. In sum, the twenty-first-century sage is a savvy interpreter of the Bible, of culture, and of people.

The Wise Person Obeys Divine Instruction to Form Habits That Mold Character

We might remember the comment from W. Willimon cited at the end of chapter 1:

28. I also recommend Brooks's more recent *Road to Character*.

> Generally, I dislike the book of Proverbs with its lack of theological content, its long lists of platitudinous advice, its "do this" and "don't do that." Pick up your socks. Be nice to salesclerks. It doesn't hurt to be nice. Proverbs is something like being trapped on a long road trip with your mother, or at least with William Bennett.[29]

Willimon's caricature, perhaps tongue-in-cheek, of wisdom presents it as simply a bunch of simplistic dos and don'ts. But this exposes a misunderstanding not only of the book of Proverbs but also of human nature.

The sages of Israel know that character is not something that is inbred or given, but must be shaped. We begin by doing the right thing (the way of wisdom) and avoiding bad behavior (the way of folly). The sages encourage us to the proper behavior by holding out the carrot (reward that leads to life) and warning about the stick (punishment that leads to death). Behaviors, however, lead to habits. If we force ourselves (often against our desires; this is called self-control, a virtue highly prized in Proverbs [4:13; 25:28]) to act in certain positive ways, then we will begin to do so naturally. And in the process we form character so that we no longer have to force ourselves; we act that way naturally.

The Wise Person Knows How to Suffer

The sage lives in the nitty-gritty of life. We have earlier described wisdom as including the ability to navigate life well (the practical level), with integrity (the ethical level), and in the fear of God (the theological level).

The book of Job in particular speaks about wisdom in relationship to suffering. While we rejected the idea that Job is about (innocent) suffering since it never answers the question of why we (Job) suffer, we acknowledged that the book speaks to how to suffer with wisdom (see chap. 3). In this, the book of Job fits well with Psalms and Lamentations. We can also see how the lives of Joseph and Daniel model a wise response to personal suffering.

Contrary to popular misconception flowing from the KJV rendition of James 5:11 ("ye have heard of the patience of Job"),[30] Job is not a patient

---

29. Willimon, *Pastor*, 255–56, quoted in Bland, *Proverbs and the Formation of Character*, 8.

30. We will not get into a detailed look at the proper understanding and source of James's reference (for this, see Balentine, *Have You Considered My Servant Job?*, 15–49). Many modern translations render the relevant Greek word as "perseverance" (NIV) or the like (an active rather than a passive response to suffering), and Job was certainly persevering. It is also possible that James reflects the depiction of Job in the *Testament of Job*, which was popular in the first century AD (see Longman, *Job*, 280–82).

sufferer. Starting in Job 3, Job complains about God and to God constantly. Indeed, God accuses Job of condemning him in order that Job might be seen to be right (40:8b). And Job knows that he is impatient and believes he is justifiably so when he asks the friends, "Why shouldn't I be impatient?" (Job 21:4).

I believe the first thing we learn from Job's example about how to suffer is that it is appropriate to complain, at least as long as that complaint is ultimately directed to God, and indeed, we see numerous times in Job's speeches that he directs his complaints to God himself. In this, the message of Job is similar to what we see in the Psalms, particularly the lament psalms (e.g., Pss. 3; 22; 69; 77; etc.). In these psalms, the composer calls out to God in the midst of life's pain. Indeed, many of these psalms complain not just to God but about God (see, e.g., Ps. 88). That laments like these appear in the Psalter indicates that God allows and even encourages his people to express their anger to and even at him.

The idea that the wise person can and, in certain situations, should lament to God is a message that many Christians need to hear today.[31] Too often God's people believe that somehow they need to stifle their complaints, but that is neither true nor healthy. The example of Job and the Psalms is to express one's heart and be brutally honest with God. The only time God gets truly angry with his complaining people is when, like in the wilderness, they complain about him but not to him.

However, the example of Job takes us even further and tells us that God does not want us to lament forever. Eventually, the suffering Job must simply bow before his God and trust him in spite of the pain (42:1–6). When we turn to the Psalms, we note, along with Brueggemann and others,[32] that once God answers a lament, then the sufferer sings a thanksgiving song (e.g., Pss. 18; 30). But what if God does not answer the lament by bringing relief? Should one go on complaining forever? The presence of songs of confidence in the Psalter suggests that the answer is no.[33] These are prayers that express trust in God in spite of ongoing trouble: "even though I walk through the darkest valley, I will fear no evil, for you are with me" (23:4; see also Ps. 131:2a: "I have calmed and quieted myself").

Thus, to suffer wisely means to acknowledge the pain and the hurt and bring it to God even if at first it comes with anger. Job's three friends turn out to be horrible counselors, not wise but foolish, because they basically

31. See Allender and Longman, *Cry of the Soul*.
32. Brueggemann, *Psalms and the Life of Faith*, 3–32.
33. For this insight I am grateful to Pemberton, *After Lament*.

told Job to stifle his rage and repent. However, wise suffering should mature into patient endurance by trusting God. While not a wisdom text per se, the author of Lamentations creates a good picture of wise suffering in the man of affliction, a personification of Judah in the aftermath of the destruction of Jerusalem:

> The LORD is good to those whose hope is in him,
>   to the one who seeks him;
> It is good to wait quietly
>   for the salvation of the LORD.
> It is good for a man to bear the yoke
>   while he is young.
> Let him sit alone in silence,
>   for the LORD has laid it on him.
> Let him bury his face in the dust—
>   there may yet be hope.
> Let him offer his cheek to the one who would strike him,
>   and let him be filled with disgrace. (3:25–30)

The Wise Person Lives with Mystery and Ambiguity

We live in a postmodern or, better, late-modern time when many people question the possibility of certain knowledge of anything. We know that our understanding of things and people is filtered by our thoughts, which are colored by our limited (and sinful) perspectives. Many, though certainly not all, people yearn for certainty. I believe this helps explain why many people are attracted to Christian teachers and preachers who teach with confident assurance about matters that are open to debate. We want absolute and unwavering answers to our questions and sometimes think that our faith ought to provide them. When we run into a life decision, we want there to be a clear-cut reason to follow one alternative over another.

But as we observed in chapter 8, the world does not work so neatly. This observation does not mean that there is no truth out there or that every belief or every decision is up for grabs. But it does mean that we have to live our lives in this (fallen) world with an appreciation for mystery and ambiguity. We will not know everything with unshakeable certainty, nor will we always navigate life's path with clarity. In terms of wisdom, we will not always be sure that this time is the right time for a certain word or action. The sage will not be paralyzed by fear or anxiety in the face of ambiguity and mystery but will live with a quiet confidence based on the fear of the Lord, in whom, like Job, we trust in the midst of our trouble.

The Wise Person Grows in Wisdom

A surface reading of wisdom books in the Bible may give a false impression that there are two possibilities: one is either wise or foolish. In other words, it sounds a bit like getting a degree. If one goes to graduate school and finishes the requirements, then one is awarded a PhD. One either has a doctorate or does not.

Wisdom is not quite the same once we dig below the surface. After all, according to the preface of the book of Proverbs, "let the wise hear and increase teaching" (1:5). In other words, a wise person can grow even more wise, and so the author of the preface of the book encourages not just the immature and the foolish but also the wise to read the book and grow.

The book of Job presents Job as wise from the start. He fears God, and he is "innocent and virtuous" (1:1). However, as we read on in the book, we see that he can become even more wise, and by the end of the book we see that he has matured far beyond where he was at the beginning of the book.

Learning never stops. If we think we have made it in terms of wisdom, we are wrong. Wisdom is a lifelong pursuit. Those who think they are wise lack humility and therefore are not wise. After all, we have already commented that wisdom is not a matter of learning a discrete set of facts. The wise persons know Scripture, but they also know how to read people and circumstances. The wise understand that wisdom is not a goal that can be reached and accomplished but a lifelong pursuit that is never completely achieved. The sage will be a lifelong student of Scripture and life.

Such pursuits will not only promote wisdom in one's life but will guard against a slide into folly. The biblical case study of the move from wisdom to folly is, of course, Solomon as he is presented in the book of Kings. At the beginning of his reign he was a monarch who wanted wisdom more than anything else, including wealth and honor. In response to God's willingness to give Solomon "whatever you want" (1 Kings 3:5), the king asked for a "discerning heart" (3:9). God was so pleased with his desire to rule his people well that he not only gave him what he asked for but also wealth and honor.

Thus, according to the book of Kings, the first part of Solomon's reign was prosperous and just. Solomon showed himself to have a discerning heart indeed (see 1 Kings 3:16–28, where he judges the claims of two prostitutes), attracting even international attention (1 Kings 10:1–13, the Queen of Sheba). However, by the end of his life, his kingdom was in shambles and on the verge of a split. Why? Because he turned away from wisdom and embraced folly. He loved foreign women who worshiped other gods and convinced him to worship those gods. This epic move from the heights of wisdom to the depths of folly became the prototype for the character Qohelet in the book of Ecclesiastes (see chap. 2) and an object lesson for others ever since.

Appendix 2

Is Wisdom Literature a Genre?

Questions have been raised in recent days about the status of wisdom literature as a separate genre in the OT. Will Kynes has stated the case against considering wisdom as a distinct category of literature, arguing that it is a modern scholarly construct created in the mid-nineteenth century.[1]

Kynes believes that the creation of a separate wisdom category has led to detrimental results. In the first place, it leads to the view that wisdom is a substantially different type of literature, presenting ideas and written by people (sages) that are radically different than other types of literature. Sages use their reason to analyze their experience to discover the most effective way to live rather than depending on revelation. If there is a theological dimension to wisdom, it is grounded in creation theology, not in the particular redemptive-historical experience of Israel. Sages and wisdom literature are thus thought to be different from the prophets, priests, and others and their ideas. In the second place, Kynes argues that the belief that there is a distinct wisdom category has led to an ever-expanding corpus of books that are identified or associated with wisdom.

As the body of the present book makes clear, I have significant agreement with Kynes's concerns, particularly the first one. In the early chapters (particularly 4–6), I have suggested that there is much overlap in the thinking

1. Kynes, *Obituary*.

of prophets, priests, sages, and others who have produced the OT over the centuries.

Because of my appreciation for the strength of Kynes's perspective, I have as much as possible avoided referring to "wisdom literature" in the book, instead focusing on the concept of wisdom as it is found throughout the OT and beyond. My hope is that this approach will make my study helpful even to Kynes and to those he will undoubtedly convince. However, I believe that Kynes's criticism is really only telling against a rather wooden (and outdated) view of genre. Thus, in this appendix I want to make a case for the consideration of wisdom literature as a generic category in biblical studies. My case must begin with a reflection on the nature of genre, something that I have worked on since the beginning of my academic career.[2]

The Nature of Genre

Before tackling the issue of wisdom literature per se, we must start with a brief discussion of the nature of genre and its use in biblical studies. Hermann Gunkel had a huge influence on the development of OT studies from the beginning of the twentieth century with his introduction of form criticism, which dominated the field for the next eighty years and still exercises great influence today.[3]

Gunkel himself was influenced by anthropological studies of the previous era, particularly the work of the Grimm brothers (early nineteenth century) well known for their collection and categorization of folktales. Gunkel felt that genres were discrete categories that had distinctive characteristics. He believed that each genre had a specific *Sitz im Leben* (setting in life).[4] Gunkel set up certain criteria for the identification of the genre of texts. He examined three factors in order to identify a text's genre: (1) the mood and thought(s) of the text; (2) the linguistic forms (grammar and vocabulary); and (3) the social setting (*Sitz im Leben*).[5]

Since the early twentieth century when Gunkel worked, however, there have been significant changes to our understanding of genre, though biblical scholars have not always (or even often) followed the lead of literary theorists.

---

2. See Longman, *Fictional Akkadian Autobiography*, particularly chap. 1, "A Generic Approach to Akkadian Literature." At the beginning of my study of this group of Akkadian texts, my advisor W. W. Hallo wisely told me to consult with his colleague in literary studies, Geoffrey Hartman, who put me in touch with recent thinking about genre in current literary theory.

3. For a history of the rise of modern form criticism, see Buss, "Study of Forms."

4. Longman, "Form Criticism."

5. Gunkel, *Psalms*, 10.

For instance, we have a better sense that generic categories are not created in heaven but are a function of authors writing in literary traditions. No one writes in a vacuum; or, to put it another way, no one writes something that is totally unique. If they did, it would not be understandable, since our reading is based on literary competence gained by our past reading experience. Indeed, there is an adage that instructs: "the individual is ineffable."[6] That is, something that is totally unprecedented is incommunicable. In literary terms, a text that bears no similarities of structure, content, or the like with anything previously written is not understandable.

Genres are texts that are grouped together because they share similarities. These similarities may be formal, structural, or based on purpose or content. Genres are not categories that fall out of heaven but are constructed because authors write with similarities to other writings, and readers are able adequately to understand the writing of authors because they know "how to take" their words based on their recognition of a text's genre and their previous reading experience.

In a phrase, genre triggers reading strategy. An author writes, sending generic signals to help the reader know how to take what he says. Heather Dubrow gives an excellent example of how our understanding of a genre affects our interpretation of a text as she asks us to give an account of the following:[7]

THE PERSONAL HISTORY OF DAVID MARPLETHORPE
The clock on the mantelpiece said ten thirty, but someone had suggested recently that the clock was wrong. As the figure of the dead woman lay on the bed in the front room, a no less silent figure glided rapidly from the house. The only sounds to be heard were the ticking of that clock and the loud wailing of an infant.

The title signals that we are dealing with a biography. Since biographies often start at birth, the most natural interpretation of the passage is that the infant is the baby David Marplethorpe and that the woman is his mother who died in childbirth. The silent figure gliding out of the house is either the doctor or the midwife.

That settled, we turn now to a second story:

MURDER AT MARPLETHORPE
The clock on the mantelpiece said ten thirty, but someone had suggested recently that the clock was wrong. As the figure of the dead woman lay on the bed in the

6. Buss, "Study of Forms," 32; and Pascal, *Design and Truth*, 2.
7. Dubrow, *Genre*, 1–2.

front room, a no less silent figure glided rapidly from the house. The only sounds to be heard were the ticking of that clock and the loud wailing of an infant.

Of course this is the same text, but now under a different title that informs us that we are reading a murder mystery and not a biography. With this understanding of the genre, the most natural interpretation is that the woman died not in childbirth but by murder, with the suspicion, which may prove wrong in the end (after all, it is a murder mystery), that the silent figure gliding rapidly from the house is the murderer. The crying baby is not newly born but is disturbed by the crime that has just been committed.

When we think of the Bible, we can see that significant debate over the interpretation of biblical texts has to do with the proper identification of their genre. Is Gen. 1 history, poetry, legend, folklore, or myth? Is the Song of Songs a love poem, a drama, or an allegory? Is the Gospel of Matthew a historical text or midrash? Of course, the debate over interpretation may also have to do with the proper understanding of how a genre, which may be agreed upon, works. For instance, while scholars may agree that, say, the book of Kings is history, they may disagree over the nature of OT historiography.[8]

Writers don't decide whether or not they are going to write in a specific genre tradition, and readers don't decide whether or not they are going to read a text in a genre category. All writing has genre(s), and all reading is influenced by the reader's identification of the genre. The question is, particularly when it comes to reading, how conscious is the reader of the genre of the text? When I read the *Wall Street Journal* in the morning before heading to my office, I don't consciously identify the genre of the piece that I am reading (news article, book review, editorial) and process my expectations. This all happens unconsciously based on my previous reading experience. When I open the novel I am enjoying, I don't consciously remind myself that it is a novel, nor do I study the history of the novel and all its conventions, but based on my previous reading experience I know "how novels work," and, for instance, I suspend my disbelief and don't balk when I read about dragons and zombies and the priestess of the fire god (OK, it is *Game of Thrones*).

When I get to my office, however, as an OT scholar I am dealing with ancient literature and need to be more mindful of genre, recognizing, as Robert Alter said, that different cultures and time periods have different literary conventions.[9] Thus, if I want to read OT books to get at the original authors' meaning, then I need to be aware of genres and how those genres work.

8. See discussion about the nature of biblical historiography in Provan, Long, and Longman, *Biblical History of Israel*, 3–152.
9. Alter, "Response."

One might think that this requires us to identify and understand ancient genres—that is, genres that the ancients would have recognized—in order for us to successfully read texts. We can do our best, but since the ancient Hebrews left scant evidence of the identification of the different types of writing, we must work inductively and create categories based on our observations of similarities between texts.[10]

As mentioned above, these similarities can be on the level of content, style, structure, topic, or tone. Over against those who are critical of the idea of a genre of wisdom literature, we respond that there are significant similarities between the books that are typically identified as the core of the genre (Proverbs, Job, and Ecclesiastes) and fewer similarities, though still present, between these books and other texts that have been called wisdom (select psalms, Song of Songs, etc.).

However, as we make our case for a wisdom genre, we need to continue our clarification of the nature of genre. Here we want to make two additional points, though the two are related and could be summarized as saying that genre is a fluid category. The first point is that genre occurs on multiple levels of abstraction from specific texts, and the second point is that texts can have more than one genre. As our example, we will use Ps. 23, which begins "The LORD is my shepherd, I lack nothing." What is the genre of Ps. 23?

1. It is *poem*, characterized by conventions such as parallelism, pervasive imagery, terse lines, and various secondary poetical devices.
2. It is *lyric poetry*, not narrative or dramatic or persuasive poetry. That is, it is a poem that expresses the inner life of the poet.
3. It is a *psalm of confidence*, not a hymn or a lament or any other type of lyric poem. It expresses trust in God in spite of danger.

We could continue, but our point is made that a text may be described by using multiple genre labels depending on the level of abstraction from the specific text. The broader the category (and poem is the broadest of all in the above analysis), the fewer similarities the texts in that category have with each other, and the narrower the category (confidence), the more they have. Thus, the same text can have a variety of genre labels based on the level of abstraction from the specific text. But, second, a text can have more than one genre as the reader/interpreter attends to differences or similarities between texts.

10. As evidence that the ancient Israelites identified genres differently than we do, we can look at the various genre terms used in the title of the Psalms (*mizmôr, šîr, təpillâ, ləhazkîr, maskîl*, and so forth).

Psalm 23 can again serve as our example. On one level of abstraction from the specific text, we can talk about seven basic types of psalms. At this level, we identified Ps. 23 as a psalm of confidence. There are six other types at this level, including hymns, laments, thanksgiving, wisdom, remembrance, and kingship psalms.[11] As we have said, Ps. 23 is a psalm of confidence. Such an identification of the genre of Ps. 23 is commonly accepted; indeed, Ps. 23 is often seen as the epitome of the genre. The psalm is first of all recognized by its tone of trust in God in the midst of adversity: "even though I walk through the darkest valley, I will fear no evil" (v. 4), and "you prepare a table before me in the presence of my enemies" (v. 5). Psalms of confidence are prayers sung by those whose laments have not been answered.[12]

Though a psalm of confidence, we can also make the case that Ps. 23 is a kingship psalm. After all, as is commonly understood, the shepherd was a common metaphor for a ruler, and most notably a king. When the psalm extols God as a shepherd of his sheep, we understand that it is referring to God as king of his people. He provides for them and takes care of them.

In summary, a genre draws together texts that share similarities of different types. Genres are not rigid and pure. Texts do not have one and only one genre, but they can be part of different literary groupings that illuminate the individual text. Genres have fuzzy boundaries. It is with this understanding of genre that we believe it is appropriate to describe a wisdom genre in the Bible.

The main identifier of the wisdom genre is simply that these texts are interested in the concept of wisdom. As the first three chapters of the present book show, Proverbs announces at the very beginning that its purpose is to instruct the reader in wisdom, Job is a debate about who has wisdom, and Ecclesiastes has the speech of two wise men who are searching for the meaning of life. As we studied these books, we saw themes and topics and interests that are very closely connected to the concept of wisdom, perhaps preeminently the "fear of the Lord." After all, Proverbs announces that "the fear of Yahweh is the beginning of knowledge/wisdom" (Prov. 1:7, etc.). Thus, when we run into the theme of the fear of the Lord, we are likely dealing with wisdom. We will discover still other themes, topics, and interests that are closely connected to wisdom in our study.

Some worry that such an approach to the question of the wisdom genre broadens the genre to include too many texts. Kynes suggests that the application of the term "wisdom" to an increasing number of biblical books and their parts "leads to the expansion of the genre and dilution of its hermeneutical

11. Longman, *Psalms*, 38–42.
12. Pemberton, *After Lament*.

significance, and therefore the potential distortion of the interpretation of its content."[13]

In the first place, I believe he overstates how all-encompassing the category "wisdom" has become in biblical studies. There are still many texts that have no relationship to wisdom. But more importantly, I suggest that there is utility in broadening the connections between the core texts that treat wisdom (Proverbs, Job, Ecclesiastes) and those in which wisdom and related themes are found (as in part 2 of this present book). However, we must be very careful at this point to remember that texts participate in more than one genre. For instance, treating the Song of Songs as a type of wisdom text should not prevent us from seeing it as love poetry, and focusing on Job as wisdom should not keep us from understanding that it also participates in a genre with lament psalms.[14]

Conclusion

Kynes and others who challenge the existence and utility of speaking of a genre called wisdom literature have presented compelling arguments against an antiquated, but still used, understanding of genre. However, in my opinion the solution is not to eradicate the term "wisdom literature" but to refine our understanding of genre as a hermeneutical tool.[15] In response to Kynes's announcement of an "obituary" for wisdom, we would borrow the words of Mark Twain: "the report of [wisdom literature's] death has been much exaggerated."[16] Ultimately, Kynes's own advocacy of an approach that uses intertextuality as the key to studying the wisdom books achieves much the same results as the genre-based approach offered here.

13. Kynes, *Obituary*.

14. Thus Dell, "Deciding the Boundaries of Wisdom," an article that also presents a nuanced understanding of genre.

15. See Sweeney and Ben Zvi, *Changing Face of Form Criticism*, which includes my article "Israelite Genres."

16. The approach I am taking here is closest to that of Sneed and Dell. See esp. Sneed, "'Grasping After the Wind.'" Compare my earlier work: *Fictional Akkadian Autobiography*; "Form Criticism"; and *Literary Approaches*.

Bibliography

Ackrill, J. L., ed. *The New Aristotle Reader.* Oxford: Oxford University Press, 1987.

Adams, J. *Competent to Counsel.* Phillipsburg, NJ: Presbyterian and Reformed, 1970. Reprint, Grand Rapids: Zondervan, 1986.

Allender, D. B., and T. Longman III. *The Cry of the Soul: How Our Emotions Reveal Our Deepest Questions about God.* 2nd ed. Colorado Springs: NavPress, 2015.

Alster, B. *Proverbs of Ancient Sumer: The World's Earliest Proverb Collections.* 2 vols. Bethesda, MD: CDL, 1997.

Alter, R. "A Response to Critics." *JSOT* 27 (1983): 113–17.

Averbeck, R. "Myth, Ritual, and Order in Enki and the World Order." *JAOS* 123 (2003): 761–62.

Balentine, S. E. *Have You Considered My Servant Job? Understanding the Biblical Archetype of Patience.* Columbia: University of South Carolina Press, 2015.

Barrett, M., and A. B. Caneday, eds. *Four Views on the Historical Adam.* Grand Rapids: Zondervan, 2013.

Bartholomew, C. G. *Ecclesiastes.* Grand Rapids: Baker Academic, 2009.

Bartholomew, C. G., and R. P. O'Dowd. *Old Testament Wisdom Literature.* Downers Grove, IL: InterVarsity, 2011.

Beaulieu, P.-A. "The Social and Intellectual Setting of Babylonian Wisdom Literature." In *Wisdom Literature in Mesopotamia and Israel*, edited by R. J. Clifford, 3–19. Atlanta: Society of Biblical Literature Press, 2007.

Beckwith, R. *The Old Testament Canon of the New Testament Church.* London: SPCK, 1985.

Beeke, J. R. "Christ, the Second Adam." In *God, Adam, and You: Biblical Creation Defended and Applied*, edited by R. D. Phillips, 141–68. Phillipsburg, NJ: P&R, 2015.

Bekkenkamp, J., and F. van Dijk. "The Canon of the Old Testament and Women's Cultural Traditions." In *A Feminine Companion to the Song of Songs*, edited by A. Brenner, 67–85. Sheffield: JSOT Press, 1993.

Besserman, L. L. *The Legend of Job in the Middle Ages*. Cambridge, MA: Harvard University Press, 1979.

Bland, D. *Proverbs and the Formation of Character*. Eugene, OR: Cascade Books, 2015.

Blenkinsopp, J. *Sage, Priest, Prophet: Religious and Intellectual Leadership in Ancient Israel*. Library of Ancient Israel. Louisville: Westminster John Knox, 1995.

Borghouts, J. F. "Witchcraft, Magic, and Divination in Ancient Egypt." In *Civilizations of the Ancient Near East*, edited by J. M. Sasson, 1775–85. Peabody, MA: Hendrickson, 1995.

Bostrom, L. *The God of the Sages: The Portrayal of God in the Book of Proverbs*. Stockholm: Almqvist & Wiksell, 1990.

Brenner, A. "Women Poets and Authors." In *A Feminine Companion to the Song of Songs*, edited by A. Brenner, 86–99. Sheffield: JSOT Press, 1993.

Brooks, D. *The Road to Character*. New York: Random House, 2015.

———. *The Social Animal: The Hidden Sources of Love, Character, and Achievement*. New York: Random House, 2012.

Brown, W. P. *Character in Crisis: A Fresh Approach to the Wisdom Literature of the Old Testament*. Grand Rapids: Eerdmans, 1996.

———. *Wisdom's Wonder: Character, Creation, and Crisis in the Bible's Wisdom Literature*. Grand Rapids: Eerdmans, 2014.

Bruch, J. F. *Weisheits-Lehre der Hebräer: Ein Beitrag zur Geschichte der Philosophie*. Strassburg: Treuttel & Würtz, 1851.

Brueggemann, W. *In Man We Trust: The Neglected Side of Biblical Faith*. Atlanta: John Knox, 1972.

———. *The Psalms and the Life of Faith*. Minneapolis: Augsburg Fortress, 1995.

———. *Solomon: Israel's Iconic Icon of Human Achievement*. Columbia: University of South Carolina Press, 2005.

Buccelati, G. "Wisdom and Not: The Case of Mesopotamia." *JAOS* 101 (1901): 35–47.

Budge, E. A. W. *Facsimiles of Egyptian Hieratic Papyri in the British Museum*. 2nd series. London: British Museum, 1923.

———. *The Teaching of Amen-Em-Apt, Son of Kanekht: The Egyptian Hieroglyphic Text and an English Translation, with Translations of the Moral and Religious Teachings of Egyptian Kings and Officials Illustrating the Development of Religious Philosophy in Egypt during a Period of about Two Thousand Years*. London: Hopkinson, 1924.

Buss, M. J. "The Study of Forms." In *Old Testament Form Criticism*, edited by J. H. Mayes, 15–56. San Antonio: Trinity University Press, 1974.

Cady, S., M. Ronan, and H. Taussig. *Sophia: The Future of Feminist Spirituality*. San Francisco: Harper & Row, 1986.

Carr, D. M. *Writing on the Tablet of the Heart: Origins of Scripture and Literature*. Oxford: Oxford University Press, 2005.

Charles, J. D., ed. *Reading Genesis 1–2: An Evangelical Conversation*. Peabody, MA: Hendrickson, 2013.

Cheney, M. *Dust, Wind and Agony: Character, Speech and Genre in Job*. Stockholm: Almqvist & Wiksell, 1994.

Childs, B. S. *Biblical Theology of the Old and New Testaments: Theological Reflection on the Christian Bible*. Minneapolis: Fortress, 1992.

———. *Introduction to the Old Testament as Scripture*. Philadelphia: Fortress, 1979.

Clifford, R. J. *The Cosmic Mountain in Canaan and the Old Testament*. Harvard Semitic Monographs 4. Cambridge, MA: Harvard University Press, 1973.

———. *Proverbs*. OTL. Louisville: Westminster John Knox, 1999.

———, ed. *Wisdom Literature in Mesopotamia and Israel*. Atlanta: SBL Press, 2007.

Clines, D. J. A. *Job 1–20*. WBC 17. Nashville: Nelson, 1989.

———. *The Theme of the Pentateuch*. 2nd ed. Sheffield: Sheffield Academic, 1997.

Cohen, Y. *Wisdom from the Late Bronze Age*. Writings from the Ancient World 34. Atlanta: Society of Biblical Literature Press, 2013.

Cole (née Cady), S., M. Ronan, and H. Taussig. *Wisdom's Feast: Sophia in Study and Celebration*. San Francisco: Harper & Row, 1989. 2nd ed., Kansas City, MO: Sheed & Ward, 1996. Reprint, Berkeley, CA: Apocryphile, 2016.

Collins, J. J. *Jewish Wisdom in the Hellenistic Age*. OTL. Louisville: Westminster John Knox, 1997.

———. "Proverbial Wisdom and the Yahwist's Vision." *Semeia* 17 (1980): 1–18.

———. "Wisdom Reconsidered, in Light of the Scrolls." *Dead Sea Discoveries* 4 (1997): 265–81.

Copan, P., et al., eds. *The Dictionary of Christianity and Science: The Definitive Reference for the Intersection of Faith and Contemporary Science*. Grand Rapids: Zondervan, forthcoming.

Crawford, S. W. "Lady Wisdom and Dame Folly at Qumran." *Dead Sea Discoveries* 5 (1998): 355–66.

Crenshaw, J. L. *Ecclesiastes*. OTL. Louisville: Westminster John Knox, 1987.

———. "Education in Ancient Israel." *JBL* 104 (1985): 601–15.

———. "Gold Dust or Nuggets? A Brief Response to J. Kenneth Kuntz." *Currents in Biblical Research* 1 (2003): 155–58.

———. "Method in Determining Wisdom Influence upon 'Historical' Literature." *JBL* 88 (1969): 129–42.

———. *Old Testament Wisdom: An Introduction*. 3rd ed. Louisville: Westminster John Knox, 2010.

———, ed. *Studies in Ancient Israelite Wisdom*. Library of Biblical Studies. New York: Ktav, 1976.

———. "Wisdom Psalms?" *Currents in Research: Biblical Studies* 8 (2000): 9–17.

Cunningham, C. *Darwin's Pious Idea: Why Ultra-Darwinists and Creationists Both Get It Wrong*. Grand Rapids: Eerdmans, 2010.

Dahood, M. J. "Proverbs 8,22–31: Translation and Commentary." *CBQ* 30 (1968): 512–21.

Day, J. "The Daniel of Ugarit and the Hero of the Book of Daniel." *VT* 30 (1980): 174–84.

Day, J., R. P. Gordon, and H. G. M. Williamson, eds. *Wisdom in Ancient Israel: Essays in Honour of J. A. Emerton*. Cambridge: Cambridge University Press, 1995.

Dell, K. J. "Deciding the Boundaries of Wisdom: Applying the Concept of Family Resemblance." In *Was There a Wisdom Tradition? New Prospects in Israelite Wisdom Studies*, ed. M. R. Sneed, 145–60. Ancient Israel and Its Literature 23. Atlanta: SBL Press, 2015.

———. "'I Will Solve My Riddle to the Music of the Lyre' (Psalm XLIX 4[5]): A Cultic Setting for Wisdom Psalms?" *VT* 54 (2004): 445–58.

Dillard, R., and T. Longman III. *Introduction to the Old Testament*. 1st ed. Grand Rapids: Zondervan, 1994.

Dressler, H. H. P. "The Identification of the Ugaritic Dnil with the Daniel of Ezekiel." *VT* 29 (1979): 152–61.

Dubrow, H. *Genre*. Critical Idiom 42. New York: Methuen, 1982.

Engelsman, J. E. *The Feminine Dimension of the Divine*. Philadelphia: Westminster, 1979.

Enns, P. *Ecclesiastes*. THOTC. Grand Rapids: Eerdmans, 2011.

———. *Exodus Retold: Ancient Exegesis of the Departure from Egypt in Wis 10:15–21 and 19:1–9*. Harvard Semitic Monographs 57. Atlanta: Scholars, 1997.

———. *Inspiration and Incarnation: Evangelicals and the Problem of the Old Testament*. 2nd ed. Grand Rapids: Baker Academic, 2015.

———. "Wisdom of Solomon." In *Dictionary of the Old Testament: Wisdom, Poetry and Writings*, edited by T. Longman III and P. Enns, 885–91. Downers Grove, IL: IVP Academic, 2008.

Estes, D. J. "Wisdom and Biblical Theology." In *Dictionary of the Old Testament: Wisdom, Poetry and Writings*, edited by T. Longman III and P. Enns, 853–58. Downers Grove, IL: IVP Academic, 2008.

Exum, J. C. *Song of Songs: A Commentary*. OTL. Louisville: Westminster John Knox, 2005.

Falk, M. *Love Lyrics in the Bible: A Translation and Literary Study of the Song of Songs*. Bible and Literature 4. Sheffield: Almond, 1982.

Farber, W. "Witchcraft, Magic, and Divination in Ancient Mesopotamia." In *Civilizations of the Ancient Near East*, edited by J. M. Sasson, 1895–1909. Peabody, MA: Hendrickson, 1995.

Farmer, K. A. "The Wisdom Books." In *The Hebrew Bible Today: An Introduction to Critical Issues*, edited by S. L. McKenzie and M. P. Graham, 129–51. Louisville: Westminster John Knox, 1998.

Fiddes, P. S. *Seeing the World and Knowing God: Hebrew Wisdom and Christian Doctrine in a Late-Modern Context*. Oxford: Oxford University Press, 2013.

Finsterbusch, K. "Yahweh's Torah and the Praying 'I' in Psalm 119." In *Wisdom and Torah: The Reception of "Torah" in the Wisdom Literature of the Second Temple Period*, edited by B. U. Schipper and D. A. Teeter, 119–36. Supplements to the Journal for the Study of Judaism 163. Leiden: Brill, 2013.

Firth, D. G. "Worrying about the Wise: Wisdom in Old Testament Narrative." In *Exploring Old Testament Wisdom*, edited by D. G. Firth and L. Wilson. Nottingham: Apollos, forthcoming.

Foh, S. "What Is the Woman's Desire?" *WTJ* 37 (1974–75): 276–83.

Fontaine, C. R. *Smooth Words: Women, Proverbs and Performance in Biblical Wisdom*. JSOTSup 356. Sheffield: Sheffield Academic, 2002.

Ford, D. F. *Christian Wisdom: Desiring God and Learning to Love*. Cambridge Studies in Christian Doctrine. Cambridge: Cambridge University Press, 2007.

Foster, B. R. *Before the Muses: An Anthology of Akkadian Literature*. 2nd ed. 2 vols. Potomac, MD: CDL, 1996.

Fox, M. V. "'*Amon* Again." *JBL* 115 (1996): 699–702.

———. *Ecclesiastes*. JPS Bible Commentary. Philadelphia: Jewish Publication Society, 2000.

———. "Frame-Narrative and Composition in the Book of Qohelet." *HUCA* 58 (1977): 83–106.

———. *Proverbs 1–9*. AB 18. New York: Doubleday, 2000.

———. *Qohelet and His Contradictions*. Bible and Literature 18. Sheffield: JSOT Press, 1989.

Fredericks, D. C. *Coping with Transience: Ecclesiastes on the Brevity of Life*. The Biblical Seminar 18. Sheffield: JSOT Press, 1993.

Gammie, J. G., and L. G. Perdue, eds. *The Sage in Israel and the Ancient Near East*. Winona Lake, IN: Eisenbrauns, 1990.

Gemser, B. "The Spiritual Structure of Biblical Aphoristic Literature." In *Adhuc Loquitur: Collected Essays of Dr. B. Gemser*, edited by A. van Selms and A. S. van der Woude, 208–19. Pretoria Oriental Studies 7. Leiden: Brill, 1968.

Goedicke, H. *The Protocol of Neferyt*. Baltimore: Johns Hopkins University Press, 1977.

———. *The Report about the Dispute of a Man with His BA: Papyrus Berlin 3024.* Baltimore: Johns Hopkins Press, 1970.

Goff, M. J. *Discerning Wisdom: The Sapiential Literature of the Dead Sea Scrolls.* Leiden: Brill, 2007.

———. *4QInstruction.* Atlanta: Scholars Press, 2013.

Goldingay, J. "The 'Salvation History' Perspective and the 'Wisdom' Perspective within the Context of Biblical Theology." *EvQ* 51 (1979): 194–207.

Goleman, D. *Emotional Intelligence.* New York: Bantam Books, 1995.

Golka, F. *The Leopard's Spots: Biblical and African Wisdom in Proverbs.* Edinburgh: T&T Clark, 1993.

Grant, J. A. "'When the Friendship of God Was upon My Tent': Covenant as Essential Background to Lament in the Wisdom Literature." In *Covenant in the Persian Period: From Genesis to Chronicles,* edited by R. J. Bautch and G. N. Knoppers, 323–39. Winona Lake, IN: Eisenbrauns, 2015.

———. "Wisdom and Covenant." In *Dictionary of the Old Testament: Wisdom, Poetry and Writings,* edited by T. Longman III and P. Enns, 860–61. Downers Grove, IL: IVP Academic, 2008.

———. "Wisdom and Covenant: Revisiting Zimmerli." *EuroJTh* 12 (2003): 103–11.

Greenfield, J. C. "The Wisdom of Ahiqar." In *Wisdom in Ancient Israel: Essays in Honor of J. A. Emerton,* edited by J. Day, R. P. Gordon, and H. G. M. Williamson, 43–52. Cambridge: Cambridge University Press, 1995.

Gunkel, H. *The Psalms.* Translated by T. M. Horner. Philadelphia: Fortress, 1967.

Gunkel, H., and J. Begrich. *An Introduction to Cultic Poetry: The Genres of the Religious Lyric of Israel.* 1933. Reprint, Macon, GA: Mercer University Press, 1998.

Hugenberger, G. *Marriage as Covenant: Biblical Law and Ethics as Developed from Malachi.* Grand Rapids: Baker, 1998.

Humphreys, W. L. "A Life-Style for the Diaspora: A Study of the Tales of Esther and Daniel." *JBL* 92 (1973): 211–23.

Hurowitz, V. "Two Terms for Wealth in Proverbs CIII in Light of Akkadian." *VT* 50 (2000): 252–54.

Isaac, E. "1 (Ethiopic Apocalypse of) Enoch." In *The Old Testament Pseudepigrapha.* Vol. 1, *Apocalyptic Literature and Testaments,* edited by J. H. Charlesworth, 5–89. Garden City, NY: Doubleday, 1983.

Jacobson, D. "Wisdom Language in the Psalms." In *The Oxford Handbook of the Psalms,* edited by W. P. Brown, 147–57. Oxford: Oxford University Press, 2014.

Jenkins, P. *The New Faces of Christianity: Believing the Bible in the Global South.* Oxford: Oxford University Press, 2006.

Jobes, K. H. "Sophia Christology: The Way of Wisdom?" In *The Way of Wisdom: Essays in Honor of Bruce K. Waltke,* edited by J. I. Packer and S. K. Soderlund, 79–103. Grand Rapids: Zondervan, 2000.

Johnston, P. S. *Shades of Sheol: Death and the Afterlife in the Old Testament*. Downers Grove, IL: InterVarsity, 2002.

Kaminsky, J. S. "Would You Impugn My Justice? A Nuanced Approach to the Hebrew Bible's Theology of Divine Recompense." *Interpretation* 69 (2015): 299–310.

Kampen, J. *Wisdom Literature*. Eerdmans Commentaries on the Dead Sea Scrolls. Grand Rapids: Eerdmans, 2011.

Kelsey, D. H. *Eccentric Existence: A Theological Anthropology*. 2 vols. Louisville: Westminster John Knox, 2009.

Kidner, D. *Proverbs*. TOTC. Downers Grove, IL: InterVarsity, 1964.

Kim, D. "Wisdom and Apocalyptic in 2 Baruch." *Henoch* 33 (2011): 250–74.

Kister, M. "Wisdom Literature and Its Relation to Other Genres: From Ben Sira to Mysteries." In *Sapiential Perspectives: Wisdom Literature in Light of the Dead Sea Scrolls; Proceedings of the Sixth International Symposium of the Orion Center for the Study of the Dead Sea Scrolls and Associated Literature, 20–22 May, 2001*, edited by J. J. Collins, G. E. Sterling, and R. Clements, 14–47. STDJ 51. Leiden: Brill, 2004.

Kitchen, K. A., and P. J. N. Lawrence. *Treaty, Law and Covenant in the Ancient Near East*. 3 vols. Wiesbaden: Harrassowitz, 2012.

Kline, M. G. *The Structure of Biblical Authority*. 2nd ed. Grand Rapids: Eerdmans, 1972.

Koch, K. *Um das Prinzip der Vergeltung in Religion und Recht des alten Testaments*. Darmstadt: Wissenschaftliche Buchgesellschaft, 1972.

Kovacs, M. C. *The Epic of Gilgamesh*. Stanford, CA: Stanford University Press, 1985.

Kramer, S. N. "'Man and His God': A Sumerian Variation on the 'Job' Motif." In *Wisdom in Israel and in the Ancient Near East*, edited by M. Noth and D. W. Thomas, 170–82. Leiden: Brill, 1955.

Krüger, T. "Law and Wisdom according to Deut 4:5–8." In *Wisdom and Torah: The Reception of "Torah" in the Wisdom Literature of the Second Temple Period*, edited by B. U. Schipper and D. A. Teeter, 35–54. Supplements to the Journal for the Study of Judaism 163. Leiden: Brill, 2013.

Kynes, W. *An Obituary for "Wisdom Literature."* Oxford: Oxford University Press, forthcoming.

LaCocque, A. *Romance, She Wrote: A Hermeneutical Essay on Song of Songs*. Harrisburg, PA: Trinity, 1998.

Lambert, W. G. *Babylonian Creation Myths*. Winona Lake, IN: Eisenbrauns, 2013.

———. *Babylonian Wisdom Literature*. Oxford: Oxford University Press, 1960. Reprint, Winona Lake, IN: Eisenbrauns, 1996.

Landy, F. *Paradoxes of Paradise: Identity and Difference in the Song of Songs*. Sheffield: Almond, 1983.

Lemaire, A. "The Sage in School and Temple." In *The Sage in Israel and the Ancient Near East*, edited by J. G. Gammie and L. G. Perdue, 165–83. Winona Lake, IN: Eisenbrauns, 1990.

———. "Sagesse et ecoles." *VT* 34 (1984): 270–81.

Levenson, J. *Creation and the Persistence of Evil*. Princeton: Princeton University Press, 1994.

———. *The Hebrew Bible, the Old Testament and Historical Criticism: Jews and Christians in Biblical Studies*. Louisville: Westminster John Knox, 1993.

Levine, E. *The Aramaic Version of Qohelet*. New York: Sepher-Hermon, 1978.

Lichtheim, M. *Ancient Egyptian Literature*, vol. 1. Berkeley: University of California Press, 1975.

———. "Didactic Literature." In *Ancient Egyptian Literature: History and Forms*, edited by A. Loprieno, 243–62. Probleme der Agyptologie 10. Leiden: Brill, 1996.

———. *Late Egyptian Literature in the International Context: A Study of Demotic Instruction*. OBO 52. Freiburg, Switzerland: Universitätsverlag, 1983.

———. *Maat in Egyptian Autobiographies and Related Studies*. OBO 120. Freiburg, Switzerland: Universitätsverlag; Göttingen: Vandenhoeck & Ruprecht, 1992.

———. *Moral Values in Ancient Egypt*. OBO 155. Fribourg, Switzerland: University Press, 1997.

Lindenberger, J. M. *The Aramaic Proverbs of Ahiqar*. JHNES. Baltimore: Johns Hopkins University Press, 1983.

Lo, A. *Job 28 as Rhetoric: An Analysis of Job 28 in the Context of Job 22–31*. VTSup 97. Leiden: Brill, 2003.

Loader, J. A. "The Bipolarity of Sapiential Theology." *OTE* 26 (2013): 365–83.

Longman, T., III. "Accuracy and Readability: Warring Impulses in Evangelical Translation Tradition." In *Biblical Translation in Context*, edited by F. W. Knobloch, 165–75. Bethesda: University Press of Maryland, 2002.

———. "Adam and Eve." In *The Dictionary of Christianity and Science: The Definitive Resource for the Intersection of Christian Faith and Contemporary Science*. Edited by T. Longman III and P. Copan. Grand Rapids: Zondervan, forthcoming.

———. *Daniel*. NIVAC. Grand Rapids: Zondervan, 1999.

———. "Determining the Historical Context of Ecclesiastes." In *The Words of the Wise Are Like Goads: Engaging Qohelet in the 21st Century*, edited by M. J. Boda, T. Longman III, and C. G. Rata, 89–102. Winona Lake, IN: Eisenbrauns, 2013.

———. *Ecclesiastes*. NICOT. Grand Rapids: Eerdmans, 1998.

———. "The 'Fear of God' in the Book of Ecclesiastes." *BBR* 25 (2015): 13–22.

———. *Fictional Akkadian Autobiography*. Winona Lake, IN: Eisenbrauns, 1993.

———. "Form Criticism, Recent Developments in Genre Theory, and the Evangelical." *WTJ* 47 (1985): 46–67.

———. *Genesis*. Story of God Bible Commentary: Old Testament Series. Grand Rapids: Zondervan, 2016.

———. *How to Read Proverbs*. Downers Grove, IL: InterVarsity, 2002.

———. "Israelite Genres in Their Ancient Near Eastern Context." In *The Changing Face of Form Criticism for the Twenty-First Century*, edited by M. A. Sweeney and E. Ben Zvi, 177–95. Grand Rapids: Eerdmans, 2003.

———. *Job*. BCOTWP. Grand Rapids: Baker Academic, 2012.

———. *Literary Approaches to Biblical Interpretation*. Foundations of Contemporary Interpretation 3. Grand Rapids: Zondervan, 1987. Reprinted as "Literary Approaches to Biblical Interpretation." In *Foundations of Contemporary Interpretation*, edited by M. Silva, 91–192. Grand Rapids: Zondervan, 1996.

———. *Proverbs*. BCOTWP. Grand Rapids: Baker Academic, 2006.

———. "Proverbs." In *The Zondervan Illustrated Bible Backgrounds Commentary*, edited by J. Walton, 5:464–505. Grand Rapids: Zondervan, 2009.

———. *Psalms: An Introduction and Commentary*. TOTC. Downers Grove, IL: IVP Academic, 2014.

———. "Qohelet as Solomon: 'For What Can Anyone Who Comes after the King Do?'" In *Reading Ecclesiastes Intertextually*, edited by K. Dell and W. Kynes, 42–56. Library of Hebrew Bible/Old Testament Studies 587. London: Bloomsbury, 2014.

———. "The Serpent." In *The Dictionary of Christianity and Science: The Definitive Resource for the Intersection of Christian Faith and Contemporary Science*. Edited by T. Longman III and P. Copan. Grand Rapids: Zondervan, forthcoming.

———. *Song of Songs*. NICOT. Grand Rapids: Eerdmans, 2001.

———. "Spirit and Wisdom." In *Presence, Power and Promise: The Role of the Spirit of God in the Old Testament*, edited by D. G. Firth and P. D. Wegner, 95–110. Downers Grove, IL: InterVarsity, 2011.

———. "Why Do Bad Things Happen to Good People? A Biblical-Theological Approach." In *Eyes to See, Ears to Hear: Essays in Memory of J. Alan Groves*, edited by P. Enns, et al., 1–16. Phillipsburg, NJ: P&R, 2010.

Longman, T., III, and R. B. Dillard. *An Introduction to the Old Testament*. 2nd ed. Grand Rapids: Zondervan, 2006.

Longman, T., III, and P. Enns, eds. *Dictionary of the Old Testament: Wisdom, Poetry and Writings*. Downers Grove, IL: IVP Academic, 2008.

Lyu, S. M. *Righteousness in the Book of Proverbs*. Forschungen zum Alten Testament 2/55. Tübingen: Mohr Siebeck, 2012.

Madueme, H., and M. Reeves, eds. *Adam, the Fall, and Original Sin: Theological, Biblical, and Scientific Perspectives*. Grand Rapids: Baker Academic, 2014.

McDowell, C. *The "Image of God" in the Garden of Eden: The Creation of Humankind in Genesis 2:5–3:24 in Light of the mīs pî pīt pî and wpr-t Rituals of Mesopotamia and Ancient Egypt*. Winona Lake, IN: Eisenbrauns, 2015.

McKane, W. *Prophets and Wise Men*. London: SCM, 1965.

———. *Proverbs: A New Approach*. OTL. London: SCM, 1992.

McKinlay, J. E. *Gendering Wisdom the Host: Biblical Invitations to Eat and Drink*. JSOTSup 216. Sheffield: Sheffield Academic, 1996.

Milik, J. "Problemes de la Literature Henochique a la Lumiere des Fragments." *HTR* 64 (1971): 333–78.

Munro, J. M. *Spikenard and Saffron: A Study in the Poetic Language of the Song of Songs*. JSOTSup 203. Sheffield: Sheffield Academic, 1995.

Murphy, R. E. *The Tree of Life: An Exploration of Biblical Wisdom Literature*. 2nd ed. Grand Rapids: Eerdmans, 1996.

———. *Wisdom Literature: Job, Proverbs, Ruth, Canticles, Ecclesiastes, and Esther*. FOTL 13. Grand Rapids: Eerdmans, 1981.

Newsom, C. A. *The Book of Job: A Contest of Moral Imaginations*. New York: Oxford University Press, 2003.

O'Donovan, O. *Resurrection and Moral Order: An Outline for Evangelical Ethics*. 2nd ed. Grand Rapids: Eerdmans, 1994.

Ogden, G. S. *Qoheleth*. Sheffield: JSOT Press, 1987.

Oppenheim, A. L. "The Intellectual in Mesopotamian Society." *Daedalus* 104, no. 2 (1975): 37–46.

Oswalt, J. N. *Isaiah*. NIVAC. Grand Rapids: Zondervan, 2003.

Overland, P. "Did the Sage Draw from the Shema? A Study of Proverbs 3:1–12." *CBQ* 62 (2000): 424–40.

Parker, S. B. "The Literatures of Canaan, Ancient Israel, and Phoenicia: An Overview." In *Civilizations of the Ancient Near East*, edited by J. M. Sasson, 2399–2400. Peabody, MA: Hendrickson, 1995.

Pascal, R. *Design and Truth in Autobiography*. Cambridge, MA: Harvard University Press, 1960.

Pearce, L. E. "The Scribes and Scholars of Ancient Mesopotamia." In *Civilizations of the Ancient Near East*, edited by J. M. Sasson, 2265–78. Peabody, MA: Hendrickson, 1995.

Pemberton, G. *After Lament: Psalms for Learning to Trust Again*. Abilene, TX: Abilene Christian University Press, 2014.

Perdu, O. "Ancient Egyptian Autobiographies." In *Civilizations of the Ancient Near East*, edited by J. M. Sasson, 2243–54. Peabody, MA: Hendrickson, 1995.

Perdue, L. G. "The Book of Qohelet 'Has the Smell of the Tomb about It': Mortality in Qohelet and Hellenistic Skepticism." In *The Words of the Wise Are Like Goads: Engaging Qohelet in the 21st Century*, ed. M. J. Boda, T. Longman III, and C. G. Rata, 103–16. Winona Lake, IN: Eisenbrauns, 2013.

———. *Wisdom and Cult: A Critical Analysis of the Views of Cult in the Wisdom Literatures of Israel and the Ancient Near East*. SBLDS 30. Missoula, MT: Scholars Press, 1977.

———. *Wisdom Literature: A Theological History*. Louisville: Westminster John Knox, 2007.

Perdue, L. G., B. B. Scott, and W. J. Wiseman, eds. *In Search of Wisdom: Essays in Memory of John G. Gammie*. Louisville: Westminster John Knox, 1993.

Phua, M. "Sirach, Book of." In *Dictionary of the Old Testament: Wisdom, Poetry and Writings*, edited by T. Longman III and P. Enns, 720–28. Downers Grove, IL: IVP Academic, 2008.

Pietersma, A., and B. G. Wright, eds. *A New English Translation of the Septuagint*. Oxford: Oxford University Press, 2007.

Pope, M. H. *Job*. AB 15. Garden City, NY: Doubleday, 1973.

———. *Song of Songs*. AB 7C. Garden City, NY: Doubleday, 1977.

Posner, R. A. "The Jurisprudence of Skepticism." *Michigan Law Review* 86 (1988): 827–91.

Poythress, V. *The Shadow of Christ in the Law of Moses*. Phillipsburg, NJ: P&R, 1995.

Provan, I., V. P. Long, and T. Longman III, *A Biblical History of Israel*. 2nd ed. Louisville: Westminster John Knox, 2015.

Rad, G. von. "The Joseph Narrative and Ancient Wisdom." In *The Problem of the Hexateuch and Other Essays*, 292–300. London: SCM, 1984.

———. *Old Testament Theology*, vol. 2. Louisville: Westminster John Knox, 1965.

———. *Wisdom in Israel*. London: SCM, 1972. Reprint, Nashville: Abingdon, 1988.

Ray, J. D. "Egyptian Wisdom Literature." In *Wisdom in Ancient Israel: Essays in Honour of J. A. Emerton*, edited by J. Day, R. P. Gordon, and H. G. M. Williamson, 17–29. Cambridge: Cambridge University Press, 1995.

Redford, D. B. *A Study of the Biblical Story of Joseph (Genesis 37–50)*. VTSup 20. Leiden: Brill, 1970.

Reed, A. H., R. R. Osmer, and M. G. Smucker. *Spiritual Companioning: A Guide to Protestant Theology and Practice*. Grand Rapids: Baker Academic, 2015.

Robertson, O. P. *The Christ of the Covenants*. Phillipsburg, NJ: Presbyterian and Reformed, 1981.

Rofé, A. "Revealed Wisdom: From the Bible to Qumran." In *Sapiential Perspectives: Wisdom Literature in Light of the Dead Sea Scrolls*, edited by J. J. Collins, G. E. Sterling, and R. Clements, 1–12. STDJ 51. Leiden: Brill, 2004.

Rogers, C. L. "The Meaning and Significance of the Hebrew Word *'Amon* in Proverbs 8:30." *ZAW* 109 (1997): 208–21.

Rollston, C. A. *Writing and Literacy in the World of Ancient Israel: Epigraphic Evidence from the Iron Age*. Archaeology and Biblical Studies 11. Atlanta: SBL Press, 2010.

Sadgrove, M. "The Song of Songs as Wisdom Literature." In *Papers on Old Testament and Related Themes*. Vol. 1 of *Studia Biblica 1978: Sixth International Congress on Biblical Studies, Oxford, 3–7 April 1978*, edited by E. A. Livingstone, 245–48. JSOTSup 11. Sheffield: JSOT Press, 1979.

Samet, N. "Religious Redaction in Qohelet in Light of Mesopotamian Vanity Literature." *VT* 65 (2015): 1–16.

Schaper, J. "*Nomos* and *Nomoi* in the Wisdom of Solomon." In *Wisdom and Torah: The Reception of "Torah" in the Wisdom Literature of the Second Temple Period*, edited by B. U. Schipper and D. A. Teeter, 293–306. Supplements to the Journal for the Study of Judaism 163. Leiden: Brill, 2013.

Scharffs, B. "The Role of Humility in Exercising Practical Wisdom." *University of California, Davis, Law Review* 32 (1998): 127–99.

Schipper, B. U., and D. A. Teeter, eds. *Wisdom and Torah: The Reception of "Torah" in the Wisdom Literature of the Second Temple Period*. Supplements to the Journal for the Study of Judaism 163. Leiden: Brill, 2013.

Schnabel, E. J. *Law and Wisdom from Ben Sira to Paul: A Tradition Historical Enquiry into the Relation of Law, Wisdom, and Ethics*. Wissenschaftliche Untersuchungen zum Neuen Testament 2/16. Tübingen: Mohr Siebeck, 1985.

Schultz, R. "Unity or Diversity in Wisdom Theology? A Canonical and Covenantal Perspective." *Tyndale Bulletin* 46 (1997): 271–306.

Schwab, G. M. *The Song of Songs' Cautionary Message concerning Human Love*. Studies in Biblical Literature 41. New York: Peter Lang, 2002.

Schwáb, Z. S. *Toward an Interpretation of the Book of Proverbs: Selfishness and Secularity Reconsidered*. JTISup 7. Winona Lake, IN: Eisenbrauns, 2013.

Scott, R. B. Y. "Wisdom in Creation: The 'AMON of viii 30." *VT* 10 (1960): 213–23.

Seow, C. L. *Ecclesiastes: A New Translation with Introduction and Commentary*. AB 18. New York: Doubleday, 1997.

Shields, M. A. *The End of Wisdom: A Reappraisal of the Historical and Canonical Function of Ecclesiastes*. Winona Lake, IN: Eisenbrauns, 2006.

———. "Wisdom and Prophecy." In *Dictionary of the Old Testament: Wisdom, Poetry and Writings*, edited by T. Longman III and P. Enns, 876–84. Downers Grove, IL: InterVarsity, 2008.

Shupak, N. "Egyptian 'Prophetic' Writings and Biblical Wisdom." *BN* 54 (1990): 81–102.

Skehan, P. W. "The Seven Columns of Wisdom's House in Proverbs 1–9." *CBQ* 41 (1979): 365–79.

Snaith, J. G. "Ecclesiasticus: A Tract for the Times." In *Wisdom in Ancient Israel: Essays in Honor of J. A. Emerton*, edited by J. Day, R. P. Gordon, and H. G. M. Williamson, 170–81. Cambridge: Cambridge University Press, 1995.

Sneed, M. "'Grasping After the Wind': The Elusive Attempt to Define and Delimit Wisdom." In *Was There a Wisdom Tradition? New Prospects in Israelite Wisdom Studies*, edited by M. R. Sneed, 39–67. Ancient Israel and Its Literature 23. Atlanta: SBL Press, 2015.

———. "Is the 'Wisdom Tradition' a Tradition?" *CBQ* 73 (2011): 50–71.

————. *The Social World of the Sages: An Introduction to Israelite and Jewish Wisdom Literature.* Minneapolis: Fortress, 2015.

————, ed. *Was There a Wisdom Tradition? New Prospects in Israelite Wisdom Studies.* Ancient Israel and Its Literature 23. Atlanta: SBL Press, 2015.

Sparks, K. L. *Ancient Texts for the Study of the Hebrew Bible: A Guide to the Background Literature.* Peabody, MA: Hendrickson, 2005.

Spittler, R. P. "Testament of Job." In *The Old Testament Pseudepigrapha.* Vol. 1, *Apocalyptic Literature and Testaments,* edited by J. H. Charlesworth, 829–68. Garden City, NY: Doubleday, 1983.

Strom, M. *Lead with Wisdom: How Wisdom Transforms Good Leaders into Great Leaders.* Melbourne: Wiley, 2014.

Strugnell, J., and D. J. Harrington. *Qumran Cave 4.XXIV: Sapiential Texts, Part 2 4QInstruction (Musar Le Mebin) 4Q415ff. with a Re-edition of 1Q26.* DJD 34. Oxford, Clarendon, 1999.

Sweeney, M. A., and E. Ben Zvi, eds. *The Changing Face of Form Criticism for the Twenty-First Century.* Grand Rapids: Eerdmans, 2003.

Tappy, R. E., and P. K. McCarter. *Literate Culture and Tenth-Century Canaan: The Tel Zayit Abecedary in Context.* Winona Lake, IN: Eisenbrauns, 2008.

Tigchelaar, E. "Sabbath Halakha and Worship in 4QWays of Righteousness: 4Q421 11 and 13+2+8 par 4Q254a 1–2." *RevQ* 18 (1998): 359–72.

Tippett, K. *Becoming Wise: An Inquiry into the Mystery and Art of Living.* New York: Penguin Press, 2016.

Toorn, K. van der. *Scribal Culture and the Making of the Hebrew Bible.* Cambridge, MA: Harvard University Press, 2007.

————. "Why Wisdom Became a Secret: On Wisdom as a Written Genre." In *Wisdom Literature in Mesopotamia and Israel,* edited by R. J. Clifford, 21–29. Atlanta: Society of Biblical Literature Press, 2007.

Treier, D. J. *Virtue and the Voice of God: Toward Theology as Wisdom.* Grand Rapids: Eerdmans, 2006.

Trible, P. *God and the Rhetoric of Sexuality.* Philadelphia: Fortress, 1978.

Tromp, N. "Wisdom and the Canticle: Ct 8,6c–7b: Text, Character, Message and Import." In *La Sagesse de l'Ancien Testament,* edited by M. Gilbert, 88–95. Louvain: Leuven University Press, 1980.

Van der Toorn, K. *See* Toorn, K. van der.

Van Leeuwen, R. "Building God's House: An Exploration in Wisdom." In *The Way of Wisdom: Essays in Honor of Bruce K. Waltke,* edited by J. I. Packer and S. K. Sunderland, 204–11. Grand Rapids: Zondervan, 2000.

————. "Cosmos, Temple, House: Building in Mesopotamia and Israel." In *Wisdom Literature in Mesopotamia and Israel,* edited by R. J. Clifford, 67–92. Atlanta: Society of Biblical Literature, 2007.

———. "Proverbs." In vol. 5 of *The New Interpreter's Bible*, ed. L. E. Keck, 15–264. Nashville: Abingdon, 1997.

———. "Wealth and Poverty: System and Contradiction in Proverbs." *Hebrew Studies* 33 (1992): 25–36.

Veldhuis, N. "Sumerian Proverbs in Their Curricular Context." *JAOS* 120 (2000): 383–99.

Von Rad, G. *See* Rad, G. von.

Waltke, B. K. "The Book of Proverbs and Old Testament Theology." *Bibliotheca Sacra* 136 (1979): 302–17.

———. "Does Proverbs Promise Too Much?" *Andrews University Seminary Studies* 34 (1996): 319–36.

Walton, J. H. "The Ancient Near Eastern Background of the Spirit of the Lord in the Old Testament." In *Presence, Power and Promise: The Role of the Spirit of God in the Old Testament*, edited by D. G. Firth and P. D. Wegner, 38–70. Downers Grove, IL: InterVarsity, 2011.

———. "The Decree of Darius the Mede in Daniel 6." *JETS* 31 (1988): 279–86.

———. *Genesis 1 as Ancient Cosmology*. Winona Lake, IN: Eisenbrauns, 2011.

———, ed. *Zondervan Illustrated Bible Backgrounds Commentary*. Vol. 5, *The Minor Prophets, Job, Psalms, Proverbs, Ecclesiastes, Song of Songs*. Grand Rapids: Zondervan, 2009.

Washington, H. C. *Wealth and Poverty in the Instruction of Amenemope and the Book of Proverbs*. SBLDS 142. Atlanta: Scholars Press, 1993.

Webb, W. *Slaves, Women and Homosexuals: Exploring the Hermeneutics of Cultural Analysis*. Downers Grove, IL: InterVarsity, 2009.

Weeks, S. *Early Israelite Wisdom*. Oxford Theological Monographs. Oxford: Clarendon, 1994.

Wenham, G. J. "Sanctuary Symbolism in the Garden of Eden Story." In *"I Studied Inscriptions from Before the Flood": Ancient Near Eastern, Literary, and Linguistic Approaches to Genesis 1–11*, edited by R. S. Hess and D. T. Tsumura, 309–404. Sources for Biblical and Theological Study 4. Winona Lake, IN: Eisenbrauns, 1994.

Wente, E. F. "The Scribes of Ancient Egypt." *Civilizations of the Ancient Near East*, edited by J. M. Sasson, 2211–21. Peabody, MA: Hendrickson, 1995.

Westermann, C. *Roots of Wisdom*. Edinburgh: T&T Clark, 1995.

———. *The Structure of the Book of Job: A Form-Critical Analysis*. Philadelphia: Fortress, 1981.

———. *Wurzeln der Weisheit: Die ältesten Sprüche Israels und anderer Völker*. Göttingen: Vandenhoeck & Ruprecht, 1990.

Whybray, R. N. *Ecclesiastes*. NCB. Grand Rapids: Eerdmans, 1989.

———. *The Intellectual Tradition in the Old Testament*. BZAW 135. Berlin: de Gruyter, 1974.

———. "Qohelet, Preacher of Joy." *JSOT* 23 (1982): 87–98.

———. *Wealth and Poverty in the Book of Proverbs.* Sheffield: JSOT Press, 1990.

Wiggermann, F. A. M. "Theologies, Priests, and Worship in Ancient Mesopotamia." In *Civilizations of the Ancient Near East,* edited by J. M. Sasson, 1857–70. Peabody, MA: Hendrickson, 1995.

Williamson, P. R. "Covenant." In *Dictionary of the Old Testament: Pentateuch,* edited by T. D. Alexander and D. W. Baker, 139–55. Downers Grove, IL: InterVarsity, 2003.

Willimon, W. *Pastor: The Theology and Practice of Ordained Ministry.* Nashville: Abingdon, 2002.

Wilson, L. *Joseph Wise and Otherwise: The Intersection of Wisdom and Covenant in Genesis 37–50.* Carlisle: Paternoster, 2004.

Winston, D. *The Wisdom of Solomon: A New Translation with Introduction and Commentary.* AB 43. Garden City, NY: Doubleday, 1979.

Witherington, B., III. *Jesus the Sage: The Pilgrimage of Wisdom.* Minneapolis: Fortress, 1994.

Wolters, A. *The Song of the Valiant Woman: Studies in the Interpretation of Proverbs 31:10–31.* Carlisle: Paternoster, 2001.

Wright, B. G., III. "Torah and Sapiential Pedagogy in the Book of Ben Sira." In *Wisdom and Torah: The Reception of "Torah" in the Wisdom Literature of the Second Temple Period,* edited by B. U. Schipper and D. A. Teeter, 157–86. Supplements to the Journal for the Study of Judaism 163. Leiden: Brill, 2013.

Wright, B. G., III, and L. M. Wills, eds. *Conflicted Boundaries in Wisdom and Apocalypticism.* SBLSymS 35. Atlanta: Scholars Press, 2005.

Zerafa, P. P. *The Wisdom of God in the Book of Job.* Rome: Herder, 1978.

Zimmerli, W. "Concerning the Structure of Old Testament Wisdom." In *Studies in Ancient Israelite Wisdom,* edited by J. Crenshaw, 175–209. New York: Ktav, 1976.

———. "The Place and Limit of Wisdom in the Framework of the Old Testament Theology." *SJT* 17 (1964): 146–58. Reprinted in *Studies in Ancient Israelite Wisdom,* edited by J. L. Crenshaw. New York: Ktav, 1986.

Zuckerman, B. *Job the Silent: A Study in Historical Counterpoint.* New York: Oxford University Press, 1991.

INDEX OF MODERN AUTHORS

INDEX OF SCRIPTURE AND OTHER ANCIENT WRITINGS

INDEX OF SUBJECTS